Diversity in the
Power Elite

Diversity in the Power Elite

How It Happened, Why It Matters

Richard L. Zweigenhaft and
G. William Domhoff

ROWMAN & LITTLEFIELD PUBLISHERS, INC.
Lanham • Boulder • New York • Toronto • Oxford

ROWMAN & LITTLEFIELD PUBLISHERS, INC.

Published in the United States of America
by Rowman & Littlefield Publishers, Inc.
A wholly owned subsidary of The Rowman & Littlefield Publishing Group, Inc.
4501 Forbes Boulevard, Suite 200, Lanham, Maryland 20706
www.rowmanlittlefield.com

PO Box 317
Oxford
OX2 9RU, UK

British Library Cataloguing in Publication Information Available

Library of Congress Cataloging-in-Publication Data

Zweigenhaft, Richard L.
  Diversity in the power elite : how it happened, why it matters / Richard L.
Zweigenhaft and G. William Domhoff.
    p. cm.
  Includes bibliographical references and index.
  ISBN-13: 978-0-7425-3698-2 (cloth : alk. paper)
  ISBN-10: 0-7425-3698-X (cloth : alk. paper)
  ISBN-13: 978-0-7425-3699-9 (pbk. : alk. paper)
  ISBN-10: 0-7425-3699-8 (pbk. : alk. paper)
  1. Elite (Social sciences) —United States. 2. Power (Social sciences) —United
States. 3. Pluralism (Social sciences) —United States. 4. Minorities—United
States. I. Domhoff, G. William. II. Title.

HN90.E4Z944 2006
305.5'20973—dc22   2005031289

Printed in the United States of America

Contents

Preface

This is an updated and theoretically revised version of the third book in a trilogy that we have written together on diversity in the power elite. It brings together and synthesizes everything that has been learned over a twenty-five-year period on this important issue. It also projects current trends into the foreseeable future.

The first book in our trilogy, *Jews in the Protestant Establishment* (1982), is a study of Jews in the American corporate elite. It shows that class is more important than ethnicity at the highest levels of the social structure. This work and our more recent findings on Jews in the United States provide a baseline from which we can measure and understand the progress of other previously excluded groups.

The second book, *Blacks in the White Establishment? A Study of Race and Class in America* (1991), updated as *Blacks in the White Elite: Will the Progress Continue?* (2003), traces the careers of African Americans who had attended elite boarding schools and universities in their youth, showing the great achievements that are possible for low-income African Americans when they are given the same opportunities granted as a matter of course to the sons and daughters of the upper-middle and upper classes. Nonetheless, the book concludes that race remained more important than class in the lives of these highly successful men and women, even though class had become more salient for them. It, too, provides a benchmark for the present study because it shows the progress that is possible when social movements and government agencies counteract the ongoing discrimination that is once again slowing down the movement of African Americans into mainstream America.

Now, in this current book, we examine the extent to which the power elite described by C. Wright Mills in 1956, a power elite that was exclusively white, male, and almost entirely Christian, has become diversified in terms of gender, race, Latino and Asian American ethnicity, and sexual orientation. To the extent that the power elite has become diversified, we explore why this has happened, who has and has not become part of the power elite, and what the implications of diversification are for understanding the workings of the American political system. We once again find that class is a more significant factor than ethnicity but that race and gender discrimination remain pervasive, even at the upper echelons of the class and power structures.

Although we conclude that there has been only a modest amount of diversification, we argue that its effects on both social movements for equal opportunity and the power elite itself have been larger than might be expected. We have discovered that there are many ironies in the battle to diversify the power positions in American society. Nothing has turned out the way anybody expected it to.

In this book, as in the previous two, we have tried to blend our appreciation of two disciplines, sociology and social psychology. We have explored structural processes related to power and class, as well as group processes related to identity formation. We use insights from these two disciplines to explain the many obstacles still facing previously underrepresented groups.

Acknowledgments

In a project like this that cuts across so many specializations and sensitive issues, we are especially grateful to the many colleagues and friends who gave us guidance throughout our research and writing. We want to thank the following people, many of whom provided us with important background information and each of whom read some or all of the manuscript, either for the first edition or this updated edition: Richard Alba, Edna Bonacich, John D'Emilio, Joe Feagin, Aida Hurtado, Jeffrey Janowitz, John Kitsuse, Rhonda F. Levine, Catherine Lew, Wendy Mink, Laura O'Toole, Perry Patterson, Vânia Penha-Lopes, Tom Pettigrew, Martha Julia Sellers, Steve Sellers, David Thomas, Deborah Woo, Lynda Woodworth, Steve Wright, and Lisa Young. We also wish to thank Carol Bowie of the Investor Responsibility Research Center (IRRC), Peter Garrett of Directorship, Kelly Glew of Steppingstone, Lory Manning of the Women's Research and Education Institute, Charles Moskos of Northwestern University, and Lynda Woodworth of Catalyst for their generous sharing of data.

In addition, we thank the twenty-one students who took "Class, Race, and Gender" at Guilford College in Greensboro, North Carolina, in the spring of 2005. Their thoughtful feedback on the first edition of this book helped us a great deal as we worked on this updated version. One of those students, the academically gifted and remarkably thorough Tess McEnery, became our research assistant in the summer of 2005, and her superlative work can only be compared to that of our research assistant from the previous summer, Samuel Beresford Williams. Both Sam and Tess scoured the Internet for credible information on the hundreds of corporate directors, members of presidential cabinets, members of the military with one-star or higher rank, and congressmen and -women about whom we write in this book. Then, they put these data in color-coded Excel files, revealing that they were not only academically gifted and thorough but also aesthetically savvy. In January 2006, Tess also provided invaluable assistance on the index.

Richie Zweigenhaft has received various forms of assistance from Guilford College for the research that went into both editions of this book. He wishes to express his appreciation for sabbatical leaves in 1995 and 2002 and for on-going, small research grants from the Office of the Academic Dean. He would also like to thank all of the librarians at Guilford for their help on this project and the following former students for their research assistance on the first edition: Cari Boram, Katharine Cannon, Michael Hamilton, Damara Luce, Patty Perez, Michael Peterson, Jennifer Simms, and Sonora Stein. In addition, he would like to express deep appreciation and affection for his departmental colleagues (past and present) who have provided both collegiality and friendship for many years.

Chapter One

Has the Power Elite Become Diverse?

Injustices based on race, gender, ethnicity, and sexual orientation have been the most emotionally charged and contested issues in American society since the end of the 1960s, far exceeding concerns about social class and rivaled only by conflicts over abortion. These issues are now subsumed under the umbrella term *diversity*, which has been discussed extensively from the perspectives of both the aggrieved and those at the middle levels of the social ladder who resist any changes.

In this book, we look at diversity from a new angle: we examine its impact on the small group at the top of American society that we call the *power elite*, those who own and manage large banks and corporations, finance the political campaigns of conservative Democrats and virtually all Republicans at the state and national levels, and serve in government as appointed officials and military leaders. We ask whether the decades of civil disobedience, protest, and litigation by civil rights groups, feminists, and gay and lesbian rights activists have resulted in a more diverse power elite. If they have, what effects has this new diversity had on the functioning of the power elite and on its relation to the rest of society?

We also compare our findings on the power elite with those from our parallel study of Congress to see whether there are differences in social background, education, and party affiliation for women and other underrepresented groups in these two realms of power. We explore the possibility that elected officials come from a wider range of occupational and income backgrounds than members of the power elite. In addition, we ask whether either of the major political parties has been more active than the other in advancing the careers of women and minorities.

According to many popular commentators, the composition of the higher circles in the United States had indeed changed by the late 1980s and early

1

1990s. Some went even further, saying that the old power elite had been pushed aside entirely.[1] Enthusiastic articles in mainstream magazines, such as one in the late 1980s in *U.S. News & World Report* entitled "The New American Establishment," have also appeared, celebrating a new diversity at the top and claiming that "new kinds of men and women" have "taken control of institutions that influence important aspects of American life." School and club ties are no longer important, the article announced, highlighting the new role of women with a picture of some of the "wise women" who had joined the "wise men" who dominated the old establishment.[2]

Then, in July 1995, *Newsweek* ran a cover story titled "The Rise of the Overclass," featuring a gallery of one hundred high-tech, media, and Wall Street stars, including women as well as men and previously excluded racial and ethnic groups as well as whites with Western European backgrounds, all of whom supposedly came from all rungs of the social ladder.[3] The term *overclass* was relatively new, but the argument—that the power elite was dead and had been superseded by a diverse meritocratic elite—was not.

More recently, David Brooks, a conservative columnist for the *New York Times*, has made the same kind of claims in two books about the upper-middle class. In the second, *On Paradise Drive: How We Live Now (and Always Have) in the Future Tense*, he refers to a time, presumably in the distant past, "back when the old WASP elite dominated," and contrasts those bad old days with the current era of a "new educated elite." He goes on to reassure the reader, "There is no single elite in America. Hence, there is no definable establishment to be oppressed by and to rebel against."[4]

We are wary about these claims announcing the demise of the old elites and the arrival of new elites because they never have been documented systematically. Moreover, they are suspect because similar claims have been made repeatedly in American history and have been proved wrong each time. In popular books and magazines from the 1830s, 1920s, and 1950s, for example, leading commentators of the day asserted that there used to be a tightly knit and cohesive governing group in the United States, but no longer. A closer look several decades later at each of these supposedly new eras invariably showed that the new power group was primarily the old one after all, with a few additions and alterations here and there.[5]

Since the 1870s, the refrain about the new diversity of the governing circles has been closely intertwined with a staple of American culture created by Horatio Alger Jr., whose name has become synonymous with upward mobility in America. Far from being a Horatio Alger himself, the man who gave his name to upward mobility was born into a patrician family in 1832; his father was a Harvard graduate, a Unitarian minister, and a Massachusetts state senator. Horatio Jr. graduated from Harvard at the age of nineteen, after which he pursued a series of unsuccessful efforts to establish himself in various careers. Finally, in 1864, Alger was hired as a Unitarian minister in Brewster, Massachusetts. Fifteen months later, he was dismissed from this position for homosexual acts with boys in the congregation.

Alger returned to New York, where he soon began to spend a great deal of time at the Newsboys' Lodging House, founded in 1853 for footloose youngsters between the ages of twelve and sixteen and home to many youths who had been mustered out of the Union Army after serving as drummer boys. At the Newsboys' Lodging House, Alger found his literary niche and his subsequent claim to fame: writing books in which poor boys make good. His books sold by the hundreds of thousands in the last third of the nineteenth century, and by 1910, they were enjoying annual paperback sales of more than one million.[6]

The deck is not stacked against the poor, according to Alger. When they simply show a bit of gumption, work hard, and thereby catch a break or two, they can become part of the American elite. The persistence of this theme, reinforced by the annual Horatio Alger Award given to such well-known personalities as Ronald Reagan, Bob Hope, and Billy Graham (who might not have been so eager to accept the award had they known that Alger did not fit their fantasy of a straight, white, patriarchal, American male), suggests that we may be dealing once again with a cultural myth.

In its early versions, of course, the story concerned the great opportunities available for poor white boys willing to work their way to the top. More recently, the story has featured black Horatio Algers who started in the ghetto, Latino Horatio Algers who started in the barrio, Asian American Horatio Algers whose parents were immigrants, and female Horatio Algers who seem to have no class backgrounds, all of whom now sit on the boards of the country's largest corporations.[7]

Few people read Horatio Alger today, but they still believe in upward mobility in an era when real wages have been stagnant for the bottom 80 percent since the 1970s, the percentage of low-income people finishing college is decreasing, and the rate of upward mobility is declining.[8] As we explain in the concluding chapter, it does not take many anecdotal examples to reinforce a strongly held cultural belief when people have a tendency to believe in a just world.

But is any of the talk about Horatio Alger and upward mobility true? Can anecdotes, dime novels, and self-serving autobiographical accounts about diversity, meritocracy, and upward social mobility survive a more systematic analysis? Have very many women or members of other previously excluded groups made it to the top? Has class lost its importance in shaping life chances?

In this book, we address these and related questions within the framework provided by the iconoclastic sociologist C. Wright Mills in his classic *The Power Elite*, published half a century ago in 1956 when the media were in the midst of what Mills called the "Great American Celebration," and still accurate today in terms of many of the issues he addressed. In spite of the Great Depression of the 1930s, Americans had pulled together to win World War II, and the country was both prosperous at home and influential abroad. Most of all, according to enthusiasts, the United States had become a relatively classless and pluralistic society, where power belonged to the people through their political parties and public opinion. Some groups certainly had more power than others, but no group or class had too much. The New Deal and World War II had forever transformed the corporate-based power structure of earlier decades.

Mills challenged this celebration of pluralism by studying the social backgrounds and career paths of the people who occupied the highest positions in what he saw as the three major institutional hierarchies in postwar America, the corporations, the executive branch of the federal government, and the military. He found that almost all members of this leadership group, which he called the power elite, were white, Christian males who came from "at most, the upper third of the income and occupational pyramids," despite the many Horatio Algeresque claims to the contrary.[9] A majority came from an even narrower stratum, the 11 percent of U.S. families headed by businesspeople or highly educated professionals like physicians and lawyers. Mills concluded that power in the United States in the 1950s was just about as concentrated as it had been since the rise of the large corporations, although he stressed that the New Deal and World War II had given political appointees and military chieftains more authority than they had exercised previously.

It is our purpose, therefore, to take a detailed look at the social, educational, and occupational backgrounds of the leaders of these three institutional hierarchies to see whether they have become more diverse in terms of gender, race, ethnicity, and sexual orientation, and also in terms of socioeconomic origins. Unlike Mills, however, we think the power elite is more than a set of institutional leaders; it is also the leadership group for the small upper class of owners and managers of large, income-producing properties, the 1 percent of American households that owned 44.1 percent of all privately held stock, 58.0 percent of financial securities, and 57.3 percent of business equity in 2001, the last year for which systematic figures are available. (By way of comparison, the bottom 90 percent, those who work for hourly wages or monthly salaries, have a mere 15.5 percent of the stock, 11.3 percent of financial securities, and 10.4 percent of business equity.) Not surprisingly, we think the primary concern of the power elite is to support the kind of policies, regulations, and political leaders that maintain this structure of privilege for the very rich.[10]

We first study the directors and chief executive officers (CEOs) of the largest banks and corporations, as determined by annual rankings compiled by *Fortune* magazine. The use of *Fortune* rankings is now standard practice in studies of corporate size and power. Over the years, *Fortune* has changed the number of corporations on its annual list and the way it groups them. For example, the separate listings by business sector in the past, like "life insurance companies," "diversified financial companies," and "service companies," have been combined into one overall list, primarily because many large businesses are now involved in more than one of the traditional sectors. Generally speaking, we use the *Fortune* list or lists available for the time period under consideration.

Second, again following Mills, we focus on the appointees to the president's cabinet when we turn to the "political directorate," Mills's general term for top-level officials in the executive branch of the federal government. We also have included the director of the CIA in one chapter because of the increased importance of that agency since Mills wrote. Third, and rounding out our portrait of the power elite, we examine the same two top positions in the military, generals and admirals, that formed the basis for Mills's look at the military elite.

As we have noted, we also study Congress. In the case of senators, we do the same kind of background studies that we do for members of the power elite. For members of the House of Representatives, we concern ourselves only with party affiliation for most groups. We include findings on senators and representatives from underrepresented groups for two reasons. First, this allows us to see whether there is more diversity in the electoral system than in the power elite. Second, we do not think, as Mills did, that Congress should be relegated to the "middle level" of power. To the contrary, we believe that Congress is an integral part of the power structure in America. Similarly, unlike Mills, because we think that the Supreme Court is a key institution within the power elite, we have added information on Supreme Court appointments.

Until the 1980s, most Northern Republicans and most Southern Democrats supported the power elite on the labor, welfare, and business-regulation issues critical to it, whereas a majority of Democrats outside of the South were sympathetic to a coalition of liberals, organized labor, and underrepresented groups. Due to the Voting Rights Act of 1965 and the gradual industrialization of the South since World War II, Southern conservatives have moved steadily into the Republican Party. At the same time, many moderate Republicans outside the South have been defeated by Democrats, leading to a situation where each of the two major power coalitions, the corporate-conservative coalition and the liberal labor coalition, is housed almost exclusively in just one of the two dominant political parties. We can therefore use party preference to gauge whether members of under-represented groups who join the power elite differ from their counterparts who are elected to Congress.

In addition to studying the extent to which women and other previously excluded groups have risen in the system, we focus on whether they have followed different avenues to the top than their predecessors did, as well as on any special roles they may play. Are they in the innermost circles of the power elite, or are they more likely to serve as buffers and go-betweens? Do they go just so far and no farther? What obstacles does each group face?

We also examine whether or not their presence affects the power elite itself. Do they influence the power elite in a more liberal direction, or do they end up endorsing traditional conservative positions, such as opposition to trade unions, taxes, and government regulation of business? In addition, in chapter 8, we argue that the diversity forced on the power elite has had the ironic effect of strengthening it by providing it with a handful of people who can reach out to the previously excluded groups and by showing that the American system can deliver on its most important promise, an equal opportunity for every individual. It is as if the diversity efforts in the final thirty-five years of the twentieth century were scripted for the arrival of a George W. Bush, the most conservative and uncompromising president since Herbert Hoover, a president with the most diverse cabinet in the history of the country; in the first five years, its members have included six women, four African Americans, three Latinos, and two Asian Americans who also held a total of ten corporate directorships and two corporate law partnerships before joining the cabinet.

The issues we address are not simple. They involve both the nature of the American power structure and the way in which people's need for self-esteem and a coherent belief system mesh with the hierarchical social structure they face. Moreover, the answers to some of the questions we ask vary greatly depending on which previously disadvantaged group we are talking about. Nonetheless, in the course of our research, a few general patterns have emerged that we examine throughout the text and then tie together in chapter 8. Six general points may help readers to see the patterns develop as we embark upon a narrative in the next six chapters that focuses on specific issues related to entry into the power elite by Jews, women, blacks, Latinos, Asian Americans, and, finally, gay men and lesbians.

1. The power elite now shows considerable diversity, at least as compared with its state in the 1950s, but its core group continues to consist of wealthy,

white, Christian males, most of whom are still from the upper third of the social ladder. Like the white, Christian males, those who are newly arrived to the power elite have been filtered through the same small set of elite schools in law, business, public policy, and international relations.

2. In spite of the increased diversity of the power elite, high social origins continue to be the most important factor in making it to the top. There are relatively few rags-to-riches stories in the groups we studied, and those we did find tended to have received scholarships to elite schools or to have been elected to office, usually within the Democratic Party. In general, it still takes the few who make it at least three generations to rise from the bottom to the top in the United States.

3. The new diversity within the power elite is transcended by common values and a subjective sense of hard-earned and richly deserved class privilege. The newcomers to the power elite have found ways to signal that they are willing to join the game as it has always been played, assuring the old guard that they will call for no more than relatively minor adjustments, if that. There are few liberals and fewer crusaders in the power elite, despite its newly acquired diversity. Class backgrounds, current roles, and future aspirations are more powerful in shaping behavior in the power elite than gender, ethnicity, race, or sexual orientation.

4. Not all the groups we studied have been equally successful in contributing to the new diversity in the power elite. Women, African Americans, Latinos, Asian Americans, and openly homosexual men and women are all underrepresented, but to varying degrees and with different rates of increasing representation. There is a real possibility that Americans are replacing the old black-versus-white distinction with a black-versus-non-black dividing line, with "white" coming to be just another word for the in-group. We will explore the reasons for this possibility in our final chapter.

5. There is greater diversity in Congress than in the power elite, especially in terms of class origins, and the majority of these more diverse elected officials are Democrats, whose presence has forced the Republicans to play catch-up by including some candidates from the previously excluded groups.

6. Although the corporate, political, and military elites have accepted diversity only in response to pressure from social-movement activists and feminists, the power elite has benefited from the presence of new members. Some serve either a buffer or a liaison function with such groups and institutions as consumers, angry neighborhoods, government agencies, and wealthy foreign entrepreneurs. More generally, their simple presence at the top serves a legitimating function. Tokenism does work in terms of reassuring the general population that the system is fair, as documented in studies discussed in chapter 8.

To provide a starting point for understanding the diversity we focus on in this book, we begin with the story of how a previously rejected and excluded out-group, the Jews, gradually became fully participating members of the power elite, especially after the 1960s. However, we recognize that the changed situation for Jews does not provide a perfect basis for comparison with the experiences of other underrepresented groups. For one thing, Jews accounted for only 3.3 percent of the population in 1950, at a time when 10 percent of the population was African American, and they make up only about 2 percent now, when African Americans constitute about 12.8 percent and Latinos about 13 percent.[11] Also, many Jews, more than are generally realized, came to the United States with economic or educational advantages, especially those who became major corporate figures.[12]

Nonetheless, the fact remains that over 40 percent of other white Americans held clearly anti-Semitic views until the years after World War II, when the full extent of the Holocaust became widely known.[13] As late as the 1940s, there were quotas on the number of Jews who were allowed to attend elite private colleges like Harvard, Yale, and Princeton, and successful Jewish business leaders were not permitted to join gentile social clubs until the civil rights movement highlighted the extent of all forms of discrimination. For example, it was not until 1977 that the most exclusive downtown club in Los Angeles accepted Jewish members, a change that was accomplished in a hurry when Harold Brown, the Jewish president of the California Institute of Technology, was selected to be the secretary of defense by the newly elected Jimmy Carter.[14] In addition, the assimilation of Jews into the power elite and Congress has been studied in great detail, which means that their experiences and pathways can serve as benchmarks.

Although anti-Catholicism nearly reached the levels of anti-Semitism in some contexts early in the twentieth century, we do not use the acceptance of Catholics into the power elite as a baseline for several reasons. Discrimination against Jews, unlike discrimination against Catholics, had cultural and racist overtones that went far beyond religious differences. Moreover, the exclusion of Jews was more complete than was the exclusion of Catholics, and the acceptance of Catholics into the establishment occurred earlier than did the acceptance of Jews. In 1954, when he published his classic work *The Nature of Prejudice*, Gordon Allport was still concerned about anti-Catholicism.[15] By the late 1950s, however, anti-Catholicism had declined dramatically, a condition that was confirmed by the election of the Irish Catholic John F. Kennedy as president in 1960. As E. Digby Baltzell pointed out in *The Protestant Establishment*, Kennedy's election "marked a definite trend toward a representative establishment as far as the Catholic community is concerned."[16] In clear contrast, Jews still faced considerable discrimination at that time, both in- and outside of the establishment.[17]

Following the chapter on Jews (chapter 2), we present empirically based chapters on women (chapter 3), blacks (chapter 4), Latinos (chapter 5), and Asian Americans (chapter 6) in the power elite. We also have included a chapter on gay men and lesbians (chapter 7), in which we faced challenging research issues. We know that there are Jews, women, blacks, Latinos, and Asian Americans in the power elite, but, unless they have chosen to be public about their sexual orientation, we can only assume that some of those in the power elite are gay or lesbian. From our perspective, the relevant issue is not how many in the power elite are gay or lesbian, or who they are, but whether or not those who are gay feel comfortable about acknowledging this publicly. Given the dependence of the researcher upon self-disclosure by gay men and lesbians, sexual orientation is a more difficult topic to study than gender or race, so the data we draw upon to address this issue are not as systematic as in other chapters. Nevertheless, the findings we draw upon, many of which are based on studies by gay and lesbian researchers, provide a solid basis for our conclusion that, as yet, there is little or no tolerance for diversity of sexual orientation within the power elite.

Because people have more than one identity and, therefore, are not solely women or black or homosexual, overlaps and cross-weavings in our presentation are inevitable. We have organized our findings into chapters that focus on a single identity at a time. When relevant, however, we attempt to address the complexity that can emerge when two or more of a person's identities seem to matter to his or her career.

Although our range of groups is a wide one, we have not tried to be completely inclusive. First, we have not analyzed the fortunes of recent immigrant groups that have fewer than a million members in the United States. These include immigrants from Thailand, refugees from Cambodia and Vietnam, and immigrants from small Pacific islands and various countries in Africa. They have not been here long enough to establish a clear pattern, and there is less information available on them than there is on the groups that we have chosen to write about. Further, we see little evidence that any of them are represented in the highest levels of the American power structure.

Second, we have not dealt with the diverse group of tribes that are variously called American Indians or Native Americans. There are several reasons for this decision. To begin with, based on data collected for the 2000 Census, there are only 2.7 million American Indians or Alaska Natives—about 1 percent of the population—and 59 percent of those who are married are married to non-Indians.[18] Moreover, those who are exclusively Native American in their heritage live separately from one another in small, culturally distinct groups in every part of the United States. Finally, 21 percent of those who identified themselves as members of one or another Native American group live on reservations apart from the rest of American society, which means that they are not likely to become part of the power elite or to be elected to Congress.[19]

Finally, we do not discuss in detail why the power elite has accepted some degree of diversification because we take it for granted that it would not have done so had it not been for the long and heroic efforts of the African American civil rights movement, a point that is all too easily overlooked in a day when corporations and elected officials in Washington, D.C., brag about their diversity. We also think that the most internationally oriented elements of the power elite, and especially the leaders of multinational corporations and in the State Department, felt compelled to accept some degree of diversity because the ongoing segregation of African Americans was an embarrassment to them in their high-stakes competition with the Soviet Union for the loyalty of people of color in the many emerging nations around the globe.[20]

NOTES

1. For example, see Nelson W. Aldrich Jr., *Old Money: The Mythology of America's Upper Class* (New York: Knopf, 1988), and Robert C. Christopher, *Crashing the Gates: The De-WASPing of America's Power Elite* (New York: Simon and Schuster, 1989).

2. "The New American Establishment," *U.S. News & World Report*, February 8, 1988, 39, 45–46.

3. "The Rise of the Overclass," *Newsweek,* July 31, 1995, 32–46.

4. David Brooks, *On Paradise Drive: How We Live Now (and Always Have) in the Future Tense* (New York: Simon & Schuster, 2004), 29, 71.

5. Edward Pessen, *Riches, Class, and Power before the Civil War* (Lexington, MA: D. C. Heath, 1973); Edward Pessen, ed., *Three Centuries of Social Mobility in America* (Lexington, MA: D. C. Heath, 1974).

6. See Richard M. Huber, *The American Idea of Success* (New York: McGraw-Hill, 1971), 44–46; Gary Scharnhorst, *Horatio Alger, Jr.* (Boston: Twayne, 1980), 24, 29, 141. For a discussion of the general pattern by which the media eulogize tycoons as "self-made," see Richard L. Zweigenhaft, "Making Rags out of Riches: Horatio Alger and the Tycoon's Obituary," *Extra!*, January/February 2004, 27–28.

7. As C. Wright Mills wrote half a century ago, "Horatio Alger dies hard." C. Wright Mills, *The Power Elite* (New York: Oxford University Press, 1956), 91.

8. See Harold R. Kerbo, *Social Stratification and Inequality* (New York: McGraw-Hill, 2006), ch. 12. See, also, the series on class in the *New York Times*, "A Portrait of Class in America," spring 2005.

9. Mills, *The Power Elite*, 279. For Mills's specific findings, see 104–105, 128–29, 180–81, 393–94, and 400–401.

10. Edward N. Wolff, "Changes in Household Wealth in the 1980s and 1990s in the U.S." (working paper 407, Levy Economics Institute, Bard College, 2004), at www.levy.org. See table 2, p. 30, and table 6, p. 34.

11. Lynette Clemetson, "Hispanics Now Largest Minority, Census Shows," *New York Times*, January 22, 2003, A1.

12. See Stephen Steinberg, *The Ethnic Myth: Race, Ethnicity, and Class in America* (New York: Atheneum, 1981); Richard L. Zweigenhaft and G. William Domhoff, *Jews in the Protestant Establishment* (New York: Praeger, 1982).

13. Seymour Martin Lipset and Earl Raab, *Jews and the New American Scene* (Cambridge, MA: Harvard University Press, 1995), 77–79.

14. Zweigenhaft and Domhoff, *Jews in the Protestant Establishment*, 51–52.

15. Gordon W. Allport, *The Nature of Prejudice*, abr. ed. (New York: Anchor, 1958), 224–26, 239.

16. E. Digby Baltzell, *The Protestant Establishment: Aristocracy and Caste in America* (New York: Random House, 1964; New Haven, CT: Yale University Press, 1987), 83.

17. Our decision to include a chapter on Jews, but not one on Catholics, does not indicate that we assume Catholics are no longer underrepresented in the power elite. In their 1982 article, drawing on 1971–1972 data about 545 "top position holders in powerful political, economic, and social institutions in the United States," Richard Alba and Gwen Moore found that non-Irish Catholics were underrepresented in most or all sectors (Irish Catholics were represented at or above their population proportion in most sectors, especially labor and politics). See Richard A. Alba and Gwen Moore, "Ethnicity in the American Elite," *American Sociological Review* 47 (1982): 373–83. Similarly, Alba has found that Italian Americans are underrepresented on the faculties of elite universities; see Richard Alba and Dalia Abdel-Hady, "Galileo's Children: Italian Americans' Difficult Entry into the Intellectual Elite, *Sociological Quarterly* 46 (2005): 3–18. In a study of the religious affiliations of the men and women listed in *Who's Who in America* from the 1930s through the 1990s, Ralph Pyle and Jerome Koch found that, as of 1992, Catholics remained underrepresented, although they have increased their representation over time, and "are likely to achieve parity shortly" (132). See Ralph E. Pyle and Jerome R. Koch, "The Religious Affiliations of American Elites, 1930s to 1990s: A Note on the Pace of Disestablishment," *Sociological Focus* 34, no. 2 (2001): 125–37. Our decision to focus on Jews, rather than Catholics, allows us to examine a group that has gone from underrepresentation in the higher circles to overrepresentation.

18. For the census figures, see Clemetson, "Hispanics Now Largest Minority." The 59 percent figure comes from Karl Eschbach, "The Enduring and Vanishing American Indian: American Indian Population Growth and Intermarriage in 1990," *Ethnic and Racial Studies* 18, no. 1 (1995): 89–108. There were only 377,000 American Indians in 1950, before the new social movements made an Indian identity both

respectable and useful. Many of those who now identify themselves as Native Americans have only one grandparent or great-grandparent who was Indian.

19. See Mary B. Davis, ed., *Native America in the Twentieth Century: An Encyclopedia* (New York: Garland, 1994). The most visible Native American in an important position in American society for the past decade or so has been Ben Nighthorse Campbell, who was elected to the U.S. Senate as a Democrat in 1992 and then switched to the Republican Party shortly thereafter. He was reelected in 1998 but chose not to run in 2004. Campbell's father was part Apache, part Pueblo Indian, and part Cheyenne. His mother was a Portuguese immigrant. Following his father's advice, as a young man, Campbell did not acknowledge his Native American heritage. He did not decide to investigate his Indian background until the mid-1960s, when he was in his thirties. In 1980, at the age of forty-seven, he became a member of the Northern Cheyenne tribe and adopted the middle name Nighthorse (*Current Biography* [1994]: 86–90).

20. See John D. Skretney, *The Minority Rights Revolution* (Cambridge, MA: Harvard University Press, 2002), for a detailed discussion of how these two factors combined to force a diversification of employment and education for African Americans that was soon expanded to include women and other previously excluded groups with much less contention.

Chapter Two

Jews in the Power Elite

When Laurence Tisch, a billionaire when he died in 2003, was growing up in the 1940s, an ambitious young Jewish man was making a mistake if he went to work for one of the large corporations, unless it was a company that had been founded by Jews. Even after he and his brother Robert parlayed a successful family business into one of the largest diversified financial corporations in America, worth billions, he still told us in a 1980 interview that "the Jews are better off not being in these big corporations because all they'll do is get bogged down."[1] A few years later, he bought CBS.[2]

Nor did it seem like a good idea for Jews to seek elected office when Stephen Isaacs published his book on Jews and American politics in 1974, in which he presented extensive evidence that Jews were more involved in the political process than any other group of Americans in terms of voter turnout, work on political campaigns, fund-raising, political polling, and political commentary. "In America," Isaacs wrote, "Jews stand out in every political area save one: holding elective office."[3] By the 1990s, however, far more Jews had been elected to the Senate and the House than would be expected on the basis of their representation in the population at large, even from districts with a relative handful of Jewish voters.

Nor was the military free of discrimination against Jews. Leonard Kaplan was one of 955 entering members of the class of 1922 at the U.S. Naval Academy. When the members of each class arrived at Annapolis in those days, each was required to write his name, hometown, date and place of birth, religion, and father's occupation in a register. Kaplan was one of seventeen midshipmen who wrote that their religion was "Jewish" or "Hebrew."[4]

Kaplan's experience at the Naval Academy consisted of four years of vicious and abominable treatment by his classmates. In the lingo of the day, he was "sent to Coventry"—no one spoke to him or even acknowledged his presence. He lived alone for four years. When the yearbook appeared at the end of his senior year, it included a crude cartoon of him, a derogatory biographical sketch (claiming, for example, that he was "born in the township of Zion, county of Cork, State of Ignorance"), and his name was omitted from the index; moreover, unlike all the other pages in the yearbook, the page about him was perforated so that it could be torn out and discarded with ease.[5] In 1995, the head of the CIA and the top admiral in the navy were both Jewish, and the fact was virtually ignored by the media.

Anti-Semitism at the Naval Academy was part of a broader pattern of prejudice and discrimination against Jews in America in the 1920s. Henry Ford, one of the most influential and respected Americans (one survey of college students found that he was rated the third "greatest man of all time," right after Napoleon and Jesus Christ), was virulently anti-Semitic. His public statements and his publications earned him the attention of many who hated Jews and presumably helped to persuade others to do so. In fact, Adolf Hitler periodically expressed his admiration for Ford, stating that "we look to Ford as the leader of the growing Fascist party in America," and "I regard Henry Ford as my inspiration."[6] Throughout the 1920s, many Jews refused to purchase Ford automobiles.[7] By the 1950s, however, after Henry Ford had died, a Jewish investment banker from Wall Street, Sidney Weinberg, was the Ford family's primary financial adviser, and he sat on the board of Ford Motors, as well as on the boards of a number of other corporations, including B. F. Goodrich, Kraft, and Cluett-Peabody.[8]

Nor were the most prestigious colleges and universities free of discrimination against Jews, either in their hiring or in their admissions policies. In 1922, the president of Harvard urged the university to adopt a quota system to solve "the Jewish problem." A similar stance by the president of Columbia University cut the percentage of Jews at Columbia from 40 to 20 percent within two years. Many medical schools and other professional schools joined a growing number of undergraduate colleges in restricting admissions for Jewish students. Jewish academicians had a difficult time obtaining positions or attaining tenure at these schools. By the mid-1970s, however, one-third of the faculty at Harvard and almost half the Yale Law School faculty were Jewish. At the same time, approximately one-fourth of the students at Harvard, Yale, Princeton, and Columbia were Jewish. Moreover, by 1993, five of the eight Ivy League institutions were headed by Jews.[9]

Anti-Semitism is not dead in America, but study after study indicates that it has diminished dramatically since World War II, and Jews have ended up more successful than any other white immigrant group. As Seymour Martin Lipset and Earl Raab write, Jews are "the best educated, the most middle-class, and, ultimately, the most affluent ethnoreligious group in the country. No other immigrant group has evinced such rapid and dramatic success."[10]

But Jews are not merely "the most middle-class" and the most affluent white immigrant group. They have become full-fledged members of the power elite, which makes it useful to look at the dramatic change Jews have experienced for clues to understanding the prejudice and obstacles that face women and people of color when they demand entry into the higher levels of society. First, however, there is a tricky preliminary question that must be addressed.

SO, WHO'S JEWISH ANYHOW?

As a girl, Dianne Goldman had a double exposure to religion: her mother was Catholic and her father was Jewish. She attended Catholic schools, graduating in 1951 from the Convent of the Sacred Heart High School in San Francisco. She recalls of her upbringing, "I was brought up supposedly with some Catholic religion and some Jewish, and I was to choose. I went to a convent and I went to a temple at the same time, but I don't think that works very well."[11] Married three times to Jewish men named Jack Berman, Bertram Feinstein, and Richard Blum,[12] she goes by the surname of her second husband. But is Dianne Feinstein, U.S. senator from California, Jewish?

Richard Darman held a series of high-level government jobs during the administrations of Ronald Reagan and George H. W. Bush, including director of the Office of Management and Budget. His grandfather had been president of his synagogue, his father, the founder and president of another synagogue. Darman himself was raised as a Jew and had a bar mitzvah. But Darman married a Gentile woman and became an Episcopalian.[13] Is Darman Jewish?

Whether Dianne Feinstein or Richard Darman is Jewish depends on whom you ask and what definition is used. It is no easy question. Indeed, the noted anthropologist Melville Herskovitz claimed that "of all human groupings, there is none wherein the problem of definition has proved to be more difficult than for the Jews."[14] Defining who is Jewish may not be the most difficult of "all human groupings"—as we will see in subsequent chapters, defining who is black, Hispanic, or Asian American is no easy task either—but it is certainly a matter of considerable complexity.

At different times, in different places, and with different political agendas, different criteria have been applied to determine whether or not someone is

Jewish. In general, four major definitions have prevailed. The first and most traditional is based on the *halacha*, the body of Jewish religious law, which states that a person is Jewish if he or she was born to a Jewish mother or has followed a prescribed set of procedures to convert to Judaism. A second way to define Jewishness is based not on birth or conversion but on conviction. According to this definition, people are Jewish if they consider themselves Jewish. This includes those whose mothers were Jewish and who see themselves as Jewish, those whose fathers were Jewish and who see themselves as Jewish, and those who have converted. A third way to define Jewishness is based on an ancestral tabulation, according to which a person who has one Jewish parent (like Dianne Feinstein) is half-Jewish, a person who has one Jewish grandparent is one-fourth Jewish, and so on. A fourth definition of Jewishness, somewhat similar to our second, is based on membership in such Jewish institutions as synagogues or Jewish clubs. Such membership not only implies that one's self-identity includes being Jewish, but it also suggests some willingness to make Jewish affiliations a part of one's public identity.

In this chapter, we generally draw on the second definition: if Dianne Feinstein thinks of herself as Jewish and Richard Darman thinks of himself as Episcopalian, those self-definitions are fine with us. But we will also pay attention to the third definition, whether one's parents or grandparents were Jewish. If, for example, a member of the political, corporate, or military elite had a parent or grandparent who was Jewish but was not told about this, or knew it and denied it, this situation is revealing, for it demonstrates just how powerful the pressures were to assimilate. It is, for example, one thing to say that the influential journalist Walter Lippman did not consider himself Jewish; it is quite another thing to say that he was born to wealthy and well-assimilated Jewish parents but would not join any Jewish organizations or even speak before any Jewish groups and refused to accept an award from the Jewish Academy of Arts and Sciences.[15]

We will also pay attention to the definition based on the religion of one's parents and grandparents because it has often been used by others to decide if a person is Jewish, and in some situations, other people's definitions of who we are take precedence over our own. As Laurence Tisch put it, "When Hitler came around he didn't ask questions whether you were or you weren't—it wasn't what you said, it was what he said."[16] Similarly, if the senior executives at a corporation did not want Jews in their midst, it was likely to be their definition of who was or was not Jewish that mattered. So, in order to understand why the power elite has been willing to accept more Jews into its ranks, we have to understand whom they have perceived as Jewish and why this is apparently no longer of such concern to them.

JEWS IN THE POWER ELITE FROM THE
ERA OF C. WRIGHT MILLS TO THE PRESENT

Americans have always believed what they still believe today, against all evidence to the contrary: Their society is different. It has no social classes. Anyone, through hard work, can be upwardly mobile. Even eminent historians contributed to this belief. In portrayals of corporate leaders and the very rich, they have stressed examples of men who had gone from rags to riches, just as in the stories Horatio Alger wrote. From this focus, the historians have proceeded to broad generalizations based on a small number of biographies. For example, in *Political and Social Growth of the American People*, Arthur Schlesinger Sr. claimed that business leaders arose "in most cases from obscure origins and unhindered by moral scruples, they were fired by a passionate will to succeed."[17]

But systematic studies have shown otherwise. When William Miller of the Harvard University Research Center in Entrepreneurial History studied the backgrounds of 190 men who were business leaders between 1901 and 1910, individuals "at the apex of some of the mightiest organizations the world up to then had seen," he found that very few had come from impoverished backgrounds or even from working-class or foreign origins. In fact, 79 percent had fathers who were businessmen or professionals; only 12 percent had fathers who were farmers, and only 2 percent had fathers who were "workers." Miller concluded that "American historians . . . stress this elite's typically lower-class, foreign, or farm origins and speculate on the forces that impelled men upward from such insalubrious environs. Yet poor immigrant boys and poor farm boys together actually make up no more than 3 percent of the business leaders who are the subject of this essay. . . . Poor immigrant and poor farm boys who become business leaders have always been more conspicuous in American history books than in American history."[18]

In another study of the backgrounds of business leaders, this one looking at the highest-ranking businessmen in 1900, 1925, and 1950, Mabel Newcomer, chairwoman of the economics department at Vassar, also found that they tended to come from the upper levels of the class structure. Fully 55.7 percent of the fathers of the 1950 executives had been business executives (seven times the proportion of business executives in the U.S. population at the time the executives were born), and another 17.8 percent had been professionals (six times the proportion of professional men in the population). When she divided the families of the 1950 executives into three classes and defined the lowest of the three as "poor," by which she meant those families that had not been able to contribute to their children's education beyond high school, she found that only 12.1 percent came from poor families. (The figure was virtually the same for the men who were top executives in 1900.[19])

When C. Wright Mills examined the backgrounds of the "very rich" in 1900, 1925, and 1950, he found no support for the prevailing myth that most were the sons of immigrants who had pulled themselves up by their own bootstraps. Instead, the data led Mills to the following characterization: "American-born, city-bred, eastern-originated, the very rich have been from families of higher class status, and, like other members of the new and old upper classes of local society . . . they have been Protestants. Moreover, about half have been Episcopalians, and a fourth, Presbyterians."[20]

The "very rich" identified by Mills were not exactly the same people who occupied positions in the political, corporate, and military elites, but there was, Mills found, considerable overlap, especially between the very rich and the corporate elite. When he looked separately at the men who made up the political, corporate, and military elites, he found, in each case, that most were Protestant and that they were especially likely to be Episcopalians and Presbyterians. For example, Mills wrote that the members of the corporate elite in 1950 were "predominately Protestant and more likely, in comparison with the proportions at large, to be Episcopalians or Presbyterians than Baptists or Methodists. The Jews and Catholics among them are fewer than among the population at large."[21]

The very rich and corporate elite also shared one other characteristic that Mills did not mention because of his purposeful neglect of political parties: they were, and still are, overwhelmingly Republican. The relatively few exceptions were wealthy Southern whites, who, until the 1970s, played a major role in the Democratic Party, where they joined with well-to-do Catholics and Jews who were Democrats due to the virulent prejudices of the Protestant rich in the first sixty years of the twentieth century.

JEWS IN THE CORPORATE ELITE

On December 14, 1973, readers of the *Wall Street Journal* awoke to the following headline: "Boss-to-Be at DuPont Is an Immigrant's Son Who Climbed Hard Way." This was news, indeed, for the boss-to-be was not merely an immigrant; nor had he merely climbed the hard way. He was Irving Shapiro, a Jew who had been named chairman of the board and chief executive officer of one of the oldest and largest corporations in America. Never before had a Jew achieved such a prominent position in a corporation that had not been founded or purchased by Jews. Shapiro assumed that his appointment was a harbinger of things to come and that the barriers that had prevented Jews from rising to the top in the corporate world were finally coming down. As he explained in an interview shortly before his retirement in 1981, "That's really been the great dividend from my position. All kinds of people have moved up in banks and other corporations simply on the premise that there is no longer a barrier."[22]

In order to show just how many doors to the corporate elite have opened for Jews, we will look at the presence of Jews in the higher circles of the corporate world throughout the twentieth century, paying special attention to their career pathways and to how their presence affected their identities as Jews. In later chapters, we will compare these pathways with those taken by women, African Americans, and other previously excluded groups.

The Overrepresentation of Jews in the Corporate Elite

For the most part, the religious makeup of the corporate elite changed very little throughout the first half of the twentieth century, though there is evidence of a slight increase in the percentage of Jews during that time. In his study of the backgrounds of business leaders between 1901 and 1910, Miller found that 90 percent were Protestant, 7 percent were Catholic, and 3 percent were Jewish.[23] In her study of the backgrounds of presidents and chairmen of the largest companies in 1900, 1925, and 1950, Newcomer found that the percentage of Jews in the corporate elite was 3.4 percent at the turn of the century and had risen to 4.3 percent by 1925 and 4.6 percent by 1950. Jews were "heavily concentrated in the merchandising, entertainment, and mass communications fields," but very few were to be found in "heavy industry or public utilities, and none at all among the railroad executives." Moreover, she estimated that 40 percent of the Jews in her 1950 sample had "organized their own enterprises."[24]

A number of studies of the postwar era reveal that the percentage of Jews in the corporate elite continued to climb. Although these studies used different samples and methods, all looked at the ethnic backgrounds of *Fortune*-level corporate directors. The results are compelling in their consistent finding that Jews have been increasingly overrepresented.

In 1972, as part of the American Leadership Study by the Bureau of Applied Social Research at Columbia University, a sample of directors of *Fortune*-level companies and "holders of large fortunes" were interviewed. Although Jews constituted only about 3 percent of the national population at that time, 6.9 percent of these business leaders and affluent men were Jewish.[25] These findings mirrored those of a 1976 survey conducted by *Fortune*, which showed that 7 percent of the chief executive officers of eight hundred American corporations were Jewish.[26] At about the same time, Frederick

Sturdivant and Roy Adler examined the backgrounds of 444 executives from 247 major American corporations. They found that 6 percent of their sample was Jewish.[27]

In a series of systematic studies performed in the late 1970s and in interviews with thirty Jewish corporate directors conducted in 1980 and 1981, we found that Jews were well represented in the corporate elite but were more likely to be in small *Fortune*-level companies than large ones. We also found that they had traveled different pathways in getting to the corporate elite than had their Gentile counterparts. Whereas Gentile executives were most likely to have advanced through the managerial ranks of the corporation, the Jewish directors were most likely to have joined the boards as outsiders with expertise in such areas as investment banking, corporate law, or public relations, unless they had risen through the ranks of companies owned or founded by Jews.[28]

It is both noteworthy and informative that many of these Jewish directors had attained skills in areas that subsequently became necessary to the corporations. Rather than merely figuring out ways to gain entry into the corridors of corporate power or waiting until the doors opened enough to let them in, many pursued less traditional areas, areas open to Jews, and the skills they developed later served as their entrée. In *A Certain People*, Charles Silberman describes the same pattern in prominent law firms and in the legal departments of large corporations in the postwar years. Both the corporations and law firms discovered that they needed lawyers who knew how to negotiate with trade unions and interpret the increasingly arcane tax laws.[29]

By the mid-1980s, studies indicated that the percentage of Jews in senior executive positions had climbed a bit higher. In a 1986 survey of the CEOs of *Fortune* 500 and Service 500 companies, modeled after Newcomer's 1955 study, *Fortune* found that 7.6 percent identified themselves as Jewish.[30] That same year, in a survey of 4,350 senior executives just below the chief executive level, Korn/Ferry International, an executive search firm, found that 7.4 percent were Jewish. More dramatic was the finding that 13 percent of those under the age of forty were Jewish.[31]

As part of his dissertation on persistence and change in the power elite, Ralph Pyle looked at the backgrounds of large samples of individuals listed in the 1950 and 1992 editions of *Who's Who in America*. When he examined the religious affiliations of those who were chief executive officers, directors, or vice presidents of *Fortune* 500 or Service 500 companies, he found that, in 1992, Episcopalians were 7.96 times as likely to be represented as their church membership figures would suggest (down from 8.42 times as likely in 1950); Presbyterians were 3.08 times as likely (down from 4.31 times as likely in 1950); and Jews were 2.76 times as likely (up from 0.76 times as likely in 1950). Episcopalians and Presbyterians were thus still very much overrepresented among corporate directors, though they had lost a little ground since 1950, but Jews had moved from being underrepresented in 1950 to being overrepresented in 1992.[32]

Pyle's systematic findings provide the most compelling evidence that the percentage of Jews in the corporate elite has increased since the 1950s. They do not, however, tell us whether Jews are less likely to be on the largest *Fortune*-level boards and more likely to be on the smaller ones because his data are based on relatively small samples.

We therefore pursued this question by applying a very different technique, one that we also employ in the chapters on Latinos and Asian Americans. For years, demographers have used the distinctive names within racial and ethnic groups to estimate the size of various populations. It is a strategy that sooner or later will lose its usefulness as distinctive groups intermarry and their children take on multiple social identities, but, for now, it is still accurate for Jews, Latinos, and Asian Americans over the age of thirty-five or so. As early as 1942, Samuel Kohs compiled a list of those names that appeared most frequently in the files of the Los Angeles Federation, an umbrella group for Jewish congregations and organizations in the Los Angeles area. Kohs found that the 106 most-common surnames accounted for about 16 percent of the names on various other Jewish Federation lists and that 35 names accounted for about 12 percent of the names on most lists. Various other researchers have since used his list of thirty-five names, or variations of it, and have found that the proportion of Jews with these distinctively Jewish names has remained relatively constant over time. Moreover, no meaningful differences in attitudes or behaviors have been found between Jews with distinctive and nondistinctive names.[33]

To determine the number of Jews on boards at the top and bottom of the *Fortune* list, we looked up each of companies ranked #1 to #100 and each of the companies ranked between #401 and #500 for 1975, 1985, 1995, and 2004 in the corresponding editions of the *Standard and Poor's Directory*, which includes all the names of the men and women who sit on boards of directors. For each, we counted names that appear on the list of distinctive Jewish names. Since the thirty-five distinctive Jewish names account for about 12 percent of the overall Jewish population, this gives us a factor of 8.33 for estimating the total number of Jews on these boards. That is, because 8.33 × 12 percent equals 100 percent, multiplying the number of times these thirty-five names appear by 8.33 provides an estimate for the total number of Jews on the boards. The results can be seen in table 2.1.

Table 2.1.   **Corporate Directors with Distinctive Jewish Names**

	Companies Ranked		
Year	1–100	401–500	Combined
1975	11	14	25
1985	8	9	17
1995	17	5	22
2004	15	15	30

If we are correct in our assumption that the distinctive Jewish name technique can be applied to corporate directors, then these figures suggest, first, that the total number of Jews with distinctive Jewish names on *Fortune* 500 boards decreased slightly, then increased, from 1975 to 2004. Second, the presence of people with distinctive Jewish names on the boards of the biggest companies (#1 to #100) has not been consistently greater than or less than the number on the boards of the smaller companies (#401 to #500). Third, if it is the case that the number of Jews with these 35 distinctive Jewish names represents about 12 percent of the total number of Jews in the population under study, then the number of Jews on the 200 *Fortune* boards we looked at was about 210 in 1975, 140 in 1985, 185 in 1995, and 250 in 2004. These figures represent 6.6 percent, 4.3 percent, 7.7 percent, and 11.1 percent, respectively, of the total number of directors of the corporations studied.[34]

The data based on distinctive Jewish names provide only an estimate of the percentage of Jews on corporate boards. Still, as table 2.2 shows, these findings, along with other findings reported in this section, demonstrate that as the percentage of Jews in America declined steadily in the twentieth century,

Table 2.2.   **Jews in the Corporate Elite**

Year	Jews in Corporate Elite (%)	Jews in Population (%)*	Source
1900	3.4	—	Newcomer 1955
1925	4.3	3.4	Newcomer 1955
1950	4.6	3.3	Newcomer 1955
1972	6.9	2.9	Alba and Moore 1982
1976	7.0	2.7	Burck 1976
1976	6.0	2.7	Sturdivant and Adler 1976
1986	7.6	2.5	McLomus 1986
1986	7.4	2.5	Bennett 1986
1995	7.7	2.3	DJN technique
2004	11.1	2.2	DJN technique

* The figures in this column are from the *American Jewish Yearbook* and the *Encyclopedia Judaica*; prior to 1925, the estimates included only those Jews who were members of Jewish congregations, so no figure appears for 1900.

the percentage of Jews on corporate boards increased. Jews are most certainly overrepresented in the corporate elite.[35]

Do Jews in the Corporate Elite Stay Jewish?

As we have indicated, the various waves of Jewish immigrants to America felt strong pressure to assimilate into the dominant Gentile culture. Many immigrants thus worked at becoming "more American" and "less Jewish." "More American" typically meant learning to speak English without an accent, dressing the way people in the new country dressed, and generally learning the cultural mores. "Less Jewish" sometimes meant decreased involvement in synagogues and other Jewish organizations, changing one's name, or having one's nose "fixed."[36]

Intermarriage patterns provide the best indicator of the extent to which American Jews have been able and willing to assimilate. Milton Gordon considers intermarriage "the keystone in the arch of assimilation"; more recently, Lipset and Raab have called it "the definitive evidence of diminished group cohesion."[37] Until the middle of the twentieth century, marriages between Jews and non-Jews were the exception rather than the rule.

In a classic study, sociologist Ruby Jo Reeves Kennedy looked at the records of more than eight thousand marriages in New Haven, Connecticut, between 1870 and 1940. She found that there had been a loosening of what she called "strict endogamy": by the end of the period, more Protestants of different denominations married one another than was the case earlier, and more Irish American Catholics married Italian American Catholics. But there had also been a strong persistence of "religious endogamy": as of 1940, the rate of in-group marriage was 80 percent for Protestants, 84 percent for Catholics, and 94 percent for Jews. Kennedy therefore proposed that the idea of America as a "melting pot" should be replaced by an alternative image, that of the "triple melting pot." Even after updating her study to include data from 1950, Kennedy argued that "cultural lines may fade, but religious barriers are holding fast."[38]

Those religious barriers eventually broke down. Richard Alba's extensive research led him to conclude that "the well-known triple–melting pot thesis . . . does not seem to be holding up," and its breakdown, though demonstrable for all non-Hispanic white Americans, is "best illustrated by the marriage patterns of Jews."[39] One study of Jews who married between 1966 and 1972 revealed that 32 percent married outside the faith.[40] As of 2004, sociologists estimated the figure to be about 50 percent.[41] Almost all those who marry non-Jews remain Jewish, but only one-seventh of their spouses convert to Judaism. Slightly less than one-third of the children of these mixed marriages are brought up Jewish, and only about 10 percent of them marry Jews. As Lipset and Raab conclude, "The cycle is downward. There is some reason to give credence to the sour joke: 'What do you call the grandchildren of inter-married Jews? Christians!'"[42]

In the context of this larger pattern of assimilation, we have found that Jews who have been successful in the corporate world have been even more likely than other Jews to assimilate, and they have done so in ways that have allowed them to fit comfortably into the power elite. For Jews at the top of the class hierarchy, class has come to supersede religious identity.[43]

In an interview study of graduates of the Harvard Business School, we asked both Jewish and Gentile managers about how Jews had been treated in their companies. For the most part, the respondents indicated that Jews had done well, but some were convinced that certain kinds of Jews were more likely to be successful than others. As one of the Jewish respondents put it, "If an individual is perceived as quite Jewish, into Jewish social events, it may have a negative impact. Those who have moved faster in this company are the less visible Jews." Another told us that one of his Jewish colleagues had never visited Israel because of his fear that it would have "political ram-ifications."[44]

The most candid comments came from one of the Gentile interviewees, who acknowledged his own prejudices as he explained his view of how things worked at his company:

> If you really want to know the way I feel, I think at the top levels, being Jew-ish will hurt a person's chances. But it depends on how he plays his cards. This one man I know is so polished, such an upper-class person, there's no way to know he's Jewish. I'll admit I'm prejudiced. There are certain aspects of Jewish people I don't like—they're pushy, they're loud, especially those damn New York bastards. Christ, I'm so sick of hearing about Israel. My friend is fine, however. He's an upper-class-type person, the kind who could make it to the top.[45]

Given this portrayal of the corporate world, we were not surprised to find, both in a series of systematic studies comparing Jews who were and were not corporate directors and in the interviews we conducted with Jewish directors, that Jews in the corporate elite are less likely to see Jewishness as a salient part of their identity than are other Jews. Moreover, we found that this was particularly true of those corporate directors whose parents or grandparents had also been in the corporate elite and that there were no differences in this regard between German Jews and the handful of Eastern European Jews who came from wealthy backgrounds. This was not only true in terms of marriage patterns but in terms of their interest in Israel, the likelihood of their having visited Israel, and the ways they chose to reveal (or not reveal) their Jewish identity in books like *Who's Who in America*.[46]

Those corporate directors we interviewed who were the first in their families to make it into the corporate elite, men like Laurence Tisch and Irving Shapiro, were still very much involved in and committed to Jewish issues. They had married Jews, for example, and had been to Israel many times. Those, however, who were of the second or third generation in their families to have been among America's economic elite—men like Joseph Frederick Cullman III, who was then chairman of the board and CEO at Philip Morris, and William Wishnick, chairman of the board and CEO at Witco Chemical, a company started by his father—had married non-Jews and were less likely to have visited Israel. We asked those we interviewed what being Jewish meant to them. The responses of the second- and third-generation members of the corporate elite were revealing. The most telling came from one man who paused and then admitted, "It really doesn't mean anything."[47]

Our research and the work of others indicate that over the past fifty years, Jews have been successful in the corporate world and have steadily increased their presence among the corporate elite. The doors that opened at DuPont for Irving Shapiro did portend the ascent of other Jews to leadership in non-Jewish companies. It did not turn heads—it certainly did not warrant shocked front-page headlines in the *Wall Street Journal*—when Richard Rosenberg, the Jewish son of a clothing salesman, became chair and CEO at the Bank of America, or when the Walt Disney Company, founded by a man who had refused to hire Jews, picked as its CEO and chairman Michael Eisner, a Jew from a wealthy New York family, to save it from the threat of a hostile takeover.[48]

At the same time, however, because of the general pressures and inducements to assimilate, being Jewish is likely to become progressively less important to these successful Jews and less important still to their children and their grandchildren. The pattern of socialization into the power elite ensures that the people who enter the higher circles do not differ significantly from those who are already there. Those who can "fit in" best are most likely to get there, and this means, at least in corporations not founded or owned by Jews, that those who put less public emphasis on their Jewishness are most likely to make it to the top. So, ironically, fifty years after Mills wrote his book, more Jews are in the corporate elite, but the longer they have been there, the less likely are they to be Jewish in any meaningful sense. Whether these same patterns will reappear for other excluded groups is a key question that we explore throughout this book.

JEWS IN THE CABINET

When we looked at the cabinets of each president from Dwight D. Eisenhower through George W. Bush (as of July 2005), we found that Jews have held 16 of the 239 cabinet positions (6.7 percent).[49] Table 2.3 lists these men (all have been men). Strikingly, there were no Jews among the seventy-eight cabinet appointees made by Ronald Reagan and both George Bushes until, in his second term, George W. Bush appointed Michael Chertoff as secretary of homeland security to replace Thomas Ridge. All of the other presidents since 1956 (Eisenhower, Kennedy, Johnson, Nixon, Ford, Carter, and Clinton) appointed at least one Jewish person to their cabinets. Whereas 14 percent of all cabinet appointments by Democratic presidents have been Jews, only 2 percent of all cabinet appointments by Republican presidents have been Jewish.[50]

Each of these sixteen Jewish men married at least once, and each had at least one child. About half of them married non-Jews, which reflects the frequency of intermarriage found among Jews and especially among successful Jewish businessmen. Wilbur Cohen married a Unitarian. Henry Kissinger's second marriage was to an Episcopalian. Michael Blumenthal, the CEO of the Bendix Corporation when President Carter appointed him, married a Presbyterian and, according to a profile in *Current Biography*, "he was baptized as a Presbyterian about the time of his marriage."[51] How-

Table 2.3. Jews in Presidential Cabinets, 1956–2005

Name	Presidency	Years Served	Department
Lewis Strauss	Eisenhower	1958–1959	Commerce
Arthur Goldberg	Kennedy	1961–1962	Labor
Abraham Ribicoff	Kennedy	1961–1962	Health Education and Welfare
Wilbur Cohen	Johnson	1968–1969	Health Education and Welfare
Henry Kissinger	Nixon-Ford	1973–1977	State
Edward Levi	Ford	1975–1977	Justice (attorney general)
Michael Blumenthal	Carter	1977–1979	Treasury
Harold Brown	Carter	1977–1981	Defense
Philip Klutznick	Carter	1980–1981	Commerce
Neil Goldschmidt	Carter	1979–1981	Transportation
Robert Reich	Clinton	1993–1997	Labor
Dan Glickman	Clinton	1995–1901	Agriculture
Mickey Kantor	Clinton	1997–1997	Commerce
Robert Rubin	Clinton	1995–1999	Treasury
Lawrence Summers	Clinton	1999–1901	Treasury
Michael Chertoff	George W. Bush	2005–present	Homeland Security

ever, the story did not end there. After serving in the cabinet, he returned to the corporate world, where he became the CEO of Burroughs Corporation, which in turn merged with Sperry to become UNISYS. When Blumenthal retired as CEO of UNISYS in 1990, he worked for five years as a limited partner for Lazard Freres. He also wrote a book about Germany and the Jews, which was a "personal exploration" that told the story of his own departure from Germany at the age of twelve to spend the war years in Shanghai, two of them in a Japanese internment camp. In 1998, he accepted an offer to head the development of the Jewish Museum, Berlin, a Holocaust memorial. Thus, after many decades of ignoring his Jewish origins, he returned to his roots through the book he wrote and through his near-total commitment to a successful memorial, which opened to high praise in 2002.[52]

The other Jewish cabinet members who have married non-Jews include Harold Brown, the person we mentioned in the opening chapter who had finally broken the anti-Semitic barrier at an exclusive Los Angeles club. Brown married an Episcopalian and, according to a profile in *Current Biography* written in 1977, he and his wife "now consider themselves 'unchurched.'" Neal Goldschmidt, Carter's secretary of transportation, married twice, both times to non-Jews. Robert Reich met his wife, who is not Jewish, when he was a Rhodes Scholar in England.[53]

These men are highly educated—almost all hold law degrees or doctorates. One of the exceptions is Lewis Strauss, who completed high school but, despite an early interest in physics, never attended college. Another exception, Wilbur Cohen, received a bachelor's degree in economics from the University of Wisconsin in 1934. He then accepted a job as a research assistant to one of his professors who had been appointed to a government position by Roosevelt to help formulate the Social Security Act. After twenty years in government service, Cohen became a professor of public welfare administration at the University of Michigan.

Most of these men came from comfortable circumstances, backgrounds that would be considered middle class or upper-middle class. Two, Kissinger and Blumenthal, were born in Germany and suffered the hardships of dislocation (especially Blumenthal, who, as we have noted, spent two years in an internment camp), but both of their families were solidly middle class. The parents of both Arthur Goldberg and Abraham Ribicoff were immigrants who had to struggle to make ends meet: Goldberg's father, who died when Arthur, the youngest of seven children, was eight, drove a horse and buggy around Chicago selling produce to hotels, and Ribicoff's father worked in a factory.[54]

JEWS IN THE MILITARY ELITE

Although Jews fought on both sides during the Civil War, by the late nine-teenth century, it was often claimed that Jews avoided or were incapable of military service. Mark Twain, for example, wrote that the Jew "is charged with a disinclination patriotically to stand by the flag as a soldier. By his make and his ways he is substantially a foreigner and even the angels dislike for-eigners."[55]

In response to such claims, in 1896, a group of seventy-eight Jewish veter-ans of the Union Army met in New York City and formed the Hebrew Union Veterans, a precursor to the Jewish War Veterans, an organization that sought to "uphold the fair name of the Jew and fight his battles wherever unjustly as-sailed" and "to gather and preserve the records of patriotic service performed by men of Jewish faith."[56] In 1984, the Jewish War Veterans opened the Na-tional Museum of Jewish History in Washington, D.C.

As we have seen, by the 1920s, when virulent anti-Semitism was wide-spread in the United States, Jews in the military were no freer from its pow-erful effects than other Jews. One of Leonard Kaplan's fellow midshipmen in the class of 1922 at the Naval Academy was Hyman Rickover, who, like Ka-plan, wrote "Hebrew" next to his name when he arrived in Annapolis in the fall of 1918. Unlike Kaplan, however, Rickover was not "sent to Coventry." Although he was seen as a "loner" and a "grind," he maintained cordial rela-tionships with his classmates. He was a competent student (he finished 106th in a class of 539), but it is unlikely that anyone would have predicted that he would become one of the most important military figures of the twentieth century.

Rickover was born in 1898 in a village north of Warsaw, Poland, and came to America as a small child, the son of a tailor. After spending his youth in Chicago, he was nominated to attend the Naval Academy by his congressman, Adolph Sabath, also an immigrant and a Jew. Rickover's career was long and distinguished. He served in the navy for more than sixty years, including thirty years in charge of the navy's nuclear power program, becoming known as the "father of the atomic submarine." His career was rife with controversy. In July 1951, he was passed over by the navy board for promotion to rear admiral; a year later, he was passed over again. Navy regulations did not permit a third try, and he would ordinarily have had to retire in mid-1953. But a massive lob-bying campaign outside the military created support for Rickover in Congress and the media, and he was promoted to rear admiral in July 1953. Twenty years later, in his mid-seventies, he became an admiral.

The opposition within the navy to promoting Rickover in the early 1950s may or may not have been based on his Jewish background. It is difficult to know for certain, for the navy boards that turned him down two years in a row held their meetings in secret. The reasons given publicly, of course, had nothing to do with his religious origins. But many of Rickover's supporters suspected that religion was a factor, and there can be no doubt that some admirals made anti-Semitic comments when speaking of Rickover. One admiral referred to him as "that little Jew," and another said of him, "When they circumcised him they threw the wrong end away."[57]

Ironically, Rickover had long since ceased thinking of himself as Jewish. In 1931, he married Ruth Masters, an Episcopalian, and left his Judaism behind. In fact, shortly after his marriage, he wrote a letter to his parents telling them of his decision to become an Episcopalian; his biographers wrote that he "lived for years without their forgiveness." Not only did he tell people that he was an Episcopalian, but when called upon to testify before congressional committees about nuclear power, he was prone to interlace his comments with references to Jesus.[58]

By the end of the twentieth century, there were Jews in the seniormost levels of the military establishment. Most striking was not merely their presence but the absence of any surprise that they were there. For many in the military, whether or not one is Jewish is simply no longer an issue. James Zimble, a former surgeon general of the navy who retired as a vice admiral (a three-star rank) and who at the time of our interview with him was president of the Uniformed Services University of the Health Sciences, asserted, "I have neither been victim of nor witnessed any anti-Semitism in the military. I know there are still redneck holdouts in the Deep South and elsewhere, but the military has gotten beyond that."[59]

Zimble's claims about the treatment of Jews in the military were echoed by others with whom we spoke, including Arnold Resnicoff, one of the two highest ranking rabbis in the navy at the time of our 1995 interview with him. As a navy rabbi for more than twenty years, he should have been aware of serious episodes of anti-Semitism in that branch of the military. In response to our question, he said, "There is no institution—and I believe this with all my heart, I'm not just giving you some company line—that fights prejudice, anti-Semitism, racism, as much as the military. Acts of overt anti-Semitism are extremely rare, and they are punished immediately. In all my years in the military, I have seen very few cases of anti-Semitism. Those were acts by individuals, and the institution reacted swiftly and forcefully." Resnicoff may have been unduly optimistic. He was called out of retirement in June 2005 to implement the recommendations of a panel that investigated and upheld charges of religious "insensitivity" at the Air Force Academy. This insensitivity included a football coach who hung a banner in the locker room declaring the players to be part of "Team Jesus Christ," pressures on cadets to attend chapel, government e-mails that cited the New Testament, and various other forms of Christian proselytizing (including comments to Jews, made by an air force chaplain, that they would burn in hell).[60]

Even with this relatively recent surge of super-Christianity at the Air Force Academy, which has made many Jewish observers nervous, the general view of those with whom we spoke was that the military fights prejudice, not only against Jews but also against blacks, Latinos, and, as one of them put it, "even women." They acknowledged that discrimination against homosexuals remains another, more difficult matter, one that we will return to in chapter 7. For now, let us consider the appointments of two Jewish men that support the assertion put forth by Zimble and Resnicoff that being Jewish is not an issue with regard to promotion in the military, even promotion to the very highest levels of the military establishment.

Jeremy Michael Boorda, who became the top-ranking naval officer in March 1994, turned out to be Jewish, though most people were unaware of that until it was mentioned in a long magazine profile about him that appeared in the *Washingtonian*. Boorda's parents, Herman and Gertrude Boorda, ran a dress shop in a small town in Illinois fifty miles south of Chicago. Their marriage was not a happy one, and there was so much tension in the home that Mike ran off and joined the navy in the middle of his junior year of high school.

Almost forty years later, married to a non-Jew and the father of three children, Boorda became a four-star admiral and the first Jewish member of the Joint Chiefs of Staff. At the time of his appointment, no one seemed to pay any attention to Boorda's Jewish background. In part, this may reflect the bureaucratic conformity demanded by the military. Mills noted that the military isolates its members, breaks down their previously acquired tastes and values, and thereby creates "a highly uniform type." The warlords, more than others in the power elite, according to Mills, come to "resemble one another, internally and externally."[61] In fact, in a celebrated case in the 1980s, the Supreme Court ruled that a military man did not have the right to wear a yarmulke. Such Jewish visibility, even as part of one's religious obligations, was deemed an inappropriate disruption of the uniformity of appearance required by the military.[62]

It is possible that no one paid attention to Boorda's Jewish background because of his own choice to assimilate. He ran away from a troubled and unhappy home, he married a non-Jewish woman, and even some of those who thought they knew him well were surprised to discover that he was Jewish. According to Retired Vice Adm. Bernard M. ("Bud") Kauderer, about a year before the *Washingtonian* article appeared, Boorda was going through a receiving line that included Adm. Sumner Shapiro, the former director of naval intelligence and a Jew. When he got to Shapiro in the line, Boorda leaned over to him and whispered, "You know, Shap, I'm one of you." Kauderer told us, "This was the first inkling we had that he was Jewish. It was a source of amazement to us."[63] But in our view, the most important reason that no one paid attention to Boorda's Jewish background was that, as Zimble and Resnicoff claimed, being Jewish is no longer an issue in the military.

The promotion of another Jewish man to a powerful position in the defense establishment provides additional support for the view that being Jewish is no longer an impediment to one's career. In March 1995, President Bill Clinton persuaded John Deutch, who had turned him down once before, to accept the nomination as director of the CIA. Deutch was born in Belgium in 1938, just thirteen months before the beginning of World War II. His family was able to escape the subsequent Nazi occupation by going first to Paris, then to Lisbon, and then, in 1940, to the United States. Deutch's father, a chemical engineer who helped invent the process for making synthetic rubber, became deputy director of the government's synthetic rubber program during the war. Deutch's mother, the daughter of diamond merchants, had a doctorate in ancient studies and allegedly spoke ten languages. Deutch attended the prominent Sidwell Friends School and received a BA from Amherst and a PhD in physical chemistry from the Massachusetts Institute of Technology (MIT). He first came to work at the Pentagon in 1961 at the age of twenty-two as one of the "whiz kids" who worked under Robert McNamara during the Kennedy administration. He left the Pentagon in 1966 to teach chemistry, first at Princeton and then at MIT. As the *New York Times* put it, since that time, "he has rotated between posts at M.I.T. and increasingly powerful positions in Democratic administrations."

In addition to his work at MIT and for the government, Deutch has also served corporations as both a board member and consultant. A lengthy profile of Deutch in the *Washingtonian* notes that, in 1992, his salary at MIT had been $207,000, but he had earned more than $600,000 from consulting and director's fees at twenty corporations, mostly defense contractors like Martin Marietta and TRW.[64]

As was true for Boorda at the time of his appointment, Deutch's religious background received virtually no mention in the press. Although a *New York Times* profile mentioned that "he and his family fled Belgium for France and eventually came to the United States," it did not state explicitly that he, or they, were Jewish. But Deutch is Jewish, as are the two women he has married, both of whom are from prominent German-Jewish families in the Washington area and were fellow students of his at Sidwell Friends.[65]

For a Jew to head the CIA is even more stunning a sign of acceptance than for a Jew to sit on the Joint Chiefs of Staff, for the CIA has historically been led by Christian men of impeccable upper-class credentials.[66] But Boorda's presence among the joint chiefs was a milestone as well, for the Joint Chiefs of Staff has also been a Gentile preserve, albeit a less socially exclusive one than the CIA. For a time during the Reagan presidency, the joint chiefs held "prayer breakfasts" led by one of Boorda's predecessors, the devout Roman Catholic four-star admiral, James Watkins.[67]

Jews, therefore, have made it to the top of the military elite. In addition to Harold Brown, Jimmy Carter's secretary of defense, Adm. Boorda, and CIA Director Deutch, numerous Jews have achieved the rank of two stars or higher (officers with a rank of two stars or higher represent only 0.2 percent of all officers).[68] Being Jewish in the military today is dramatically different from being Jewish at the Naval Academy in the early 1920s, or even from being Jewish in the military during the 1950s when Mills wrote *The Power Elite*.

JEWS IN CONGRESS AND ON THE SUPREME COURT

The Senate

Between 1844 and 1913, six men of Jewish background served in the U.S. Senate.[69] Then, for the next thirty-six years, there were no Jews until Herbert Lehman, having served as governor of New York for ten years and lost a Senate race in 1946, won a special election in 1949 after the incumbent resigned.

Table 2.4 lists the Jews elected to the Senate since 1950. As the table shows, three Jewish men were elected in the second half of the 1950s: Richard Neuberger of Oregon in 1955, Jacob Javits of New York in 1956 (replacing Lehman, who, at the age of seventy-eight, declined to run for a second full term), and Ernest Gruening of Alaska in 1958. Another, Abraham Ribicoff of Connecticut, was elected in 1962. By 1992, there were ten Jews in the Senate, and as of July 2005, there were eleven.[70] This list does not include William Cohen, who served as a senator from Maine from 1979 to 1996, whose father was Jewish.[71]

As is true for the Jews in presidential cabinets, there is a notable distinction between the two major political parties: seventeen of the twenty-three Jewish senators have been Democrats. Democrat or Republican, however, the increase in the number of Jewish senators not only means that the percentage is considerably higher than the percentage of Jews in the general population, but it also reflects a sea change in the political role played by Jews in America, who were once limited to behind-the-scenes parts.[72]

Table 2.4.   Jews in the Senate Since 1956

Name	Party/State	Years Served
Herbert Lehman	D-NY	1949–1956
Richard Neuberger	D-OR	1955–1960
Jacob Javits	R-NY	1957–1980
Ernest Gruening	D-AL	1959–1969
Abraham Ribicoff	D-CT	1963–1981
Howard Metzenbaum	D-OH	1974; 1977–1994
Richard Stone	D-FL	1975–1980
Edward Zorinsky	D-NE	1976–1987
Rudy Boschwitz	R-MN	1979–1990
Carl Levin	D-MI	1979–present
Warren Rudman	R-NH	1980–1993
Arlen Specter	R-PA	1981–present
Frank Lautenberg	D-NJ	1982–2001; 2003–present
Jacob (Chic) Hecht	R-NV	1983–1989
Herb Kohl	D-WI	1989–present
Joseph Lieberman	D-CT	1989–present
Paul Wellstone	D-MN	1991–2002
Dianne Feinstein	D-CA	1992–present
Barbara Boxer	D-CA	1993–present
Russell Feingold	D-WI	1993–present
Ron Wyden	D-OR	1996–present
Charles Schumer	D-NY	1999–present
Norm Coleman	R-MN	2003–present

Jews who have been elected to the Senate differ dramatically from one another in the degree to which they have been involved in Judaism. At one pole is Ernest Gruening, whose father was a prominent surgeon with a summer home in Rockport, Massachusetts. Gruening went to Hotchkiss and then to Harvard, first as an undergraduate and then as a medical student. Isaacs reports that Gruening "never paid the slightest attention to things Jewish," and there is no mention of his Jewish heritage in his lengthy autobiography.[73]

At the other pole is Joseph Lieberman, an Orthodox Jew married to a woman named Hadassah, a man who, in accordance with the regulations of his faith, does not use electrical appliances or ride elevators on the Sabbath. When Lieberman was elected in 1988 to the Senate, it was clear that things had changed, at least in Connecticut politics.

In 1992, eight months into his first term as mayor of Philadelphia, Ed Rendell was in the midst of a battle with unions as he tried to prevent the city from going into bankruptcy. In a heated moment, as a way to assert to the labor leaders that he was not going to budge, Rendell angrily informed them, "I'm Jewish, so I don't have the slightest chance of national office." He may have been correct in 1992, but four years later, his fellow Jewish Pennsyl-vanian, Senator Arlen Specter, became a candidate for the Republican presi-dential nomination, and eight years later, Lieberman (not just Jewish but, as noted, an orthodox Jew) had more than the "slightest chance" of winning na-tional office: he and his running mate, Al Gore, actually won the popular vote (though not the election). As one writer assessed Lieberman's vice presiden-tial candidacy, "one of the nation's most enduring truths — that Jews could ad-vance to the very top in American finance, journalism, and the arts, but not in politics — had become yesterday's myth."[74]

Although commitment to Orthodox Judaism is now acceptable, it is neither required nor expected. This was demonstrated by one of the more conse-quential episodes in the political life of two Jews in the Senate, one that took place in the Minnesota senatorial election of 1990. The Democratic nominee was Paul Wellstone, a liberal activist and professor of political science at Car-leton College who had never held political office and whose father had emi-grated from Russia in 1914. (His mother was born in the United States, but her parents were Russian Jewish immigrants.) The Republican nominee and incumbent was Rudy Boschwitz, who was born in Berlin in 1930 and fled to America with his family when he was very young. Boschwitz was heavily fa-vored, not only because he was the incumbent and not only because Well-stone was so inexperienced but because his campaign was much more heav-ily financed; Boschwitz raised seven times as much money as Wellstone.

But Wellstone ran an extremely effective and resourceful campaign, draw-ing on more than ten thousand volunteers, many of whom had been his stu-dents. Boschwitz, meanwhile, made a series of blunders, the worst of which was described by two Minnesota journalists as "one of the most memorable pratfalls ever witnessed in Minnesota politics."[75] He sent a letter to Jewish voters one week before the election to remind them of his own Jewish her-itage and support for Israel and to denounce Wellstone for raising his children as non-Jews and for having "no connection whatsoever with the Jewish com-munity or our communal life." This attack backfired, for it seemed to confirm Wellstone's claims that Boschwitz had been running a negative campaign.[76] By 1990, then, a Senate seat from a state with a very small percentage of Jew-ish residents could be contested by two Jews and could be decided in part by an apparent perception among voters, including many Jewish voters, that it was inappropriate for one candidate to criticize the other for the way he chose to live his life as a Jew.

Wellstone ran against Boschwitz again in 1996 and was reelected. He was campaigning for a third term, when he, his wife and daughter, three staff mem-bers, and two pilots died tragically in a plane crash in October 2002. Well-stone's Republican opponent, Norm Coleman, also Jewish, won the election against former senator Walter Mondale, who agreed to run at the last minute.

The twenty-three Jewish senators are similar to others in the power elite in a number of ways. Almost all have been married, some more than once. Of the six marriages by the five Jewish men elected to the Senate between 1949 and 1963, half were to non-Jews (Gruening's wife, Neuberger's wife, and Javits' first wife). In contrast, almost all of the Jewish men and women elected to the Senate after 1963 have married Jews. Although the national trend has revealed an increasing likelihood of marrying outside the faith, the more recently elected Jewish senators have been more, not less, likely to marry Jewish partners. This, too, suggests that the pressures for Jewish politicians to assimilate may have decreased over time.

All of the Jewish senators earned at least a bachelor's degree, and two-thirds have gone on to earn higher degrees (thirteen received law degrees, one a business degree, one a medical degree, and one a doctorate.). They differ from Jews in the corporate community and the executive branch of government, however, in that they come from a broader range of socioeconomic backgrounds. Some, like Javits, Ribicoff, and Lautenberg, were second-generation Americans who grew up in real poverty. Others, like Neuberger, Metzenbaum, Lieberman, and Boxer, had parents who owned small businesses. And some, like Lehman, Gruening, Kohl, and Feinstein, grew up in very comfortable economic settings. By the time they ran for the Senate, many had become millionaires.[77]

The House

There has been a similarly dramatic increase in the number of Jews elected to the 435-member House of Representatives, although the number has declined in the last decade. In 1975, there were only ten Jewish members of the House (2.3 percent), most of whom were elected in Jewish districts in New York. By 1993, there were thirty-three Jewish men and women in the House (7.6 percent), and they served districts scattered across the country, including many in which less than 1 percent of the voting population was Jewish. As of 2005, the number had dropped to twenty-six (5.9 percent), only one of whom was a Republican (the others were all Democrats, with one exception, Bernie Sanders of Vermont, a socialist who has run as an Independent).[78]

Supreme Court

In 1853, Millard Fillmore nominated Judah P. Benjamin, a Jew, to be on the Supreme Court, but Benjamin declined the nomination. It was more than sixty years before another president, Woodrow Wilson, nominated another Jew, Louis D. Brandeis, in 1916. Brandeis accepted, and, despite considerable opposition, he was confirmed. He served until 1939, the first of seven Jews to have served on the Supreme Court (as of July 2005, 108 men and women had served on the Court; therefore, 6.5 percent had been Jewish).[79]

Another Jew, Benjamin N. Cardozo, joined Brandeis on the Court in 1931 (he was nominated by Herbert Hoover, the only Republican president to have nominated a Jew to the Supreme Court). When Cardozo died, eight years later, Franklin Delano Roosevelt named Felix Frankfurter, who served until 1963. When Frankfurter left the Court, Arthur Goldberg replaced him and, when Goldberg left the Court after only two years, his replacement was Abe Fortas. When Fortas resigned in 1969, there were no Jews on the Court until 1993, when Clinton appointed Ruth Bader Ginsburg (the first Jewish woman Supreme Court justice) and then Stephen G. Breyer.[80]

Not surprisingly, these seven have had excellent academic credentials — four attended Harvard Law School, one attended Yale, two attended Columbia, and one attended Northwestern (the total is eight because Ginsburg attended both Harvard and Columbia). They come from varied class backgrounds. Brandeis is described by a current professor of law at the Yale Law School as "a well-educated, financially prosperous son of well-educated, commercially successful immigrants who had left Germany after the failure of the liberal revolutions of 1848."[81] Cardozo was from a well-to-do New York Sephardic Jewish family that arrived in America in 1654. Benjamin's father was a prominent lawyer, and the family lived in a fashionable neighborhood near Fifth Avenue.[82]

In contrast, Frankfurter's family emigrated from Austria when he was twelve and had little money. His father, Leopold, was descended from six generations of rabbis but was somewhat of a dreamer; after arriving in New York in 1894, he started a retail fur and silk business, which enabled the family to make it "from Seventh Street to the middle-class environs of Yorkville on East Seventy-first Street in only five years," but the family was never secure or economically comfortable (in contrast, Leopold's brother, who stayed in Vienna, became a prominent author and scholar). Like many Jewish immigrants of his generation, Frankfurter attended the City College of New York (CCNY). He did so well (he graduated third in his class of 774) that he went on to Harvard Law School (where he subsequently taught, at times as the only Jew on the faculty).[83] Similarly, Goldberg and Fortas were both American-born children of Eastern European Jewish immigrants. As noted above, Goldberg was the youngest of seven children born to Russian immigrant parents (his father was a peddler who drove a horse-drawn wagon), worked at odd jobs, and received scholarships to a junior college and DePaul before studying law at Northwestern. Fortas, the youngest of five children, was the son of Orthodox Jews who emigrated from England. His father "scratched out a living" at various jobs, including work as a jeweler, shopkeeper, pawnbroker, and cabinetmaker. Fortas, too, attended college on a scholarship (Southwestern University, from which he graduated first in his class), and then he graduated second in his class at Yale Law School.[84]

Ginsburg and Breyer are both the grandchildren of Eastern European immigrants. Ginsburg, born Joan Ruth Bader, was born in Brooklyn, where her parents lived in a working-class neighborhood. During her senior year of high school, her mother died of cancer and left her the "relatively large sum of $8,000 for her college tuition," which, because she had won a scholarship to Cornell, she gave to her father. Breyer grew up in San Francisco, where his father was a lawyer and his mother volunteered for the Democratic Party and the League of Women Voters. He attended Stanford and then Harvard Law School.[85] Both Ginsburg and Breyer were among the six millionaires on the Court in 2005. Ginsburg reported assets of between $6 million and $24 million, and Breyer listed holdings worth between $4 million and $15 million.[86]

These seven also vary in terms of the extent of their observation of the tenets of Judaism. Brandeis grew up in a secular home and had virtually no sense of Jewish affiliation. Shortly before he became a member of the Court, he stated, "I have been to a great extent separated from Jews. I am very ignorant in things Jewish." Cardozo was bar mitzvahed but did not practice Judaism as an adult (he remained a member of his Sephardic congregation but did not attend services; he referred to himself privately as a "heathen" and publicly as an agnostic). Frankfurter recounted that he went to the synagogue during the High Holidays while he was a student at CCNY, but he "left the service in the middle of it, never to return," for Judaism "ceased to have inner meaning." Fortas always identified himself as Jewish, but Judaism had little spiritual meaning for him; according to one biographer, "he viewed his religion as a handicap to disclose rather than as a heritage to claim."[87] Goldberg was the first Jew on the Supreme Court to remain observant throughout his adult life, though (unlike, say, Joseph Lieberman) he was not Orthodox; nor did he go to a synagogue every week. He did, however, attend services on the High Holidays of Rosh Hashanah and Yom Kippur, he and his wife held seders in their house during Passover, and, shortly after he became a member of the Supreme Court, when a scheduling conflict arose, he consulted his hometown rabbi back in Chicago about whether it would be acceptable to hear arguments on Yom Kippur.[88] Breyer attended religious school, but his family was not especially observant.[89]

CONCLUSION

The clear evidence of representation, or overrepresentation, of Jews in the corporate elite, the cabinet, and the military elite reflects a dramatic reversal of the discrimination experienced by Jews in these arenas until the final third of the twentieth century. Although Jews may still be underrepresented in some business sectors within the corporate community, the data we have examined reveal that Jews are overrepresented overall in the corporate elite. Jews are also now overrepresented in both the Senate and the House, where they tend to be Democrats. These findings lead to an important question: how have Jews been able to become part of what was formerly a Christian power elite and Congress?

They have done so in a number of ways, each of which might provide a basis of comparison in subsequent chapters as we consider the experiences of women and other previously excluded groups. First, Jews have had both the ability and the willingness to assimilate into what Alba has called the emerging ethnic category of "European Americans." Almost all Jews are white (there are almost one hundred thousand African Americans who are Jewish).[90] Virtually all of the Jews who have moved into the power elite, however, are white. The ethnic prejudice against Jews, therefore, was not accompanied by the added feature of race that African Americans, Asian Americans, and others of color have had to contend with. This may have made it easier for Jews to assimilate generally and, more specifically, to be accepted by those in the power elite. And this, we believe, is reflected by the dramatic increase in intermarriages between Jews and Gentiles.

A second factor is the strong cultural emphasis among Jews on academic success and the resulting overrepresentation of Jews among college graduates. This is even more the case for the best colleges and universities in America, which are golden highways to positions in the power elite and Congress. To the degree that women and people of color graduate from the best schools, we should see them in the power elite and in Congress.[91]

Related to the emphasis on academic success is the fact that many Jews came to America with experience as employers or shopkeepers in their own communities.[92] Some of them or their children had achieved financial success before doors began to open for them, primarily in retailing but also in fields like investment banking. It became difficult to exclude members of the Jewish community when they had the financial wherewithal to buy their way into the corporate elite. Once in, they were asked to join other boards as outside directors. And over time, especially with the various waves of mergers and acquisitions that make it difficult to know whether or not a company was founded or is owned by Jews, they have simply become part of the corporate elite. Similarly, because Jews were well educated, politically active, and had acquired all kinds of valuable expertise, as they became a potent group economically, more and more they began to appear in presidential cabinets and, by the 1990s, in Congress.

Alba refers to Jews as "the outstanding instance of a group that is managing to swim to some degree against the assimilatory tide."[93] This may be true when Jews are compared with other white non-Hispanic ethnic groups who are melding into European American homogeneity. But we have seen that Jews who have made it to the power elite have been likely to assimilate. In contrast to this pattern, however, we did find that recent Jewish senators were less likely than former Jewish senators to have married Gentiles.

A number of factors, then, seem to be important in understanding the successful entry by Jews into the power elite and Congress. They have light skin, and those who rise the highest are likely to have been born into relatively privileged circumstances. They have excellent educational credentials. They often have managerial skills, and they have made an effort to blend in. There is also a factor we have not mentioned: time. Second- and third-generation American Jews tend to have become fully acculturated, and non-Jewish whites seem to have become more accepting of them. In the chapters that follow, then, we shall focus on various factors, namely, class background, education, managerial experience, and color, as well as whether one was born in the United States (or one's parents were), to assess the importance of these variables in understanding why members of other previously excluded groups do or do not gain entry into the power elite and Congress.

NOTES

1. Laurence Tisch, interviewed by Richard Zweigenhaft, New York City, July 23, 1980.

2. Jonathan Kandell, "Laurence A. Tisch, Investor Known for Saving CBS Inc. from Takeover, Dies at 80," *New York Times*, November 16, 2003, 28.

3. Stephen D. Isaacs, *Jews and American Politics* (Garden City, NY: Doubleday, 1974), 10.

4. Norman Polmar and Thomas B. Allen, *Rickover: Controversy and Genius* (New York: Simon and Schuster, 1982), 39–40, 54.

5. Not all Jewish midshipmen at the Naval Academy in the early 1920s were "sent to Coventry," but various forms of hazing were widespread, and no one escaped it completely. Two members of the class of 1923 who may have been Jewish (one was named Seltzer and the other Wetherstine, but neither had listed himself as Jewish on arrival) attempted suicide as a result of the vicious hazing they experienced. This led to a congressional investigation (Polmar and Allen, *Rickover*, 51–52, 55–57).

6. Albert Lee, *Henry Ford and the Jews* (New York: Stein and Day, 1980), 3, 46.

7. Stanley Feldstein, *The Land That I Show You: Three Centuries of Jewish Life in America* (Garden City, NY: Anchor Press, 1978), 224–27.

8. Richard L. Zweigenhaft and G. William Domhoff, *Jews in the Protestant Establishment* (New York: Praeger, 1982), 31–33.

9. E. Digby Baltzell, *The Protestant Establishment: Aristocracy and Caste in America* (New York: Random House, 1964), 210–11; M. G. Synnott, *The Half-Opened*

Door: Discrimination at Harvard, Yale and Princeton, 1900–1970 (Westport, CT: Greenwood Press, 1979), 14–17; Dan A. Oren, *Joining the Club: A History of Jews and Yale* (New Haven, CT: Yale University Press, 1985); Susanne Klingenstein, *Jews in the American Academy, 1900–1940* (New Haven, CT: Yale University Press, 1991); Jerome Karabel, *The Chosen: The Hidden History of Admission and Exclusion at Harvard, Yale, and Princeton* (Boston: Houghton Mifflin, 2005). The estimate on Harvard's faculty is from Seymour Martin Lipset and David Reisman, *Education and Politics at Harvard* (New York: McGraw-Hill, 1975), 307. The estimate on Yale's law school faculty is from Robert A. Burt, *Two Jewish Justices: Outcasts in the Promised Land* (Berkeley: University of California Press, 1988), 1. The estimate on the percentage of Jewish students at Harvard, Yale, Princeton, and Columbia and the information about the Ivy League presidents are from Edward S. Shapiro, "The Friendly University: Jews in Academia Since World War II," *Judaism* 46, no. 3 (1997): 365–74.

10. Seymour Martin Lipset and Earl Raab, *Jews and the New American Scene* (Cambridge, MA: Harvard University Press, 1995), 27.

11. "Dianne Feinstein," *Current Biography* (1979): 128.

12. Jerry Roberts, *Dianne Feinstein: Never Let Them See You Cry* (New York: HarperCollins West, 1994).

13. Marjorie Williams, "The Long and the Short of Richard G. Darman," *Washington Post Magazine*, July 29, 1990, 25. Williams writes, "Darman grew touchy when asked about his grandfather and his religion, explaining that his background is 'complex,' including Jewish and Catholic forebears. He is, he said, 'a mongrel and currently a practicing Episcopalian.'" See, also, Barry Rubin, *Assimilation and Its Discontents* (New York: Knopf, 1995), 218.

14. Melville Herskovits, "Who Are the Jews?" in *Jewish-American Literature: An Anthology*, ed. Abraham Chapman, 471–93 (New York: New American Library, 1974), 473.

15. Ronald Steel, *Walter Lippman and the American Century* (Boston: Little, Brown & Co., 1980), 195. For a fascinating account of how Steel came to realize that Lippman's Jewish background was a source of great personal anguish and should be an important component of his biography, see Ronald Steel, "Living with Walter Lippman," in *Extraordinary Lives: The Art and Craft of American Biography*, ed. William Zinsser, 121–60 (Boston: Houghton Mifflin, 1986).

16. Tisch, interview with Zweigenhaft; see also Zweigenhaft and Domhoff, *Jews in the Protestant Establishment*, 102.

17. Arthur M. Schlesinger Sr., *Political and Social Growth of the American People: 1865–1940* (New York: Macmillan, 1941), 129.

18. William Miller, "American Historians and the Business Elite," in *Men in Business*, ed. William Miller, 309–28 (New York: Harper and Row, 1952), 328.

19. Mabel Newcomer, *The Big Business Executive: The Factors That Made Him, 1900–1950* (New York: Columbia University Press, 1955), 55, 62–63.

20. C. Wright Mills, *The Power Elite* (New York: Oxford University Press, 1956), 106.

21. Mills, *Power Elite*, 127–28.

22. Irving Shapiro, interviewed by Richard Zweigenhaft, Wilmington, Delaware, February 23, 1981. When Shapiro died twenty years later, the *New York Times* obitu-

ary made no mention that Shapiro was the first Jewish CEO of a major *Fortune* 500 company not founded by Jews, or even that he was Jewish. The obituary referred to Shapiro's father as "a Lithuanian immigrant who ran a dry-cleaning business in Minneapolis." Claudia H. Deutsch, "Irving Shapiro, 85, Lawyer and Ex-Chairman of DuPont," *New York Times*, September 15, 2001, B7.

23. Miller, "American Historians," 324.

24. Newcomer, *Big Business Executive*, 46–49.

25. Richard D. Alba and Gwen Moore, "Ethnicity in the American Elite," *American Sociological Review* 47 (1982): 373–83.

26. Charles G. Burck, "A Group Profile of the Fortune 500 Chief Executive," *Fortune*, May 1976, 174–75.

27. Frederick D. Sturdivant and Roy D. Adler, "Executive Origins: Still a Gray Flannel World," *Harvard Business Review*, November–December 1976, 125–33.

28. See Zweigenhaft and Domhoff, *Jews in the Protestant Establishment*, 25–46.

29. Charles E. Silberman, *A Certain People: American Jews and Their Lives Today* (New York: Summit Books, 1985), 96–97.

30. Maggie McComus, "Atop the Fortune 500: A Survey of the C.E.O.," *Fortune*, April 28, 1986, 26–31. In 1956, in addition to its list of the top five hundred industrial corporations, *Fortune* began to publish a list of nonindustrial companies. By 1983, that list had become the Service 500, with companies grouped in several categories (banks, diversified financial services, life insurance, etc.). In 1995, because of the considerable blurring of lines that had been caused by mergers and acquisitions, *Fortune* decided to combine the industrial and service companies into a single list. See Thomas A. Stewart, "A New 500 for the New Economy," *Fortune*, May 15, 1995, 166.

31. Robert A. Bennett, "No Longer a WASP Preserve," *New York Times*, June 29, 1986, F28.

32. Ralph E. Pyle, "Persistence and Change in the Establishment: Religion, Education and Gender among America's Elite, 1950 and 1992" (PhD dissertation, Purdue University, 1995), 143; see, also, Ralph E. Pyle, *Persistence and Change in the Protestant Establishment* (Westport, CT: Praeger, 1996), 62.

33. Harold S. Himmelfarb, R. Michael Loar, and Susan H. Mott, "Sampling by Ethnic Surnames: The Case of American Jews," *Public Opinion Quarterly* 47 (1983): 247–60. They conclude that the distinctive Jewish name (DJN) technique is particularly useful for those who are interested "in explanatory rather than descriptive studies (i.e., studies which are interested in explaining patterns rather than making accurate estimates of population characteristics") (254).

The thirty-five distinctive Jewish names are Berman, Bernstein, Caplan, Cohen, Cohn, Epstein, Feldman, Friedman, Ginsberg, Gold, Goldberg, Goldman, Goldstein, Greenberg, Grossman, Horowitz, Kahn, Kaplan, Katz, Levin, Levine, Levinson, Rosen, Rosenbaum, Rosenbloom, Rosenthal, Rothman, Rubin, Samuels, Shapiro, Siegel, Silverman, Weinberg, Weiner, and Weinstein.

Ira Rosenwaike, in "Surnames among American Jews," *Names* 38 (1990): 31–38, demonstrates not only that many Jews have names that are not at all distinctively Jewish, such as "Gordon" and "Miller," but that even among those people with distinctive

Jewish names, like Cohen, a small percentage are not Jewish. His data, based on a 1982 survey of 1.2 million American men and women, conducted by the American Cancer Society, indicate that about 89 percent of those with the names on the thirty-five-name DJN list are Jewish. Even taking this into account, the estimates that we will present of the number of Jewish directors on *Fortune* 500 boards are still substantially higher than the percentage of Jews in the larger population.

34. These percentages are based on an average board size of 16 in 1975 and 1985, 14 in 1995, and 11.2 in 2004. For the 1975, 1985, and 1995 estimates, see Murray Weidenbaum, "The Evolving Corporate Board," *Society*, March/April 1995, 12; for the 2004 estimate, we summed the number of board members on these two hundred boards and divided by two hundred. The figure we came up with (11.2) corresponded to that reported in Mark Thomsen, "Fortune Names Worst Corporate Boards," *Institutional Shareowner*, May 3, 2001, at www.institutionalshareowner.com.

35. Just how much the percentage of Jews in the general population has decreased is the topic of much debate in the Jewish community. A major report released in 2002 by the National Jewish Population Survey estimated that the number of American Jews had dropped by 300,000 from 1990 to 2000, reducing the number to 5.2 million. Critics claimed that the number of Jews was actually considerably higher ("It's utter nonsense," said one). The disagreements were based largely on how one defines who is a Jew. See Daniel J. Wakin, "A Count of U.S. Jews Sees a Dip; Others Demur," *New York Times*, October 9, 2002, A25. For our estimate of the number of Jews in 2004 (2.2 percent in table 2.2), we have used the 6.2 million estimate provided in the *American Jewish Yearbook* for 2002. The National Jewish Population Survey estimate of 5.2 million would lower the percentage to 1.9. Either way, the percentage of Jews in the larger population has declined.

36. Rubin, *Assimilation and Its Discontents*, 64.

37. Milton Gordon, *Assimilation in American Life* (New York: Oxford University Press, 1964), 8; Lipset and Raab, *Jews and the New American Scene*, 53.

38. Ruby Jo Reeves Kennedy, "Single or Triple Melting Pot? Intermarriage Trends in New Haven, 1870–1940," *American Journal of Sociology* 49, no. 4 (1944): 331–39; Ruby Jo Reeves Kennedy, "Single or Triple Melting Pot? Intermarriage in New Haven, 1870–1950," *American Journal of Sociology* 58, no.1 (1952): 56–59.

39. Richard Alba, *Ethnic Identity: The Transformation of White America* (New Haven, CT: Yale University Press, 1991), 14.

40. Steven M. Cohen, "The Coming Shrinkage of American Jewry: A Review of Recent Research," in *Renascence or Oblivion: Proceedings of a Conference on Jewish Population, 1978*, ed. J. Zimmerman and B. Trainin, 1–25 (New York: Federation of Jewish Philanthropies).

41. For an estimate of 50 percent, see Steven Steinberg, "The Melting Pot and the Color Line," in *Reinventing the Melting Pot: The New Immigrants and What It Means to Be American*, ed. Tamar Jacoby (New York: Basic Books, 2004), 239. Lipset and Raab cite a National Jewish Population Survey (NJPS) survey that found that, for the five-year period prior to 1990, the figure was 57 percent (*Jews and the New American Scene*, 45). These estimates have been controversial. When the NJPS released its "long-anticipated" study in 2003 based on data gathered in 2000 and 2001, the au-

thors of the study explained that the previous estimates were inflated because they had included people who said they were not raised as Jews. The revised estimates were 38 percent for 1980 to 1984 and 43 percent for 1985 to 1990; the new report estimated a 43 percent rate of intermarriage from 1990 to 1995 and a 47 percent rate by 2001. According to the project manager, among the "thorniest issues" was "how to define who is a Jew." Laurie Goodstein, "Survey Finds Slight Rise in Jews Intermarrying," *New York Times*, September 11, 2003, A13.

42. Lipset and Raab, *Jews and the New American Scene*, 72–73.

43. See Zweigenhaft and Domhoff, "Identity and Class in the Corporate Elite," ch. 5 in *Jews in the Protestant Establishment*," 89–111.

44. Richard L. Zweigenhaft, *Who Gets to the Top? Executive Suite Discrimination in the Eighties* (New York: Institute of Human Relations, 1984), 14–15.

45. Zweigenhaft, *Who Gets to the Top?* 12.

46. Zweigenhaft and Domhoff, *Jews in the Protestant Establishment*, 89–111.

47. Zweigenhaft and Domhoff, *Jews in the Protestant Establishment*, 110.

48. See Carrie Dolan, "BankAmerica's Rosenberg Will Succeed Clausen as Chief; Dividend Lifted 66%," *Wall Street Journal*, February 6, 1990, B8. This article does not mention Rosenberg's religion; nor was his religion mentioned in the much briefer announcement of his appointment in the *New York Times*. Rosenberg does, however, include that he is Jewish in his *Who's Who in America* biographical sketch. The information on Eisner is from *Current Biography* (1987): 154–57.

49. This is higher than the percentage of Jews in presidential cabinets from 1897 through 1972. In her study of presidential cabinets during those years, Beth Mintz found that, of the 166 people whose religion she could identify, 6 were Jewish. Jews, therefore, represented 3.6 percent of the total, a figure that was slightly higher than the percentage of Jews in the larger population at that time. Two were in the cabinets of Republican presidents (Oscar S. Straus, secretary of commerce and labor, 1906–1909, and Lewis L. Strauss, secretary of commerce, 1958–1959) and four were in the cabinets of Democratic presidents (Henry Morganthau Jr., secretary of the treasury, 1934–1945; Arthur J. Goldberg, secretary of labor, 1961–1962; Abraham A. Ribicoff, secretary of health, education, and welfare, 1961–1962; and Wilbur J. Cohen, secretary of health, education, and welfare, 1968–1969). Beth Mintz, "The President's Cabinet, 1897–1972: A Contribution to the Power Structure Debate," in "New Directions in Power Structure Research," ed. G. William Domhoff, special issue, *Insurgent Sociologist* 5, no. 3 (1975): 131–48.

50. For this analysis, we have included only cabinet positions, not "cabinet-level" positions such as ambassador to the United Nations or secretary for veterans' affairs, even though those who hold cabinet-level positions typically attend cabinet meetings. Nor have we counted Madeleine Albright, secretary of state during Clinton's second term, as Jewish. Albright was raised as a Catholic and later became an Episcopalian. Shortly after her confirmation as secretary of state, she learned that her parents had converted to Catholicism from Judaism and that three of her grandparents had died in the Holocaust. Her history adds another dimension to the difficult question of who is Jewish. Steven Erlanger, "Albright Grateful for her Parents' Painful Choices," *New York Times*, April 5, 1997. For Albright's reflections on this discovery, see Madeleine Al-

bright, "Names on the Synagogue Wall," ch. 15 in *Madam Secretary: A Memoir* (New York: Hyperion, 2003), 298–316. It should be noted that, although he appointed no Jews to his cabinet until Chertoff joined the cabinet in 2005, a number of Jews played important roles in the development of George W. Bush's foreign policy, especially Paul Wolfowitz, deputy secretary of defense, and Richard Perle, a resident fellow at the American Enterprise Institute. Also Jewish (though it is a surprise to many) is Lewis ("Scooter") Libby, who resigned as Vice President Dick Cheney's chief of staff hours after he was indicted for perjury related to the leak of the name of a CIA agent married to a critic of the White House. Libby, like George Bush, a graduate of Andover, has been a member of Temple Rodef Shalom, a Reform congregation in Falls Church, Virginia, for many years, although he apparently only attends services on the High Holidays. He is also a member of the Republican Jewish Coalition. See Ron Kampeas, "Libby Jewish? Some Wonder How Neo-con's Faith Impacts Leak Scandal," *JTA: Global News Service of the Jewish People* (online: www.jta.org), November 2, 2005.

51. "W. Michael Blumenthal," *Current Biography* (1977): 77.

52. W. Michael Blumenthal, *Invisible Wall: German and Jews, A Personal Exploration* (New York: Counterpoint, 1998).

53. "Harold Brown," *Current Biography* (1977): 89.

54. Like many Jewish immigrants who came to America, Goldberg's father came with skills that stood him in good stead, even though he had to do menial work. He had been the town clerk in the Ukrainian village from which he immigrated, and, as Goldberg's biographer writes, "In order to provide for their transit and his own survival, Joseph Goldberg quickly obtained work as a peddler. For an educated man, it was a less than ideal way to make a living, but the only paying job he could find." David L. Stebenne, *Arthur J. Goldberg: New Deal Liberal* (New York: Oxford University Press, 1996), 4.

55. Gloria R. Mosesson, *The Jewish War Veterans Story* (Washington, D.C.: The Jewish War Veterans of America, 1971), 17. In a subsequent article, in response to pressure from veterans' groups, Twain retracted these statements.

56. Mosesson, *The Jewish War Veterans Story*, 19.

57. Polmar and Allen, *Rickover*, 192, 194.

58. Polmar and Allen, *Rickover*, 80, 637.

59. Dr. James Zimble, interviewed by Richard Zweigenhaft, Bethesda, Maryland, August 25, 1995.

60. Rabbi Arnold Resnicoff, interviewed by telephone by Richard Zweigenhaft, August 25, 1995; Laurie Goodstein, "Air Force Chaplain Tells of Academy Proselytizing," *New York Times*, May 12, 2005, A22; "Air Force Names Rabbi to Bias Post," *New York Times*, June 28, 2005, A18; Clarence Page, "Thou Shalt Aim for Clarity," *Greensboro News & Record*, June 30, 2005, A7.

61. Mills, *The Power Elite*, 195.

62. *Goldman v. Weinberger*, 475 U.S. 503 (1986).

63. Bernard M. Kauderer, interviewed by telephone by Richard Zweigenhaft, October 27, 1995.

64. Tim Weiner, "Reluctant Helmsman for a Troubled Agency: John Mark Deutch," *New York Times,* March 11, 1995, A8. Nick Kotz, "Mission Impossible," *Washingtonian*, December 1995, 134.

65. In his cover article for *Parade* magazine, titled "Is He the CIA's Last, Best Hope?" November 19, 1995, Peter Maas makes no mention of Deutch's Jewish background. Nor is there any mention of Deutch's having attended an elite prep school: Deutch and his wife, we are told, went "to the same high school" (5). In a long article in the *New York Times Magazine* titled "The CIA's Most Important Mission: Itself," December 10, 1995, Tim Weiner did include information about Deutch's Jewish background (84). Kotz's *Washingtonian* article mentions that Deutch's family was Jewish and that his father was on the board of directors of the Washington Hebrew Congregation (66).

Days after Deutch stepped down as director of the CIA in December 1996, CIA technicians discovered highly classified information on five computers in his home. In August 1999, Deutch's security clearance was suspended, which was the first time in the agency's fifty-two years that a former director had been stripped of access to highly classified information. Deutch was the subject of a criminal investigation over the security lapses, but the Justice Department decided not to press charges. A searing report by the Senate Select Committee on Intelligence revealed that Deutch "had problems before becoming director with regard to the handling of classified information." Steven Lee Myers, "Former Chief of CIA Is Stripped of Right to Classified Information," *New York Times*, August 21, 1999, A1; Steven Lee Myers, "Former CIA Director Left Secrets Open to Theft, Agency Investigator Says," *New York Times*, February 23, 2000, A17.

66. See, for example, Burton Hersh, *The Old Boys: The American Elite and the Origins of the CIA* (New York: Scribner's, 1992).

67. Richard Halloran, "Navy's Chief Discusses Morality and Weapons," *New York Times*, May 6, 1983.

68. "Distribution of Active Duty Forces by Service, Rank, Sex, and Ethnic Group," 05/31/95, Washington, D.C.: Department of Defense. For more information, see ch. 3, n. 76.

69. They were David Levy Yulee, Florida, 1844–1860; Judah Benjamin, Louisiana, 1852–1860; Benjamin Franklin Jonas, Louisiana, 1879–1885; Joseph Simon, Oregon, 1897–1903; Isidor Rayner, Maryland, 1905–1912; and Simon Guggenheim, Colorado, 1907–1913. See Eli N. Evans, *Judah P. Benjamin: The Jewish Confederate* (New York: Free Press, 1988), xx, 32, 47–48, and 399; Isaacs, *Jews and American Politics*, 235; and L. Sandy Maisel, ed., *Jews in American Politics* (Lanham, MD: Rowman & Littlefield, 2001), 447.

70. *Congressional Quarterly*, November 7, 1992, 9; *Congressional Quarterly*, January 25, 2003, 192. As various writers have noted, with ten or more Jews in the Senate, there are enough for a "minyan," the requirement for public prayer services.

71. Cohen's father was Jewish and his mother was, as he describes her, "Irish, Protestant, and proud." Because his father wanted him to have a Jewish upbringing, Cohen began to prepare for his bar mitzvah when he was seven, and only at the age of twelve did he discover that he would have to undergo a special conversion ceremony because his mother was not Jewish. He refused to do so and became a Unitarian. William S. Cohen, *Roll Call: One Year in the United States Senate* (New York: Simon and Schuster, 1981), 60–62.

In a book about his two terms in the Senate, Warren Rudman (R-NH), who is Jewish, writes the following: "The irony was that most people outside Washington didn't know I was Jewish, while a lot of people mistakenly thought my friend Bill Cohen, the senator from Maine, was, because of his name. In fact his father is Jewish, but Bill's mother is an Irish Protestant. Bill received mountains of anti-Semitic mail. He would say, 'Rudman, you SOB, I'm going to take out an ad and tell people you're Jewish and they should write to you!'" Warren B. Rudman, *Combat: Twelve Years in the Senate* (New York: Random House, 1996), 32.

72. Isaacs, *Jews and American Politics,* 10.

73. Isaacs, *Jews and American Politics,* 202. Ernest Gruening, *Many Battles: The Autobiography of Ernest Gruening* (New York: Liveright, 1973).

74. Buzz Bissinger, *A Prayer for the City* (New York: Vintage Books, 1997), 131. Rendell served as mayor of Philadelphia until 1999. In 2002, he was elected governor of Pennsylvania. Elizabeth Kolbert, "It's Not the Most Conventional Run, But Specter Asserts He's in It to Win," *New York Times*, October 29, 1995, 13. David M. Shribman, "The Lieberman Candidacy," in Maisel, *Jews in American Politics*, xxvi.

75. Dennis J. McGrath and Dane Smith, *Professor Wellstone Goes to Washington: The Inside Story of a Grassroots U.S. Senate Campaign* (Minneapolis: University of Minnesota Press, 1995), 253.

76. McGrath and Smith, *Professor Wellstone Goes to Washington*, 253. See, also, Brent Staples, "Dirty Political Ads, Reconsidered," *New York Times*, November 11, 1990, section IV, 16; and "Ousted Senator Apologizes for Letter to Jews," *New York Times*, November 10, 1990, A10.

77. Among the millionaires are Lehman, Metzenbaum, Kohl, Lautenberg, and Feinstein. See R. W. Apple Jr., "Never Mind the Log Cabin," *New York Times*, October 16, 1994, E3.

78. *Congressional Quarterly*, November 7, 1992, 9; November 12, 1994, 11; January 4, 1997, 29; January 9, 1999, 63; January 20, 2001, 181; January 25, 2003, 193; January 31, 2005, 241; see, also, Michael Hoffman, "More Jews in Congress: Does It Make a Difference?" *Moment*, February 1993, 32–39. Many consider Sanders, who was reelected in 2004 with more than two-thirds of the vote, to be the front-runner for the vacant Senate seat in Vermont created by the decision of Republican-turned-Independent senator Jim Jeffords to step down in 2006. See John Nichols, "Being Like Bernie," *The Nation*, August 15 and 22, 2005, 15–18.

79. Robert A. Burt, "On the Bench: The Jewish Justices," in *Jews in American Politics*, ed. L. Sandy Maisel, 65–80 (Lanham, MD: Rowman & Littlefield, 2001). See, also, Robert A. Burt, *Two Jewish Justices: Outcasts in the Promised Land* (Berkeley: University of California Press, 1988), 7, and Allon Gal, *Brandeis of Boston* (Cambridge, MA: Harvard University Press, 1980), 195.

80. Burt, "On the Bench," 66.

81. Burt, "On the Bench," 67.

82. Burt, "On the Bench," 67. Andrew L. Kaufman, *Cardozo* (Cambridge, MA: Harvard University Press, 1998), 6. As was not unusual at the time, Cardozo spent two years at Columbia Law School but did not graduate (two-thirds of his classmates also left after the second year); see Kaufman, *Cardozo*, 49. Kaufman also

notes that prior to entering Columbia as an undergraduate, Cardozo and his brother were tutored by Horatio Alger. This was some years after Alger had been fired by the Unitarians for sexual misconduct. As Kaufman notes, "the fact that Alger committed pedophilia at the age of thirty-four casts a shadow over his subsequent yearning for relationships with boys and young men, but there is no evidence of any later misconduct" (25).

83. Michael E. Parrish, *Felix Frankfurter and His Times: The Reform Years* (New York: Free Press, 1982), 8–9, 14–15.

84. Burt, "On the Bench," 71–73. Also, Bruce Allen Murphy, *Fortas: The Rise and Ruin of a Supreme Court Justice* (New York: William Morrow, 1988), 3–4, 6–7, 13. See, also, http://goldberg.law.northwestern.edu/mainpages/bio.htm.

85. See www.oyez.org/oyez/resource/legal_entity/107/biography and www.oyez.org/oyez/resource/legal_entity/108/biography.

86. "Financial Portrait of the Justices Shows at Least Six Millionaires," *New York Times*, June 11, 2005, A11.

87. Burt, "On the Bench," 67, 71, 77; Kaufman, *Cardozo*, 25, 69. See, also, www.oyez.org/oyez/resource/legal_entity/108/biography.

88. David L. Stebenne, author of *Arthur J. Goldberg*, in phone conversation, June 6, 2005.

89. We do not know how observant Ruth Bader Ginsburg is.

90. See Bernard J. Wolfson, "The Soul of Judaism," *Emerge*, September 1995, 42–46. See, also, Karen Brodkin, *How Jews Became White Folks and What That Says about Race in America* (New Brunswick, NJ: Rutgers University Press, 1998).

91. See Karen D. Arnold, "Getting to the Top: What Role Do Elite Colleges Play?" in *About Campus* (San Francisco: Jossey-Bass, November–December 2002), 4–12.

92. Stephen Steinberg, *The Ethnic Myth: Race, Ethnicity and Class* (New York: Atheneum, 1981), 93–103.

93. Alba, *Ethnic Identity*, 309.

Chapter Three

Women in the Power Elite

The power elite depicted by C. Wright Mills was, without doubt, an exclusively male preserve. On the opening page of *The Power Elite*, Mills stated clearly that "the power elite is composed of men whose positions enable them to transcend the ordinary environments of ordinary men and women."[1] Although there were some women in the corporate, political, and military worlds, very few were in or near the higher circles that constituted the power elite. Are they there now? If so, how substantial and how visible is their presence? When did they arrive, and how did they get there? What are their future prospects? Do they fare better in Congress? These are some of the questions we will address in this chapter.

WOMEN IN THE CORPORATE ELITE

Women on Corporate Boards

In a chapter entitled "The Chief Executives," Mills described the men who owned and ran the largest corporations in the United States: "Large owners and executives in their self-financing corporations hold the keys of economic power. Not the politicians of the visible government, but the chief executives who sit in the political directorate, by fact and proxy, hold the power and the means of defending the privileges of their corporate world. If they do not reign, they do govern at many of the vital points of everyday life in America, and no powers effectively and consistently countervail against them, nor have they as corporate-made men developed any effectively restraining conscience."[2]

Who were these "corporate-made men" who occupied the "top two or three command posts" in each of the largest "hundred or so corporations"? As we indicated in chapter 2, when Mills systematically studied their backgrounds, the evidence showed clearly that they were not "country boys who [had] made good in the city" or the Horatio Alger types of popular myth; nor were they immigrants or even the sons of immigrants. Instead, Mills wrote, these executives, "today as in the past, were born with a big advantage: they managed to have fathers on at least upper-middle-class levels of occupation and income; they are Protestant, white, and American-born. These factors of origin led directly to their second big advantage: they are well-educated in the formal sense of college and post-college schooling."[3]

It went without saying that these "typical executives" were men. Although there were a handful of women on the boards of the top corporations, they were wives or daughters in family-controlled companies or presidents of prestigious women's colleges, and they were unlikely to sit in one of the few most important positions (the top two or three "command posts"). Mills virtually ignored women in the corporate elite because there were so few of them. His failure to make an issue of the absence of women in the corporate elite is evidence that he, too, was a product of his time. If Mills had seen this as an issue of importance, there can be no doubt that he would have addressed it. It was, for Mills as for most others, a given.

Mills died in 1962, a year before the publication of Betty Friedan's influential *The Feminine Mystique* and a few years before the rise of feminism on university campuses. By the 1970s, women had entered the corporate world in far greater numbers than ever before. Indeed, the sociologist Jerry A. Jacobs wrote in the early 1990s that "the increasing representation of women among the ranks of managers in organizations in the U.S. is perhaps the most dramatic shift in the sex composition of an occupation since clerical work became a female-dominated field in the late nineteenth century."[4] The progress of women in the highest levels of management was of interest to many. Journalists and academics asked with some frequency whether women had made it into the corporate elite, and, if not, why not?

In 1978, *Fortune* magazine presented the results of a systematic study of women on boards of directors of the thirteen hundred companies that made up the *Fortune* 500, the *Fortune* Second 500, and the six lists of the top fifty retailers, utilities, banks, life insurance companies, transportation companies, and diversified financial companies. Drawing on the proxy-statement lists, which, as required by law, include the names and salaries of the three highest-paid officers and any board members who earned more than $40,000 in the previous year, *Fortune* found that ten of the sixty-four hundred people identified were women, representing "a measly 0.16 percent." Nor did the presence of ten women in those corporate ranks represent progress: a similar study five years earlier had "turned up" eleven women.[5]

Mills's focus, as we have noted, was on the top two or three positions in the top "hundred or so" corporations. By this rather stringent standard, only one person in the 1978 survey came close to qualifying for membership in the corporate elite: Katharine Graham was the chief executive officer of the *Washington Post* (though it was ranked only #435 on the *Fortune* list in 1978, so it was not exactly in the top "hundred or so"). As *Fortune* put it, Graham was "catapulted from housewife to president of the company after her husband's suicide in 1963."[6] This was hyperbole, however, because Graham was not just a "housewife" before her husband's death. Educated at Vassar and the University of Chicago, the daughter of the multimillionaire former owner of the paper, and an experienced journalist herself, she found that her main challenge was being catapulted into a position that had always been held by a male, not being catapulted from the role of housewife.[7]

In 1962, Felice Schwartz founded Catalyst, a nonprofit agency specializing in women's job issues. Over the years, Catalyst developed a dual mission: to assist women in business and the professions in achieving their maximum potential, and to help employers capitalize on the abilities of their female employees. In 1977, responding to requests from some major corporations, Catalyst began its Corporate Board Resource. This program was designed to draw on Catalyst's database of women of achievement "to help board chairmen carefully select and recruit female directors."[8] By the late 1970s, then, Catalyst was systematically monitoring the progress of women on boards and simultaneously working with boards to increase the presence of women.

Using a slightly broader sample than *Fortune* did in 1973 and 1978, one that included all directors of the top thirteen hundred companies, not just those who had earned $40,000 or more that year, Catalyst found that in 1977 there were forty-six women on boards. By 1984, that figure had climbed to 367, 2.3 percent of all directors in the study.[9]

Starting in 1993, Catalyst began to publish its annual *Census of Female Board Directors* based on the top one thousand companies, namely, the *Fortune* 500 and the *Fortune* Service 500, as a way of calling attention to how few women sit on corporate boards. As Sheila Wellington, president of Catalyst, wrote in *Directorship Newsletter*, "Hardly had the ink dried on the *1993 Census* before more corporations were calling to alert us to the fact that they'd added a woman to their boards. For months, we fielded calls relaying names of female additions to boards. The day we began the 1994 count, the fax began a steady six-week hum, with company after company telling of their new women directors."[10] Clearly, by 1994 "company after company" felt the need to demonstrate that they had included women on their boards.

There has been a steady increase in the number of corporate directorships held by women, from 9.5 percent in 1995 to 13.6 percent in 2003. In 2003, almost all of the *Fortune* 500 companies had at least one woman director (446 of the 500, or 89.2 percent), and 47.6 percent had two or more, but only in 54 companies (10.8 percent) were 25 percent of the board seats filled by women. The larger *Fortune* companies tend to have more women on their boards than the smaller ones. In a separate analysis of the directors on *Fortune* 100 companies as of September 30, 2004, a Catalyst-sponsored study found that women held 16.9 percent of the total seats. Although the increases over the past decade have been steady, it is clear that it will take a long time before women, who own 48 percent of all stock in the United States, will achieve parity. Many women executives, not surprisingly, have been disappointed by these data.[11]

Moreover, various Catalyst studies have shown that within the *Fortune* 500 corporations, even fewer women hold the most senior and highest-paying positions. For example, in 2002, 5.2 percent of the top earners were women (up from 2.4 percent in 1995), and 7.9 percent of those holding the most important positions in the corporation (what Catalyst calls the "clout titles," such as chairman, chief executive, vice chairman, president, chief operating officer, and executive vice president) were women (up from 6.2 percent in 1997, the first year Catalyst assessed such data).[12]

Who are these women, and how did they come to be corporate directors? Do they come from backgrounds similar to or different from those of the white, Protestant, American-born sons of businessmen and professionals who constituted the corporate elite in 1956? What role do they play on the corporate boards: are they tokens, or have they assumed positions of importance equal to those of their male counterparts on their boards?

Three studies help answer these questions. The first was performed in 1977 by Burson-Marsteller, a public relations and advertising firm, for a client. The second was a 1986 doctoral dissertation by Beth Ghiloni. The third was done by Catalyst in 1991. Although their methods and samples differ, together these studies suggest some patterns and some changes over time in the characteristics of women on corporate boards.

All three studies found that the women directors were highly educated, better educated, in fact, than the male directors who sat on boards with them. Moreover, using attendance at exclusive prep schools, listing in the *Social Register*, or membership in an exclusive club as evidence of membership in the social upper class, and using ownership of large amounts of stock in a *Fortune*-level firm as evidence of membership in the economic upper class, Ghiloni concluded that 33 percent of her sample were from either the economic or the social upper class or both. This figure is similar to overall findings for samples of predominantly male directors for 1963 by G. William Domhoff and for 1970 by Thomas Dye.[13]

At the time the three studies were done, the women directors tended to take one of four routes to the corporate elite. The first and, at that time, most frequently traveled was the business route. About 40 percent classified themselves as businesswomen, but they had traveled different paths than the businessmen who sat on boards. Whereas the men had typically spent fifteen to twenty years moving up the ranks of a large corporation, the women were more likely to have been heads of non-*Fortune*-level companies. Many referred to themselves as "consultants," which was a grab bag category that included both large and small projects.[14] Some women directors had risen through the ranks of a single corporation to the level of vice president and had then been asked to join boards of firms other than the ones in which they held executive positions—they became outside directors even though they did not sit on the boards of their own firms.

The academic path was the second most frequently traveled route to the corporate board. Many of the directors were or had been university presidents, vice presidents, or deans.[15]

The volunteer career was the third most frequently traveled path to the corporate board. These women were especially likely to be members of the social upper class, to have attended one of the seven sister schools, and to have been in the Junior League, an exclusive service organization for women. Their experiences at the head of various nonprofit charitable and cultural organizations often put them in contact with directors and executives from the corporate world who sat on their boards of trustees. This, in turn, gave the women volunteers entrée onto the corporate boards.[16]

Finally, a legal career provided the fourth most frequently traveled pathway to the corporate board. The lawyers were the least likely of those in Ghiloni's study to have come from upper-class backgrounds ("only" 20 percent qualified as upper class by Ghiloni's criteria), and only a few had gone to prestigious law schools.[17]

Our look at the pathways traveled by more recent women directors indicates that all four pathways still hold, though more women are moving up through the corporations than in the past.

The Pressure to Assimilate

Obviously, a woman cannot pass as a man in the same way that a Jewish man can pass as a Gentile. A woman in the corporate world may have to find other ways to show that she is "one of the boys," even while struggling to maintain her sense of femininity.

This can put her in no-win situations. In the early 1970s, Cecily Cannan Selby, the national executive director of the Girl Scouts of America, became the first woman to sit on the board of Avon. One of the first meetings she attended was a dinner meeting, and the atmosphere was rather tense. After the meal, one of the men offered her a cigar. "When I accepted," she recalls, "I could feel them all relax."[18]

Rosabeth Moss Kanter has suggested that the need to reduce uncertainty in large and impersonal institutions leads to the strong emphases on conformity in behavior and homogeneity in background: "It is the uncertainty quotient that causes management to become so socially restricting; to develop tight inner circles excluding social strangers; to keep control in the hands of socially homogenous peers; to stress conformity and insist upon a diffuse, unbounded loyalty; and to prefer ease of communication and thus social certainty over the strains of dealing with people who are 'different.'"[19]

A few years after Kanter's book appeared, when we interviewed black and white Jewish and Gentile men and women who had MBAs from Harvard and were in (or had been in) the corporate world, this theme emerged again and again. Notably, the Jewish women we interviewed agreed that being a woman posed more of a hurdle than being Jewish. A number of them, however, explained that this did not mean that their Jewishness was completely without significance. As one put it, "It's not irrelevant. It's part of the total package. Ultimately, in the fishbowl-type environment you're in, they scrutinize you carefully. It's part of the question of whether you fit the mold. Are you like me or not? If too much doesn't fit, it impacts you negatively." Another explained, "It's the whole package. I heard second-hand from someone as to how I would be perceived as a pushy Jewish broad who went and got an MBA. Both elements, being Jewish and being a woman, together with having the MBA, were combined to create a stereotype. I had to work against that stereotype from the first day." Another summed the situation up by saying, "Anything that makes you different is more likely to be a factor at senior levels because it's so much more homogeneous there."[20]

In 1990, Elizabeth Dole, then secretary of labor (and, since January 2003, a member of the Senate), initiated a department-level investigation into the question of whether or not there was a "glass ceiling" blocking women and minorities from the highest ranks of U.S. corporations. When the report was issued by the Federal Glass Ceiling Commission in 1995, comments by the white male managers who had been interviewed and surveyed supported the earlier claims that upper management was willing to accept women and minorities only if they were not too different. As one manager explained, "What's important is comfort, chemistry, relationships, and collaborations. That's what makes a shop work. When we find minorities and women who think like we do, we snatch them up."[21]

One *Fortune* 500 labor relations executive used the phrase "comfort zone" to make the same point about "chemistry" and reducing "uncertainty": "You need to build relationships," she said, "and you need to be pretty savvy. And for a woman or a person of color at this company, you have to put in more effort to get into this comfort zone."[22]

Much has been made of the fact that men have traditionally been socialized to play competitive team sports and women have not. In *The Managerial Woman*, Margaret Hennig and Anne Jardim argue that the experience of having participated in competitive team sports provides men with many advantages in the corporate world. Playing on sports teams teaches boys such things as how to develop their individual skills in the context of helping the team to win, how to develop cooperative, goal-oriented relationships with teammates, how to focus on winning, and how to deal with losing. "The experience of most little girls," they wrote in the mid-1970s, "has no parallel."[23] Although the opportunities for young women to participate in competitive sports, including team sports like basketball and soccer, have increased dramatically in recent years, far fewer opportunities were available when many of the women now in higher management in U.S. corporations were young.[24]

Just as football is often identified as the classic competitive and aggressive team sport that prepares men for the rough-and-tumble (and hierarchical) world of the corporation, an individual sport, golf, is the more convivial, but still competitive, game that allows boys to play together, shoot the breeze, and do business. As Marcia Chambers shows in *The Unplayable Lie*, the golf course, and especially the country club, can be as segregated by sex as the football field. Few clubs bar women, but some clubs do not allow women to vote, sit on their governing boards, or play golf on weekend mornings.[25]

Many women managers are convinced that their careers suffer because of discrimination against them by golf clubs. In a study of executives who manage "corporate-government affairs," Denise Benoit Scott found that the women in such positions "share meals with staff members and other government relations officials but never play golf." In contrast, men in such positions "play golf with a broad range of people in business and government, including legislators and top corporate executives." As one of the women she interviewed put it, "I wish I played golf. I think golf is the key. If you want to make it, you have to play golf."[26]

Similarly, when the editors of *Executive Female* magazine surveyed the top fifty women in line-management positions (in sales, marketing, production, and general management with a direct impact on the company's bottom line), they asked them why more women had not made it to the "upper reaches of corporate America." The most frequently identified problem was the "comfort factor"—the men atop their corporations wanted others around them with whom they were comfortable, and that generally meant other men similar to themselves. One of the other most frequently identified problems, not unrelated to the comfort factor, was the exclusion from "the social networks—the clubs, the golf course—where the informal networking that is so important to moving up the ladder often takes place."[27]

Based on the interviews they conducted for *Members of the Club*, Dawn-Marie Driscoll and Carol Goldberg also conclude that there is an important connection between golf and business. Both Driscoll and Goldberg have held directorships on major corporate boards. They establish their insider status at the beginning of their book: "We are both insiders. We always have been and probably always will be." In a section entitled "The Link That Counts," they explain how they came to realize the importance of golf: "We heard so many stories about golf that we began to pay more attention to the interaction between golf and business. We realized the importance of golf had been right in front of our eyes all the time, but because neither of us played golf, we had missed it as an issue for executive women. But golf is central to many business circles."[28]

A few months before Bill Clinton was elected president, his future secretary of energy had some pertinent comments about the importance of fitting into corporate culture and the relevance of playing golf. "Without losing your own personality," said Hazel O'Leary, then an executive vice president at Northern States Power in Minnesota, "it's important to be part of the prevailing corporate culture. At this company, it's golf. I've resisted learning to play golf all my life, but I finally had to admit I was missing something that way." She took up golf.[29]

There is evidence that the golf anxiety expressed by women executives has its counterpart in the attitudes held by male executives: in its 1995 report, the Federal Glass Ceiling Commission found that many white male executives "fretted" that minorities and women did not know how to play golf.[30]

Whether or not playing golf is necessary to fit in, it is clear that women who make it into the corporate elite must assimilate sufficiently into the predominantly male culture to make it into the comfort zone. As Kathleen Jamieson points out, however, this can place them in a double bind. On the one hand, women in the corporate world are expected to be competitive and tough-minded, but not too competitive or tough-minded, or they risk being called ballbusters. On the other hand, women in the corporate world are expected to be feminine enough to be seen as attractive and caring, but not too feminine, lest their appearance and behavior be seen as inappropriate or as an indication that they are tender-minded.[31]

Another factor helps smooth the way into the comfort zone for some women: family connections. In 1980, when we interviewed multimillionaire

Jay Pritzker for *Jews in the Protestant Establishment*, we asked him about his extremely successful and wealthy family. By the 1980s, the Pritzkers' businesses included the Hyatt hotels, Braniff Airlines, *McCall's* magazine, casinos, cable television systems, vast tracts of real estate, and hundreds of thousands of acres of timberland. At the time of our interview, various male members of the next generation had entered the family businesses, but none of the women had. Although we talked about where his children and nieces and nephews had attended high school, whether or not they had married Jews, and the fact that some of the sons had joined the family business, no mention was made of the daughters' doing so.[32]

Penny Pritzker, Jay's niece, was at that time a twenty-year-old senior at Harvard. After graduating in 1981 with a degree in economics, she went to Stanford, where, by 1985, she had earned both an LLB and an MBA. By the early 1990s, she had become the head of Classic Residence by Hyatt, a chain of upscale homes for the elderly, and chairman (the term she then preferred) of Coast-to-Coast Financial Savings and Loan, which managed over $1 billion in assets. After Jay Pritzker's death in 1999, she and two of her cousins emerged as those making key decisions about how to manage the $15 billion family pie; some of those decisions were successfully challenged in court by an eighteen-year-old female cousin, who, two years later, received $450 million in a settlement (as one lawyer put it, "Clearly, a divorce is taking place here").[33]

Penny Pritzker is just one of a number of nieces and daughters to emerge at the top of some of America's largest corporations and financial institutions. Another is Abigail Johnson; born in 1961 and holding a BA from Hobart and William Smith Colleges and an MBA from Harvard, she manages one of the portfolios of Fidelity Investments, a company owned by FMR Corp. In 1994, her father, Edward C. ("Ned") Johnson III, gave her a voting stake in FMR equal to his own and put her on the board. *Business Week* speculated at the time, "It's looking increasingly likely that Abby will eventually succeed him as chairman of the nation's largest mutual-fund firm." The official line is that her father (though seventy-five) has no plans to retire and that she is, as she claimed late in 2004, "100 percent focused on the job at hand."[34] Yet another daughter of an aging tycoon is Shari Redstone, whose father, Sumner Redstone, controls Viacom, the giant media company. After receiving a BA from Tufts in 1975, she went to law school at Boston University, focusing on tax law. She worked briefly for a law firm as a defense attorney, got married, got divorced, and began to work for her father, first in the family's privately owned business, National Amusements, and then for Viacom. She has had conflicts with Mel Karmazin, the company's president, and it is not clear that she will succeed her father; either way, she will emerge as a woman with considerable corporate clout. As one writer put it, "Whatever happens with Mr. Karmazin, Mr. Redstone, who is 80, has dynastic goals that could leave his daughter a very powerful player at the table: she will one day control Viacom shares that have a current value of $7.5 billion and 71 percent of the shareholders' vote."[35]

Aside from wanting their companies to appear diverse (especially if they cater to a diverse clientele), does something more drive corporations to include women in higher management and on their boards? We think there is. It has to do with the use of women to create a "buffer zone."

As part of his analysis of the transition from a pure patriarchal system, in which all power is held by males, to modern capitalism, Michael Mann proposes that "a kind of compromise between patriarchy and a more gendered stratification hierarchy has emerged," both in the households and in the marketplace. In this compromise, women now occupy buffer zones between the men of their own class and the men in the classes below. This phenomenon appears at every point in the class hierarchy. Women who are part-time and unskilled manual laborers in low-income jobs, for example, serve as a buffer between the mostly male unemployed below them and the mostly male skilled manual workers above them. Secretaries and other white-collar women interact with the blue-collar workers who do maintenance jobs and deliver packages for the male managers. Women are the nurses and paralegals for physicians and lawyers. And women in the higher reaches function as a buffer between "capital and all labor" by serving as volunteers, fundraisers, and board members for a wide range of charitable and social service organizations.[36]

Drawing on this analysis, we conclude that the men who run America's corporations have women in higher management and on their boards not only to present a corporate image of diversity but to provide a valuable buffer between the men who control the corporation and the corporation's labor force (and the general public). It is not surprising, therefore, that Catalyst has found that relatively few of the women officers who hold the titles of executive vice president, senior vice president, or vice president have positions with operational responsibility for profit and loss. Instead, many are channeled into positions specializing in such areas as labor relations and public relations.[37] It is in these jobs especially that women are used as effective buffers. Because these staff jobs seldom lead to positions in top management, Ghiloni concluded her study of the velvet ghetto of public affairs in a top-fifty corporation by noting that "women can play an increasingly important role in the corporation and still not gain power."[38]

Long before women joined corporate boards or were employed in personnel and public relations, women of the upper class interceded in the social system in ways that smoothed out the hard-edged, profit-oriented impact of a business-driven economy. In the Progressive Era, some upper-class women argued for protective labor legislation, maximum hours, and more respectful treatment of labor. They came to call themselves "volunteers" as they took a hand in running health, cultural, and social welfare agencies that added a humane, socially concerned dimension to their lives of wealth and privilege. First in nonprofit institutions and now in corporations, we see the intersection of gender and class in a way that serves the power elite by providing a buffer zone between the wealthy few and the rest of society.[39]

Women as CEOs, in the Legal World, and on Wall Street

In 1978, the futurist Herman Kahn was asked how long he thought it would take before 25 percent of the chief executives of the *Fortune* 500 were women. "About two thousand years," he replied, "but make it 10 percent, and I'll say within twenty years."[40] Kahn was not the only one in the late 1970s to predict that before the turn of the century, more than just a few women would become CEOs of *Fortune*-level companies. In 1976, *Business Week* identified the "top 100 corporate women" and claimed that it would not be long until some became chief executive officers of *Fortune*-level companies. But when the magazine interviewed these one hundred women eleven years later, it found that their progress up the corporate ladder had been quite slow. As *Business Week* summed up the situation in 1987, "Many are sticking it out, though, resigned to the idea that they may advance—but never to the highest corporate offices. Others have abandoned big companies to start their own businesses, new careers, or families."[41]

In that 1987 article, *Business Week* acknowledged that "now, more than a decade later, it is clear that the optimism was overblown." Optimism, however, springs eternal in the *Business Week* breast, for the very article that acknowledged the previous "overblown" optimism was titled "Corporate Women: They're About to Break Through to the Top," and it listed "fifty women to watch." Only one of the fifty had been on the 1976 list of one hundred. The fifty corporate women on the 1987 list, *Business Week* assured its readers, were different from the hundred on the 1976 list: "These women are vastly different—better educated, more single-minded, and more confident about their prospects. They have reason to be: Their generation has achieved far greater success in the corporate world in much less time than the original 100, and many are poised at the CEO's doorway."[42]

The *Wall Street Journal* chimed in with its own prediction in 1987. In an article entitled "Five Future No. 1's" the *Journal* identified five women who were likely to become CEOs of *Fortune* 500 companies within a decade: Deborah Coleman (then vice president of operations for Apple Computer), Karen

Horn (then chairman and CEO-elect of Banc One Corp's Cleveland Unit), Kay Koplovitz (then president and CEO of USA Network, which was jointly owned by Time, Inc., Paramount Pictures, and MCA), Colombe Nicholas (then president of the American arm of Christian Dior), and Linda Wachner (president of Warnaco).[43]

The envelopes, please. From 1977 until 1986, Katharine Graham of the *Washington Post* was the only woman CEO of a *Fortune* 500 company. By late 1996, when we completed work on the first edition of this book, there had been four women CEOs of *Fortune* 500 companies: Katharine Graham of the *Washington Post* (she retired in 1991); Marion Sandler, co-CEO and co-founder with her husband of Golden West (#491 in 1996); Linda Wachner, president and CEO of Warnaco from 1986 to 2001; and Jill Barad, who was named CEO of Mattel (#342 in 1996) in August 1996.[44]

In the years since the publication of the first edition of this book, another nine women have become CEOs of *Fortune* 500 companies. Table 3.1 lists the names of the thirteen women who have been CEOs of *Fortune* 500 corporations. As of November 2005, eight women were CEOs of *Fortune* 500 companies (thus making up 1.6 percent of the five hundred CEOs of *Fortune* 500 companies).

All of the thirteen earned their BAs in a variety of liberal arts disciplines. About 40 percent went to elite schools (including Wellesley, Vassar, Georgetown, Princeton, and Stanford), and the others attended local colleges and universities (such as Queens College, Marymount, University of Southern Arkansas, William Paterson University, and the State University of New York, Buffalo). Two earned master's degrees and one attended Harvard's Advanced Management Program. Carly Fiorina, who was CEO at Hewlett-

Table 3.1. Women CEOs of *Fortune* 500 Companies

Name	F500 Company	F500 Rank in 2005	Years of Service
Marion O. Sandler	Golden West Financial	#435	1963–present
Katherine Graham	Washington Post	#526	1977–1991
Linda J. Wachner	Warnaco	#939	1986–Nov. 01
Jill E. Barad	Mattel	#383	Oct. 97–Feb. 00
Carleton S. Fiorina	Hewlett-Packard	#11	July 99–Feb. 05
S. Marce Fuller	Mirant	#424	July 99–present
Andrea Jung	Avon	#278	Nov. 99–present
Cinda A. Hallman	Spherion	#698	Apr. 01–Apr. 04
Anne M. Mulcahy	Xerox	#132	Aug. 01–present
Patricia F. Russo	Lucent	#247	Jan. 02–present
Eileen Scott	Pathmark Stores	#467	Oct. 02–present
Mary Sammons	Rite Aid	#128	June 03–present
Brenda C. Barnes	Sara Lee	#114	Feb. 05–present

Packard (#11 in 2005) from 1999 through February 2005, for example, earned a BA from Stanford in medieval history and philosophy (she started law school but hated it and dropped out). Katherine Graham spent a year at Vassar and then transferred to the University of Chicago, where she majored in American history, and Andrea Jung, CEO of Avon since 1999, studied English literature at Princeton.

Most came from privileged circumstances. Marion Sandler's parents owned successful hardware and real estate businesses (she met her husband, Herb, a lawyer, vacationing in the Hamptons on Long Island). Katharine Graham, as noted above, was the daughter of the millionaire founder of the *Washington Post*. Jill Barad's father was an Emmy-award-winning television producer, and her mother was a pianist and an artist. Carly Fiorina's father was a judge and a law professor, and her mother was an artist. Andrea Jung's mother was a chemical engineer, and her father, an architect. Xerox CEO Anne Mulcahy's father was an English professor who became an editor for a New York publisher.

Three of the thirteen come from less privileged backgrounds. Cinda Hallman, former CEO of Spherion (#698 in 2005, but #443 in 2001), grew up in Texarkana, a town on the border of Texas and Arkansas. Neither of her parents graduated from college, though her father's family had been well-off, and he had inherited one of a number of farms owned by his parents. Her father, who died when she was fifteen, owned a couple of small farms and, when the family needed cash, hired himself out as a carpenter. She went to college on a scholarship and worked while in college to make ends meet.[45] Eileen Scott, CEO at Pathmark (#467 in 2005), is the daughter of a policeman. She grew up in a large Catholic family (she is one of eleven children) and started working for Pathmark in 1969 while she was in high school as a cashier and part-time bookkeeper; she graduated from William Paterson in 1976 with a degree in business administration, moved up through the management ranks of the company, and became CEO in October 2002. Brenda Barnes, who became CEO of Sara Lee (#114 in 2005) in February 2005, is the daughter of a factory worker father and a homemaker mother.[46]

If we expand our focus to include the entire *Fortune* 1000, another nine women are, or have been, CEOs of companies that have not made the top 500 list but ranked between 501 and 1,000. They, like the women who have been CEOs of *Fortune* 500 companies, tend to have been born to privilege and to be well educated (this group includes one woman with an MBA from Harvard, another with an MS in engineering, one with a law degree, and one with a PhD in clinical pharmacology).[47]

Eight of these nine women are white. The exception is Loida Lewis, a Filipina who took over TLC/Beatrice when her husband, Reginald Lewis, the company's founder, died. Lewis is from an upper-class Filipino family. Her wedding to Reginald Lewis in August 1969 was "a lavish ceremony that made the society pages of Philippine newspapers [and whose guests] included many of the country's top business and social elite. The country's then Vice President, Fernando Lopez, acted as one of the godfathers of the couple."[48] Two years after she took over, TLC/Beatrice liquidated its assets, and the company dropped out of the *Fortune* 1000.

It is noteworthy that in the early 1990s, relatively few male CEOs believed that their companies would select women to run their companies in the near future. In a study of 201 chief executives at the country's largest corporations, the respondents were asked, "How likely is it that your company will have a female CEO in the next ten years?" Only 2 percent said "very likely," and 14 percent said "somewhat likely." Correspondingly, at that time, women constituted only about 5 percent of the participants in the executive training seminars run by business schools, considered at many companies to be "an indispensable credential for future CEOs."[49]

Therefore, more than twenty-five years after futurist Herman Kahn made his prediction that within twenty years 10 percent of the *Fortune* 500 CEOs would be women, less than 2 percent are. Women now constitute about 14 percent of all directors of *Fortune*-level boards but a smaller percentage of the top-earning senior officers working within these corporations. Moreover, there is evidence that even those women who are on *Fortune*-level boards have been marginalized in terms of the actual board responsibilities that they have—or have not—been given. A number of studies have demonstrated that male directors are more likely than female directors to serve on the more important committees (such as the executive, finance, and compensation committees) and female directors are more likely to serve on the less important ("softer") committees like public relations.[50]

Women have made it into the highest circles of the legal world and Wall Street to about the same degree as women in the corporate elite. One study found that 13.6 of all partners in the country's largest law firms were women, but only 54 percent of these women were equity partners, which means those who share in their firm's profits (74 percent of the male partners were equity partners). Similarly, a study of the leading Wall Street investment and brokerage houses found that only about 8 percent of the managing directors were women. The study found that "the more glamorous and high paying jobs, such as investment banking and trading," were "even more of a male preserve than Wall St. itself."[51]

Just how much a male preserve Wall Street remains was highlighted in July 2004 when Morgan Stanley agreed to pay $54 million to settle a sex discrimination case rather than stand trial. This was the second largest settlement the Equal Employment Opportunity Commission had ever reached with a company. Nor was Morgan Stanley the only Wall Street firm to settle out of court for discrimination. In previous lawsuits, both Merrill Lynch and Smith Barney paid more than $200 million in settlements to women who worked in their brokerage operations. None of these firms was eager to have it said in court that it had tolerated "frat-house behavior" or to have the embarrassing numbers on compensation and promotion appear in the official court record. As the *New York Times* concluded, "Wall Street is still dominated by the white men who fill the bulk of the most powerful and highest-paying jobs in the industry."[52]

We return to the prospects for further advancement for women in corporations at the end of the chapter.

WOMEN IN THE CABINET

Since the Eisenhower administration, 20 women and 212 men have served in the cabinets of 10 presidents. Table 3.2 lists the names of all the women who have served in cabinets and the positions they held. *inner/outer Cabinet*

Table 3.2.   Women in Cabinets

Name	Presidency	Years Served	Department
Frances Perkins	Roosevelt	1933–1945	Labor
Post 1950			
Oveta Culp Hobby	Eisenhower	1953–1955	Health, Education, and Welfare
Carla Anderson Hills	Ford	1975–1977	Housing and Urban Development
Juanita A. Kreps	Carter	1977–1980	Commerce
Patricia R. Harris	Carter	1977–1979	Housing and Urban Development
Patricia R. Harris	Carter	1979–1981	Health, Education, and Welfare
Shirley M. Hufstedler	Carter	1979–1981	Education
Elizabeth H. Dole	Reagan	1983–1987	Transportation
Margaret M. Heckler	Reagan	1983–1985	Health and Human Services
Ann D. McLaughlin	Reagan	1987–1989	Labor
Elizabeth H. Dole	Bush	1989–1990	Labor
Lynn M. Martin	Bush	1990–1992	Labor
Barbara Franklin	Bush	1992–present	Commerce
Hazel R. O'Leary	Clinton	1993–1997	Energy
Janet Reno	Clinton	1993–2001	Justice (attorney general)
Donna E. Shalala	Clinton	1993–2001	Health and Human Services
Madeline K. Albright	Clinton	1997–2001	State
Alexis Herman	Clinton	1997–2001	Labor
Elaine Chao	Bush 2	2001–present	Labor
Gale Norton	Bush 2	2001–present	Interior
Ann Veneman	Bush 2	2001–present	Agriculture
Condoleezza Rice	Bush 2	2005–present	State
Margaret Spellings	Bush 2	2005–present	Education

Eisenhower appointed only one woman (as compared with twenty men). The next three presidents, John F. Kennedy, Lyndon Johnson, and Richard Nixon, named seventy people to their various cabinets, but not one woman, so the cabinet was an exclusively male club from 1955 until 1975, when Gerald Ford appointed a woman to be secretary of housing and urban development (HUD). Of Jimmy Carter's twenty-one cabinet members, three were women, one of whom held two different positions. Reagan's cabinets included thirty-three people, three of whom were women. Three of George H. W. Bush's twenty appointments were women (including Elizabeth Dole, who had also served in Reagan's cabinet), and five of Clinton's twenty-seven appointments were women. Of George W. Bush's twenty-four cabinet appointments (as of July 2005), five have been women. The number of women in presidential cabinets has thus increased since Mills wrote his book, especially under Clinton (19 percent) and George W. Bush (21 percent).[53]

The number of cabinet positions held by women is but one measure of their presence in the political elite. Another, perhaps more important, measure is the specific cabinet positions they have held. As the political scientist Thomas Cronin has written, "Vast differences exist in the scope and importance of cabinet-level departments. The three-million-person Defense Department and the sixteen-thousand-person or so departments of Labor or Housing and Urban Development are not similar." Cronin acknowledges that one can rank-order the cabinet positions in a variety of ways, including longevity, annual expenditures, and number of personnel, but his view is that the "contemporary cabinet" is best differentiated into "inner and outer cabinets." The inner cabinet includes the secretaries of state, defense, and treasury and the attorney general, all of whom cover "broad-ranging, multiple interests" and serve in a counseling role to the president. The remaining members of the cabinet are part of the outer cabinet; their departments tend to focus on domestic policy issues, and they tend to assume an advocacy role rather than a counseling role.[54]

Seventeen of the twenty women cabinet members have been in the outer cabinet—only Janet Reno, Clinton's attorney general, Madeleine Albright, Clinton's secretary of state beginning in 1997, and Condoleezza Rice, George W. Bush's secretary of state in his second term, have held positions in the inner cabinet. In their 1981 study of women in the power structure, Faye Huerta and Thomas Lane concluded that the women in the cabinet have held the "so called 'soft issue' areas such as housing, commerce and welfare." With the appointments of Reno, Albright, and Rice, this has changed.[55]

In her study of the social backgrounds of all members of the cabinet between 1897 and 1973, Beth Mintz found that almost two-thirds (63 percent) had fathers who held professional or managerial positions, 80 percent were Protestants (48 percent were either Episcopalian or Presbyterian), and 86 percent had completed four years of college or more. Many had direct links to the business community. "Typically," she noted, "a cabinet position is one of several governmental positions held in a process of business-government interchange."[56]

The twenty women who have served in the cabinet since 1953 have backgrounds similar to those Mintz found when she studied all cabinet members from 1879 through 1973. Most were born into economically secure families in which the fathers, or both parents, were well-educated professionals. The father of Oveta Culp Hobby, Eisenhower's secretary of health, education, and welfare, was a lawyer, and her husband owned the major newspaper in Houston. Both parents of Hazel O'Leary, Clinton's secretary of energy, were physicians. The parents of Barbara Franklin, George H. W. Bush's secretary of commerce, were both educators, as were the parents of Condoleezza Rice. The parents of Janet Reno were both journalists, and the fathers of Carla Hills (Ford's secretary of housing and urban development), Elizabeth Dole (Reagan's secretary of transportation and George H. W. Bush's secretary of labor), and Ann McLaughlin (Reagan's secretary of labor) were successful businessmen. Although Ann Veneman, George W. Bush's secretary of agriculture in his first term, likes to claim, "I was born a poor little peach farmer's daughter," her father owned a successful farm with peach orchards and grapes. During Veneman's childhood, he was elected to the California general assembly, and he then became undersecretary for health, education and welfare in the Nixon administration. "By the middle 1970s," writes Laura Flanders, "her father had become an influential man with powerful friends and he connected her to most of them."[57]

Two of the twenty were born outside the United States. Madeleine Albright, Clinton's secretary of state, was born in Czechoslovakia, where her father was a diplomat (she grew up speaking Czech, French, and some Polish), and Elaine Chao, George W. Bush's secretary of labor, was born in Taiwan and came to the United States at the age of eight. Her father left China as an apprentice merchant seaman about the time of the Chinese revolution in 1949 and went to Taiwan. The conventional story notes that he married, had three children, came to the United States, worked three jobs, sent for the wife and children, and then started a business that became wildly successful, allowing the family to rise through the class structure, moving from Queens, to Long Island, and ultimately to Westchester County. When Chao was nominated as secretary of labor, various politicians and commentators could not say the words "American dream" often enough.[58]

But there is a bit more to the story, namely, the suggestion that James Chao had more to draw on when he arrived in the United States than the conventional version indicates. Laura Flanders provides more details about what led

to this immigrant success story. Since Flanders has clearly done her home-
work, we will quote her at some length:

> Elaine Chao was born in Taiwan in 1953, to a family who fled from Shanghai
> after the Chinese revolution in 1949. These were difficult years for Chinese anti-
> communists, but Elaine's father, James, had had the luck not only to attend one
> of his country's finest universities with Jiang Zemin, the future leader of the
> People's Republic, but also to fall in with the immensely powerful Shanghai-
> born family the Tungs, who shifted their operations to Taiwan for a time. The
> Tung dynasty is powerful in Chinese politics and business to this day. Hong
> Kong's first chief executive after reunification with mainland China was Tung
> Chee Hwa, the first child of the magnate Tung Chao Yung, in whose Maritime
> Trust company James Chao got his start. James Chao married into another pow-
> erful family: the Hsus (pronounced "shoe"). His wife's family would later oper-
> ate a shipping empire in Hong Kong. Did James Chao arrive in the U.S. with
> nothing? Quite possibly, but Chao had, as one who knows his history put it, "ac-
> cess to plenty." Chao was connected to powerful families in Taiwan—the cen-
> ter of U.S.-Sino relations during the embargo against mainland China—and in
> trade, connections translate into freight.[59]

Both Albright and Chao, then, were born in other countries and made the
difficult transition to a new culture, but each began her journey in a family
with advantages.

Only two of the twenty seem to have come from genuine working-class
origins. The father of Margaret Heckler (Reagan's secretary of health and human services) was a doorman at a New York City hotel, and Patricia Harris's
father was a waiter on a railroad (both Heckler and Harris attended college on
scholarships). Four others were from middle-class backgrounds. The father of
Shirley Hufstedler (Carter's secretary of education) was a contractor, who had
to move frequently during the Depression to find work, and her mother was
a teacher. The father of Donna Shalala (Clinton's secretary of health and human services) was a real estate salesman and a leader in the Syrian-Lebanese
community in Cleveland, Ohio; her mother was a physical education teacher
who put herself through law school at night while Shalala and her twin sister
were young girls. The father of Alexis Herman (secretary of labor under Clinton) was a mortician and political activist—after suing the state's Democratic
Party to secure for blacks the right to vote, he became the first black ward
leader in Alabama—and her mother was a reading teacher. The father of Gale
Norton (secretary of the interior under George W. Bush) learned aviation me-
chanics in the army and then worked for various aviation firms.[60]

It is a bit harder to categorize the class background of Juanita Kreps (secretary of commerce under Carter): her father was a "struggling mine opera-
tor" in Kentucky. Her parents were divorced when she was four, and she lived

qualities 4 ?

with her mother until she was twelve, at which time she attended a Presbyterian boarding school. She later said of her childhood (during the Depression), "Everyone was having economic problems, and we weren't any worse off than anyone else."[61]

All twenty of these women graduated from college, and fifteen did postgraduate work. Nine graduated from law school (two went to Harvard and one each went to Boston College, George Washington University, Hastings, Rutgers, Stanford, Denver University, and Yale). Four did doctoral work (Kreps received a PhD in economics from Duke; Shalala, a PhD in political science from Syracuse University; Albright, a PhD in international affairs from Columbia; and Rice, a PhD in international studies at Denver University), and three attended MBA programs (McLaughlin at the University of Pennsylvania, and Franklin and Chao at Harvard).

Kreps and Shalala came to the cabinet after rising through the academic hierarchies of large research universities (Kreps had been a vice president at Duke, and Shalala was chancellor of the University of Wisconsin). Rice, too, had been a university administrator, but she did not exactly rise through the academic ranks: after working in Washington with the National Security Council during the administration of George H. W. Bush, Rice was offered tenure at Stanford in May 1993 and became provost a month later. Margaret Heckler and Lynn Martin had served a number of terms in Congress and then been defeated in reelection bids before Republican presidents named them to their cabinets. Janet Reno had also been elected to office: she served four terms as state attorney in Dade County, Florida.

Most of the rest came to the cabinet from other government positions or from the corporate world, and some had spent time in both settings. Hills was a partner in a law firm and had been working in the Justice Department; Hufstedler was a U.S. Court of Appeals justice; McLaughlin had been the highest-ranking woman executive at Union Carbide and then worked at high-level positions in the Treasury and Interior departments; O'Leary was an executive vice president at Northern States Power, one of the largest gas and electric utility companies in the Midwest.

Chao worked as an investment banker at the Bank of America and Citicorp, served in the department of transportation while George H. W. Bush was president, and then headed the Peace Corps and United Way before joining the Heritage Foundation, a conservative think tank. Gale Norton also had worked at a conservative think tank (the Mountain States Legal Foundation) and had been attorney general of Colorado (she ran for the Republican Senate nomination in 1996 but was defeated in the primaries). Anne Veneman moved back and forth between various state and federal government positions in California and Washington and private law practice.[62]

Many of these women had served on major corporate boards before being nominated for cabinet positions. Before she was nominated by Carter to be secretary of commerce, Juanita Kreps held an endowed chair in economics at Duke University, but her income from that chair was only half what she earned as a director on boards that included R. J. Reynolds, Eastman Kodak, and J. C. Penney. In 1976, her income as a professor at Duke was $30,106, and her income from boards was $61,150.[63] When George H. W. Bush appointed Barbara Franklin to be secretary of commerce, the *New York Times* described her as "a well-connected management consultant, corporate director and Republican fund-raiser." Franklin was, at the time, a director on seven boards, which provided her with as much as $327,000 a year, depending on how many meetings she attended. Only one woman in history had served on more *Fortune* 1000 boards simultaneously, Ann McLaughlin, who was secretary of labor during Reagan's second term.[64] Before returning to Washington to work in the George W. Bush administration, Rice served on the boards of Chevron, Transamerica, and Charles Schwab.

Not surprisingly, many of these women, like the men who have served in presidential cabinets, have been asked onto boards after leaving their cabinet positions. If one eliminates those women still serving in the cabinet, Elizabeth Dole (who, as we will discuss below, is now in the Senate), and those who have died, seven of the remaining eleven former women cabinet members served on twenty-one *Fortune* 500 boards in 2003. For example, Carla Hills served on the boards of AOL Time Warner (#25 in 2003), American International Group (#9), ChevronTexaco (#7), and Lucent Technologies (#141); Ann McLaughlin (now Ann McLaughlin Korologos) served on the boards of AMR (#104), Fannie Mae (#316), Host Marriott (#431), Kellogg (#225), and Microsoft (#47).[65]

Some also sit on other boards, and service on these boards can also be very lucrative. When it was revealed in 2003 that many charitable foundations pay their trustees quite handsomely, Juanita Kreps defended the fact that she received payment for such work. She said that she would not remain on the board of the $6 billion Duke Endowment if she were not paid to do so (in 2001, she received $132,800 plus expenses from that endowment). "I don't think we're being overpaid," she said. "We do a lot of work. We meet two full days 10 times a year in Charlotte which isn't the easiest place to get to, and there's a good bit of correspondence to deal with in between."[66]

All but Reno, Shalala, Herman, and Rice have been married. Most have had children. A few have been in major Washington power marriages. Hills's husband, Roderick Hills, also a lawyer, was head of the Securities and Exchange Commission from 1975 to 1977. Elizabeth Dole met Senator Robert Dole of Kansas while she was working in the White House Office of Consumer Affairs during the Nixon administration. They were married in 1975. During the Reagan years, some considered them "the second-most powerful couple in the nation's capital."[67] Ann McLaughlin was married to John McLaughlin, a former Jesuit priest turned Nixon speechwriter turned television talk show host. ("Father McLaughlin," we are told in one profile of Ann McLaughlin, "defended Nixon throughout the Watergate scandal, predicting publicly that the president would eventually come to be regarded as 'the greatest moral leader of the last third of this century.'"[68]) Elaine Chao is married to Mitch McConnell, senator from Kentucky, referred to by the *New York Times* as "perhaps best known for his opposition to campaign reform" (as of 2001, the two of them were considered "Washington's newest power couple").[69]

Patricia Harris was African American, as are Hazel O'Leary, Alexis Herman, and Condoleezza Rice. Elaine Chao is Chinese American. The others are (or were) white. Three are (or were) Episcopalians (Hobby, Hills, Kreps), one is a Congregationalist (Franklin), and one is a Presbyterian (Rice, although she went to a Catholic high school). Elizabeth Dole was a lifetime Methodist until, in an apparent effort to help her husband please the right wing of his party as he campaigned for the 1996 Republican nomination, she left the Methodist Church in Washington that she had attended for years (the same church the Clintons attended) and joined a more "traditional Christian church."[70] Five have been Catholics (Heckler, Herman, O'Leary, McLaughlin, and Martin). Albright, as we have noted, was born to Jewish parents, raised a Catholic, and became an Episcopalian when she married (see chapter 2, note 50).

WOMEN IN THE MILITARY ELITE

As was typically the case, Mills did not mince words when he wrote about those at the top of the military hierarchy. Mills referred in general to military men throughout history and throughout the world as "warlords," and he referred more specifically to "the men of violence: the United States warlords."[71]

In 1956, there were no women among the warlords. The only mention Mills made of women when he wrote about the military was to demonstrate the importance of rank in such an extremely hierarchical institution. Even the social lives of the women married to military men were affected by the rank of their husbands. Mills quotes the wife of Gen. George C. Marshall describing a social event for military wives between the two world wars: "At a tea such as this one you always ask the highest-ranking officer's wife to pour coffee, not tea, because coffee outranks tea."[72]

Indeed, it was not until 1967 that Congress passed legislation allowing women to be promoted to any general officer grade in the army and the air force. (The sanction of corresponding promotions for women in the navy and the Marines took another decade.) When Gen. William Westmoreland officiated at the 1970 ceremony at which the first two women were promoted to the rank of brigadier general, he surprised everyone present. First, as he pinned the stars on Anna Hays, a twenty-eight-year army veteran who had served in three wars, he kissed her "squarely on the mouth." A few minutes later, after pinning stars on the second woman in history to become a general, he intoned, "And now, in accordance with a new Army custom . . . " and kissed her, too.[73]

In their 1981 study of women in power, Huerta and Lane looked at those positions in the military hierarchy mentioned by Mills for the years 1958, 1965, 1972, and 1978. Of the 478 positions they examined in the Department of Defense, the army, the navy, and the air force, they found only seven that had been occupied by women. Five of these were with the women's branches of the army and the Marines (since eliminated by the integration of the women's corps with the formerly all-male military). The other two were positions identified as "general counsel." These findings, they concluded, were "not unexpected," given that the military is "almost universally recognized as a 'man's world.'"[74]

In large part as a result of the shift from conscription to an all-volunteer military in 1973, the U.S. military has become less a "man's world," at least in terms of the number of men and women on active duty. In 1972, there were slightly fewer than 45,000 women on active duty (1.9 percent of the total force); by 2003 that number had increased to more than 210,000 (about 15 percent). The percentage of women officers was about the same as that of enlisted personnel (15 percent), but the percentage of female officers in the different branches ranged from a high of 17.8 percent in the air force to a low of 5.4 percent in the Marine Corps.[75]

In spite of their increased numbers in recent decades, women have not yet been promoted to the very highest military ranks. As of September 2004 (the most recent data available), of the 898 people in the army, navy, air force, and Marine Corps who had achieved the rank of general officer, only 39, or 4.3 percent, were women (in the previous edition of this book, based on 1995 data, only 11 women, or 1.2 percent, were general officers).[76]

It was not until March 1996, when Clinton nominated Maj. Gen. Carol Mutter of the Marine Corps to be the first woman three-star general, that a woman achieved officer rank higher than two-star.[77] A few months later, Patricia Tracey became the first vice admiral in the navy; in June 1997, Claudia Kennedy became the first three-star general in the army; and in 1999, Leslie

F. Kenne became the first three-star general in the air force.[78] Mutter retired in 1999, Kennedy retired in 2000, and Kenne retired in 2003, so as of July 2004, Tracey was the only woman with three-star rank in all the armed services. It appears that it will be a long time before the percentage of women general officers moves out of the token range.

There have been so few women who have achieved two-star rank or higher that it is hard to draw conclusions about their backgrounds, but we can look at the first seventy women who became general officers and ask how they got there. All but five were white: four were African American, and one was Hispanic. Most were from middle-class backgrounds, and a disproportionate number came from the personnel field. When we asked one of these women, Brig. Gen. Wilma Vaught, president of the Women in Military Service Memorial Foundation, why this was so, she focused on what has been an important issue with regard to military promotions at the highest levels: combat experience. "The types of problems you have in personnel women can handle as well as men," she told us, "and, of course, you don't need combat experience to do well in personnel." Vaught also noted that with the exception of those who had been nurses, almost all of the seventy women had come from administrative rather than technical backgrounds.[79]

The presence of women in the modern American military was highlighted painfully in the spring of 2004 when the world learned, with graphic and extensive photographic evidence, of the sadistic and humiliating treatment of Iraqi prisoners at Abu Ghraib prison. Three of the first seven soldiers charged with the abuse of prisoners were women: Pvt. 1st Class Megan Ambuhl, Pvt. 1st Class Lynndie England, and Specialist Sabrina Harman.

Women also served in senior levels of authority at Abu Ghraib prison. In fact, two of the twelve women generals in the army played prominent roles. The prison was directed by one of the nine one-star generals, Brig. Gen. Janis Karpinski. Karpinski, who served in the Special Forces and holds a bronze star, was in charge of three U.S.-British-led prisons, eight battalions, and thirty-four hundred army reservists. Karpinski was first suspended from her command; then, after an internal army review found that she had been derelict in "all aspects of command responsibilities," she was demoted to the rank of colonel. In addition, one of the army's three women who held two-star rank, Maj. Gen. Barbara Fast, was the top intelligence officer in Iraq, in charge of the interrogators at Abu Ghraib. The allegations of dereliction of duty against Fast were found to be "unsubstantiated."[80]

The presence of women in both junior and senior positions at the prison demonstrated quite clearly that the mere addition of women to a previously all-male culture does not necessarily change the culture. As writer and commentator Barbara Ehrenreich put it, lamenting "a certain kind of feminist naiveté" that assumes that the presence of women in leadership roles automatically changes the nature of the organization they lead, "Women do not change institutions simply just by assimilating into them."[81]

There are, then, very few women in the military who have made it to what Mills considered warlord status, and prospects are not good for more than token presence in the highest military circles for a long time. The percentage of women officers remains quite small, the system of promotion remains riddled with biases against women, and there is extensive evidence of sexual harassment against women. Jeanne Holm, the third woman promoted to the rank of general and the first in the air force, concluded in the 1992 revised edition of her 1982 book *Women in the Military*, "It would be unrealistic to believe that a system still so heavily weighted toward operational experience of the kind as yet available on only a limited basis for women will be able to operate in an unbiased fashion."[82] Laurie Weinstein and Francine D'Amico, who have written extensively about women in the military, are more direct than Holm in their condemnation of the ways that military culture works against women: "When American women enter the United States military institution, they enter hostile territory: it is, quite literally, No-*Woman's*-Land."[83]

WOMEN IN CONGRESS AND ON THE SUPREME COURT

The Senate

As table 3.3 shows, twenty-seven women have served in the Senate since 1950. They fall into two clusters: those who served in the Senate before 1978, when Nancy Kassebaum was elected, and those who have been elected since then.

From the time Mills wrote *The Power Elite* until 1972, only one woman served in the U.S. Senate: Margaret Chase Smith of Maine.[84] Smith's husband, a Maine politician "who ran for office 48 times in his lifetime without a defeat," was a member of the House from 1937 to 1940.[85] He became gravely ill and, dying, asked his constituents to elect his wife, a former teacher and newspaperwoman. They did, and she served in the House for eight years before successfully running for the Senate in 1948.

During her long tenure in the Senate, Smith had some female company, but it tended to be brief, and it was invariably the result of the death of a male senator during his elected term of office.[86] Several of them were widows appointed to take the place of their deceased husbands, and they did not serve for long. Maurine Neuberger, widow of the senator from Oregon, won a special election to complete his term and won the seat in the regular election in 1960; she then chose not to run again in 1966. When Smith was defeated in her bid for reelection in November 1972, in large part because of

over his dead body

Table 3.3.   Women in the Senate

Name	Party/State	Years Served
Margaret Chase Smith	R-ME	1949–1971
Eva Bowring	R-NE	1954–1954 (aptd)
Hazel Abel	R-NE	1954–1954
Maurine Neuberger	D-OR	1961–1967
Elaine Edwards	D-LA	1972–1972 (aptd)
Muriel Humphrey	D-MN	1978–1978 (aptd)
Maryon Pittman Allen	D-AL	1978–1978 (aptd)
Nancy Kassebaum	R-KS	1979–1997
Paula Hawkins	R-FL	1981–1987
Barbara Mikulski	D-MD	1987–present
Jocelyn Burrdick	D-ND	Sept. 1992–Dec. 1992
Dianne Feinstein	D-CA	1992–present
Barbara Boxer	D-CA	1993–present
Carol Moseley-Braun	D-IL	1993–1998
Patty Murray	D-WA	1993–present
Kay Bailey Hutchison	R-TX	1995–present
Olympia Snowe	R-ME	1995–present
Sheila Frahm	R-KS	June 1996–Nov. 1996
Susan Collins	R-ME	1997–present
Mary Landrieu	D-LA	1997–present
Blanche Lincoln	D-AR	1999–present
Debbie Stabenow	D-MI	2001–present
Jean Carnahan	D-MO	2001–2003
Hillary Clinton	D-NY	2001–present
Marie Cantwell	D-WA	2001–present
Lisa Murkowski	R-AL	2002–present
Elizabeth Dole	R-NC	2003–present

her support for the war in Vietnam, the Senate was again, for six years, an all-male club.[87]

Nancy Landon Kassebaum's election to the Senate in 1978 represented a genuine breakthrough, for she was the first woman to be elected who did not replace a deceased male. Kassebaum was not, however, without valuable political connections. Her father, Alf Landon, had been governor of Kansas and had run for president against Franklin Delano Roosevelt in 1936. The *New York Times* asserted in an editorial that if her "middle name were Jones her campaign would have been a joke."[88] In addition to a name familiar to the voters of Kansas, she had something else that helps one become a member of the Senate, a net worth of millions of dollars that enabled her to finance her campaign.

Two years later, the number of women senators doubled when Paula Hawkins was elected from Florida. Hawkins had run for the Senate in 1974 and for lieutenant governor in 1976. She lost both of those races, but she won

woman who is too strong is a ball buster

the Republican primary in 1980 and was elected as part of the Reagan landslide that year. Six years later, she was defeated by Governor Bob Graham.
Another woman senator was elected in 1986, Barbara Mikulski, a Democrat
from Maryland who had previously served five terms in the House of Representatives, so there continued to be two women in the Senate (Kassebaum
was the other).

In 1992, on the heels of the Clarence Thomas confirmation hearings, which
captivated the nation and demonstrated quite persuasively to many that the
Senate Judiciary Committee (and, by extension, the U.S. Senate) consisted of
white men determined to ignore women's concerns while professing empathy
with them, four women were elected to the Senate, tripling the number of
women in that body from two to six. Kassebaum and Mikulski were joined by
Carol Moseley-Braun, the first African American woman ever to be elected to
the Senate; Barbara Boxer, who had served five terms in the House; Dianne
Feinstein, the former mayor of San Francisco; and Patty Murray, a former pre-
school teacher, state legislator, and self-described "mom in tennis shoes."[89]

In June 1993, the number of women in the Senate climbed to seven when
Kay Bailey Hutchison, a Republican, won a special election after Clinton selected Lloyd Bentsen, a Democratic senator from Texas, as secretary of the
treasury. In November 1994, when Maine elected Olympia Snowe, who had
been an aide to Senator William Cohen when he served in the House, she became the eighth woman in the Senate.[90] When Bob Dole resigned from the
Senate in May 1996 to pursue his quest for the presidency full-time, the Republican governor of Kansas selected Sheila Frahm, a moderate, pro-choice
Republican, to replace him, increasing the number of women in the Senate to
nine, but she soon lost any chance of continuing when an antiabortion ultraconservative defeated her in the Republican primary. In that 1996 election,
Mary Landrieu was elected to the Senate from Louisiana. Like Nancy Kassebaum, who had been elected to the Senate eighteen years earlier (and who
chose not to run for reelection in 1996), Landrieu was the daughter of a successful politician whose name was well-known throughout the state: her father, Moon Landrieu, had been mayor of New Orleans and secretary of housing and urban development in the Carter administration. Susan Collins, also
elected in 1996, had worked for more than a decade as adviser on business affairs to William Cohen when he served in the House of Representatives.

Seven more women have been elected since the first edition of this book.
In the 1998 election, Blanche Lincoln, a Democrat from Arkansas, was
elected. In 2000, three women were elected: Debbie Stabenow (D-MI), Maria
Cantwell (D-WA), and Hillary Clinton (D-NY). In addition, when Mel Carnahan was killed prior to the 2000 election, the residents of Missouri elected
him, a dead man, rather than his opponent John Ashcroft; Carnahan's widow,

Jeanne, was appointed to his seat, and Ashcroft became attorney general in George W. Bush's first cabinet. In 2002, when Frank Murkowski, longtime Republican senator from Alaska, was elected governor, he appointed his daughter Lisa to take over his Senate seat; despite accusations of nepotism, she was reelected in 2004. In the November election of 2002, Elizabeth Dole, former cabinet member and wife of former senator and presidential contender Bob Dole, was elected to the Senate in North Carolina.

Clearly, there have been two eras, each bringing women to the Senate via very different routes. In the pre-Kassebaum era, women had to be in the right place at the right time when a male senator died, and these requirements were best met by being his widow. The post-Kassebaum era, from 1978 to the present, includes women whose elections did not require such a morbid prerequisite.

The women who have been elected to the Senate differ from those who have been appointed to the cabinet in some obvious ways. For one, they are much less well educated and less likely to have attended prestigious colleges and universities. With the exception of Paula Hawkins, who attended Utah State but did not receive a degree, all of the women elected to the Senate earned undergraduate degrees, but only four attended elite undergraduate institutions (Feinstein's degree is from Stanford, Clinton went to Wellesley, Murkowski went to Georgetown, and Dole went to Duke), and only two have postgraduate degrees from Ivy League schools (Clinton went to law school at Yale, and Dole went to Harvard). Seven have advanced degrees: Mikulski and Stabenow have MSWs, Kassebaum has a master's in history, and Moseley-Braun, Hutchison, Clinton, and Dole have law degrees.

Correspondingly, women in the Senate are less likely than the women in the cabinet to have come from privileged backgrounds and much more likely to have come from genuinely working-class families. About one-third, including Kassebaum, Feinstein, Landrieu, Murkowski, Clinton, and Dole, came from upper-middle-class or upper-class backgrounds. Most, however, grew up in middle-class or working-class families. Maria Cantwell, for example, grew up in a working-class Irish neighborhood and was the first in her family to earn a college degree. Patty Murray's father ran a local five-and-dime store on the main street of the small town in which she grew up, one of seven children. Carol Moseley-Braun's father was a policeman, and Paula Hawkins' father was a navy chief warrant officer.

These women are from much more heterogeneous religious backgrounds than the women of the cabinet (or the men of the Senate). There are seven Catholics, three Episcopalians, three Methodists, two Jews, one Mormon, and one Greek Orthodox among them. All but Mikulski and Collins have been married, and all but Mikulski, Collins, Hutchison, and Snowe have had children.

The House

There has been a corresponding increase in the number of women elected to the House. In the November 1990 election, twenty-nine women were elected or reelected to the House, twenty Democrats and nine Republicans. The dramatic increase in the number of women senators in 1992 was accompanied by a sharp increase in the number of women elected to the House: forty-seven, thirty-five Democrats and twelve Republicans. Two years later, when the Republicans gained control of the House, the number of women increased by one, to forty-eight, but the number of Republicans increased by six, to eighteen. In 1996, fifty-one women were elected, thirty-five Democrats and sixteen Republicans. Eight years later, in 2004, sixty-five women were elected to the House (forty-two Democrats and twenty-three Republicans).[91]

A systematic look at the eighty-seven women who have been elected to the House since 1990 indicates that they, like the women elected to the Senate in the post-Kassebaum era, are less educated and much less likely to have attended elite schools; they are also less likely to have come from privileged backgrounds and more diverse religiously than the women in the cabinet and the corporate elite.

The Supreme Court

Only two Supreme Court justices have been women: Sandra Day O'Connor and Ruth Bader Ginsburg. In chapter 2, we noted that Ginsburg, who is Jewish, grew up in a working-class neighborhood in Brooklyn. She earned a scholarship to Cornell and then began law school at Harvard. When her husband (now a professor of law at Georgetown University) accepted a job in New York City, she transferred to Columbia. Clinton appointed her to the Court in 1993.

The first woman to join the Court, however, was Sandra Day O'Connor, an Episcopalian appointed in 1981 by Ronald Reagan, who had promised during the 1980 campaign that, if elected, he would appoint a woman to the Supreme Court. O'Connor grew up on a huge, 160,000-acre ranch in southeastern Arizona that had been founded by her grandfather in 1880, thirty years before Arizona became a state, on land that the United States had obtained from Mexico (after the Mexican American War of 1846–1848) through the Gadsden Purchase. By the time Sandra was born, in 1930, it was, as she and her brother describe it in their jointly written memoir, "the largest and most successful ranch in the region." Because of the ranch's isolation, she went to live with her grandmother in El Paso, where she attended the Radford School for Girls, an exclusive private academy, and then the local high school. After she graduated from high school at the age of sixteen, she went to Stanford for her bachelor's degree (in economics) and then for law school.[92]

While in law school, she briefly dated her future Supreme Court colleague, William Rehnquist, a fellow law school student, but she married another fellow law school student, John Jay O'Connor III, the son of a physician from a wealthy San Francisco family. After they spent a few years in Germany (he was a lawyer in the army), they returned to Arizona, where he joined a "prosperous and prestigious Phoenix law firm," and she raised three sons. As one biographer described this period in her life, "O'Connor maintained her contacts with the legal world through the traditionally female vehicle of community volunteer work. She was president of the Phoenix Junior League and active in a variety of civic organizations." In addition, and perhaps most importantly for her future career, she became active in Republican Party politics, including working as a precinct organizer for Barry Goldwater in his presidential bid in 1964. She was appointed to the state senate and then won reelection, and she cochaired the statewide committee to elect Richard Nixon in 1972.[93]

She then was elected as a judge, appointed to the Arizona Court of Appeals, and chosen by Reagan in 1981.

CONCLUSION

The power elite is no longer the all-male enclave it was in the 1950s. The presence of women has increased most clearly and steadily in the corporate world and cabinets, but the percentage of women on corporate boards has only recently topped 13 percent; in some presidential cabinets it has been higher, with the peak thus far being the Clinton cabinet at 31 percent at the beginning of his second term. Although women made up almost 13 percent of the officers in the military at the end of 1993, less than 2 percent of those who achieved the rank of general officer (the equivalent of a one-star general) were women. There have been no women among the highest-ranking military officers, the Joint Chiefs of Staff. The women in the corporate, cabinet, and military elites are thus very much still in the minority, even though a few, like Carly Fiorina of Hewlett-Packard, Anne Mulcahy of Xerox, Janet Reno, Madeleine Albright, and Condoleezza Rice, clearly have attained positions of real power.

The participation of women in Congress increased dramatically after 1978, with the strongest surge coming in the 1990s. Still, women make up less than 15 percent of the Senate and the House. Most have been Democrats, though this is not as pronounced a majority as is the case for Jews in Congress.

To put the slow progress of women in electoral office in the United States into a larger perspective, as of 2003, the United States, with Congress consisting of 14.3 percent women, tied for sixtieth (with Andorra) internationally. Rwanda, with 48.8 percent women legislators, edged out Sweden, with 45 percent, for first place; Germany, with 32.2 percent, was in eleventh place; Britain, with 17.9 percent, was in fiftieth place. In order to increase the pace by which women are represented electorally, some countries have enacted legislation guaranteeing a certain number of positions to women (some countries have done the same thing for corporate directorships).[94]

Unlike Jewish men, who, over the generations, can become virtually indistinguishable from the Christian men in the power elite, the women in the power elite and Congress remain identifiably different. Still, the more similar they are to the men who have long dominated the power elite in terms of attitudes and values, class background, and education, the more acceptable they are, and the more likely to move into the higher circles. The women who have been elected to Congress have come from more varied backgrounds, as have both the women and the men who have gone the furthest in the military.

Despite the gains that women have made in the corporate world, the hopeful projections by corporate leaders and magazine editors about continuing advances are not likely to be borne out. They fly in the face of several sobering realities, beginning with the fact that the extreme gender segregation of the occupational structure has not improved since the early 1990s. Even the occupations that have more women, such as management, law, and medicine, remain highly segregated in terms of specializations and functions. There is also the fact that women have continued since 1993 to make just 76 percent of what men make when all possible extraneous factors are carefully controlled. The same Jerry A. Jacobs who was quoted earlier in this chapter concerning the dramatic increases of women in management now says that further changes in gender segregation and wage differentials have not come as rapidly as he thought they would: "Indeed, the closer you look within nominally integrated occupations, the more segregation you find. Men and women are segregated by occupation, by firms within occupation, and by jobs and specializations within firms. There are 'men's jobs' and 'women's jobs' at all levels of education, skills, and experience, and at each level, the women's jobs tend to be paid less."[95]

Experts argue over the varying weights to assign to the several factors that perpetuate this situation, but they usually begin with the inflexible way in which work is structured and the increasing hours that have been demanded of executives and professionals in recent decades, which force women to choose between career advancement and their families since they remain the primary caregivers at home. There is also the fact that women soon see the obvious preference that male colleagues and clients have for associating with other men ("homophily"), leaving them outside the information and contact networks that can lead to business deals or better jobs. They also have to suffer the ongoing coarseness of the male-centered "culture" that prevails in most corporations. They face insinuations about their femininity, putting their self-images on the line. Finally, they often must endure negative remarks about the capabilities of women, as well as outright discrimination.[96]

The idea that the chief problem for women in the corporate elite is the nature of the workplace, not an allegedly temporary lack of supportive female colleagues, is reinforced by the fact that men who are tokens in female-dominated work settings do not suffer the same kinds of problems as women who are tokens in male-dominated work settings, as would be expected if the cause were essentially being a part of a small minority. According to Christine Williams, a sociologist who has studied both women who do traditionally men's work and men who do traditionally women's work, "Discrimination is not a simple by-product of numbers: The social organization of work tends to benefit certain groups of workers over others, regardless of their proportional representation in an occupation. Consequently some groups (like women) suffer because of their minority status; other groups (like men) do not."[97]

So, as long as the social organization of work benefits men but creates impossible choices and unpleasant personal experiences for women, few women will ever make it to the top because many of the most likely candidates will have been driven out. This problem was demonstrated once again by the resignations of several high-level women executives at Ford Motors in 2004. These women explained to a reporter that the company had an almost militaristic structure in which there was little or no cooperation or sense of decency: "Aside from the long hours, frequent moves and disruptive work schedules that seem to come with a job in a global industry, there are complaints about the fear of retribution, temper tantrums, and a general lack of humanity and understanding that you have to have a life outside the office. "As one refugee put it, 'How can people with master's degrees scream at each other?'"[98]

However, the series of gauntlets that keep very many women from becoming CEOs does not mean that women will cease to have a key function within the power elite. Indeed, they now seem to have the ideal role from the male point of view. They serve as tokens, buffers, and experts until they reach their early forties or fifties; then, they become the consultants and advisers who are the role models and instructors for the new generation of buffers. They will, for the most part, continue to follow the pathways to boards of directors in the same ways they have since the 1970s, not as CEOs of major corporations but as university presidents, heads of high-status charitable organizations, partners in law firms, officers in public relations firms, and former political appointees and elected officials.

Thus, whether or not very many of them make it to the innermost corporate circles, we believe that the corporate world is strengthened by the presence of women. They take some of the sting out of an impersonal business system that can be hard on workers at the lowest levels (and those beneath them who cannot find work). In addition, their presence helps to legitimate the system because it feeds into the Horatio Alger mythology that anyone who works hard can rise to the top. A close look at the class backgrounds of those women who have made it to the top, however, demonstrates that the upper classes are overrepresented by a factor of about ten or fifteen to one.

It also seems unlikely that the military will become a more open pathway of advancement for women into the power elite. The premium on extensive combat experience and command of combat troops is just too great. We therefore think that the main avenue for women into seats of power will be within the political arena, where they have more control over the pace and timing of work. The increasing number of women serving in city governments and state legislatures will mean a growing number of able and experienced women candidates who will have credibility with voters and financial support from women in business and the professions. We think that members of the Democratic Party will continue to lead the way in this regard but that the Republicans will have to follow suit to some extent, just as they have in the past.

NOTES

1. C. Wright Mills, *The Power Elite* (New York: Oxford University Press, 1956), 3–4.

2. Mills, *Power Elite*, 125.

3. Mills, *Power Elite*, 129.

4. Jerry A. Jacobs, "Women's Entry into Management: Trends in Earnings, Authority, and Values among Salaried Managers," *Administrative Science Quarterly* 37 (1992): 282–301.

5. Wyndham Robertson, "The Top Women in Big Business," *Fortune*, July 17, 1978, 58–63.

6. Robertson, "Top Women."

7. Graham's father was Jewish, though she did not discover this until she enrolled at Vassar. She, like her parents, was married in a Lutheran ceremony, and she does not consider herself Jewish. See Howard Bray, *The Pillars of the Post: The Making of a News Empire in Washington* (New York: Norton, 1980), 211; Carol Felsenthal, *Power, Privilege, and the Post: The Katharine Graham Story* (New York: Putnam, 1993), 68, 98, 334, 443. Katharine Graham, *Personal History* (New York: Knopf, 1997), 52–53.

8. "Women on Corporate Boards: The Challenge of Change," Catalyst, 250 Park Avenue South, New York, NY 10003-1459, or, as below in n. 11 (New York: Catalyst), 1993, 4. See, also, Enid Nemy, "Felice N. Schwartz, 71, Dies; Working Women's Champion," *New York Times*, February 10, 1996, 52.

9. "You've Come a Long Way, Baby—But Not as Far as You Thought," *Business Week*, October 1, 1984, 126.

10. Sheila Wellington, "Women on Corporate Boards: The Challenge of Change," *Directorship Newsletter*, December 1994. Directorship describes itself as a "data-based firm specializing in corporate governance." In business since 1975, the company uses proxy statements to provide detailed information to its clients (mostly corporations, but also magazines and researchers) on more than seven thousand directors.

11. *2003 Catalyst Census of Women Board Directors: A Call to Action in a New Era of Corporate Governance* (New York: Catalyst, 2003); Kirstin Downey, "Survey Finds Few Female Directors," *Washington Post*, June 18, 2004, E3; "Women and Minorities on Fortune 100 Boards," Alliance for Board Diversity, May 17, 2005, at http://216.15.177.66/ABDReport.pdf. In contrast to these data for board memberships in the United States, in Norway, when it became apparent that businesses were slow to include women in executive positions, the government passed a law requiring that at least 40 percent of corporate board seats be filled by women; see Alan Cowell, "Oslo Journal: Brewmaster Breaks One Tradition but Upholds Another," *New York Times*, December 24, 2005, A4; see, also, the conclusion of this chapter about women elected to national office, which includes some cross-cultural comparisons.

12. *2002 Catalyst Census of Women Corporate Officers and Top Earners in the Fortune 500* (New York: Catalyst, 2003), 8, 12.

13. Beth Ghiloni, "New Women of Power: An Examination of the Ruling Class Model of Domination" (PhD dissertation, University of California, Santa Cruz, 1986), 122–36; G. William Domhoff, *Who Rules America?* (Englewood Cliffs, NJ: Prentice Hall, 1967), 51, 57; Thomas R. Dye, *Who's Running America? The Carter Years*, 2nd ed. (Englewood Cliffs, NJ: Prentice Hall, 1979), 169–70.

14. Ghiloni, "New Women of Power," 156.

15. Ghiloni, "New Women of Power," 157.

16. Ghiloni, "New Women of Power," 159–62.

17. Ghiloni, "New Women of Power," 163–64.

18. "Women on Board: Survey Indicates Inroads into the Male-Dominated Business World," *Los Angeles Times*, April 19, 1995. Such insensitivity on the part of the men in the corporate world is not rare. At one point, as she rose through the management ranks, Carly Fiorina, former CEO of Hewlett-Packard, was told by a colleague that a business lunch had been scheduled at a strip club and that she therefore could not attend. Because the lunch was with an important client, Fiorina showed up anyway and sat through the uncomfortable lunch. Nate DeGraff, "Former CEO Offers Advice for Rough Times," *Greensboro News & Record*, May 8, 2005, B1. Fiorina's willingness to tolerate male boorishness paid off: even though she was fired from her job as CEO of Hewlett-Packard in February 2005, she left the company with a compensation package worth more than $42 million. See Eric Dash, "Fiorina Exiting Hewlett-Packard with More Than $42 Million," *New York Times*, February 12, 2005, B10.

19. Rosabeth Moss Kanter, *Men and Women of the Corporation* (New York: Basic, 1977), 49.

20. Richard L. Zweigenhaft, *Who Gets to the Top? Executive Suite Discrimination in the Eighties* (New York: Institute of Human Relations, 1984), 17.

21. *Good for Business: Making Full Use of the Nation's Human Capital* (Washington, D.C.: U.S. Government Printing Office, 1995), 28.

22. Peter T. Kilborn, "A Leg Up on Ladder, but Still Far from Top," *New York Times*, June 16, 1995.

23. Margaret Hennig and Anne Jardim, *The Managerial Woman* (New York: Pocket, 1976), 45.

24. Title IX was enacted by Congress in 1972, when many women in senior management today were in high school. At that time, one in twenty-seven high school girls participated in high school sports. As of 2004, the figure was one in three. Bill Pennington, "Title IX Trickles Down to Girls of Generation Z," *New York Times*, June 29, 2004, C22.

However, many of the youngest women entering the corporate elite did grow up playing sports. Some played in high school, and some have participated at the most competitive levels of intercollegiate sports. Stephanie Streeter, a 1979 graduate of Stanford and CEO of Banta Corp (#911 in 2005) since October 2002, provides a classic example. Streeter was a four-year starter for Stanford's women's basketball team. Joel Dresang, "Full-Court Press: Streeter Brings Skills Honed by Sports to the Business World," *Milwaukee Journal Sentinel* (online), July 3, 2004, at www.findarticles.com/p/articles/mi_qn4196/is_20040704/ai_n10975727.

25. Marcia Chambers, *The Unplayable Lie: The Untold Story of Women and Discrimination in American Golf* (New York: Golf Digest/Pocket, 1995). See, also, Marcia Chambers, "For Women, the Country Club Is the Big Handicap," *New York Times*, May 14, 1995, and Marcia Chambers, "The High Price of Victory," *New York Times*, April 4, 2001, C19.

Some golf clubs continue to deny memberships to women. The best known is Augusta National Golf Club, the home of the Masters Golf Tournament. When the club's policies were challenged in 2003 by the National Council of Women's Organizations, the nation's oldest and largest organization of women's groups, its chairman (William ["Hootie"] Johnson) reacted defiantly. In order to avoid legal challenges based on the acceptance of funds from public corporations, the tournament was telecast with no television advertisements.

The club admitted its first black members in 1990. The handful of black members, including some of the CEOs discussed in the section titled "Black CEOs of *Fortune* 500 Companies" in ch. 4, were under intense pressure either to persuade the club to change its policies or to resign their memberships. See Clifton Brown, "Augusta Answers Critics on Admitting Women," *New York Times*, July 10, 2002, C18; Richard Sandomir, "Women's Group Lobbies Seven Augusta Members," *New York Times*, September 28, 2002, B18; Bill Pennington and Dave Anderson, "Some at Augusta National Quietly Seek a Compromise," *New York Times*, September 29, 2002, section 8, 1; Bill Pennington with Clifton Brown, "Members of Club Who Favor Change Told to Back Off," *New York Times*, November 13, 2002, C19.

26. Denise Benoit Scott, "The Power of Connections in Corporate-Government Affairs: A Gendered Perspective" (paper presented at the annual meeting of the American Sociological Association, Los Angeles, 1994), 16; see, also, Denise Benoit Scott, "Women at the Intersection of Business and Government: Are They in Places of Power?" *Sociological Spectrum* 18, no. 3 (1998): 333–63.

27. Basia Hellwic, "Executive Female's Breakthrough 50," *Executive Female*, September–October 1992, 46.

28. Dawn-Marie Driscoll and Carol R. Goldberg, *Members of the Club: The Coming of Age of Executive Women* (New York: Free Press, 1993), 163. See, also, Janet Lever, "Sex Differences in the Games Children Play," *Social Problems* 23 (1976): 478–87; Janet Lever, "Sex Differences in the Complexity of Children's Play and Games," *American Sociological Review* 43 (1978): 471–83; Kathryn Ann Farr, "Dominance Bonding through the Good Old Boy Sociability Group," *Sex Roles* 18 (1988): 259–77.

29. Anne B. Fisher, "When Will Women Get to the Top?" *Fortune*, September 21, 1992, 44–56 (quotation appears on p. 56).

30. Lena Williams, "Not Just a White Man's Game," *New York Times*, November 9, 1995.

31. Kathleen Hall Jamieson, *Beyond the Double Bind: Women and Leadership* (New York: Oxford University Press, 1995), 120–45. For some more recent empirical research on the dilemmas faced by "agentic" women in management positions, see Laurie A. Rudman, "Self-promotion as a Risk Factor for Women: The Costs and Benefits of Counterstereotypical Impression Management," *Journal of Personality & Social Psychology* 74 (1998): 629–45; Laurie A. Rudman and Peter Glick, "Prescriptive Gender Stereotypes and Backlash toward Agentic Women," *Journal of Social Issues* 57 (2001): 743–62; Laurie A. Rudman and Kimberly Fairchild, "Reactions to Counterstereotypic Behavior: The Role of Backlash in Cultural Stereotype Maintenance," *Journal of Personality and Social Psychology* 87 (2004): 157–76.

32. Jay Pritzker, interviewed by Richard Zweigenhaft, Chicago, Illinois, October 20, 1980. See, also, "The Hustling Pritzkers," *Business Week*, May 5, 1975, 55–62; "Billionaire Philanthropist A. N. Pritzker Dies," *Washington Post*, February 9, 1986.

33. See Jodi Wilgoren and Geraldine Fabrikant, "Knives Drawn for a $15 Billion Family Pie," *New York Times*, December 11, 2002, A1; Suzanna Andrews, "Shattered Dynasty," *Vanity Fair*, May 2003, 181–85, 231–36; Jodi Wilgoren, "$900 Million Accord Enables Breakup of Pritzker Dynasty," *New York Times*, January 7, 2005, A17. See, also, Anthony Ramirez, "Jay Pritzker, Who Built Chain of Hyatt Hotels, Is Dead at 76," *New York Times*, January 25, 1999, A21. Penny Pritzker was ranked #152 on Forbes 2004 list of the four hundred richest Americans, with an estimated worth of $1.6 billion; there was one Pritzker ahead of her (Thomas, at #142, with an estimated worth of $1.7 billion) and eight Pritzkers behind her (all tied for #165, each with an estimated worth of $1.5 billion).

34. "The Daughter Also Rises," *Business Week*, July 17, 1995, 82–83; Danny Hakim, "Fidelity Picks a President of Funds Unit: Scion of the Founder Seen as Next Chairman," *New York Times*, May 22, 2001, C1; and John Hechinger, "Abigail P. Johnson, President, Fidelity Management & Research Co.," November 9, 2004, at www.thestate.com (the e-mail quote is from Hechinger).

35. Geraldine Fabrikant, "Redstone Heir Steps Further into Viacom Territory," *New York Times*, May 10, 2004, C1; Joe Flint, "Shari Redstone, President, National Amusements," November 9, 2004, at www.thestate.com. See, also, Nancy Hass, "Hey Dads, Thanks for the Love and Support (and the Credit Card): Being Daddy's Girl

Doesn't Just Lead to the Mall; It Can Lead to the Boardroom, Too," *New York Times*, June 16, 2002, section 9, 1; Weld Royal, "When a Daughter Is Groomed for Chief," *New York Times*, October 6, 2002, Business section, 12.

36. Michael Mann, "A Crisis in Stratification Theory? Persons, Households/Families/Lineages, Genders, Classes, and Nations," in *Gender and Stratification*, ed. Rosemary Crompton and Michael Mann, 40–56 (London: Polity, 1986), 47. See, also, Peta Tancred-Sheriff, "Gender, Sexuality, and the Labour Process," in *The Sexuality of Organization*, ed. Jeff Hearn, Deborah L. Sheppard, Peta Tancred-Sheriff, and Gibson Burrell, 45–55 (London: Sage, 1989). Tancred-Sheriff suggests that women in corporations use "implicit sexuality" as a form of "adjunct control" that serves to "facilitate the operation of the capitalist enterprise" (53).

37. *2002 Catalyst Census of Women Corporate Officers and Top Earners*, 8.

38. Beth W. Ghiloni, "The Velvet Ghetto: Women, Power, and the Corporation," in *Power Elites and Organizations*, ed. G. William Domhoff and Thomas R. Dye, 21–36 (Newbury Park, CA: Sage, 1987).

39. See G. William Domhoff, *The Higher Circles* (New York: Random House, 1970), 35; Susan Ostrander, *Women of the Upper Class* (Philadelphia: Temple University Press, 1984); and Diana Kendall, *The Power of Good Deeds: Privileged Women and the Social Reproduction of the Upper Class* (Lanham, MD: Rowman & Littlefield, 2002.)

40. Robertson, "Top Women," 59.

41. "Where Are They Now? Business Week's Leading Corporate Women of 1976," *Business Week,* June 22, 1987, 76.

42. "Where Are They Now?" 76.

43. Carol Hymowitz, "Five Future No. 1's: It's a Good Bet That One of These Women Will Lead a Fortune 500 Firm in the 1990s," *Wall Street Journal,* March 20, 1987. Surprisingly, only two of the five on the *Wall Street Journal* list were on the list of fifty women identified by *Business Week*.

44. Although Mattel announced in August that Barad would become CEO, she did not officially take charge until January 1997. See Lisa Bannon, "Mattel Names Jill Barad Chief Executive," *Wall Street Journal,* August 23, 1996; Judith H. Dobrzynski, "Women Pass Milestone in the Board Room," *New York Times*, December 12, 1996, D4.

45. We do not have information about the parents of Fuller, Russo, and Sammons (the public relations representatives of Russo and Sammons told us they could not provide such personal information). In a phone interview, however, Cinda Hallman made it clear that it was quite rare for women from working-class backgrounds to make it to the highest positions in the corporate world, and that doing so was difficult: "It was extremely hard. At the time I didn't know that, and I'm glad I didn't. If you don't have the privileged background, you have to compensate in other ways. If I fell down on my face I knew I was going to get back up on my feet and try again. One other thing: how you look is important. I know how to do the hair, the make-up. Most people think I come from a rich family" (Cinda Hallman, interviewed by telephone by Richard Zweigenhaft, July 26, 2004).

46. Cait Murphy, "Sara Lee Cleans Out Its Cupboards," *Fortune*, March 7, 2005, 38, and Del Jones, "Sara Lee Biggest Company (For Now) with Female CEO," *USA Today,* February 11, 2005, Money section, 4B.

47. As in the case of the women *Fortune* 500 CEOs, there is at least one exception in terms of class background: Patricia Gallup, the president, CEO, and cofounder of PC Connection (#984 in 2005), is the daughter of a carpenter and union mediator. She has a BA in anthropology from the University of Connecticut.

48. Reginald F. Lewis and Blair S. Walker, *"Why Should White Guys Have All the Fun?" How Reginald Lewis Created a Billion-Dollar Business Empire* (New York: Wiley, 1995), 106–107. See, also, Jonathan P. Hicks, "Reginald F. Lewis, 50, Is Dead; Financier Led Beatrice Takeover," *New York Times,* January 20, 1993.

49. Fisher, "When Will Women Get to the Top?" 44.

50. See, for example, Diana Bilimoria and Sandy Kristin Piderit, "Board Committee Membership: Effects of Sex-Based Bias," *Academy of Management Journal* 37, no. 6 (1994): 1453–77. For a similar conclusion based on a study of senior executives, see Karen S. Lyness and Donna E. Thompson, "Above the Glass Ceiling? A Comparison of Matched Samples of Female and Male Executives," *Journal of Applied Psychology* 82, no. 3 (1997): 359–75.

In a study of men and women directors based on a national network that included the largest corporations, nonprofit organizations, and federal advisory boards, Olga Mayorova and Gwen Moore found that the women were more likely to sit on boards that did not interlock with other boards and were less likely to provide ties between organizations. See Olga Mayorova and Gwen Moore, "Interlocking Directorates: Gender and Social Capital," unpublished manuscript.

51. Claudia H. Deutsch, "Women Lawyers Strive for Chance to Make It Rain," *New York Times*, May 21, 1996; Peter Truell, "Success and Sharp Elbows," *New York Times*, July 2, 1996.

52. Patrick McGeehan, "Morgan Stanley Settles Bias Suit with $54 Million," *New York Times,* July 13, 2004, A1, C9. Both data from the Equal Employment Opportunity Commission and the industry's own Security Industry Association showed that white men filled the large majority of executive management positions at major Wall Street firms. For a discussion of the frat-house behavior and settlement agreements that prevent disclosure, see Susan Antilla, "Money Talks, Women Don't," *New York Times*, July 21, 2004, A23; see, also, Susan Antilla, *Tales from the Boom-Boom Room: Women Vs. Wall Street* (Princeton, NJ: Bloomberg Press, 2002). The Morgan Stanley settlement is merely part of a "deluge" of class-action suits for sex discrimination that have included Mitsubishi (settled for $34 million), Home Depot (settled for $104.5 million), Merrill Lynch (settled for an undisclosed sum), American Express (settled for $42 million), and Boeing (settled for $72.5 million). See Betsy Morris, "Sex Discrimination: How Corporate America Is Betraying Women," *Fortune*, January 10, 2005, 64–74.

53. These figures are based on those with official cabinet status (but not those with "cabinet-level" status who do not hold cabinet positions). Thus, for example, Carol Browner and Christine Todd Whitman, who served as the heads of the Environmental Protection Agency under Clinton and George W. Bush, respectively, are not included; nor are a number of other highly visible women like Jeane Kirkpatrick, ambassador to the U.N. under Reagan. We did not include Condoleezza Rice when she was George W. Bush's national security adviser, but we did include her when she became secretary

of state in 2005. After the position was created, we included secretary of homeland security to the list of cabinet appointments.

54. Thomas E. Cronin, *The State of the Presidency,* 2nd ed. (Boston: Little, Brown,
1980), 275–76.

55. Faye C. Huerta and Thomas A. Lane, "Participation of Women in Centers of
Power," *Social Science Journal* 18, no. 2 (1981): 71–86. In this respect, the United
States has lagged beyond much of the world. As Jeffreys-Jones wrote in *Changing
Differences* (New Brunswick, NJ: Rutgers, 1995), prior to Albright's appointment
as secretary of state, "Since 1960 there have been twenty-two women prime ministers and presidents worldwide, but the United States has had no women as president, vice-president, secretary of state, secretary of defense, or chair of the Senate Foreign Relations Committee. According to this measurement American
women are among the missing sisters of world politics, a predicament they have
shared with the female citizens of Italy, Australia, and Chile, as well as of such
supposedly less democratic countries as the former Soviet Union, Iraq, and North
Korea" (2–3).

56. Beth Mintz, "The President's Cabinet, 1897–1972: A Contribution to the
Power Structure Debate," in "New Directions in Power Structure Research," ed. G.
William Domhoff, special issue, *Insurgent Sociologist* 5, no. 3 (1975): 131–48.

57. Laura Flanders, *Bushwomen: Tales of a Cynical Species* (New York: Verso,
2004), 113–15. See, also, Elizabeth Becker, "Candidate Vows to Aid Beleaguered
Farmers," *New York Times*, January 19, 2001, A21.

58. See, for example, Steven Greenhouse, "Senate Panel Gives Warm Reception to
New Labor Nominee," *New York Times*, January 25, 2001, A18; "Elaine Chao," *Current Biography* (2001): 84–87; Elizabeth Becker, "Family History Forges Labor Secretary's Convictions," *New York Times,* February 26, 2001, A10.

59. Flanders, *Bushwomen,* 150–51.

60. See "Margaret M. Heckler," *Current Biography* (1983): 182–84; "Patricia
Roberts Harris," *Current Biography* (1965): 189–91; "Donna Shalala," *Current Biog-
raphy* (1991): 515; Michael Wines, "Friend Helped Labor Nominee Move Up, Then
Almost Brought Her Down," *New York Times,* March 12, 1997.

61. "Juanita Kreps," *Current Biography* (1977): 259.

62. "Elaine L. Chao," *Current Biography* (2001): 84–87; "Gale A. Norton," *Current Biography* (2001): 391–93; Becker, "Candidate Vows to Aid Beleaguered Farmers," A21; Flanders, *Bushwomen,* 113–46, 147–82, and 218–51.

63. Flanders, *Bushwomen,* 261.

64. Keith Bradsher, "Bush Picks Nominee for Commerce Post," *New York Times,*
December 27, 1991.

65. *2003 Catalyst Census of Women Board Directors: A Call to Action in a New
Era of Corporate Governance* (New York: Catalyst, 2003). The *Fortune* rankings in
this paragraph in the text, as well as those in this endnote, are all for 2003. The other
former women cabinet members and their corporate boards were Lynn Martin on
Procter & Gamble (#31), Ryder Systems (#345), SBC Communications (#27), and
Ryder System (#345); Barbara Franklin on Aetna (#88) and Dow Chemical (#51);
Hazel O'Leary on AES (#181) and UAL (#132); Donna Shalala on Gannett (#275),

Lennar (#256), and Unitedhealth Group (#63); Alexis Herman on Cummins (#296) and MGM Mirage (#397).

66. Stephanie Strom, "Fees and Trustees: Paying the Keepers of the Cash," *New York Times*, July 10, 2003, A16.

67. "Elizabeth Dole," *Current Biography* (1983): 117.

68. "Ann McLaughlin," *Current Biography* (1988): 368.

69. Christopher Marquis, "A Washington Veteran for Labor; a Tested Negotiator for Trade," *New York Times*, January 12, 2001; Becker, "Family History Forges Labor Secretary's Convictions," A10.

70. Richard Reeves, "Church and Statesmen: Sen. Bob Dole's Church Isn't Politically Correct," *Greensboro News and Record,* May 15, 1995.

71. Mills, *Power Elite,* 186.

72. Mills, *Power Elite*, 190.

73. Jeanne Holm, *Women in the Military: An Unfinished Revolution,* rev. ed. (Novato, CA: Presidio, 1992), 203.

74. Huerta and Lane, "Participation of Women," 75.

75. Lory Manning and Vanessa R. Wight, *Women in the Military: Where They Stand*, 4th ed. (Washington, D.C.: Women's Research and Education Institute, 2003), 9, 11. See, also, *1993 Handbook on Women Workers: Trends and Issues* (Washington, DC: U.S. Department of Labor), 22–23; Department of Defense, *Defense 94 Almanac,* issue 5 (1994): 30. According to Holm, the end of the draft "more than any other factor during the seventies produced an expansion of women's participation in the armed forces that was of unexpected and unprecedented proportions" (*Women in the Military,* 246).

76. The George W. Bush administration has classified many formerly public documents—in fact, as of July 2005 it was classifying such documents at the rate of 125 per minute (see "The Dangerous Comfort of Secrecy," *New York Times*, July 12, 2005, A22). Among those that have been classified were the previously easily accessible annual reports produced by the Department of Defense showing the number of active-duty forces by service, rank, sex, and ethnic group. These data are now available only through the Freedom of Information Act. We thank Capt. Lory Manning, the director of the Women in the Military Project at the Women's Research & Education Institute, for sharing the 2004 data with us ("Distribution of Active Duty Forces by Service, Rank, Sex, and Ethnic Group," 09/30/04, DMDC-3035EO).

77. John Mintz, "President Nominates 1st Woman to Rank of Three-Star General," *Washington Post,* March 27, 1996.

78. John Mintz, "Clinton Nominates First Black Admiral: Woman in Line to Become Vice Admiral," *Washington Post,* May 14, 1996.

79. Wilma Vaught, interviewed by Richard Zweigenhaft, Arlington, Virginia, August 2, 1995. Unfortunately, the war in Iraq has provided many women in the military with combat experience. Even though the military's 1994 rules limit women's exposure to combat by barring them from frontline units, the tactics of ambush in Iraq, as one army captain put it, meant that "the front line is everywhere." As of April 2005, 35 women in the military had been killed (23 by hostile fire), more than 250 had been wounded, and 2 had been prisoners of war (women represented 15 percent of all military personnel and

about 10 percent of those deployed to the Iraq theater of operations). See Lory Manning, *Women in the Military: Where They Stand*, 5th ed. (Washington, D.C.: Women's Research and Education Institute, April 2005), 9. See, also, Lawrence J. Korb and Nigel Holmes, "Two Years and Counting," *New York Times*, March 20, 2005, A13, and "More Women Dying in Iraq Combat's 'Front Line,'" *Greensboro News & Record*, December 16, 2004, A10. As of May 2005, the role of women in combat was still under debate in Congress. See Thom Shanker, "House Bill Would Preserve, and Limit, the Role of Women in Combat Zones," *New York Times*, May 20, 2005, A21.

80. In a fifty-five-page "scathing report on prisoner abuse" written by Maj. Gen. Antonio Taguba, Fast was mentioned only briefly though Karpinski's leadership was extensively and severely critiqued. Some speculated that this was because the report was written by a two-star general and Fast, unlike Karpinski, was of equal rank. As one former military man explained, "If you want to investigate a major general you need a lieutenant general" to do the investigation. See Susan Taylor Martin, "Report Steers Clear of Interrogators' Boss," *St. Petersburg Times* (online), May 8, 2004, at www.sptimes.com/2004/05/08/Worldandnation/Report_steers_clear_o.shtml. Susan Taylor Martin, in an article titled "Military Sidesteps Scandal," *St. Petersburg Times* (online), May 28, 2004, at www.sptimes.com/2004/05/28/Worldandnation/Military_star_sideste.shtml, claimed that Fast was "still on track to become commander of a key U.S. military base and only the second three-star female in Army history." As of May 2005, Fast had not become a three-star but had become commander of the Army Intelligence Center at Ft. Huachuca, Arizona. Richard A. Serrano and Mark Mazzetti, "General Demoted over Prison Scandal," *Los Angeles Times*, May 6, 2005, A20.

In an additional weird twist, it was revealed that several years prior to her assignment to oversee the prison at Abu Ghraib, Karpinski had been arrested for shoplifting at a domestic air force base. Somehow, the military missed, or ignored, this incident when it promoted her to brigadier general. As *New York Times* columnist Bob Herbert concluded, "The same army that's scouring Iraq for insurgents and terrorists was apparently unaware of the arrest record of the woman assigned to such a sensitive position at Abu Ghraib." Bob Herbert, "Stranger Than Fiction," *New York Times*, May 9, 2005, A23.

81. Barbara Ehrenreich, "What Abu Ghraib Taught Me," *AlterNet*, May 2004, at http://alternet.org/story/18740. See, also, Carol Burke, *Camp All-American, Hanoi Jane, and the High and Tight: Gender, Folklore, and Changing Military Culture* (Boston: Beacon Press, 2004); Rita James Simon, ed., *Women in the Military* (New Brunswick, NJ: Transaction, 2001); and Francine D'Amico and Laurie Weinstein, eds., *Gender Camouflage* (New York: New York University Press, 1999).

The same general point can be made about women in Congress. As Michele L. Swers shows in *The Difference Women Make: The Policy Impact of Women in Congress* (Chicago: University of Chicago, 2002), although women in Congress expand the range of issues included on the congressional agenda, "simply increasing the number of women and other minorities in Congress will not automatically lead to enhanced influence on policy design" (133); nor will it necessarily change the way Congress functions.

82. Holm, *Women in the Military,* 278.

83. Laurie Weinstein and Francine D'Amico, introduction to *Gender Camouflage,* 5. Their edited anthology includes many examples of women who have been mistreated in and by the military.

84. Donald E. Matthews, *U.S. Senators and Their World* (New York: Vintage, 1960), 13.

85. Martin Gruberg, *Women in American Politics* (Oshkosh, WI: Academia, 1968).

86. See Diane Kincaid, "Over His Dead Body: A Positive Perspective on Widows in the United States Congress," cited in Barbara Boxer, *Strangers in the Senate: Politics and the New Revolution of Women in America* (Washington, D.C.: National Press Books, 1994), 90.

87. Rhodri Jeffreys-Jones, *Changing Differences: Women and the Shaping of American Foreign Policy, 1917–1994* (New Brunswick, NJ: Rutgers University Press, 1995), 128.

88. "Nancy Kassebaum," *Current Biography* (1982): 192.

89. Jamieson, *Beyond the Double Bind,* 193. Because of the number of women elected to the Senate, the House, and state legislatures in the 1992 election, the media incessantly designated 1992 as "the year of the woman."

90. Snowe and her second husband, John R. McKernan Jr., who served as governor of Maine for two terms, were referred to as "Maine's political power couple" in the *Congressional Quarterly,* November 12, 1994, 13.

91. *Congressional Quarterly,* November 10, 1990, 3836; November 7, 1992, 8; November 12, 1994, 10; January 4, 1997, 29; January 31, 2005, 243. These figures are based on voting members of the House; therefore, we have not included Eleanor Holmes Norton, Democrat from the District of Columbia.

92. Sandra Day O'Connor and H. Alan Day, *Lazy B: Growing Up on a Cattle Ranch in the American Southwest* (New York: Random House, 2002).

93. The fact that she dated Rehnquist is drawn from Lou Cannon, "When Ronnie Met Sandy," *New York Times,* July 7, 2005, A27; see, also, Nancy Maveety, *Justice Sandra Day O'Connor: Strategist on the Supreme Court* (Lanham, MD: Rowman & Littlefield, 1996), 12–14 (quotation appears on p. 14).

94. Alexander G. Higgins, "Rwanda Women Knock Sweden out of Top Spot in Parliamentary Share," Associated Press Worldstream, October 22, 2003; see, also, Will Laster, "United States Lag behind Europe in Including Women in Politics," Associated Press (online: www.ap.org), February 28, 2003; Alan Cowell, "Oslo Journal," A4.

95. Jerry Jacobs, "Detours on the Road to Equality: Women, Work, and Higher Education," *Contexts* 1, no 2 (Winter 2003): 32–41 (quotation appears on p. 33).

96. Jacobs, "Detours on the Road"; see, also, Louise M. Roth, "Engendering Inequality: Processes of Sex-Segregation on Wall Street," *Sociological Forum* 19, no. 2 (2004): 203–28; Louise M. Roth, "The Social Psychology of Tokenism: Status and Homophily Processes on Wall Street," *Sociological Perspectives* 47, no. 2 (2004): 189–214; and Gail M. McGuire, "Gender, Race and the Shadow Structure: A Study of Informal Networks and Inequality in a Work Organization," *Gender & Society* 16, no. 3 (June 2002): 303–22.

97. Christine L. Williams, *Still a Man's World: Men Who Do "Women's Work"* (Berkeley: University of California Press, 1995), 20–21. See, also, Christine L. Williams, *Gender Differences at Work: Women and Men in Nontraditional Occupations* (Berkeley: University of California Press, 1990); Christine L. Williams, ed., *Doing "Women's Work": Men in Nontraditional Occupations* (Newbury Park, CA: Sage, 1993); Joel Heikes, "When Men Are the Minority: The Case of Men in Nursing," *Sociological Quarterly* 32, no. 3 (1991): 389–401; Janice Yoder, "Is It All in the Numbers? A Case Study of Tokenism," *Psychology of Women Quarterly* 9, no. 3 (1985): 413–18.

98. Edward Lapham, "Women at Ford: What's the Problem? The Company's Culture Drove Them Out; It Must Be Changed," *Automotive News*, December 20, 2004, 14.

Chapter Four

Blacks in the Power Elite

Militant change

On June 23, 1964, a headline on the business page of the *New York Times* read, "Negro Lawyer Joining U.S. Industries Board." The subject of the story was Samuel R. Pierce Jr., a graduate of Cornell University, where he had been a Phi Beta Kappa student and a star halfback on the football team. When Pierce joined the board of U.S. Industries, he became the first black to sit on the board of a *Fortune* 500 company.[1]

The same week Pierce joined the board of U.S. Industries, another African American, Asa T. Spaulding, became a member of the board of W. T. Grant, a nationwide chain of more than one thousand general merchandise stores. Spaulding was the president of the North Carolina Mutual Life Insurance Company of Durham, the largest black-owned business in the country.[2]

BLACKS IN THE CORPORATE ELITE

Obviously, the appointment of two black men to corporate boards in 1964 was a product of the civil rights movement, but why these particular companies at this particular time? The chairman and chief executive officer of U.S. Industries, John I. Snyder Jr., was both atypical and ahead of his time. The *New York Times* described him the following way: "Soft-spoken and scholarly, Mr. Snyder presented a rather contradictory picture of a millionaire businessman. He was an industrialist who cared deeply about labor. He was a stanch Democrat among Republicans. He believed strongly in the union shop as a necessity for good labor-management relations."[3] Or, as *Business Week* rather scornfully described Snyder a few years later, comparing him unfavorably to his more profit-oriented successor, "he dabbled in liberal politics, engaged in civil rights work, and argued that private business should try to fulfill its 'social responsibilities.'"[4]

91

The reason for the integration of the W. T. Grant board was as obvious as it was vigorously denied. The company had been under attack because many of its Southern stores operated segregated lunch counters. There had been both picketing and sit-ins at Grant lunch counters, and neither had been good for business. Although the chairman of the board claimed that Spaulding's appointment had nothing to do with the "lunch counter policy," it was clearly an effort to defuse an embarrassing and potentially costly situation.[5]

Has it been more typical for boards to integrate because of socially conscious CEOs or as a reaction to protest? According to sociologist Sharon Collins, who has conducted extensive interviews with black executives, most were hired not because of a commitment to equality and diversity on the part of senior management, though some senior managers may have had such a commitment, but because of pressures of one kind or another on their companies. In addition to the specific protests against individual companies for particular policies, like the refusal of some W. T. Grant stores to serve blacks at their lunch counters, federal laws created general pressures to integrate the higher levels of management. Not only did companies have to deal with overt protests, or the threat of them, but they had to adhere to newly legislated guidelines in order to obtain government contracts. Most of Collins's interviewees attributed the opportunities that opened up for them to both overt protests and federal policies against discrimination. As she puts it in *Black Corporate Executives,* the black executives she interviewed "believe that new job opportunities emerged because of this federal affirmative action legislation and because of community-based political pressures, including urban violence."[6]

Our look at the first dozen companies to add black directors to their boards leads us to conclude that the same pattern Collins observed at the senior executive levels held for board appointments. In some cases, like U.S. Industries, boards were driven by what Collins calls a "moral commitment," but more often, as was the case with W. T. Grant, the companies were responding to external pressures.[7]

But why Samuel R. Pierce Jr. and Asa T. Spaulding? What led the boards of U.S. Industries and W. T. Grant to choose these two men among the many possible candidates for integrating the American corporate elite? As was the case for the first Jews asked to join all-Christian boards and the first women to join all-male boards, the two men selected were not likely to make those already in the boardroom uncomfortable: they were highly educated, they were assimilated into the mainstream (that is to say, white) culture, and they were not prone to rock the boat.

Samuel Pierce grew up in comfortable circumstances on Long Island. His father had parlayed a menial job at the elegant Nassau Country Club into a valet service for members of the club; subsequently, he opened his own dry-cleaning store, began to buy real estate, and became a devoted Republican, an affiliation that he passed on to his son. In 1943, midway through his under- graduate work at Cornell, the younger Pierce dropped out to join the army, serving in North Africa and Italy during World War II. After the war, he re- turned to Cornell, where he completed his bachelor's and law degrees.

In 1955, one of his former law professors brought him to Washington, D.C., to work in the Eisenhower administration. In 1959, Nelson Rockefeller, the governor of New York, appointed him to fill a vacancy as a judge. Two years later, he became the first black partner of a major New York law firm, Battle, Fowler, Stokes & Kheel. Theodore Kheel, a well-known labor arbitra- tor who did work for U.S. Industries, was a close friend of CEO John Snyder. Aware of Snyder's willingness to add a black to the U.S. Industries board, Kheel suggested Pierce. Snyder had served with Pierce on the New York State Banking Board and thought it a good suggestion.[8]

Asa Spaulding, born in 1902, was sixty-two when he joined the W. T. Grant board. His father owned a farm in rural North Carolina and also ran a general store, cut timber, and operated a still that produced both turpentine and rosin.[9] His great-uncle, A. M. Moore, was a physician who lived in Durham and founded a small insurance company. Dr. Moore realized that Asa was profi- cient in math, so he persuaded Asa's parents to let their son move to Durham, where the schools were better. After receiving a bachelor's degree from New York University and a master's degree in mathematics and actuarial science from the University of Michigan, he returned to Durham in 1932 to be the ac- tuary at North Carolina Mutual. In 1959, Spaulding became president of the company after the death of his cousin Charles C. Spaulding, who had been the president for some thirty years.

A 1967 *New York Times Magazine* profile of Spaulding stressed his "cautious way of life," contrasting him to the militant Black Power types prone to demon- strations and boycotts. "No, sir, I didn't get out and picket or demonstrate any- where during the civil-rights drive," Spaulding told the reporter. "I felt I could contribute much more toward racial advancement in other ways. . . . We mustn't get impatient. We've made progress, though not everyone is satisfied."[10]

U.S. Industries and W. T. Grant did not exactly open the floodgates, but by mid-1971, there were a dozen blacks on *Fortune* 500 boards. A close look at their backgrounds reveals a few general patterns that characterize them as a group: they were highly educated, many were from families that were eco- nomically comfortable or even quite wealthy, and some had developed valu- able political connections.

Clifton R. Wharton Jr., who joined the board of Equitable Life in 1969, and William T. Coleman Jr., who joined the boards of Penn Mutual in 1969 and Pan Am in 1970, are examples of those among the first wave of black corporate directors who came from highly educated and economically privileged families. Wharton's father, a lawyer, was the first African American to pass the Foreign Service Exam, and in the early 1960s, he became the country's first black career ambassador when he was named ambassador to Norway.[11]

Because of his father's postings around the globe, Wharton's early education was unusually cosmopolitan. He was trilingual from his childhood, graduated from Boston Latin, a prestigious public high school, and entered Harvard at the age of sixteen. While at Harvard, he was active with the radio station and helped to found the National Student Association. In 1947, at the age of twenty, he graduated with a BA in history.[12]

After receiving an MA in international affairs from Johns Hopkins, Wharton spent five years working for Nelson Rockefeller's American International Association for Economic and Social Development. He then enrolled in a PhD program in economics at the University of Chicago. Five years later, PhD in hand, he went to work for another Rockefeller, John D. Rockefeller III, who had established a nonprofit organization called the Agricultural Development Council.

In 1970, a year after he joined the board of Equitable Life, Wharton became the first black president of a major American university when he assumed that post at Michigan State. After eight years there, he became chancellor of the State University of New York from 1978 to 1987, then chairman and chief executive officer at TIAA-CREF, the country's largest private pension fund.[13] Along the way, Wharton joined a number of other *Fortune*-level boards (Ford Motor Company and Burroughs in 1973, Time, Inc., in 1983, Federated Department Stores in 1985, and TIAA-CREF in 1986).[14] He became deputy secretary of state in Clinton's administration, the number-two position under Warren Christopher, but Christopher was said to have considered Wharton's performance "lackluster," and he was asked to resign after only ten months in office.[15]

William T. Coleman Jr. had impeccable educational, professional, and social credentials. From a solidly middle-class family that claimed six generations of teachers and Episcopal ministers on one side and numerous social workers on the other, Coleman grew up outside Philadelphia, where his father was the director of the Germantown Boys Club. Through his father and other members of the family, he met many of the most distinguished black leaders of the 1920s and 1930s, including W. E. B. Du Bois and Thurgood Marshall. After graduating from the University of Pennsylvania summa cum laude in 1941 and the Harvard Law School in 1946 (interrupted by a stint in the Army Air Corps during the war), Coleman became a law clerk to Supreme Court Associate Justice Felix Frankfurter.

One of Frankfurter's other law clerks was Boston Brahmin Elliot Richardson, whom Coleman had met when they both served on the editorial board of the *Harvard Law Review*. Each morning, before turning to their legal work for Justice Frankfurter, Coleman and Richardson spent about an hour reading poetry together. Richardson became the godfather to Coleman's daughter. When his clerkship ended, Coleman joined the prestigious New York law firm of Paul, Weiss, Rifkind, Wharton & Garrison; a few years later, he returned to his hometown to join a prominent Philadelphia law firm, and he soon became a partner in Dilworth, Paxson, Kalish, Levy & Coleman. As a high-powered and socially connected Republican corporate lawyer, Coleman was an unsurprising choice when corporate boards sought to integrate in the late 1960s and early 1970s. In addition to his seats on the boards of Penn Mutual and Pan Am, over the years Coleman served on the boards of the First Pennsylvania Corporation, the First Pennsylvania Banking and Trust Company, the Philadelphia Electric Company, International Business Machine (IBM), Chase Manhattan, PepsiCo, the American Can Company, AMAX, and INA. Coleman was such a successful corporate lawyer and had served on so many boards that when he agreed to become secretary of the treasury under President Ford, his income dropped dramatically: he sold his shares of Pan Am stock, gave up all his directorships, and accepted a salary that was one-fifth what he had earned in private life.[16]

Others among the first wave of black corporate directors had valuable political connections that made them even more desirable additions to corporate boards that wished to integrate. Hobart Taylor Jr., who joined his first *Fortune* 500-level board in 1971, was from a wealthy Texas family with long-standing political connections to Lyndon B. Johnson. Hobart Taylor Sr., a businessman, became a multimillionaire and a longtime friend and early political supporter of Johnson.[17] When Johnson first ran for the Senate in 1948, Hobart Taylor Sr. was one of his key financial backers.[18] Johnson appointed him as a delegate to the 1956 Democratic National Convention, and in 1960, Hobart Taylor Jr., by then a Detroit lawyer, was one of Johnson's key supporters in his quest for the presidency.

Hobart Taylor Jr. attended Prairie View State College and then earned an MA at Howard before attending the University of Michigan Law School, where he was editor of the *Law Review*. After law school, he stayed in the Detroit area, spending a decade as chief legal and financial adviser for public improvements in Wayne County. In 1961, Taylor went to Washington, D.C., to become special assistant to Vice President Johnson, and in 1964 he became associate counsel to President Johnson. One of Johnson's biographers described Taylor as "a mild, go-slow civil-righter and son of the Houston Negro millionaire."[19]

After leaving the Johnson administration in 1965 to become a director of the Export-Import Bank and then a partner at a Washington law firm, Taylor became a director of the Realty Equities Corporation in 1968.[20] In 1971, he joined the boards of Standard Oil of Ohio, A&P, and Westinghouse Electric. He was later to serve on the boards of Aetna, Eastern Airlines, and Burroughs. He died in 1981 of amyotrophic lateral sclerosis (Lou Gehrig's disease).

The first eleven black corporate directors had one characteristic in common: they were all men. By early 1971, there was much speculation about which *Fortune*-level board would be the first to name a black woman and which woman would be named. Many assumed the woman would be Patricia Roberts Harris, who had served as ambassador to Luxembourg. Indeed, in May 1971, it was announced that Harris had agreed to join the boards of Scott Paper and IBM. The following year, she went on the board of Chase Manhattan.[21]

Harris was born in Mattoon, Illinois. Her father was a waiter on a Pullman railroad car. In 1977, in the hearings to confirm her nomination as secretary of housing and urban development, she bristled when Senator William Proxmire suggested that she might not be able to defend the interests of the poor. "You do not seem to understand who I am. I am a black woman, the daughter of a dining-car worker. I am a black woman who even eight years ago could not buy a house in parts of the District of Columbia. I didn't start out as a member of a prestigious law firm, but as a woman who needed a scholarship to go to school. If you think I have forgotten that, you are wrong."[22]

After graduation from Howard University summa cum laude in 1945, and after working as program director of the YWCA in Chicago, she returned to Washington and worked first with the American Council on Human Rights and then with Delta Sigma Theta, a sorority. In 1955, she married a Howard law professor and decided to attend law school at George Washington University.

After law school, Harris worked in the Department of Justice, then left to teach law at Howard. John F. Kennedy appointed her cochairwoman of the National Women's Committee for Civil Rights, and in May 1965, Lyndon Johnson, whose nomination she had seconded at the 1964 Democratic convention, selected her to be ambassador to Luxembourg. As a law professor and former ambassador, Harris was an unsurprising choice as the first black woman to join a corporate board, though some were surprised at how long it took the corporations to ask her.

One intriguing exception exists to the general early pattern of blacks named to corporate boards. Unlike his mostly well-educated, well-off, and in some cases well-connected predecessors, this corporate director came from an impoverished background and attended a nonelite college in West Virginia. He was also a minister who had led public boycotts as a means of confronting large corporations. Yet, he was named to the board of the largest company in the world. This might not have come about if not for a racist slip of the tongue.

By January 1971, blacks had joined the boards of seven major corporations, but none was as major as General Motors (GM), ranked number one by *Fortune* since the magazine began publishing its list of the top five hundred companies in 1955. At the annual GM stockholders meeting in spring 1970, an antimanagement group calling itself the Campaign to Make General Motors Responsible attacked the company for its minority-hiring policies and its lack of corporate responsibility. As part of its protest, the group emphasized that there were no blacks on GM's board of directors and that only eleven of its thirteen hundred automobile dealerships were owned by blacks.[23]

Campaign GM, as the group came to be known, managed to place some proposals on the annual shareholder ballot, including one that would have added three public representatives to GM's board and another that would have created a one-year Shareholders' Committee for Corporate Responsibility. None of the proposals garnered support on more than 3 percent of the ballots cast, but some shareholders who voted the proposals down acknowledged sympathy with Campaign GM's principles. Various colleges and foundations holding substantial shares of GM stock cautioned management that their continued support depended upon improved corporate responsibility. The Rockefeller Foundation, for example, criticized GM for its "defensive and negative attitude" toward its critics.[24]

At that stockholders meeting, James Roche, CEO and chairman at GM, who had been on his feet for most of the troubled six-and-a-half-hour meeting, made an embarrassing slip of the tongue. He was challenged by a young minister from Dayton, Ohio, about GM's failure to send a representative to a television station in Dayton to respond to Campaign GM's proposals. Was GM not, the minister asked, a "public corporation"? Roche responded by claiming, "We are a public corporation owned by free, white . . . " At this point, as some people in the audience gasped and others laughed at his use of a well-known racist phrase, Roche lamely added, "umm . . . and . . . and . . . and black and yellow people all over the world." Though Roche later tried to downplay any meaningfulness to the slip and asserted that he simply had become confused by the audience's laughter, it was clearly an embarrassing episode in a long and difficult day.[25]

A few months later, with unhappy memories of the annual stockholders meeting and well aware that the Rockefeller Foundation and other institutional stockholders were watching closely, Roche called Leon Sullivan, an activist minister in Philadelphia, and asked him to come to New York to discuss joining the GM board. Sullivan told Roche that he was too busy but that Roche was welcome to visit him in Philadelphia. Roche accepted this demand for respect, and Sullivan agreed to go on the board.

Who was Leon Sullivan? Born in Charleston, West Virginia, in 1922, he grew up poor. His parents divorced when he was young, and he was able to attend college because he received a football scholarship to West Virginia State University. He injured his knee during his sophomore year and lost the scholarship but was able to stay in school by working in a steel mill. During his sophomore year, he also became the minister for a small Baptist congregation in Charleston. The following year, learning that the New York politician and minister Adam Clayton Powell Jr. was coming to town on a lecture tour, Sullivan invited him to speak to his congregation. Powell accepted and was so impressed with Sullivan that he offered him a job in New York after he graduated. Two years later, Sullivan became an assistant minister at Powell's church. He also worked on Powell's initial campaign for Congress and earned a master's degree in sociology from Columbia and a divinity degree from the Union Theological Seminary.[26]

In 1950, Sullivan became the pastor of the Zion Baptist Church in North Philadelphia. His congregation grew from six hundred to six thousand at Zion, and by the late 1950s, he was leading four hundred other ministers in boycotts of Philadelphia businesses that refused to hire blacks. (In the 1930s, Powell had led boycotts of New York–area white businesses.) In 1964, Sullivan set up a job-training program called Opportunities Industrialization Centers, designed to train high school dropouts; by 1971, it had training centers in seventy cities.

Roche's decision to pursue Sullivan for the GM board is revealing, for Sullivan certainly differed from the other early black corporate directors both in his academic background and in his professional and political experience. It is likely that Roche and the GM board assumed that naming a highly visible and politically active minister would serve as an effective response to those shareholders who were protesting various of the company's policies. In 1964, W. T. Grant could name a sixty-two-year-old African American who was willing to tell a *New York Times* writer that "we mustn't get impatient," but General Motors in 1971, facing vociferous and embarrassing shareholder protests, needed to make a stronger statement as it integrated its board.

One of Sullivan's first acts as a board member was to vote against the entire board on a controversial resolution. In its coverage of GM's 1971 shareholders meeting, the *Wall Street Journal* reported, "The meeting's dramatic highlight was an impassioned and unprecedented speech by the Rev. Leon Sullivan, GM's recently appointed Negro director, supporting the Episcopal Church's efforts to get the company out of South Africa. It was the first time that a GM director had ever spoken against management at an annual meeting."[27] This challenge to boardroom hegemony may have been just what Roche needed to demonstrate GM's willingness to tolerate criticism. As

Forbes magazine explained, "such public dissent is rare in big business, and it certainly didn't harm GM's reputation."[28]

By June 1972, GM had started the General Motors Minority Dealer Development Academy, part of a program to encourage and provide support for minority members to become automobile dealers.[29] Years later, the guidelines that became known as the Sullivan Principles were used by many institutions, especially universities, when they decided whether or not to divest the holdings of companies that did business in South Africa.[30]

Blacks on *Fortune*-level Boards, 1971–2005

In the early 1970s, with doors to some boardrooms finally opened, more and more *Fortune*-level companies added black directors to their boards, though few companies added more than one. By March 1971, the biweekly newsletter *Business and Society* identified only sixteen "major corporations" (not all of these made the annual *Fortune* list) that had black directors, and eleven of the sixteen had added those black directors within the previous eight months. By the end of 1971, more than thirty companies had added black members to their boards, and by 1972, that number was up to fifty-four.[31] When *Black Enterprise* magazine ran an article in September 1973 on black directors, there were sixty-seven black men and five black women on the boards of slightly more than one hundred "major U.S. companies." As the article noted, with approximately fourteen thousand directors on the boards of the one thousand companies that appeared on *Fortune*'s annual list, black directorships represented less than 1 percent of the total.[32]

As was the case with many other indicators of educational and economic advancement for blacks in the 1970s, this rate of increase did not continue.[33] *Business and Society Review* prefaced "A Listing of Black Directors" in its fall 1981 issue with the observation that "in the early 1970s there was a sudden flurry of appointments for blacks to the boards of major corporations. Today the flurry has quieted down considerably, and the current tally of black directors is not very much longer than the last one we published—four years ago." The list included 73 blacks who held seats on 112 companies.[34]

Nor had there been a dramatic increase in the number of blacks moving up the corporate ladder. In 1980, the *Wall Street Journal* summarized the findings of two studies that demonstrated how few blacks had moved into the higher ranks of management. In one, a survey by Korn/Ferry International, only three of seventeen hundred senior executives were black. In the other, only 117 blacks out of 13,000 managers were ranked as "department head" or higher in Chicago companies.[35] George Davis and Glegg Watson wrote in their 1982 book, *Black Life in Corporate America,* that after three years of extensive interviewing, "We heard of only a few of the [*Fortune*] five hundred that had a Black in what could be considered senior management."[36] Also in the early 1980s, John Fernandez reported that in his study of more than four thousand managers drawn from twelve large corporations, he had found only four blacks at the five highest levels.[37] Similarly, in a study of more than one thousand business executives promoted to the positions of chairman of the board, president, or vice president of leading corporations during the fiscal year 1983–1984, Floyd Bond, Herbert Hildebrandt, and Edwin Miller found that 99.2 percent were white, and only 0.2 percent were black (the other 0.6 percent were Hispanic, "Oriental," or "other").[38]

It is therefore important to keep in mind the distinction between *inside directors*, those who move up through the corporate ranks and become directors of the companies they work for, and *outside directors*, those who are asked onto a board on the basis of visibility they have achieved outside the company. The first African Americans to sit on major corporate boards were outside directors, though a few had been successful businessmen in black-owned companies.

In chapter 3, we presented data on women directors of *Fortune* 1000 companies tabulated by Catalyst. During the 1990s, an organization called Directorship monitored the presence of various minority groups on corporate boards. The data they gathered show a steady increase in the presence of blacks on *Fortune* 1000 boards from 118 in 1992 to 220 in 1999 (an increase from 1.6 percent to 3.4 percent).

Far more seats were held by blacks than there were blacks who held those seats—that is to say, many sat on more than one board. In fact, on average, blacks who sat on *Fortune* 1000 boards in the 1990s sat on two of them. A breakdown by sex reveals that black men who were directors sat on an average of 1.9 boards, and black women who were directors sat on an average of about 2.4 boards. Though she was referring to her appointment as ambassador to Luxembourg and not to her corporate directorships, a comment by Patricia Harris may help to explain why so many corporate boards, seeking to appear diversified, select black women: "When I'm around, you get two for the price of one—a woman and a Negro."[39]

Directorship no longer monitors the number of African Americans on corporate boards, but a study was done of African American directors on *Fortune* 500 boards in 2004 for the Executive Leadership Council (ELC), an organization of African Americans who hold senior executive positions in *Fortune* 500 companies. This study found that among the 5,572 board seats on *Fortune* 500 companies, 449 (or 8.1 percent) were held by African Americans. About three-fourths of these seats were held by men, although, as was the case in the 1990s, on average women held more seats than the men did. Revealingly, when the researchers broke the *Fortune* 500 into five groups based on annual revenue, there was a steady decline in the percentage of African Americans on the boards as the companies got smaller. Thus, 10.9 percent of the directors of those companies ranked #1 to #100 were African Americans, but the corresponding figures were 9.0 percent for the companies between #101 and #200, 7.9 percent for the companies between #201 and #300, 6.2 percent for the companies between #301 and #400, and 5.5 percent for those between #401 and #500.[40]

The overall 8.1 percent figure, therefore, masks a pattern whereby the larger, more visible companies are more likely to include African American directors, and the smaller, less visible ones are less likely to include them. This helps to explain why, as recently as 1999, the data from Directorship, which included the entire *Fortune* 1000, indicated that only 3.6 percent of the directors were African Americans.

It also explains the findings from another data set we have drawn on, that obtained from the Investor Responsibility Research Center (IRRC), which yields an estimate well below 8.1 percent. The IRRC list is not based on five hundred or one thousand companies, but the fifteen hundred largest companies included on the annual Standard & Poor's (S&P) list. The IRRC data indicated that 499 of the total number of seats, 13,820, were held by African Americans (3.6 percent). As was the case for the data gathered by Directorship and the data gathered by the ELC, more African American men were directors than women (373 of the 499 seats, or 75 percent, were held by men), but, on average, the women sat on more boards than did the men (2.0 versus 1.7).[41]

Black Interlocking Directors, 1994

In 1994, *Ebony* magazine, drawing on data provided by Directorship, published an article titled "Top Black Corporate Directors." The article included the names of and directorships held by the thirty-four black men and women who sat on three or more corporate boards. A comparison of this elite group of interlockers with the earliest black directors reveals some of the changes that took place during the last three decades of the twentieth century.

The most obvious difference between the blacks who became directors between 1964 and 1971 and those who were interlocking directors in 1994 is that far more of the 1994 group were female. Only one of the first twelve black *Fortune*-level directors, Patricia Roberts Harris, was female, but eleven of the 1994 interlockers were women (an increase from 8 percent to 32 percent).

About 40 percent of the 1994 black interlockers came from families that were economically comfortable, a slightly lower figure than for those who became directors between 1964 and 1971. One of the 1994 interlockers, for example, was former congressman William H. Gray III, who sat on seven boards, including those for Chase Manhattan, Warner-Lambert, and Westinghouse. Gray's father and grandfather were clergymen; his father had also been a college president, and his mother taught high school. Another was Barbara Scott Preiskel, a graduate of Wellesley and Yale Law School, who sat on five boards, including those for General Electric and the *Washington Post*. Preiskel's father was a lawyer who became a real estate broker, and her mother taught high school chemistry.

About 25 percent were from solidly working-class backgrounds. One was Walter E. Massey, a physicist who became the head of the National Science Foundation and then president of Morehouse College; by 1994, he sat on the boards of Amoco, BankAmerica, and Motorola. Massey's father was a steelworker and his mother, a teacher. Another interlocker with a working-class background was Delano Lewis, president and CEO of National Public Radio, who sat on the boards of Colgate-Palmolive, Chase Manhattan, and GEICO. Lewis's father worked for the Santa Fe railroad, and his mother was a domestic who became a beautician. Steven Minter, a foundation executive who sat on the boards of Goodyear Tire and Rubber, Consolidated Natural Gas Company, Keycorp, and Rubbermaid, came from a similar background. Minter's father, whose last year of formal education was the eleventh grade, was a county supervisor of highways, and his mother, who dropped out of school after the eleventh grade but subsequently earned a high school equivalency degree, became an accounts manager for a small company.

The other 35 percent came from poverty. Although their families had very little money, some emphasized that their parents had "middle-class values." John Jacob, former head of the National Urban League, who sat on five corporate boards in 1994, including those for Anheuser-Busch and Coca-Cola, grew up as one of five sons in a three-room house with an outhouse in the front yard. His father was a Baptist minister who helped make ends meet by doing carpentry. Jacob explained that his parents, though poor, had "very rigid middle-class standards" in addition to their "southern Baptist principles—no drinking, no dancing, no card playing, no movies on Sunday."[42]

The former UN ambassador Donald McHenry, who in 1994 sat on the boards of AT&T, Bank of Boston, Coca-Cola, and International Paper, grew up in East St. Louis, Illinois. His father, an autoworker, left the family when McHenry was a small boy, and his mother, a cook, raised him and his two siblings alone. John Slaughter, the president of Occidental College from 1988 to 1999, grew up in Topeka, Kansas, where his father, whose last year of formal education was the third grade, worked as a custodian; in 1994, Slaughter sat on five *Fortune*-level boards, including Atlantic Richfield, IBM, and Monsanto.

Four of the thirty-four were the children of immigrants. (As we shall discuss in our final chapter, we consider being an immigrant, or the child of an immigrant, an important factor in overcoming the psychological impact of white prejudice in the United States.) Clifford Alexander's father came from Jamaica in 1919. After starting out as a waiter, he "worked his way up to becoming in succession, business manager of the Harlem YMCA, branch manager of a group of apartment buildings, and manager of the Harlem branch of the New York Bank for Savings." Alexander was a student at the exclusive Fieldston School, Harvard, and Yale Law School.[43] The mother of Franklin A. Thomas emigrated from Barbados. Ernesta Procope's parents were from the West Indies, and Lois Rice Dickson's parents came to the United States from Jamaica.

As was true of the first twelve black corporate directors, the 1994 black interlockers were very well educated. All but two were college graduates, and thirty-one of the thirty-four had earned postgraduate degrees. In a careful study of the pathways to the top positions in the corporate world, Michael Useem and Jerome Karabel examined the backgrounds of 2,729 senior officers and outside directors of 208 companies on *Fortune*'s 1978 lists. They found that within this group, those who had attended various top-ranked undergraduate institutions, business programs, or law schools were significantly more likely to become chief executive officers and to sit on multiple boards. Their research demonstrated that even within such a high-achieving group of corporate managers, the school that one attended was an effective predictor of who attained the highest levels of success.[44]

In table 4.1, we have used Useem and Karabel's categories to summarize the educational credentials of their sample as well as those of the first black *Fortune*-level directors and the 1994 interlocking black directors. More than half of those in Useem and Karabel's sample either did not complete college (16.4 percent) or completed only a BA (38.8 percent); in contrast, this was true of less than 10 percent of both groups of black directors. Useem and

Table 4.1. Educational Backgrounds of Corporate Directors

Educational Background	All directors, 1977[a]	First black directors, 1964–1971	Interlockers, 1994[b]
No college or dropped out	16.4%	8%	3%
BA only (from top-ranked school)	38.8% (11.2%)	0	6% (3%)
MBA (from top-ranked school)	17.1% (14%)	0	24% (24%)
LLB or JD (from top-ranked school)	17.4%	42% (25%)	33% (12%)
Other degrees	10.1%	50%	36%

The first number in each column refers to the percentage who earned the degree; the numbers in parentheses refer to the percentage who attended top-ranked schools.
Notes:
[a] Useem and Karabel, "Pathways to Top Corporate Management."
[b] *Ebony*, 50th anniversary issue, November 1995.

Karabel's study also revealed that upper-class credentials contribute to one's chances of rising to the top of the corporate hierarchy. Those with fewer academic credentials were more likely to be from upper-class backgrounds, suggesting that their class-linked personal contacts overcame their relative lack of education. Useem and Karabel concluded, "Upper-class origins confer a significant advantage on the career prospects of senior managers with the same educational credentials. Credentials also make a substantial independent difference in the careers of senior managers, though less so for the minority of managers from upper-class backgrounds than for the majority who are not."[45]

Not surprisingly, then, because virtually none of the black directors had the kind of upper-class credentials Useem and Karabel refer to (either inclusion in the *Social Register* or attendance at one of fourteen exclusive prep schools), the black directors were more likely than those in Useem and Karabel's sample to have gone on to earn higher degrees (especially law degrees and doctorates). This not only demonstrates that the black directors needed more education to get to the same place, but it alerts us to the fact that they traveled different pathways to get there—though, as we shall see shortly, it is not really the same place.

Pathways to the Corporate Elite for Black Directors

As we look at the career pathways the 1994 interlockers took to the corporate elite, seven different routes emerge. The first and most prominent pathway was via the academic hierarchy, starting as a researcher or professor and then becoming a senior administrator (most likely a college president). Just as Clifton Wharton earned his PhD and later became a college president, five of the 1994 directors were, or had been, college presidents. We have already mentioned John Slaughter, former president of Occidental College. Another was Jewell Plummer Cobb, the former president of California State University, Fullerton, who in 1994 sat on the boards of Allied-Signal, CPC International, First Interstate Bancorp, and Georgia-Pacific. In addition to the five who were or had been college presidents, three others were senior administrators at academic institutions; one headed a business school, and two headed medical schools.

Some of the 1994 directors followed a second pathway, the same one that Asa Spaulding traveled: they founded, or rose to the top of, black businesses. This category included Jesse Hill Jr., the former president, CEO, and chairman of the board of Atlanta Life, the nation's second-largest black-owned insurance company, who sat on the boards of Delta, National Service Industries, and Knight-Ridder, and Ernesta Procope, the president and founder of E. G.

Bowman Company, the nation's largest black-owned insurance brokerage agency, who sat on the boards of Avon, the Chubb Corporation, and Columbia Gas Systems.

Some followed the path of Leon Sullivan: their work as civil rights activists led to their invitation to join corporate boards. Two men on the 1994 list had been the head of the National Urban League (Vernon Jordan, who was first on the list with seats on ten major companies, and John E. Jacob, sixth on the list with five).

Some followed the path that Samuel Pierce and William Coleman had traveled: they were lawyers who had experience in high-powered corporate law firms and in government. C. Wright Mills and others have noted that it is not unusual for members of the power elite to move from one of the higher circles to another and back again. Indeed, Mills wrote that "the inner core of the power elite" included men "from the great law factories and investment firms, who are almost professional go-betweens of economic, political and military affairs, and who thus act to unify the power elite."[46] Consider, for example, the career of Aulana Peters, one of the 1994 interlockers. After finishing law school, she worked for a decade for the Los Angeles law firm Gibson, Dunn & Crutcher. She then spent four years during the Reagan administration working for the U.S. Securities and Exchange Commission. In 1988, she returned to Gibson, Dunn & Crutcher as a partner, and in 1994 she sat on the boards of Mobil, Merrill Lynch, Minnesota Mining and Manufacturing, and Northrop Grumman.

The fifth pathway—that of the person who has been asked onto boards because of his or her work as a management consultant—is one of the newer routes to the corporate elite. Among those who have taken that route are Arthur Brimmer, a Harvard-trained economist who became president of Brimmer and Company, an economic and financial consulting firm, and Claudine Malone, a graduate of Wellesley and the Harvard Business School, who became president of Financial Management Consulting, Inc. (Brimmer, who sat on eight boards in 1994, was second on the 1994 list after Vernon Jordan; Malone was seventh on the list, sitting on five.)[47]

The 1994 interlockers took two additional pathways that were not available to the earlier black directors but have long been standard routes to the corporate board for white men. The first is rising through the ranks of white corporations. The second is having been born to someone who founded a major corporate enterprise.

In 1994, two of the interlockers, A. Barry Rand and Richard D. Parsons, were among the highest-ranking executives in *Fortune* 500 companies. Rand, the only child of college-educated, middle-class parents in Washington, D.C., went to work for Xerox at the age of twenty-four, shortly after he graduated from American University with a degree in marketing. After two years as a sales representative and ten years as a regional sales representative (during which time he earned an MBA from Stanford), Rand became corporate director of marketing in 1980, and in 1984 he became vice president of eastern operations. In 1986, he became corporate vice president and president of U.S. marketing, and in 1992, he became executive vice president, a promotion that placed him as one of the four most senior executives at the company. As early as 1987, *Black Enterprise* asserted that "he has a good chance of doing what no other black professional has ever done: become president of a *Fortune* 500 company."[48] As we will see in the next section, Rand did become the CEO of a *Fortune* 500 company—but it was not Xerox, the company for which he worked for thirty-one years.

Four years younger than Rand, by 1994 Richard D. Parsons also had emerged as a senior executive at a major American corporation, Time Warner, though his route to this position was quite different from Rand's steady rise at Xerox. Parsons, one of five children, was born in the Bedford-Stuyvesant area of Brooklyn, New York. His father was an electrician and his mother, a homemaker. Parsons graduated from the University of Hawaii and attended Albany Law School. After law school, he took a job as an assistant counselor to New York governor Nelson Rockefeller. When Rockefeller became vice president in 1974, Parsons went to Washington, D.C., as his deputy counsel. (Parsons, whose parents were Democrats, says, "I wasn't born a Republican, I became a Republican.")[49]

In 1977, Parsons left the White House to join what the *New York Times* called a "blue chip New York law firm," and in 1988, he became the chairman and chief executive of Dime Savings Bank. Under his guidance, the bank overcame $1 billion in bad debts, and when Dime merged with Anchor Savings Bank in 1994, Parsons became the chairman and CEO of Dime Bancorp, the fourth-largest savings bank in the nation and the largest on the East Coast. A mere six months later, Parsons became the highest-ranking black at any *Fortune* 500 company—he was named president of Time Warner, second in command behind chairman Gerald M. Levin. As *Black Enterprise* put it, "Parsons' appointment may signal a crack in the wall that has traditionally prevented black executives from attaining the highest level positions in corporate America."[50] It did signal a crack in the wall—Parsons became CEO at AOL Time Warner in May 2002.

Rand and Parsons were among the three youngest people on the 1994 list of directors. The youngest, born in 1958 and thus ten years younger than Parsons, was Linda Johnson Rice. Her route to multiple seats on *Fortune*-level boards was one that has been a traditional pathway for white men and has recently been traveled by women: she was born into a family that founded a successful business. Rice is the daughter of John H. and Eunice W. Johnson, who in 1942 founded the Johnson Publishing Company, the largest black-owned publisher of magazines in the United States.[51] Rice's father is one of only a handful of blacks to have appeared on the annual list published by *Forbes* magazine of the four hundred richest Americans.[52]

When she graduated at twenty-two from the University of Southern California (USC) with a degree in journalism, Linda Rice (then Linda Johnson) became vice president of the company; when she received her MBA from Northwestern University in 1987, she became, at the age of twenty-nine, the president and chief operating officer. Her father, who was then sixty-nine, remained CEO and chairman until 2002, when she took over the company as CEO.[53]

The two data sets we have for African American corporate directors in 2004, the one that we obtained from the IRRC and the "2004 Census of African Americans on Corporate Boards," a list that results from the study done for the ELC, allowed us to look at those African American interlockers who sat on at least three boards in 2004. The two lists are not identical, but, as one would assume, there is a great deal of overlap (there is also overlap between the 1994 list and these two lists; about one-fourth of the men and women who were on the 1994 list appear on the 2004 lists). The ELC study, based on the *Fortune* 500, identified forty-five interlockers, and the IRRC list, based on the S&P 1500 companies, included fifty-six. In both cases, about 75 percent of the interlockers were men, and, on average, the women held slightly more seats. Based on the two lists, three men emerged as holding the most seats (between six and eight, depending on which list one used): William Gray III, Vernon Jordan, and former professional football player, Willie D. Davis.[54]

Though none of the 1994 interlocking directors was the beneficiary of the social programs that emerged in the 1960s to enhance educational opportunities for academically promising black youngsters from economically impoverished circumstances, we predicted in the first edition of this book that over the next decade some black corporate directors were likely to be the graduates of such programs. We were thinking especially of A Better Chance (ABC), a program about which we have written, which has placed more than ten thousand youngsters in elite prep schools.[55] The earliest graduates of the program are in their fifties, and we assumed that some were likely to be named to corporate boards.

We were right. As of July 2005, two ABC graduates had been asked onto the boards of *Fortune*-level corporations. The first, Deval Patrick, has served on the boards of United Airlines and Reebok. Born in Chicago in 1956, he lived with his mother and his sister in a low-income neighborhood where he was attending the local public school when one of his teachers recommended him to ABC.

He graduated from Milton Academy in 1974 and went to Harvard and then Harvard Law School. After working for the Legal Defense and Educational Fund of the National Association for the Advancement of Colored People (NAACP), he joined a prestigious corporate law firm in Boston, Hill & Barlow.

Patrick came to national prominence when Bill Clinton nominated him to be the assistant attorney general in charge of the Civil Rights Division of the Department of Justice. Unlike Clinton's previous two nominees, Lani Guanier and John Payton, both of whom faced such strong opposition that Clinton withdrew his nominations, Patrick won bipartisan support and was confirmed easily.[56] As head of that division from 1994 to 1997, Patrick directed the work of 240 lawyers. In early 1997, he returned to private practice as a partner with another Boston law firm, Day, Berry & Howard.

Shortly thereafter, Patrick moved to the center of the battle over racial fairness in corporate America when he was asked to chair a task force created as part of the settlement in a huge racial discrimination suit against Texaco. As chair of the Independent Equality and Fairness Task Force, he was responsible for helping Texaco create and implement a human resources program that would ensure fairness and equal opportunity for all employees. It had to report annually on Texaco's progress to the Federal District Court for five years. After submitting two such reports to the Federal District Court, Patrick resigned from his role as chair of the task force and accepted a position as Texaco's vice president and general counsel. From February 1999 to April 2001, he headed Texaco's legal department, which had more than seventy lawyers in offices around the world.[57]

In April 2001, Patrick left Texaco to become executive vice president and general counsel at Coca-Cola, where he and four other senior vice presidents were on the executive committee. According to the *Atlanta Journal and Constitution*, Patrick received $1 million to compensate him for payments he would have received had he stayed at Texaco. His five-year contract paid him an annual base salary of $475,000.[58] After three tumultuous years, during which a number of contentious cases were filed against Coca-Cola, Patrick resigned in 2004.[59] In April 2005, Patrick announced that he was planning to run for governor of Massachusetts.[60]

William M. Lewis Jr., another graduate of the ABC program, is also on a *Fortune* 500 board. Lewis, whose father was a construction worker, attended Andover Academy through the ABC program and then earned both an AB and an MBA from Harvard. He worked for Morgan Stanley, where he became a managing director in 1988. In 1997, a *Fortune* magazine feature titled "The New Black Power: The Players" referred to him as "a managing director on the rise." A July 2002 article in *Fortune* on the "50 most powerful black executives in America" ranked Lewis number thirteen on the list.[61]

When we asked him in an interview in 2001 why he had not yet been asked to serve on a *Fortune*-level board, he explained that Morgan Stanley had "a flat prohibition against managing directors sitting on a board." But, he also told us, there was probably "a 75% chance you won't find me here in five years," and, if he were to leave, "in terms of a platform or a launch pad, post Morgan Stanley, yeah, there's no question. I would assume that I would be a reasonable candidate for somebody's board."[62]

His predictions proved accurate. In April 2004, after twenty-four years with Morgan Stanley, Lewis became cochairman of investment banking at another global investment firm, Lazard Freres and Company. (Vernon Jordan is the senior managing director at Lazard.) In November 2004, he joined the board of the Federal Home Loan Mortgage Corporation, known as Freddie Mac, and in June 2005, he joined the board of Darden Restaurants, which owns and operates 1,350 restaurants (including Red Lobster, Olive Garden, and Smokey Bones Barbeque & Grill) and ranked #386 on the *Fortune*-list in 2005.[63]

Black CEOs of *Fortune* 500 Companies

In 1991, we predicted, "it seems unlikely that more than two or three blacks will make it to the very top of a *Fortune* 1000 corporation in the next two decades, even with the cultural capital of prep school and Ivy League educations."[64] Were we right? It appeared that we were in 1998 when the first edition of this book came out. At that time, there had been only one African American CEO of a *Fortune* 1000 company, Clifton Wharton, of TIAA-CREF.[65]

But by 2001 we had been proven wrong. By the end of that year, there had been no fewer than seven black CEOs of *Fortune* 1000 companies (including Wharton), and by June 2005, another six had been named. The arrival of these CEOs on the corporate scene went as follows: in 1998, Errol Davis was appointed CEO at Alliant Energy; in 1999, Franklin D. Raines was appointed CEO at Fannie Mae, John W. Thompson at Symantec, Lloyd Ward at Maytag, and A. Barry Rand at Avis; in 2001, Kenneth Chenault became CEO at American Express; in 2002, Richard Parsons became CEO at Time Warner, and Stanley O'Neal at Merrill Lynch; in 2004, Robert L. Wood became CEO at Crompton Corporation, and Aylwin Lewis became CEO at K-Mart; and in 2005, Clarence Otis Jr. became CEO at Darden Restaurants, and James Bell became interim CEO at Boeing.

A look at these African American CEOs reveals some clear patterns. First, and most obviously, there are no women among them. Though some African American women have at times been identified as likely to become CEOs of *Fortune* 1000 companies (most frequently mentioned has been

Ann Fudge, chairman and CEO at Young & Rubicam), as of July 2005, it had yet to occur.[66]

Second, it is striking how well educated these men are. All are college graduates, and ten have advanced degrees (four have LLBs or JDs, six have MAs or MBAs, and one has a PhD). Four of the thirteen attended Harvard, either as undergraduates or for law or business degrees (or both), and others attended such schools as Williams, Bowdoin, Johns Hopkins, the University of Michigan, and Stanford.

Third, these African Americans come from a wide range of class backgrounds. About half grew up in families that faced difficult economic circumstances. Franklin Raines's father was a custodian for the city of Seattle, and his mother worked as a cleaning woman; at one point, when his father fell ill, the family was on welfare for two years. Lloyd Ward's father was a postman by day who also worked a night job as a janitor at the local movie theater in a small town in southern Michigan (he died when Ward was eighteen). Stanley O'Neal's father worked on a farm in Alabama, and his mother worked as a domestic; as a boy, O'Neal contributed to the family finances by delivering newspapers and picking corn and cotton. When he was twelve, his family moved to a housing project in Atlanta, and his father found work at a General Motors factory. Clarence Otis's father was a custodian for the city of Los Angeles and worked a second full-time job cleaning the office of a local dentist; his mother, though not licensed as a day care worker, took care of the children of friends and neighbors who worked during the day. Errol Davis grew up in a working-class family in the Homewood neighborhood in Pittsburgh. John W. Thompson, whose father was a postal worker who liked to hunt and whose mother was a teacher, still tells people that he is just a "country boy."[67]

In sharp contrast, some of these CEOs grew up in quite comfortable circumstances. Clifton Wharton's father was a lawyer and an ambassador, Kenneth Chenault's father was a dentist, and Barry Rand's parents were "college educated." Clearly, a higher percentage of the black CEOs came from working- or lower-class backgrounds than was the case for the first black directors or the 1994 interlockers.[68]

It is even more revealing to contrast the backgrounds of these thirteen men with the twenty-two women who are or have been CEOs of *Fortune* 1000 companies. As we showed in chapter 3, almost all of the women who have become CEOs have come from privileged backgrounds.

Fourth, no matter what their circumstances at birth, whether they went to public or private high schools, Ivy League colleges or state universities, these African American CEOs seem to have developed what a friend of one them called "smoothness." They appear to be, as she put it, "entirely at ease with white people."[69] In an ethnographic study of African American executives at a "major financial service corporation in center city, Philadelphia," sociologist Elijah Anderson observed that the black executives at the highest ranks appeared to be "utterly polished." "Their demeanor in the presence of whites," he wrote, "seems almost casual and certainly confident. During such interactions, they leave no doubt that they are the social and intellectual equals of their white counterparts."[70]

A fifth pattern emerges as one looks at the backgrounds of these men: at least six were excellent athletes who participated in team sports. Franklin Raines was the quarterback of his high school football team, and Lloyd Ward attended Michigan State on a basketball scholarship. Barry Rand was all-metropolitan in the Washington, D.C., area in football, basketball, and track and told one interviewer that he went to Rutgers expecting to become a professional football player. Richard Parsons was an all-around athlete in high school and played freshman basketball at the University of Hawaii. Kenneth Chenault played three sports in high school and ran track and played soccer at Bowdoin. Clarence Otis played both football and tennis in high school.[71]

There is, of course, much debate about whether or not the amount of time young African American males devote to playing and watching sports detracts from the quality of their educations. As sports sociologist Harry Edwards and others have argued over the past few decades, many young African Americans end up with nothing when their athletic careers come to an end, and the athletic careers of most young athletes end long before they ever receive a paycheck as a professional athlete.[72] Indeed, as of 2000, there were only fourteen hundred black athletes playing professional basketball, football, and baseball (compared to more than thirty-one thousand black physicians and surgeons, thirty-three thousand black lawyers, and five thousand black dentists).[73] Ward's story is particularly revealing in this respect because when he played basketball at Michigan State, he had to reject pressures to take Mickey Mouse courses.

Whatever the merits of athletic participation for most young black students, the fact that at least six of the African American CEOs participated in athletics at the high school or collegiate level suggests that having been good athletes and playing on teams did not hurt them and probably helped them in their adult careers. Perhaps it taught them leadership skills; perhaps it taught them to compete against and play alongside white teammates; perhaps it taught them self-confidence. Or, as Barry Rand noted, perhaps it taught them how to be in the limelight. As he said of his high school athletic career, "I was used to being at the center of athletic attention."[74]

It is also noteworthy that many former professional athletes have become very successful businessmen. Their route, of course, is quite different from

team sports
comfort zone

that of the CEOs we have discussed, for they accumulated considerable economic capital as professional athletes, as well as valuable contacts and name
recognition. Still, when we did a study of the African American directors of
the most successful black-owned corporations, the list included a number of
former professional athletes. For example, basketball players Dave Bing and
Julius Erving and NFL defensive lineman Charlie W. Johnson were founders
of three of the largest African American–owned corporations in the United
States. Similarly, when we looked at the African Americans who sat on S&P
1500 boards in 2004, the list included a number of former professional football players (as we noted above, Willie Davis sat on many boards, but also on
the list were Calvin Hill and Lynn Swann) and former professional basketball
players (including Dave Bing, Julius Erving, and Wayne Embry). These men
are part of what the *Wall Street Journal* has called the "growing fraternity of
athletes-turned-entrepreneurs."[75]

Are the Barriers Coming Down and for How Many?

As the data we have presented make clear, much has changed since the first
African Americans joined corporate boards in 1964. At the same time, blacks
(like women, but not Jews) remain underrepresented on corporate boards. Although blacks accounted for about 11 percent of the U.S. population in 1964
and about 13 percent in 2005, the percentage of seats held by blacks on *Fortune* 1000 boards during that same period rose from zero to somewhere between 3.6 and 8.1 percent.

But what about the pipeline? Are other younger blacks, like Rand, Parsons,
and Rice, moving through the ranks? Studies in the early 1980s revealed that
there were very few blacks at the higher levels of management in the largest
companies. A 1990 study by the executive search firm Korn/Ferry International indicated that the number of blacks in "high-level management positions" had increased during the previous decade, but only from 0.2 percent to
0.6 percent.[76]

In 1998, the Joint Center for Political and Economic Studies surveyed 750
black professionals in corporate America. Although most expressed optimism
about their own professional futures in America's largest corporations, 81
percent said discrimination in their jobs was common. When asked to rate
how well corporate America was doing in terms of promoting blacks on an
equitable basis, 40 percent said "poor," 33 percent said "fair," 18 percent said
"good," and 1 percent said "excellent." Tellingly, 78 percent said that they believed top black executives were "often in those positions for appearance's
sake." Almost two-thirds (64 percent) advised black youngsters to pursue careers as entrepreneurs, far more than the 24 percent who encouraged them to

enter the corporate world. And more than two-thirds (68 percent) said they wanted to leave the corporate world and start their own businesses.[77]

In its July 2002 feature story titled "50 Most Powerful Black Executives," *Fortune* asserted that there are "more on the way." The article noted that the ELC (consisting of senior black executives in *Fortune* 500 companies who are "no more than three steps away from CEO") had 275 members as of that date, compared with nineteen members when it was founded in 1986. There are, however, several thousand executives within three steps of the top in *Fortune* 500 companies, so the 275 represents less than 5 percent of the total.[78]

Thus, there are blacks in the pipeline, though they seem to be leaving at higher rates than others, and those who remain represent a percentage that is well below that of blacks in the larger population. Sociologist Sharon Collins has demonstrated how the very forces that led to the hiring of many African Americans—a federal commitment to affirmative action and the enforcement of equal opportunity guidelines—fell by the wayside in the 1980s and 1990s.[79]

Collins concluded in 1993 that "the gains blacks have made over 25 years may be in jeopardy." And, indeed, we believe that these gains would have been in even greater jeopardy were it not for a new set of private-sector programs that begin in elementary schools in some areas of the country and continue through to corporate internships for black college students. These efforts, which we discuss further in chapter 8, have been funded primarily by the major corporations. Essentially, the corporations have gone into partnerships with various educators who have come to them for funding to help prepare students of color for prep schools, elite colleges, and the corporate world. The corporations and their foundations, we believe, have been motivated by the threat of lawsuits for racial discrimination in the workplace, the increasing purchasing power of black consumers, and the need for diverse management teams in an increasingly globalized economy.[80]

The decreased support from the government and the increased support from the corporate world was demonstrated when the George W. Bush administration fought affirmative action in cases that challenged the admissions policies at the University of Michigan Law school, but briefs from *Fortune* companies, as well as one from military officers, supported the university and argued that affirmative action was necessary. Moreover, the majority decision, written by Sandra Day O'Connor, expressly mentioned these briefs from members of the power elite. She wrote,

Major American businesses have made clear that the skills needed in today's increasingly global marketplace can only be developed through exposure to widely diverse people, cultures, ideas, and viewpoints. High-ranking retired officers and civilian military leaders assert that a highly qualified, racially diverse officer corps is essential to national security. Moreover, because universities, and in particular, law schools, represent the training ground for a large number of the Nation's leaders (*Sweatt v. Painter*), the path to leadership must be visibly open to talented and qualified individuals of every race and ethnicity. Thus, the Law School has a compelling interest in attaining a diverse student body.[81]

For the time being, however, there are black CEOs, there are black directors, and there are blacks in the corporate pipeline, though the numbers are small and show very little, if any, increase in any of these categories. It is likely that for the foreseeable future, many or most of the blacks in the corporate elite will have arrived there from the outside, as has been true since the 1960s. Some, like Rand, Parsons, Chenault, Ward, O'Neal, and Lewis will rise through the ranks of major corporations, but most African Americans in the corporate elite will be outside directors who are lawyers, university presidents (or the deans of medical schools or business schools), successful in businesses founded by blacks, or "management consultants."

In this respect, black corporate directors, even those who are interlocking directors, continue to constitute a distinctly different group from white corporate directors in the innermost circles. Unlike the thirty-four black interlocking directors we looked at, most white interlocking directors are themselves the CEOs of major corporations; two-thirds of all outside directors are themselves senior officers of other corporations, and half are chairmen, presidents, or CEOs.[82] Of the 1994 black interlocking directors, only Rand and Parsons qualified as senior officers of major corporations. There are more now, but still not that many. Blacks on corporate boards thus face a double whammy: they are statistically underrepresented, and they have traveled different, less respected pathways to their positions. As a result, they are likely to continue to play marginal roles.

The array of blacks with some potential to join the corporate elite seems to be diverse. The first twelve black directors included both conservative Republican lawyers like Samuel Pierce and William Coleman and longtime liberal activists like Leon Sullivan, and the 1994 group of interlocking directors included conservative Republicans and liberal activists, although, in both groups, the traditionalists far outnumbered the activists. As we indicated, Sullivan was an exception, for the general tendency has been to select directors who will not rock the boat too much. Even the few activists who have been asked and agreed to join corporate boards are likely over time to have become part of the establishment. In a 1993 profile in *Current Biography,* Vernon Jordan's willingness to join corporate boards was explained in the following way: "During his ten years at the helm, he greatly expanded the influence of the National Urban League by enlisting the cooperation of some of the largest corporations in the United States. As part of the effort, he began serving on the boards of directors of such corporate giants as J. C. Penney, Xerox, and American Express."[83] Maybe so. But Jordan was also expanding his own influence, and by 1995, as a partner in a major Washington, D.C., law firm, wearing shirts "custom-made in London," a confidant and golfing buddy of the president, and a director of ten corporations, Jordan had become an influential insider rather than an outsider activist.[84]

BLACKS IN THE CABINET

Before Bill Clinton's election in 1992, only five blacks had served in presidential cabinets (see table 4.2). The first was Robert Weaver, who in 1966 became the secretary of housing and urban development. Weaver grew up in a suburb of Washington, D.C., in one of the few black families among some three thousand neighbors. His white neighbors went to nearby all-white schools, but he and his brother had to commute forty-five minutes each day to attend black schools in the city. "Their one ambition," Weaver said of his parents, "was to send us to New England schools."[85]

Weaver went to a New England school, Harvard, where he earned a BA, an MA, and a PhD. (He was not the first in his family to attend Harvard; his grandfather had gone there.) He then went to Washington, D.C., to be a part of Roosevelt's New Deal, serving in a variety of positions as adviser to

Table 4.2. Blacks in Cabinets

Name	Presidency	Years Served	Department
Robert Weaver	Johnson	1966–1968	Housing and Urban Development
William Coleman	Ford	1975–1977	Transportation
Patricia Harris	Carter	1977–1979	Housing and Urban Development
Patricia Harris	Carter	1979–1981	Health, Education, and Welfare
Samuel Pierce	Reagan	1981–1989	Housing and Urban Development
Louis Sullivan	George H. W. Bush	1989–1993	Health and Human Services
Ronald Brown	Clinton	1993–1996	Commerce
Michael Espy	Clinton	1993–1995	Agriculture
Hazel O'Leary	Clinton	1993–1997	Energy
Alexis Herman	Clinton	1997–2001	Labor
Rodney Slater	Clinton	1997–2001	Transportation
Colin Powell	George W. Bush	2001–2005	State
Rod Paige	George W. Bush	2001–2005	Education
Alphonso Jackson	George W. Bush	2003–present	Housing and Urban Development
Condoleezza Rice	George W. Bush	2005–present	State

agency heads on minority issues. He was the architect and leader of the "black cabinet," a group of blacks who lobbied for and assisted in the integration of the federal government.[86]

After World War II, Weaver held teaching positions at Northwestern, Columbia, and New York universities. In 1955, he became the state rent commissioner in New York, and in 1960, he was appointed vice chairman of the New York City Housing and Development Board. When John F. Kennedy was elected president, he named Weaver to head the Housing and Home Finance Agency, at the time the highest federal administrative position ever held by an African American. Although Kennedy attempted to elevate the agency to cabinet status, Congress blocked his efforts. Five years later, Lyndon Johnson succeeded where Kennedy had failed; the agency, with its name changed to the Department of Housing and Urban Development, achieved cabinet status, and in 1966, Weaver became the first African American to hold a cabinet position.[87]

After Weaver left his position as secretary of housing and urban development, there were no black cabinet members for another seven years. There were no blacks in Nixon's cabinets. In 1975, Gerald Ford selected William Coleman Jr. as his secretary of transportation. The third black in a presidential cabinet, Patricia Roberts Harris, held two cabinet positions during Carter's presidency: first she was secretary of housing and urban development, and later she became secretary of health, education, and welfare (HEW).

In 1981, twenty-seven years after he had become the first black corporate director on a *Fortune*-level board, Samuel Pierce Jr. became secretary of housing and urban development under Ronald Reagan. In this capacity, Pierce came under investigation for corruption. Although other senior housing officials were convicted, an independent counsel ultimately decided not to prosecute Pierce because of his age (he was then seventy-two), his poor health, and the absence of "clear criminal intent." Pierce did, however, release a statement that read, in part, "I realize that my own conduct contributed to an environment in which these events could occur. I must take the blame for problems."[88]

George H. W. Bush's only black cabinet appointee was Louis Sullivan, a physician whom Barbara Bush had come to know well when she joined the board of trustees of the Morehouse School of Medicine, where Sullivan was dean. After Sullivan gave a speech introducing her at the Republican National Convention in August 1988, Barbara Bush successfully lobbied for his appointment as secretary of health and human services.

Clinton was the first president to appoint more than one black to his cabinet. His initial cabinet included three: Ron Brown, the former chair of the Democratic National Committee; Mike Espy, a former congressman from

Mississippi, who was one of the first black leaders to endorse Clinton's presidential candidacy; and Hazel O'Leary, the corporate vice president discussed in chapter 3. After his reelection in 1996, Clinton appointed Alexis Herman to replace Robert Reich as secretary of labor and Rodney Slater to replace Frederico Peña as secretary of transportation.

There have been four African Americans in George W. Bush's cabinet as of November 2005: Colin Powell, secretary of state from 2001 to 2005; Roderick Paige, secretary of education from 2001 to 2005; Alphonso Jackson, who replaced Mel Martinez as secretary of housing and urban development in March 2004; and Condoleezza Rice, Bush's replacement for Powell as secretary of state.

Whereas about 50 percent of the first twelve black directors on *Fortune*-level boards, 40 percent of the 1994 black interlockers, and 43 percent of the first seven black CEOs of *Fortune* companies had been born into economically comfortable circumstances, nine of the fourteen (or 64 percent) cabinet members came from relative privilege.

As we have already seen, William Coleman Jr. came from generations of educators, ministers, and social workers; Samuel Pierce's father was a successful businessman and property owner; and Robert Weaver, whose Harvard-educated grandfather was the first black in the United States to earn a doctoral degree in dentistry, grew up in a comfortable Washington, D.C., suburb. Louis Sullivan's father was an undertaker and his mother a teacher. Ron Brown's parents were both graduates of Howard University; his father managed the Theresa Hotel in Harlem, which catered to many prominent entertainers and professionals. Mike Espy's maternal grandfather was one of the most prosperous blacks in the South: he founded a chain of funeral homes and, at the time of his death, was one of the largest landowners in Mississippi. Both of Hazel O'Leary's parents were physicians. Roderick Paige's father was a high school principal, and his mother was a librarian, and Condoleezza Rice's parents were both educators (her father was a college dean).

Alexis Herman grew up in Alabama, where (as noted in chapter 3) her father was a mortician who became the first black elected to Alabama's Democratic Party organization, and her mother was a reading teacher. Colin Powell's parents, Jamaican immigrants, lived in the South Bronx, and they both worked in the New York garment industry. As writer David Halberstam explained in a profile of Powell, "With two incomes and two children, the Powells were not poor in the classic sense. They lived in the South Bronx, and Colin and his sister, Marilyn, never did without anything important."[89]

Three of the fourteen, Patricia Roberts Harris, Rodney Slater, and Alphonso Jackson, came from poverty. As noted in chapter 3, Harris's father worked as a waiter on a railroad, Slater grew up picking cotton and peaches

in Marianna, Arkansas, and Jackson was the youngest of twelve children—
his father did not graduate from high school and, as Jackson explained, "jug-
gled three jobs to keep food on the table."[90]

All fourteen went to college, four to prestigious "white" schools (Weaver
to Harvard, Coleman to the University of Pennsylvania, Pierce to Cornell, and
Brown to Middlebury) and four to prestigious "black" schools (Harris and
Espy to Howard, Sullivan to Morehouse, and O'Leary to Fiske). Eight of the
fourteen went to law school, one (Sullivan) went to medical school, and three
completed doctoral work—Weaver received a PhD in economics from Harvard, Paige a DPEd (doctor of physical education) at Indiana University, and
Rice a PhD from the University of Denver.

BLACKS IN THE MILITARY ELITE

In chapter 2, we told of the Jewish Midshipman Leonard Kaplan's being "sent
to Coventry" in the 1920s, which meant that no one spoke to him during his entire four years at the Naval Academy. Benjamin O. Davis Jr., the first black to
graduate from the U.S. Military Academy in the twentieth century, had a parallel experience during his four years at that institution in the 1930s. After he had
been at West Point for a short time, there was a knock on his door announcing
a meeting in the basement in ten minutes. Davis painfully recalled that meeting
and its long-term effects in the autobiography he wrote almost sixty years later:

> As I approached the assembly where the meeting was in progress, I heard some-
> one ask, "What are we going to do about the nigger?" I realized then that the
> meeting was about me, and I was not supposed to attend. I turned on my heel
> and double-timed back to my room.
>
> From that meeting on, the cadets who roomed across the hall, who had been
> friendly earlier, no longer spoke to me. In fact, no one spoke to me except in the
> line of duty. Apparently, certain upperclass cadets had determined that I was get-
> ting along too well at the Academy to suit them, and they were going to enforce
> an old West Point tradition—"silencing"—with the object of making my life so
> unhappy that I would resign. Silencing had been applied in the past to certain
> cadets who were considered to have violated the honor code and refused to re-
> sign. In my case there was no question of such a violation; I was to be silenced
> solely because cadets did not want blacks at West Point. Their only purpose was
> to freeze me out.
>
> Except for the recognition ceremony at the end of plebe year, I was silenced
> for the entire four years of my stay at the Academy.[91]

Davis stuck it out at West Point and graduated near the top of his class.
Even after graduation in 1936, his classmates (among them, William West-

moreland, who commanded U.S. troops in Vietnam from 1964 to 1968 and came from a wealthy textile family in South Carolina) continued their silent treatment of him for years. In fact, for the next fifteen years, as his assignments took him to different locations in the United States and around the world, not only did his classmates continue to give him the silent treatment, but they and their wives also shunned Davis's wife.[92]

Davis was to become the second black to hold the rank of brigadier general (and the first to hold that rank in the air force). The first was his father, whose military career spanned a fifty-year period from the Spanish American War to World War II. The senior Davis enlisted in the cavalry in 1899, soon passed the tests to become an officer, and over the years rose through the military ranks, with various stints teaching military science at Wilberforce University in Ohio and the Tuskegee Institute in Alabama.

Pioneers like the Davises helped prepare the way for a military that some have called a model of integration. According to Charles Moskos and John Sibley Butler in *All That We Can Be*, "By the mid-1950s, a snapshot of 100 enlisted men on a typical parade would have shown twelve black faces; integration had become a fact of Army life. At a time when Afro-Americans were still arguing for their educational rights before the Supreme Court and marching for their social and political rights in the Deep South, the Army had become desegregated with little fanfare."[93]

By 1985, of the 1,067 men with general officer rank, 36, or 3.4 percent, were black. By 1995, there were still only thirty-six blacks with general officer rank, but there were fewer generals overall, so the percentage of blacks was a bit higher at 4.0 percent.[94] In May 1996, when Bill Clinton nominated Vice Adm. J. Paul Reason to become a four-star admiral, he became the first black four-star in that branch of the service. (The air force had promoted a black to four-star rank twenty years earlier, and the army had done so in the mid-1980s; the Marines as yet had not.[95]) By September 2004, of the 898 men and women with general officer rank, 47, or 5.2 percent, were black. Thus, over the past twenty years, there has been a slight increase in the percentage of blacks with general officer rank, and there has been a handful at the seniormost levels, but the increase has been small, and blacks remain underrepresented.[96]

Some indication of the future of African Americans in the military elite can be seen in the number of graduates from the three military academies, which produce a disproportionate number of generals and admirals. At West Point, the number of black graduates increased from an average of two or three a year between 1955 and 1967 to an average of seventy per year from 1990 through 1994. The class of 2008, which had 1,235 entering students, included 72 African Americans (5.8 percent). The starting point was even lower at the

Naval Academy, which graduated fewer than two a year until 1967, but the average was seventy-seven a year from 1990 through 1994. The class of 2007, which started with 1,227 students, included 69 African Americans (5.6 percent). At the Air Force Academy, there were, on average, fewer than two black graduates a year until 1967, but the figure reached sixty-two between 1986 and 1989. The Air Force Academy's entering classes of 2005 through 2009 included a total of 6,570 students, 295 of whom (4.5 percent) were African Americans. Thus, African Americans are underrepresented at all three academies, and the numbers have either stayed about the same or declined since the early 1990s.[97]

One might expect that those blacks who have achieved general officer status, almost all of them men, would become, at the time of their retirement, prime candidates for senior corporate positions. As Mills pointed out back in the 1950s, there was "increased personnel traffic . . . between the military and the corporate realms" because of "the great cultural shift of modern American capitalism toward a permanent war economy."[98] As a result, Mills added, "Get me a general" became the slogan of corporate recruiters. But Moskos and Butler found, much to their surprise, that this has not been the case for black generals. In numerous interviews with retired generals over the years, they found that "even the most qualified black generals" have not been hired as consultants and have not been asked onto corporate boards. "This is particularly puzzling," they write, "considering that most of these retired generals once had responsibility for thousands of soldiers and oversaw logistic systems of enormous cost and complexity. . . . It is difficult not to conclude that the discrimination these people overcame in the military overtakes them again when they return to civilian life."[99]

Still, a retired black general has become one of the best-known and most admired Americans. It was a major breakthrough in 1989 when Colin Powell was named chairman of the Joint Chiefs of Staff. And, indeed, Powell's ascendance to the top of the military hierarchy has had as much impact for civilians as for soldiers. According to Moskos and Butler, "the elevation of Colin Luther Powell to the chairmanship of the Joint Chiefs of Staff in 1989 was an epic event in American race relations, whose significance has yet to be fully realized."[100]

Powell's parents were both Jamaican immigrants, a fact he makes much of, and so will we when we explore the reasons for the success and failure of minorities in the United States in chapter 8.[101] While a student at the City College of New York, Powell joined the Reserve Officers' Training Corps (ROTC), and when he graduated in 1958, he was commissioned as a second lieutenant. Powell has emphasized that he "found himself" in ROTC: "Suddenly everything clicked. . . . I had found something I was good at. . . . For the first time, in the military I always knew exactly what was expected of me."[102] Equally important, the military had become a place where blacks could do well. "I had an intuitive sense that this was a career which was beginning to open up for blacks," says Powell. "You could not name, in those days, another profession where black men routinely told white men what to do and how to do it."[103]

Powell rose through the ranks. He served as a junior officer in Vietnam, then held a series of command and staff jobs. In 1972, he became a White House fellow; noting that race worked to his advantage in this appointment, he said to a friend, "I was lucky to be born black."[104] Four years later, Jimmy Carter appointed Clifford Alexander secretary of the army, and the number of black generals tripled while Alexander held that position. "My method was simple," Alexander revealed. "I just told everyone that I would not sign the goddam promotion list unless it was fair."[105] In 1979, at the age of forty-two, Colin Powell achieved the rank of general. By 1987, he had become national security adviser under Reagan, and in 1989, under George H. W. Bush, he became the first black—and the youngest man ever—to be chairman of the Joint Chiefs of Staff. After the Gulf War, polls consistently indicated that Powell was among the most admired people in America.[106]

"THING IS, I AIN'T THAT BLACK" *Colin Powell*

Throughout the century, scholars have demonstrated that a disproportionate number of black professionals have been light skinned, and that blacks with darker skin are more likely to be discriminated against. Horace Mann Bond found, for example, that many "early Negro scholars" were "light-complexioned" individuals from families that had been part of the antebellum "free colored population" or born to "favored slaves." He explained their success in the following way: "The phenomenon was not due, as many believed, to the 'superiority' of the white blood; it was a social and economic, rather than a natural selection. Concubinage remained an openly sustained relationship between white men and Negro women in the South for fifty years after the Civil War; the children of such unions were more likely to have parents with the money, and the tradition, to send a child to school, than the former field hand slaves who were now sharecroppers and day laborers."[107]

The authors of the Glass Ceiling Commission's report argue that "gradations in skin color" have continued to affect the career chances of men and women of color. They write,

Color-based differences are inescapable but nobody likes to talk about them. These are complicated differences because they are not exclusively racial and not exclusively ethnic. The unstated but ever-present question is, *"Do they look like us?"*

Though it is mostly covert, our society has developed an extremely sophisticated, and often denied, acceptability index based on gradations in skin color. It is not as simple a system as the black/white/colored classifications that were used in South Africa. It is not legally permissible, but it persists just beneath the surface, and it can be and is used as a basis for decision making, sometimes consciously and sometimes unconsciously. It is applied to African Americans, to American Indians, to Asian and Pacific Islander Americans, and to Hispanic Americans, who are described in a color shorthand of black, brown, yellow, and red.[108]

Although this issue is generally not commented upon directly, some accounts of African Americans in positions of power allude to it indirectly. For example, Patricia Roberts Harris is described as follows in *Current Biography*: "Among her ancestors were Negro slaves, Delaware and Cherokee Indians, and English and Irish settlers. . . . In some of her facial features she resembles Sophia Loren."[109]

Not surprisingly, therefore, when we looked at photographs of those black Americans who had made it into the power elite, we noted that they were lighter skinned than many other black Americans. We were able to confirm this observation more systematically by asking two raters, working independently, to use the Skin Color Assessment Procedure, a skin-color rating chart developed by two psychologists, to rate the skin color of many of those we have identified as members of the power elite and various control groups of other black Americans. The differences were powerful: the blacks in the power elite were rated as lighter skinned than the blacks in the control groups, and this was especially true for the black women in the power elite, who were rated as lighter than any of the other groups.[110] In fact, when the raters scored the photographs in *Ebony* magazine's 1996 list "100 Most Influential Black Americans and Organization Leaders," Hazel O'Leary had the lowest score (and was thus seen as the lightest) of anyone on the list.

These findings not only make sense in terms of the earlier research on skin color among eminent black Americans, but they are also consistent with our findings on Jews and women in the power elite. As we have indicated in the previous two chapters, those Jews who have made it into the power elite are likely to have been highly assimilated in the first place. The longer they have been in the power elite, especially the corporate and military elites, the less distinguishable they become from their Gentile counterparts. Similarly, the women who have made it into the corporate elite are those who fit in the best, and though it is certainly easy enough to distinguish them from men in terms of their appearance, they tend to be (or to become) quite similar to the men surrounding them in terms of class background, values, and behaviors. In chapter 3, we quoted a woman executive who explained to us that although she perceived her gender to pose the most substantial obstacle to her advancement in her career, this did not mean that being Jewish was irrelevant. "It's part of the total package," she told us. "It's part of the question of whether you fit the mold. Are you like me or not? If too much doesn't fit, it impacts you negatively."

In the same way, being black makes it hard to "fit the mold," and being a dark-skinned black makes it even harder. This is not the only factor operating in terms of what can make one different, but it contributes to whether "too much doesn't fit." This may explain why light skin is more prevalent among black women in the power elite than among black men, for black women are already different from the white male power elite norm because of their sex. It is as if one can accumulate only so many points of difference from the norm, and a combination of gender points and skin-color points can exceed the acceptable limit.

Colin Powell captured the essence of skin color's role in the broader context of not being too different from, and thus threatening to, whites. In a lengthy *New Yorker* profile, Henry Louis Gates Jr. asked Powell to explain polls that showed him having greater appeal among whites than among blacks. Powell, described by Gates as "light-skinned and blunt-featured," cut through sociological jargon and the need for statistical analyses:

> One, I don't shove it in their face, you know? I don't bring any stereotypes or threatening visage to their presence. Some black people do. Two, I can overcome any stereotypes or reservations they have, because I perform well. Third thing is, *I ain't that black.* . . . I speak reasonably well, like a white person. I am very comfortable in a white social situation, and I don't go off in a corner. My features are clearly black, and I've never denied what I am. It fits into their general social setting, so they do not find me threatening. I think there's more to it than that, but I don't know what it is.[111]

BLACKS IN CONGRESS AND ON THE SUPREME COURT

The Senate

The three blacks who have served in the U.S. Senate in modern times represent three eras. Indeed, if Edward Brooke, born in 1919, was a product of the old black middle class of the mid-twentieth century, and Carol Moseley-Braun, born in 1947, was a product of the race-conscious 1960s, Barack Obama, born in 1961, is a product of the increasingly biracial and bicultural world of the 1980s and 1990s.[112]

Edward Brooke was a Republican who represented the state of Massachusetts from 1967 until 1979. His father was a lawyer, and Brooke grew up in upper-middle-class neighborhoods in the Washington, D.C., area. The family lived mostly in black neighborhoods, though for a while they lived in a white neighborhood that was so rigidly segregated that blacks who did not live there could not pass through the neighborhood without a note from a white person. According to one account, "He spent his boyhood summers on his mother's family plantation in Virginia, where his grandparents told the light-skinned youth that he was a descendant of Thomas Jefferson and of a British admiral, Sir Philip Bowes Brooke, and that he was related to Rupert Brooke, the English poet."[113]

After graduating from Howard in 1941 and serving in the army during World War II, he attended Boston University Law School, where he edited the *Law Review*. After he graduated in 1948, he started a one-man law practice outside Boston, and a few years later, he entered state politics. In 1948 and again in 1952, he ran for the state legislature both as a Democrat and as a Republican (it was then legal to do so); both times he lost the Democratic nomination but won the Republican one, then lost in the general election. In 1960, he ran for secretary of state as a Republican, losing by fewer than twelve thousand votes. Two years later, he won the election for attorney general, the second-highest office in the state. (He gained the Republican nomination on the second ballot over Boston blue blood Elliot Richardson.) In 1966, he ran for the U.S. Senate and won, defeating the former governor, Endicott ("Chub") Peabody.

In running for state attorney general, Brooke downplayed his race. He was, he asserted, an American first, a Republican second, and "a black incidentally." He declared, "I'm not running as a Negro. I never have. I'm trying to show that people can be elected on the basis of their qualifications and not their race."[114] A few years later he remarked, "I am not a civil rights leader and I don't profess to be one."[115]

Brooke lost his bid for a third term in the Senate when he was ensnared in a set of allegations about financial impropriety, fueled by bitter divorce proceedings with his wife, an Italian he met during the war. Although he was never convicted of a crime, his reputation suffered, and he lost that election to Paul Tsongas. He subsequently worked as a consultant and lawyer for various Washington, D.C., law firms and real estate developers. According to one account, in the early 1990s he was living in Virginia with his second wife and son and describing himself as a "retired country gentleman."[116]

Carol Moseley-Braun, the second African American elected to the Senate in modern times, has never been prone to downplay race. As a teenager in Chicago in the 1960s, she staged a one-person sit-in at a restaurant that would not seat her, refused to leave an all-white beach even when whites threw stones at her, and marched with Martin Luther King Jr. in a demonstration calling for open housing in an all-white neighborhood. She describes her upbringing in the following way: "They raised us in a world that did not acknowledge or legitimize racism. Ethnic pride was part and parcel of that world—my maternal grandparents had been Garveyites and Muslims, 'race men' as they were called at the time."[117]

Born to a middle-class family on the South Side of Chicago—her father was a policeman and her mother a medical technician—Moseley-Braun received a BA from the University of Illinois at Chicago and a JD from the University of Chicago Law School.

Six years after graduating from law school she was elected to the Illinois House of Representatives, and a decade later, she was elected Cook County recorder of deeds. When, four years later, she decided to run for the U.S. Senate, entering the Democratic primary against the incumbent, Alan J. Dixon, who had voted to confirm Clarence Thomas, few at first thought she had a chance. As one account puts it, Moseley-Braun's candidacy "appeared so unpromising that political organizations created to provide seed money to women's campaigns across the country gave her nothing or just token contributions late in the race."[118] Nonetheless, she defeated Dixon, and when she won the general election, she became one of seven women in the Senate (see chapter 3) and the only African American. She was defeated in 1998 in her attempt for a second term, and, once again, the Senate had no African American members.

Barack Obama's mother, a white woman born in Kansas, met his father, a Kenyan, in 1959 when they were students at the University of Hawaii. When Obama was a toddler, his father left Hawaii to do graduate work in economics at Harvard (the scholarship he won was not big enough to enable him to take his wife and son with him), and upon completing his doctoral degree, he returned to Africa.

His parents divorced, and a few years later, Obama's mother met and married an Indonesian. She and six-year-old Barack moved to Jakarta, where Barack lived for four years before returning to Hawaii to live with his maternal grandparents (his grandfather sold insurance and his grandmother worked in a bank).

Despite his family's middle-class background, he was accepted at Punahou Academy, Hawaii's most exclusive prep school. He began college at Occidental before transferring to Columbia, from which he graduated in 1983. After three years working in Chicago as a community organizer, he went to the Harvard Law School, where he became the first black editor of the *Harvard Law Review*. After graduating from law school in 1991, and before returning to Chicago, he spent a year working on the book that was to become *Dreams from My Father*, a memoir that describes his growing up in Hawaii and Indonesia and his search as a young adult to learn more about his father, his family in Kenya, and his own racial identity.[119] He returned to Chicago, practiced civil rights law, and taught at the University of Chicago Law School. When the opportunity arose, he ran for and was elected to the state senate representing a district that included both Hyde Park (home of the university) and some of the most impoverished ghettos on the South Side.[120]

Seven years after his election to the state senate, Obama burst upon the national scene in March 2004 when he beat six others to win the Democratic primary for Senate (he won 53 percent of the vote). The polls indicated that he was well ahead of Jack Ryan, his wealthy, white, Republican opponent, when a sex scandal led Ryan to withdraw from the race. The Illinois Republicans had a hard time finding someone to run against him, and, thus, with no opponent back in Illinois, in July 2004 Obama traveled to Boston to deliver an electrifying keynote address at the Democratic National Convention.

Finally, after various possible candidates turned them down, including former football coach Mike Ditka, the Illinois Republicans came up with Alan Keyes, a hard-core, right-wing, conservative African American who had been an unsuccessful candidate in many previous political races, even though he was a resident of Maryland and a few years earlier had railed against Hillary Clinton for running for the Senate in New York when she was not a resident of that state. When November rolled around, Barack Obama won a landslide victory, with 70 percent of the vote.[121]

Obama is immensely popular with whites, in part, because he is so comfortable among them. As he said about the white voters from rural areas and small towns in Illinois, "I know those people. Those are my grandparents. The food they serve is the food my grandparents served when I was growing up. Their manners, their sensibility, their sense of right and wrong—it's all totally familiar to me."[122]

Whites are also comfortable with him, in part for the same reasons they are comfortable with Colin Powell. His biracial and multicultural background (and his light skin) insulate him from the stereotypes they hold of African Americans, and, as a result, like Powell, he is perceived as nonthreatening.[123]

The House

In the November 1990 election, twenty-five blacks were elected or reelected to the House; in 1992, that number rose to thirty-eight, and it has stayed at about that number since that time (it was thirty-seven in 2002, and forty in 2004). As of 2005, all forty of the blacks in the House were Democrats.[124] Although they are not proportionally represented in the House of Representatives, they do constitute 9.2 percent of that body, a figure that is certainly higher than the figures we have cited for blacks on boards of directors, in most presidential cabinets, and in the Senate.

When we looked more systematically at the sixty-six blacks who have served in the House since 1990, some revealing patterns emerged. First, only two of the sixty-six have been Republicans, Gary Franks of Connecticut and J. C. Watts of Oklahoma. Franks, however, was defeated in 1996, and Watts decided not to run in 2002, so, as of July 2005, there were no black Republicans in the House. Second, only sixteen (24 percent) have been female.[125] Third, although more than 90 percent have been college graduates, relatively few did their undergraduate work at elite colleges or universities. Six graduated from Ivy League schools: three went to Yale (Franks, Sheila Jackson Lee [D-TX] and Denise Majette [D-GA], two went to the University of Pennsylvania (Chaka Fattah [D-PA] and Harold Ford Jr. [D-TN]), and two went to Harvard (Robert Scott [D-VA] and Arthur Davis [D-AL]). Another eight attended prestigious black colleges (Elijah Cummings [D-MD] and Mike Espy, a Democratic congressman from Mississippi before he was named to the Clinton cabinet, went to Howard; Major Owens [D-NY], Sanford Bishop [D-GA], and Earl Hilliard [D-AL] went to Morehouse; John Lewis [D-GA] and Alcee Hastings [D-FL] went to Fisk; and Bennie Thompson [D-MS] went to Tougaloo). The roster of the schools from which the others received their undergraduate degrees reads like a sampling of four-year colleges in America and includes Arkansas A&M; Florida A&M; California State, Los Angeles; New York University; North Carolina A&T; St. Louis University; Seton Hall; South Carolina State; Tennessee State; Texas Christian University; University of California, Los Angeles (UCLA); the University of the Redlands; and Western Michigan.

These sixty-six men and women had earned fifty postgraduate degrees among them. Not surprisingly, the largest number of these degrees (twenty-four) came from law schools. Again, a few attended the country's most elite law schools, including Harvard, Yale, Georgetown, and the University of Virginia, but most went to less prestigious schools like Cleveland Marshall Law School, Southwestern, Texas Southern, the University of Maryland, the University of Santa Clara, St. John's, and Wayne State. Twenty-one earned various kinds of master's degrees, and three had doctorates.

The schools attended suggest that, as a group, the black men and women who have been elected to the House have come from less privileged backgrounds than those who have been appointed to *Fortune*-level boards of directors or presidential cabinets. We were able to corroborate this by looking at the family backgrounds for a sample of those about whom we could find information.[126]

About 20 percent of them grew up in economically comfortable back-grounds (compared, for example, with a corresponding figure of 40 percent for the interlocking directors we looked at earlier in this chapter). This in-cludes Mike Espy, who, as we have seen, came from a wealthy Mississippi family. It includes Harvard graduate Robert Scott, whose father was a doctor and whose mother was a teacher, and Sanford Bishop, whose father was a col-lege president and whose mother was the head librarian at the college. It also includes seven who are the children of men or women who have been suc-cessful politicians: the father of Harold E. Ford Jr. (D, TN) served in the House of Representatives for twenty years (Ford was elected to his father's seat); similarly, the father of William Clay Jr. (D, MO) served in the House for thirty-two years; Carrie Meek, the mother of Kendrick Meek (D, FL), served in the House for ten years; the father of Walter R. Tucker III (D-CA) was the mayor of Compton, California; the father of Cynthia McKinney (D-GA) was a longtime legislator in the state house in Georgia; and the father of Jesse Jackson Jr. (D-IL), though not an elected official, has been a powerful political figure in the United States for decades and entered the Democratic presidential primaries in 1984 and 1988.

About half are from stable working-class families. These include men and women whose fathers were career military men (Corrinne Brown [D-FL] and Alan Wheat [D-MO]), insurance salesmen (Eva Clayton [D-NC]), longshore-men (Ronald Dellums [D-CA]), steelworkers (Earl Hilliard [D-AL] and Edol-phus Towns [D-NY]), policemen (Diane Watson [D-CA]), and elevator oper-ators (Charles Rangel [D-NY]). In most of these families, the mother also worked; some were hairdressers, some were clerk typists, some were maids.

About one-third came from real poverty. This includes, for example, Kweise Mfume (D-MD), who was thirteen when his stepfather, a truck driver, left home, and sixteen when his mother, who worked as a maid, died (he changed his name from Frizzell Gray to Kweise Mfume at the age of twenty)[127]; Carrie Meek (D-FL), whose parents were sharecroppers in Florida; and Mel Watt (D-NC), who grew up in a fatherless household and lived in a tin-roofed shack without running water or electricity in rural Meck-lenburg County in North Carolina.

The Supreme Court

Just as the three African Americans to have served in the Senate provide a study in contrasts and reveal the tenor of the times, so, too, do the two African American men to have served on the Supreme Court, Thurgood Marshall and Clarence Thomas. Marshall, appointed by Lyndon Johnson, a Democratic president, in 1967, was from a stable home, was politically liberal, and was tall and light skinned. Thomas, appointed in 1991 by George H. W. Bush, a Republican president, grew up in a very unstable home, is extremely conservative, and is short and dark skinned.

Marshall grew up in Baltimore. His father, a "pale-skinned blue-eyed man," dropped out of elementary school and worked as a railroad porter. His mother, also light skinned, was a college graduate and, like her mother before her, was a teacher. After graduating from Colored High and Training School, he attended Lincoln University and then graduated from law school at Howard University. As the chief counsel for the NAACP, Marshall had won the landmark *Brown v. Board of Education of Topeka, Kansas* decision in 1954 that forced the desegregation of the country's public schools. John F. Kennedy named him to the U.S. Court of Appeals, and in 1965, Lyndon Johnson named him to the office of U.S. Solicitor General before nominating him two years later for the Supreme Court.[128]

Thomas was born to a teenage mother in Pin Point, Georgia, and never really knew his father. His childhood was one of hardship and abandonment. When he was seven, his mother left him with his grandparents, who raised him (his grandfather, he later told colleagues, rarely spoke to him as a boy except to order him to do chores, whipped him with an electrical cord, and locked him in a closet when he misbehaved). Raised a Baptist, his grandmother had converted to Catholicism, and Thomas was able to attend Catholic schools, first a school run for black children by Franciscan nuns and then a seminary. He attended Holy Cross (his acceptance was clearly the result of the college's late-1960s commitment to affirmative action) and then Yale Law School (ditto).

After graduating from Yale, Thomas worked first for John Danforth (then state attorney general in Missouri) and then as a corporate lawyer in the pesticide and agricultural division of Monsanto Company. When Danforth won a Senate seat, Thomas went to Washington, D.C., to be his legislative aide. After attending a conference for black conservatives, he came to the attention of Ronald Reagan, who appointed him assistant secretary for civil rights in the Department of Education. Not long thereafter, Reagan appointed him to head the Equal Employment Opportunity Commission, where he did everything he could to dismantle the agency, much to the dismay of its staff and the African American community across the United States. George H. W. Bush nominated Thomas to the U.S. Court of Appeals in Washington, D.C., in 1990, and then, a year later, when Thurgood Marshall announced his retirement, he nominated him for the Supreme Court. This turned out to be one of the most controversial Supreme Court appointments in history (the final vote in the Senate was 52–48, the most votes ever cast against a successful nominee).[129]

Whereas Marshall was so light skinned that he was once called a "tall, yeller nigger" by a redneck sheriff in Tennessee, Thomas was quite dark skinned. As one woman who attended elementary and junior high school with him said, "He was darker than most kids, and in that generation, people were cruel. He was teased a lot, they'd call him 'Nigger Naps' . . . and a lot of girls wouldn't want to go out with him." Another childhood friend said, "Clarence had big lips, nappy hair, and he was almost literally black. Those folks were at the bottom of the pole."[130]

Marshall married twice. His first wife was an African American from a middle-class family (when they met, she was a student at the University of Pennsylvania). After she died, he married one of the secretaries in the NAACP office, Cissy Suyat, born in Hawaii of Filipino parents.[131] Thomas, to date, has been married twice. His first wife, from whom he is now divorced, was a light-skinned black woman (one of her four grandparents was Japanese), and his second wife, Virginia ("Ginni") Lamp, is a white woman from a well-to-do, Republican, Nebraska family who works for the right-wing Heritage Foundation (they were strong Goldwater supporters in 1964).[132]

Marshall ridiculed Thomas and other black conservatives as "the goddam black sellouts." According to African American journalist Carl Rowan, "Marshall would shake his head in wonderment that a black man who grew up in Jim Crow Georgia, and who had benefited from a thousand affirmative actions by nuns and others, and who had attended Yale Law School on a racial quota, could suddenly find affirmative action so destructive of the character of black people."[133]

CONCLUSION

Three patterns emerge from our examination of blacks in the power elite and Congress. First, as was the case for Jews and women, it is apparent that social background is important. Although some have authentic stories to tell of going from rags to riches, as do some whites, most are from either working-class or middle-class families, and many are from economically privileged backgrounds. Whether one is white or black, the advantages of being born into privilege are apparent.

Second, education is important. As we have seen repeatedly in this chapter, the blacks who have made it into the power elite and Congress are quite well educated. This not only underscores the importance of education, which we also found to be the case in the chapters on Jews and women, but reinforces the oft-heard claim that blacks have to be better educated than whites to get ahead.

Third, the same pattern holds for blacks that held for Jews and women in the cabinet and Congress. Cabinet members tend to be from families higher in the socioeconomic spectrum than elected officials, and they include Republicans as well as Democrats. In keeping with their lower social-class origins, almost all of those who have been elected to Congress have been Democrats.

Before we can make an adequate assessment of how well-to-do and well-educated African Americans are likely to fare in the future in terms of access to the power structure, we need to compare their progress to that of Latinos and Asian Americans.

NOTES

1. "Negro Lawyer Joining U.S. Industries Board," *New York Times,* June 23, 1964. U.S. Industries was #465 in the *Fortune* 500 that year.

2. Leonard Sloane, "Negroes in Business: A New Era Is Signaled by Election of 2 Directors by Big Corporations," *New York Times*, June 26, 1964.

3. "John Snyder Jr., Industrialist, 56," *New York Times,* April 25, 1965.

4. "Taking USI out of the Limelight," *Business Week,* January 21, 1967, 51.

5. Sloane, "Negroes in Business."

6. Sharon M. Collins, *Black Corporate Executives: The Making and Breaking of a Black Middle Class* (Philadelphia: Temple University Press, 1997), 58.

7. Collins addresses "moral commitment" in Sharon M. Collins, "Blacks on the Bubble: The Vulnerability of Black Executives in White Corporations," *Sociological Quarterly* 34, no. 3 (1993): 434.

8. "Negro Lawyer Joining U.S. Industries Board"; Sloane, "Negroes in Business"; "Personality: Pierce Causes Insurance Stir," *New York Times,* December 13, 1964.

9. John Ingham and Lynne B. Feldman, "Asa T. Spaulding," *African-American Business Leaders: A Biographical Dictionary* (Westport, CT: Greenwood, 1994), 395.

10. Bill Surface, "The World of the Wealthy Negro," *New York Times Magazine,* July 23, 1967, 10, 35, 38, 40.

11. "Clifton R. Wharton, Jr.: The Nation's Highest-Paid Black Executive," *Ebony,* September 1987, 32.

12. "Clifton R. Wharton, Jr.," *Current Biography Yearbook* (1987): 598.

13. Gerald H. Rosen, "TIAA-CREF: Declining Returns," *Academe* 78, no. 1 (January–February 1992): 8. According to Rosen, this was "an astonishing salary figure for the not-for-profit community."

14. As Wharton became part of the corporate elite, so, too, did his wife, Delores. The daughter of a Harlem undertaker, Delores, who once studied dance with Martha Graham, became a director on numerous *Fortune*-level boards, including Kellogg, Phillips Petroleum, and Gannett. In 1980 she founded the Fund for Corporate Initiatives,

designed to help minorities and women become CEOs and corporate directors. As of the early 1990s, each year she organized a weeklong retreat for twenty or so promising young executives from *Fortune* 500 companies. Patricia O'Toole, "Another Kind of Wharton School," *Lear's,* March 1991, 26–27.

15. Elaine Sciolino, "With Foreign Policies under Fire, Top State Dept. Deputy Is Ousted," *New York Times,* November 9, 1993. See, also, Lee A. Daniels, "Abrupt Exit: Racism, Leaks, and Isolation Drove Clif Wharton to Resign from the State Department," *Emerge*, February 1994, 28–33.

16. "William T. Coleman, Jr.," *Current Biography* (1976): 89.

17. "Hobart Taylor, Jr.," *Annual Obituary* (New York: St. Martin's, 1981), 232–33.

18. Robert Dallek, *Lone Star Rising: Lyndon Johnson and His Times, 1908–1960* (New York: Oxford University Press, 1991), 398.

19. Alfred Steinberg, *Sam Johnson's Boy: A Close-Up of the President from Texas* (New York: Macmillan, 1968), 563. Rowland Evans and Robert Novak say in *Lyndon B. Johnson: The Exercise of Power* (New York: New American Library, 1966) that when it came to civil rights, "like Johnson, Taylor was a gradualist" (317).

20. "Realty Equities Corp. Picks a Board Member," *New York Times,* April 30, 1968.

21. Marylin Bender, "Woman Lawyer Still Awaits a Bid to Board," *New York Times,* May 3, 1971.

22. Michael E. Mueller, "Patricia Roberts Harris: Former U.S. Cabinet Secretary, Ambassador, Attorney," in *Contemporary Black Biography: Profiles from the International Black Community*, ed. Barbara C. Bigelow, vol. 2 (Detroit, MI: Gale, 1992), 99.

23. "A Black for GM's Board," *Time,* January 26, 1970, 72.

24. "After the Courtesy, a Crisis of Costs," *Fortune,* June 1970, 31.

25. William Serrin, "For Roche of G.M., Happiness Is a 10% Surcharge," *New York Times Magazine,* September 12, 1971, 36–37, 109–25 (quotation appears on p. 116).

26. Ernest Holsendolph, "A Profile of Leon Sullivan," *Black Enterprise,* May 1975, 47–51.

27. Quoted in Ralph Nader and Joel Seligman, "The Myth of Shareholder Democracy," in *The Big Business Reader: Essays on Corporate America*, ed. Mark Green and Robert Massie Jr., 447–56 (New York: Pilgrim, 1980).

28. "Roche of General Motors: Thus Far and No Further," *Forbes,* May 15, 1971, 48.

29. Herschel Johnson, "The Making of Black Car Dealers," *Black Enterprise,* May 1974, 14.

30. When Sullivan died in 2001, the *New York Times* obituary began by highlighting the work he did to fight apartheid by developing guidelines for corporate investment in South Africa. Paul Lewis, "Leon Sullivan, 78, Dies; Fought Apartheid," *New York Times*, April 26, 2001, C17.

31. Milt Moskowitz, "The 1982 Black Corporate Directors Lineup," *Business Society Review* (fall 1982): 54.

32. Lester Carson, "Black Directors: The 72 Black Men and Women Who Sit on the Boards of Major U.S. Corporations," *Black Enterprise,* September 1973, 17–28.

33. As an example of another indicator, the number of blacks at the Harvard Business School rose from less than 1 percent in 1965 to more than 10 percent in the early 1970s but fell to less than 4 percent by 1980. Similarly, the percentage of blacks at

many elite prep schools rose until the mid-1970s but then leveled off or dropped. See Richard L. Zweigenhaft, *Who Gets to the Top? Executive Suite Discrimination in the Eighties* (New York: Institute of Human Relations, 1984), 25; Richard L. Zweigenhaft and G. William Domhoff, *Blacks in the White Elite: Will the Progress Continue?* (Lanham, MD: Rowman & Littlefield, 2003), 2.

34. "A Listing of Black Directors," *Business and Society Review* (fall 1981): 63–64.

35. Jonathan Kaufman, "Black Executives Say Prejudice Still Impedes Their Path to the Top," *Wall Street Journal,* July 9, 1980.

36. George Davis and Glegg Watson, *Black Life in Corporate America* (Garden City, NY: Anchor, 1982), 77.

37. John Fernandez, *Racism and Sexism in Corporate Life* (Lexington, MA: Lexington, 1981), 10.

38. Floyd A. Bond, Herbert W. Hildebrandt, and Edwin L. Miller, *The Newly Promoted Executive: A Study in Corporate Leadership, 1983–1984* (Ann Arbor: University of Michigan, Division of Research, Graduate School of Business Administration, 1984), 26.

39. Bender, "Woman Lawyer." See, also, Cynthia Fuchs Epstein, "Positive Effects of the Multiple Negative: Explaining the Success of Black Professional Women," *American Journal of Sociology* 78 (1973): 912–35.

40. Erika Hayes James and Lynn Perry Wooten, "The Executive Leadership Council 2004 Census of African Americans on Boards of Directors," Executive Leadership Council, 1010 Wisconsin Avenue NW, Washington, D.C. 20007.

41. The IRRC data includes ethnicity for most but not all of the 13,280. These data, therefore, can be seen only as educated estimates. We wish to thank Carol Bowie, the director of Governance Research, for her assistance in obtaining the data.

42. "John E. Jacob," *Current Biography* (1986): 247.

43. "Clifford L. Alexander, Jr.," *Current Biography* (1977): 10.

44. Michael Useem and Jerome Karabel, "Pathways to Top Corporate Management," *American Sociological Review* 51 (1986): 184–200. See pp. 187–88 for the lists of the top-ranked undergraduate institutions, MBA programs, and law schools.

45. Useem and Karabel, "Pathways," 193.

46. C. Wright Mills, *The Power Elite* (New York: Oxford University Press, 1956), 289.

47. Malone is part of a sizable contingent of Wellesley women who sit on *Fortune*-level boards. In fact, as of the mid-1990s, more women who sat on *Fortune* 500 boards attended Wellesley than any other college. See Judith H. Dobrzynski, "How to Succeed? Go to Wellesley," *New York Times,* October 29, 1995. Two of the eleven black women interlockers went to Wellesley, Claudine Malone and Barbara Preiskel.

48. Alfred Edmond Jr., "Can This Man Keep Team Xerox No. 1?" *Black Enterprise,* August 1987, 60. The following year, *Business Week* singled out Rand as one of four black executives who might become chief executive officers of major U.S. corporations in the next decade ("The Black Middle Class," *Business Week,* March 14, 1988, 63).

49. Fonda Marie Lloyd and Mark Lowery, "The Man Behind the Merger," *Black Enterprise,* October 1994, 76.

50. Mark Lowery, "Second in Command at Time Warner," *Black Enterprise,* January 1995, 15. The November 1995 issue of *Ebony* notes that, in January 1995, Kenneth I. Chenault became vice chairman of American Express and, thus, "the highest-ranking Black executive of a Fortune 500 company." *Ebony* quotes an assertion in the *Wall Street Journal* that "many executives of the company predict that Mr. Chenault . . . will eventually become American Express chairman" (114). In February 1997, Harvey Golub, the chairman of American Express, wrote a letter to employees indicating that Chenault was "the primary internal candidate to succeed me when the time comes" but also indicating that he did not plan to step down for another eight years. See Saul Hansell, "American Express Names Apparent Successor to Chief," *New York Times,* February 28, 1997. The Associated Press article referred to this as "the first public anointment of a black executive to run one of the country's biggest companies." Patricia Lamiell, "American Express Names Black CEO as First in Position," *Greensboro News and Record,* February 28, 1997.

51. John H. Johnson was no relation to George E. Johnson, the founder of Johnson Products Company and one of the first twelve black corporate directors (he joined the board of Commonwealth Edison in 1971). These two Johnsons were the two richest black men in Chicago and, for a time, perhaps the two richest black men in the country. In a chapter titled "Johnson vs. Johnson," Stephen Birmingham describes the "long-standing friction between the two men." See Stephen Birmingham, *Certain People: America's Black Elite* (Boston: Little, Brown, 1977), 29–40. See, also, Douglas Martin, "John H. Johnson, 87, Founder of Ebony, Dies," *New York Times,* August 9, 2005, C22.

52. Andrew Hacker, "Who They Are," *New York Times Magazine,* November 19, 1995, 71. At that time, the other four were Berry Gordy (of Motown Records), Reginald Lewis (of Beatrice Foods), Oprah Winfrey, and Bill Cosby.

53. Laurie Freeman, "Linda Johnson Rice: Publishing Company Executive," in *Contemporary Black Biography: Profiles from the International Black Community,* ed. L. Mpho Mabunda, vol. 9, 194–96 (New York: Gale Research, 1995).

54. Sonia Alleyne, "Count on This: New Report on the Number of Blacks on Corporate Boards," *Black Enterprise* 35 (June 2005): 80.

55. See Zweigenhaft and Domhoff, *Blacks in the White Elite.*

56. Steven A. Holmes, "Street Survivor via Harvard: Deval Laurdine Patrick," *New York Times,* February 2, 1994, A12.

57. As of October 1999, Texaco was one of ten *Fortune* 500 companies with legal counsel who were minorities (nine of the ten were men). See Darryl Van Duch, "Minority GCs are Few, Far Between," *National Law Journal,* October 18, 1999, 1ff.

58. Henry Unger, "Ex-Coke President Got $3.5 Million; Stahl's Separation Deal Also Gave Stock Access," *The Atlanta Journal and Constitution,* May 2, 2001, 1C.

59. There was considerable controversy surrounding Patrick's departure. It was not clear whether he resigned or was fired. The *Wall Street Journal* reported that "displeasure from higher-ups" played a role in his resignation, and the *New York Post* claimed he "was canned." After an initial announcement that he had been replaced by an interim general counsel, the company's CEO and chair (who himself was leaving the company) made another announcement saying Patrick had Coke's "full confidence and support" and that Patrick had agreed to stay until the end of 2004. Ten days

later, at the annual meeting, during which stockholders were handed leaflets by demonstrators chanting "Coca-Cola, killer Cola, toxic Cola, racist Cola" and at which one shareholder activist was wrestled to the floor by security guards and arrested, Jesse Jackson addressed the meeting about his concerns over Patrick's resignation, calling Patrick (who resigned on Easter) "another Easter victim." See Kenneth Gilpin, "Executive Quits as Turmoil Continues at Coke," *New York Times*, April 13, 2004, C1; Paul Tharp, "Coca-Cola Fizzles as Top Lawyer Is Canned," *The New York Post*, April 13, 2004, 31; Scott Leith, "Exodus of Coke Counsel Delayed," *The Atlanta Journal and Constitution*, April 15, 2004; "Trouble at Coke's Annual Meeting," *Atlanta Business Chronicle*, April 21, 2004; Theresa Howard, "Coke's Search for CEO Still Up in Air," *USA Today*, April 22, 2004; and Betsy Morris, "The Real Story: How Did Coca-Cola's Management Go from First-rate to Farcical in Six Short Years?" *Fortune*, May 31, 2004, 84–98.

Whatever the inside story of Patrick's departure from Coke was, he apparently left a very wealthy man. According to one article, Patrick's "contract suggests that he's likely to walk away with at least $22.9 million in stock options, and a $1.55 million payment due because he resigned just days before his third anniversary as a company officer." See Sue Reisinger, "Deval Patrick's Exit: The Long Goodbye," *National Law Journal*, May 10, 2004, 11.

60. "Massachusetts: Prosecutor to Run for Governor," *New York Times*, April 15, 2005, A14. Some labor leaders were unhappy with Patrick's role as chief legal counsel at Coca-Cola. See Frank Phillips, "Labor Leaders Critical of Patrick," *The Boston Globe*, February 8, 2005, B1.

61. Eileen P. Gunn, "No Boundaries," *Fortune*, August 4, 1997, 77; Cora Daniels, "50 Most Powerful Black Executives: Unprecedented Clout," *Fortune*, July 22, 2002, 65.

62. William M. Lewis, interviewed by Richard L. Zweigenhaft, New York City, October 19, 2001.

63. Melissa S. Monroe, "Top Black Executive Leaves Morgan Stanley for Lazard," *Black Enterprise*, July 2004, 22; "Freddie Mac Announces Four Nominees to Stand for Election as New Directors," *Freddiemac.com*, at www.freddiemac.com/news/archives/corporate/2004/newdirectors_092004.html; "William M. Lewis, Jr. Elected to Darden Restaurants Board," PR Newswire Association, March 22, 2005, LexisNexis.

64. Richard L. Zweigenhaft and G. William Domhoff, *Blacks in the White Establishment?: A Study of Race and Class in America* (New Haven, CT: Yale University Press, 1991), 136.

65. "Clifton R. Wharton, Jr.," *Current Biography* (1987): 597–99. Wharton was also, as of the mid-1980s, the country's highest paid black executive. See "Clifford R. Wharton, Jr.: The Nation's Highest Paid Black Executive," *Ebony*, September 1987, 29–33.

66. In 1999, when she was an executive vice president at Kraft, Fudge was #34 on the *Fortune* "50 Most Powerful Women in American Business" list. See Patricia Sellers, "These Women Rule," *Fortune*, October 25, 1999, 94–123; Ann M. Fudge, "Nuns, Bicycles and Berries," *New York Times*, January 12, 2000, C12. See, also, Claudia H. Deutsch, "An Apparent Heir at Xerox," *New York Times*, June 1, 2003, Business section, 2, an article about Ursula M. Burns, an African American woman.

"Even though," writes Deutsch, "Anne M. Mulcahy, Xerox's first female chief executive, is only 50, many people have already pegged Ms. Burns as her successor."

The February 2005 issue of *Black Enterprise* included its annual "Most Powerful African Americans in Corporate America" list. Among the 75 on the list were 18 CEOs "culled from the 1,000 largest domestic and international corporations traded publicly on the U.S. equities market." Of the 18, 3 were women: Ann Fudge of Young & Rubicom, Renetta McCann of Starcom Americas, and Pamela Thomas-Graham of CNBC. See "Meet 17 High-Powered CEOs," at blackenterprise.com.

67. Richard W. Stevenson, "A Homecoming at Fannie Mae," *New York Times*, May 17, 1998, Business section, 10; David Leonhardt, "The Saga of Lloyd Ward: His Remarkable Journey to Become Maytag's CEO," *Business Week*, August 9, 1999, 59–61, 64–66, 68, 70; David Rynecki, "Putting the Muscle Back in the Bull," *Fortune*, April 5, 2004, 162–70. The information on Clarence Otis's parents is from an e-mail from Otis to Richard Zweigenhaft, June 13, 2005.

68. "Clifton R. Wharton, Jr.," *Current Biography* (1987): 597–99; Timothy L. O'Brien, "Successor Is Selected to Run American Express," *New York Times*, April 27, 1999, C6; Claudia H. Deutsch, "Former Xerox Officer Gets Top Avis Job: Chairman's Post Fulfills a Long Aim," *New York Times*, November 10, 1999, C8; Lisa C. Jones, "Winning the Power Game: Erroll B. Davis, Jr., Head of WPL Holdings, Inc.," *Ebony* (online), November 1994, at www.findarticles.com/p/articles/mi_m1077/ is_n1_v50/ai_15885848; Carrie Kirby, "Newsmaker Profile: John Thompson, Man with a Plan," at sfgate.com.

69. The quote is from Gwendolyn Parker, a graduate of Radcliffe and the New York University business school, writing about Kenneth Chenault. She wrote, "Ken had an additional skill, which people often called his smoothness. As I saw it, that smoothness came from his recognition that his ease with white people was not merely a neutral ability, but something he could turn to his advantage." See Gwendolyn M. Parker, *Trespassing: My Sojourn in the Halls of Privilege* (Boston: Houghton Mifflin, 1997), 192–3.

70. Elijah Anderson, "The Social Situation of the Black Executive: Black and White Identities in the Corporate World," in *The Cultural Territories of Race: Black and White Boundaries*, ed. Michele Lamont (Chicago: University of Chicago Press, 1999), 12. Anderson explores the difficulties the executives he studied had negotiating relationships with other blacks in the corporation and with whites who were both "wise" and "not so wise" to the difficulties blacks encounter in such a predominantly white setting. Among other things, they were worried "about appearing 'too black' in one set of circumstances and 'too white' in another" (15).

71. For Rand, see Caroline V. Clarke, *Take a Lesson: Today's Black Achievers on How They Made It & What They Learned along the Way* (New York: John Wiley and Sons, 2001), 162. For Parsons, see David Carr, "No Use Crying Over Spilled Billions," *New York Times*, June 20, 2004, 5. For Chenault, see Nelson D. Schwartz, "What's in the Cards at AMEX?" *Fortune*, January 22, 2001, 59–70, 62. There is no mention of Wharton's interest or participation in sports in the extensive biographical material we have read about him. In one article about O'Neal, he says that he sometimes finds time to "pay a bad game of golf." Susan Young, "A Long Road of Learn-

ing: Merrill Lynch's Stan O'Neal," *Harvard Business School Bulletin* (online), June 2001, 2, at www.alumni.hbs.edu/bulletin/2001/june/profile.htm. For Clarence Otis, e-mail, June 13, 2002. (We have no information about whether or not Lewis participated in sports in high school or college.)

72. See, for example, Harry Edwards, "Athletic Performance in Exchange for an Education—A Contract Unfulfilled," *The Crisis*, May 1983, 10–14, and, more recently, Harry Edwards, "Crisis of Black Athletes on the Eve of the 21st Century," *Society* 37, no. 3 (March–April 2000): 9–13. For a critique of Edwards' position, see Earl Smith, "There Was No Golden Age of Sport for African American Athletes," *Society* 37, no. 3 (March–April 2000): 45–48.

73. Henry Louis Gates Jr., "Breaking the Silence," *New York Times*, August 1, 2004, A11.

74. Clarke, *Take a Lesson,* 162.

75. See Richard L. Zweigenhaft, "'Penetrators' and 'Internal Elites': A Comparison between African Americans on the Boards of the Ten Largest Companies on the *Fortune* 500 and Those on the Boards of the Ten Largest Companies on the *Black Enterprise* List" (paper presented at the annual meeting of the Pacific Sociological Association, Portland, Oregon, April 16, 1999). See, also, Udayan Gupta, "Minority Suppliers Are Getting a Boost from Big Firms," *Wall Street Journal*, November 10, 1994, B2.

76. Lena Williams, "Not Just a White Man's Game," *New York Times,* November 9, 1995.

77. See Shelley Branch, "What Blacks Think of Corporate America," *Fortune*, July 6, 1998, 140, 142–43.

78. Daniels, "Most Powerful Black Executives," 63. The estimate of less than 5 percent is our best guess, based on interviews we conducted for *Blacks in the White Elite* with African American executives working for *Fortune*-level companies (see *Blacks in the White Elite*, ch. 7, n. 15).

79. Collins, "Blacks on the Bubble," 438.

80. For a detailed account of these "corporate-mediated" programs, which include the A Better Chance program and the Summer Venture in Management Program (SVMP) at the Harvard Business School, see Zweigenhaft and Domhoff, *Blacks in the White Elite*, 166–72. See, also, the section on these programs in ch. 8.

81. See http://caselaw.lp.findlaw.com/scripts/getcase.pl?court=US&vol=000&invol=02–241 and www.umich.edu/~urel/admissions/legal/gru_amicus-ussc/um.html.

82. Michael Useem, *The Inner Circle: Large Corporations and the Rise of Business Political Activity in the U.S. and U.K.* (New York: Oxford University Press, 1984), 3, 38–39.

83. "Vernon Jordan," *Current Biography* (1993): 297.

84. "Vernon Jordan," 299. See, also, Jeff Gerth, "Being Intimate with Power, Vernon Jordan Can Wield It Quietly but Effectively," *New York Times,* July 14, 1996.

85. Robin Armstrong, "Robert C. Weaver: Government Administrator, Scholar," in *Contemporary Black Biography: Profiles from the International Black Community*, ed. L. Mpho Mabunda, vol. 8 (New York: Gale Research, 1995), 259.

86. Richard Bardolph, *The Negro Vanguard* (New York: Rinehart, 1959), 255.

87. Armstrong, "Robert C. Weaver," 261.

88. "Former Secretary Pierce Spared Trial in HUD Corruption Case," *New York Times,* January 12, 1995.

89. David Halberstam, "There Is Something Noble to It," *Parade Magazine*, September 17, 1995, 5.

90. Richard A. Oppel Jr., "Nominee Is Picked to Replace Departing HUD Secretary," *New York Times,* December 13, 2003.

91. Benjamin O. Davis Jr., *Benjamin O. Davis, Jr., American: An Autobiography* (Washington, DC: Smithsonian Institution Press, 1991), 27.

92. Davis, *Benjamin O. Davis, Jr.,* 52. See, also, Richard Goldstein, "Lt. Gen. Benjamin O. Davis Jr., 89, Dies; in World War II, Led First Black Pilots Unit," *New York Times*, July 7, 2002, A19.

93. Charles C. Moskos and John Sibley Butler, *All That We Can Be: Black Leadership and Racial Integration the Army Way* (New York: Basic, 1996), 31.

94. Moskos and Butler report that, in 1995, the 145,000 blacks in the army were about half of all blacks in military uniform and accounted for about 27 percent of all those on active duty in the army. The percentage of blacks in the army, they note, was "approximately twice the proportion found in the navy, air force, or marine corps" (6).

95. John Mintz, "Clinton Nominates First Black Admiral," *Washington Post,* May 14, 1996.

96. For the September 2004 data, see "Distribution of Active Duty Forces by Service, Rank, Sex and Race, 09/30/04," Department of Defense document DMDC-3035EO (see, also, ch. 3, n. 76).

97. *Black Americans in Defense of Our Nation* (Washington, D.C.: U.S. Government Printing Office, 1991). The recent data for the Naval Academy and the U.S. Military Academy are from their websites; the data for the Air Force Academy were provided by the public affairs office at the school.

98. Mills, *Power Elite,* 215.

99. Moskos and Butler, *All That We Can Be,* 50.

100. Moskos and Butler, *All That We Can Be*, 114.

101. In 1994, when he received the Order of Jamaica, the highest honor given to non-Jamaicans, after reminding those attending that he was an American citizen, Powell added, "But let it be clear to all present that I consider myself a Jamaican, a true son of Jamaica." "Colin Powell Honored with Order of Jamaica," *New York Times*, December 2, 1994, A6.

102. Halberstam, "There Is Something Noble," 5.

103. Halberstam, "There Is Something Noble," 5.

104. John F. Stacks, "The Powell Factor," *Time,* July 10, 1995, 25.

105. Henry Louis Gates Jr., "Powell and the Black Elite," *New Yorker,* September 25, 1995, 63–80. In 1993, Clinton named Togo West Jr., a black, as secretary of the army. Noting that since Alexander's appointment in the late 1970s, there had been other blacks in senior positions on the civilian side of the army, Moskos and Butler observed "with the appointment of Togo West, Jr., as secretary of the Army in 1993, the presence of a black in the senior Army Secretariat had become almost the norm" (*All That We Can Be,* 35).

106. Moskos and Butler, *All That We Can Be,* 115.

107. Horace Mann Bond, "The Negro Scholar and Professional in America," in *The American Negro Reference Book*, ed. John P. Davis (Englewood Cliffs, NJ: Prentice Hall, 1966), 559. See, also, Franklin E. Frazier, *The Black Bourgeoisie: The Rise of the New Middle Class* (New York: Free Press, 1957); Horace Mann Bond, *Black American Scholars: A Study of Their Beginnings* (Detroit, MI: Balamp, 1972); H. Edward Ransford, "Skin Color, Life Chances, and Anti-White Attitudes," *Social Problems* 18 (1970): 164–78; Elizabeth Mullins and Paul Sites, "The Origins of Contemporary Eminent Black Americans: A Three-Generation Analysis of Social Origins," *American Sociological Review* 49 (1984): 672–85; Cedric Herring, Verna M. Keith, and Hayward D. Horton, eds., *Skin Deep: How Race and Complexion Matter in the "Color-Blind" Era* (Urbana: University of Illinois Press, 2004); Margaret Hunter, *Race, Gender, and the Politics of Skin Tone* (New York: Routledge, 2005).

108. Glass Ceiling Commission, *Good for Business: Making Full Use of the Nation's Human Capital, a Fact-Finding Report of the Federal Glass Ceiling Commission* (Washington, D.C.: U.S. Government Printing Office, 1995), 29.

109. "Patricia Robert Harris," *Current Biography* (1965): 191. Recent research demonstrates that "Afrocentric facial features," such as a wide nose or full lips, contribute to stereotyping of individuals within, as well as between, racial groups. See Irene B. Blair, Charles M. Judd, M. S. Sadler, and C. Jenkins, "The Role of Afrocentric Features in Person Perception: Judging by Features and Categories," *Journal of Personality and Social Psychology* 83 (2002): 5–25; Irene B. Blair, Charles M. Judd, and Kristine M. Chapleau, "The Influence of Afrocentric Facial Features in Criminal Sentencing," *Psychological Science* 15 (2004): 674–79.

110. The Skin Color Assessment Procedure is described in Selena Bond and Thomas F. Cash, "Black Beauty: Skin Color and Body Images among African-American College Women," *Journal of Applied Social Psychology* 22, no. 1 (1992): 874–88.

The two raters had a high rate of interrater agreement (the interjudge reliability, as determined by a Pearson product moment correlation, was $r = 0.87$). The ninety magazine-quality photographs used were drawn from *Current Biography,* from various articles in *Ebony*'s fiftieth-anniversary issue in November 1995, and from the October 1994 *Ebony* article on the black interlocking directors. A regression analysis looking at the effect of both power-elite status and gender on skin-color rating was highly significant ($F = 20.23$, $p < 0.0001$). Gender was a stronger predictor (beta = 0.50, $p < 0.0001$) of skin color than power-elite status (beta = 0.20, $p < 0.02$).

111. The description of Powell is in Gates, "Powell and the Black Elite," 66 (quotation appears on p. 70).

112. Two blacks from Mississippi, Hiram Revels and Blanche Cruce, served in the Senate during Reconstruction. They were both selected by the state's legislature, not by the voters. "Edward W. Brooke," *Current Biography* (1967): 42.

113. "Edward W. Brooke," 41.

114. Isaac Rosen, "Edward Brooke: Former U.S. Senator, Lawyer, Consultant," in *Contemporary Black Biography: Profiles from the International Black Community*, ed. L. Mpho Mabunda, vol. 8 (New York: Gale Research, 1995), 28.

115. Rosen, "Edward Brooke," 28.

116. Rosen, "Edward Brooke," 29.

117. Carol Moseley-Braun, "Between W. E. B. Du Bois and B. T. Washington," *Ebony,* November 1995, 58.

118. Isaac Rosen, "Carol Moseley Braun: Politician, Lawyer," in *Contemporary Black Biography: Profiles from the International Black Community*, ed. Barbara C. Bigelow, vol. 4 (Detroit, MI: Gale, 1993), 28.

119. Barack Obama, *Dreams from My Father: A Story of Race and Inheritance* (New York: Times Books, 1995). Very few of the students at Punahou were poor, and almost none were black. Obama notes that his first experience with affirmative action had little to do with race: he was not accepted at Punahou because he was black but, rather, because his grandfather worked for an alumnus who had clout at the school (54).

120. William Finnegan, "The Candidate: How the Son of a Kenyan Economist Became an Illinois Everyman," *The New Yorker*, May 31, 2004, 34.

121. Some political consultants claimed Obama's speech was "the best keynote address they had heard in years." According to the *New York Times* the next day, "As he moved through rooms and hallways, whispers followed: perhaps the man who had just passed would be the first black president of the United States." Randal C. Archibold, "Day After, Keynote Speaker Finds Admirers Everywhere," *New York Times*, July 29, 2004, 6. See, also, "Plan B for Illinois," *New York Times*, August 10, 2004, A22, and David Mendell and John Chase, "Barack Obama's Landslide Victory Sets Stage for National Role," *Chicago Tribune*, November 3, 2004.

122. Finnegan, "The Candidate," 36.

123. For these very reasons, many African American voters in Chicago were at first wary about Obama. He was defeated in 2000 when he ran for Congress against Bobby Rush, a former Black Panther (see Finnegan, "The Candidate," 36), and, as Salim Muwakkil, a senior editor at *In These Times,* put it, in 2004 some black voters "initially withheld support for Obama because he was projected as such a post-race candidate" ("Shades of 1983," *In These Times*, April 26, 2004, 13).

124. Gregory L. Giroux, "A Touch of Gray on Capitol Hill," *Congressional Quarterly*, January 31, 2005, 243.

125. Twenty-four percent of the blacks in the House since 1990 have been women; this represents a higher percentage than the percentage of women in the House, which was about 14 percent in 2005. Moreover, Katherine Tate notes in *Black Faces in the Mirror: African Americans and Their Representatives in the U.S. Congress* (Princeton, NJ: Princeton University Press, 2003) that "perhaps the single most striking difference between Black women members and all other members of the House" is that they are more likely to be unmarried. Whereas almost 90 percent of the members of the House were married at the time they were elected, since 1973, only about one-third of the black women were married at the time they were elected (the other two-thirds have been widowed, separated, divorced, or single) (46).

126. The various published sources yielded information on slightly more than one-third of them. We therefore phoned the congressional offices of the remainder and re-

quested the relevant information from press secretaries. We were able to obtain sufficient information about the parents of fifty of the sixty-six.

127. Peter J. Boyer, "The Rise of Kweise Mfume," *The New Yorker*, August 1, 1994, 28–29.

128. Juan Williams, *Thurgood Marshall: American Revolutionary* (New York: Times Books, 1998), 15, 21–22, 34–35.

129. Jane Mayer and Jill Abramson, *Strange Justice: The Selling of Clarence Thomas* (Boston: Houghton Mifflin, 1994), 37–52, 348.

130. Howard Ball, *A Defiant Life: Thurgood Marshall and the Persistence of Racism in America* (New York: Crown, 1998), 15. Mayer and Abramson, *Strange Justice*, 45.

131. Williams, *Thurgood Marshall*, 50, 229, 242–44.

132. Mayer and Abramson, *Strange Justice*, 54–55, 144.

133. Mayer and Abramson, *Strange Justice*, 14.

Chapter Five

Latinos in the Power Elite

When Roberto Goizueta left his native Havana, Cuba, in 1949 to begin his freshman year at Yale University, he had no idea that by the 1980s he would be running one of the largest corporations in the United States. Basque and Spanish in racial and cultural heritage and a member of the wealthy upper class in Cuba, he returned home to Havana after he had earned a degree in engineering, and from 1954 to 1960, he worked for the Coca-Cola subsidiary.

But Goizueta and other wealthy young Cubans did not count on the actions of another Cuban-born son of a successful Spanish immigrant, Fidel Castro, who turned his back on his father's large ranch and his own elite education to create the revolutionary army that overthrew Cuban dictator Fulgencio Batista in January 1959. By the early 1960s, Castro was threatening major capitalist enterprises, leading Goizueta and more than 380,000 other Cubans to emigrate to the United States by 1980.[1] In 1960, Goizueta became assistant to the senior vice president of Coca-Cola in the Bahamas, and by 1964, he was assistant to the vice president for research and development at the company's headquarters in Atlanta.

It took only a few years before Goizueta became a vice president for engineering; shortly thereafter, he was a senior vice president, then an executive vice president. He was named president and chief operating officer in 1980 and became chairman of the board and CEO in 1981. When he died in October 1997, he was one of the most powerful corporate chieftains in the United States, atypical though he may be of most of the 41.3 million people identified as of July 2004 as Hispanic Americans.[2]

Vilma S. Martínez, born to Mexican American parents in 1943 in San Antonio, Texas, had a very different experience. As a young girl, she was bitter about the discrimination she experienced. She recalls that her junior high school counselor recommended that she go to a vocational or technical high school, her high school counselor would not advise her about applying to college, and her father, a construction worker, was skeptical about the usefulness of college for a woman, saying that she "would not complete school, that she would get married and have children." But she insisted on an academic high school, graduated from the University of Texas in two and a half years, and did not have the first of her two children until 1976, nine years after she had earned a law degree from Columbia University.[3]

Martínez practiced civil rights law as a staff attorney for the NAACP Legal Defense Fund from 1967 to 1970 and for the New York State Division of Human Rights after that. After two years as a labor lawyer with the Wall Street firm of Cahill, Gordon & Reindel, she became one of the prime movers in establishing the Mexican American Legal Defense and Education Fund (MALDEF). In 1973, she became MALDEF's general counsel and president. Three years later, the liberal Democratic governor of California, Jerry Brown, surprised everyone by appointing Martínez, only thirty-two years old, regent of the University of California, where she rubbed elbows with a cross-section of the California corporate rich and lobbied for greater diversity in the faculty and student body. In May 1982, she joined the Los Angeles law firm of Munger, Tolles & Olson, where her clients have included Pacific Telephone, Blue Cross, and Allstate Insurance.[4] As of 2005, she sat on the boards of three *Fortune* 500 corporations: Anheuser-Busch (#139 in 2005), Burlington Northern Santa Fe (#200), and Fluor (#241).

But not all Latinas from the Southwest are liberal enough to work for the NAACP or MALDEF. Those from New Mexico, whose ancestors were sometimes landholders before the American conquest of the territory, are often quite conservative. Patricia Díaz, born in Santa Rita, New Mexico, in 1946, was the daughter of an army sergeant who was transferred frequently. She spent her teenage years in Japan, graduated from a high school in Santiago, Chile, and received her BA in 1970 from UCLA and a law degree in 1973 from Loyola University in Los Angeles. After three years with a large corporate firm in Los Angeles, she became a management attorney specializing in labor disputes, first with Pacific Lighting and then with ABC in Hollywood. She was working for ABC in 1983 when Ronald Reagan unexpectedly named her as a "Democratic" appointee to the National Labor Relations Board, the second female and first Latina member in its forty-seven-year history. There she joined the majority in a wide range of decisions that were extremely damaging to labor organizing.[5] In 1986, she became a member of the Federal Communications Commission (FCC). After an equally conservative three-year tenure as an FCC commissioner, she returned to the private sector as a corporate lawyer for U.S. Sprint. In 1992, George H. W. Bush tried to improve his appeal to Mexican Americans in the Southwest by appointing Díaz as assistant secretary of state for human rights and humanitarian affairs. When Bush lost his bid for reelection, Díaz joined the Washington, D.C., office of the venerable Wall Street law firm of Sullivan & Cromwell and became a director of Telemundo, the second-largest Hispanic radio and television corporation in the United States. Married to Michael Dennis, a lawyer, and going by the name of Patricia Díaz Dennis, she left Sullivan & Cromwell to become senior vice president and general counsel for SBC Pacific Bell/SBC Nevada Bell. Her being a conservative Democrat has served Díaz Dennis—and the Republicans—extremely well.

Goizueta, Martínez, and Díaz Dennis are prime examples of why social scientists stress that it is very risky to generalize about the Hispanic or Latino experience in the United States. The 1.4 million Cuban Americans, many of whom were quite well off in Cuba, have one story, while the 3 million immigrants from Puerto Rico usually have another. (Actually, a few of the Puerto Rican immigrants are also wealthy, but most arrived poor.) Similarly, people of Mexican descent in New Mexico, many of whom have ancestors who have lived in the area for more than one hundred years and who sometimes call themselves "Spanish Americans," are different from the Mexican American immigrants to Texas and California. Moreover, the Mexican Americans of the Southwest range from middle-class entrepreneurs to migrant farm workers, and they vary greatly in color and appearance as well because of a history of intermarriage with the indigenous Indian populations of Mexico. The Latino population in the United States also includes some immigrants from Spain and various Latin American countries. On a 1995 list of the seventy-five richest Hispanics, which was dominated by twenty-seven Cuban Americans and twenty-five Mexican Americans, there were also eight people identified as Spanish and one person each from Chile, Colombia, Costa Rica, the Dominican Republic, Ecuador, Uruguay, and Venezuela. Five Puerto Rican immigrants and three residents of Puerto Rico rounded out the list. At the top was Roberto Goizueta of Coca-Cola, whose net worth was estimated at $574 million.[6]

There is even disagreement among scholars and political activists about what general name, if any, should be used to characterize a group whose main common heritage is the Spanish conquest and the Spanish language. The term *Hispanic* is favored by some, especially on the East Coast; others prefer *Latino*, especially on the West Coast. In a 1990 survey, however, it was found that neither term was liked by most Americans of Cuban, Mexican, or Puerto Rican extraction. Most preferred labels that reflected their specific backgrounds. Moreover, the three groups have "little interaction with each other, most do not recognize that they have much in common culturally, and they do not profess any strong affection for each other." The authors of the survey wrote that "it is particularly noteworthy that more respondents prefer to be called 'American' than 'Latino,' the label that many members of the Latino intelligentsia, including ourselves, have insisted is both the 'correct' and the preferred label."[7]

Given these disagreements, we will continue to use the terms *Latino/Latina*, *Hispanic American*, and *Hispanic* interchangeably when a general term is needed. When possible, we will use specific ethnic identifications.

Underlying this diversity of national origins and the tendency to identify primarily with one's own subgroup, there are nonetheless two factors that powerfully shape the degree of acceptance and assimilation of all Latino immigrants. The first is their religion. The 70 percent who are Catholics can blend in easily with the largest single church in the United States (67.3 million strong, making up 23 percent of the U.S. population). Their Catholic heritage is an important piece of cultural capital because it provides entrée into new social circles as they attain education or a higher-status occupation. True, local parishes are sometimes differentiated by status and income levels, but new social connections can be made through new parishes if a person is climbing the social ladder.[8]

The second major factor influencing the fate of Hispanic Americans is skin color and facial features. As two sociological studies note, there is great variation in the appearance of Latinos, ranging from a pure "European" look to a Native American look.[9] In most Latin American countries, the lighter-skinned and more European-looking people tend to be in the higher social classes, and the darker-skinned and more Indian-looking people in the lower classes.[10]

Several journalists and social critics have concluded that darker-skinned Hispanics are also at a disadvantage in the United States. To test this claim, E. A. Telles and Edward Murguia used information from a nationwide survey of Hispanics in 1979 to see whether those rated as light skinned by the interviewer had higher average earnings than those who were darker. Since the lightest-skinned group was too small for sound statistical comparisons, it was merged with a group judged to be of medium skin color, and a comparison was then made with the darkest group. The researchers found that there was a strong tendency for the lighter group to earn more than the darker one, and they argue that this cannot be explained in terms of educational differences because the two groups had very similar educational backgrounds.[11] A more recent study, based on the 2000 Census, showed that Latinos who identified themselves as white had higher levels of education and income than those who selected the "some other race" category.[12] As we shall show, our own study of the skin color of Hispanics in the corporate elite leads to the same conclusion: it is advantageous to be light skinned.

LATINOS IN THE CORPORATE ELITE

From 1990 through 2002 in its January issue, *Hispanic Business* published an annual list of "the boardroom elite." The list included Hispanics who served on "the boards of *Fortune* 1000 corporations, divisions, and subsidiaries." The inclusion of "divisions and subsidiaries" made these lists less exclusive than the ones we have used in previous chapters. In 2004, after skipping 2003, *Hispanic Business* published a list that only included directors on *Fortune* 500 companies.[13] We have gone back to the 1998 and 2001 lists and eliminated those seats on divisions and subsidiaries of *Fortune* 500 boards and those seats on boards that were ranked between #501 and #1000. The results reveal that the number of Hispanic directors on *Fortune* 500 boards increased from forty-seven in 1998 (these forty-seven held sixty-two seats), to fifty in 2001 (they held fifty-eight seats), and to sixty-nine in 2005 (they held ninety-five seats). Thus, although Hispanics now make up about 13.5 percent of the U.S. population, even with the gains made during this six-year period, only 1.6 percent of the approximately fifty-nine hundred *Fortune* 500 directors are Hispanic. Almost all are outside directors (only five were inside directors in 2001, and only three were in 2005).[14]

Although we have considerable confidence in these findings, it is important to stress that they are not perfect. Deciding who is and who is not Hispanic is not an exact science. As with Jews, names can be misleading. When a reader of *Hispanic Business* wrote to complain that John Castro, the CEO of Merrill Corporation, had been omitted from a list of corporate executives published in the January 1995 issue (along with the list of the "boardroom elite"), the editors replied that "company officials tell us he is not Hispanic."[15] Similarly, Arthur Martinez, the seemingly Latino CEO of Sears, Roebuck from 1992 to 2000, is mostly Irish. As a company spokesperson explained to us when we inquired, "He is mostly of Irish descent. A family member married someone from Spain generations ago, and that is where the name comes from."[16] There are also Hispanics whose names do not reveal that they are Hispanic: in 1994, H. B. Fuller Company selected Walter Kissling, born and raised in Costa Rica, as its CEO.[17]

We analyzed the social, educational, and career backgrounds of the 103 Latinos and Latinas who sat on *Fortune* 500 boards in 1998, 2001, 2004, and 2005. The gender difference was large: 81 percent were men, and 19 percent were women. Still, the 19 percent is considerably higher than the comparable percentage for non-Hispanic white women on boards (less than 14 percent in 2003), but lower than the figure for African American women (25 percent). As is the case for African Americans, the Hispanic women were more likely to sit on multiple boards than are the men (on average, the women held 1.53 seats, and the men 1.35).[18]

Although the available biographical information is not complete in all cases, a majority of the men and women on our list seem to have been raised in at least middle-class circumstances. Many others had an elite education at the undergraduate or graduate levels that gave them the social connections and educational credentials to move quickly into responsible positions in the corporate community. Only a few people on the list of directors could be considered genuine bootstrappers, making their way to the top of corporations without the benefit of family backing or an elite education.

As might be expected from our account of Roberto Goizueta's appointment as CEO at Coca-Cola and the large number of Cuban Americans among the wealthiest Hispanics, many of the successful entrepreneurs and executives on our list come from Cuban American backgrounds. Most had the advantage of being born to parents who were wealthy, well educated, or both. This was true, for example, for Roberto Mendoza, who, like Roberto Goizueta, was born in Cuba and educated at Yale and who became the head of mergers and acquisitions at Morgan Guaranty Trust in 1987, earning him a seat on the board.

And it was also true for Alfonso Fanjul. He and his brother José manage a fifth-generation, privately held family business, Flo-Sun, with cane fields in Florida and Puerto Rico, that is a leading sugar producer in the United States and the Dominican Republic. Forced to relocate to the United States when Castro came to power, the Fanjuls have by far the worst labor record of any sugar-producing company in the country, frequently violating minimum wage and labor laws with their predominantly Latino migrant labor force. In brushing off criticism of the Fanjuls, a New York friend of theirs said, "They are completely accepted by society [in Palm Beach]—they hang out with all the best people."[19] As of 2004, the family was estimated to be worth more than $500 million, with an estimated $65 million of its income each year due to government subsidies (and "untold hundreds of millions" from price supports).[20]

In 1996, the *New York Times* reported that, despite his permanent residency in the United States, Alfonso Fanjul (known as "Alfy") had Spanish citizenship. Some critics suggested that he preferred having Spanish citizenship to avoid U.S. estate taxes, but a flap over his large campaign finance donations—Alfy is a major donor to the Democratic Party—led him to claim that he was applying for American citizenship. His brother José (known as "Pepe") contributes to the Republicans (according to the Center for Responsive Politics, the Fanjuls gave $2.6 million to politicians and political committees between 1979 and 2004). Though they describe themselves as having political differences, political analysts attribute their donations to both parties simply as a calculated strategy to make sure that, no matter who is elected, they will have political clout.[21]

With the death of Roberto Goizueta, the most prominent Cuban American in corporate America is now Armando Codina. He, too, was born to privilege in Cuba—his father was the president of the Senate prior to the revolution—but Codina's route to the corporate elite was more difficult than Goizueta's. Codina's parents, who had divorced when he was young, were able to arrange for him to leave the island in the early 1960s as part of a program run by the Catholic Church called "Operation Peter Pan" (fourteen thousand youngsters participated in this program). He was sent to an orphanage in New Jersey, where he reports that he had a difficult time mixing with children from troubled backgrounds (when he arrived, he recalls, with "fine English flannel suits" that had been made specially for him by a tailor his mother had taken him to in Cuba, many of the other kids gave him a very hard time).[22]

He spent a few years in a foster home in New Jersey and then began college at Jacksonville University in Florida. His mother, who spoke no English and had never worked, was able to leave Cuba, and she came to live with him in Florida. In order to support the two of them, he dropped out of school, worked two jobs, and, with $18,000 that he borrowed from the Small Business Administration, he started a small business, a computer company that handled billing and processed forms for doctors. The business did well; he sold it in 1978 for $4 million and started the Codina Group, a real estate development company that was to be his ticket to the big time.[23]

Active in Republican politics, he became the chairman of the 1980 Bush campaign in Florida. After Bush lost that campaign and became Reagan's vice president, he asked Codina to hire his son, Jeb, as president of his company, which Codina did. Subsequently, as Jeb Bush ran for various offices in Florida—successfully for secretary of commerce and unsuccessfully for governor—he worked intermittently for the firm. While he worked for Codina, however, he made a lot of money. As William Finnegan wrote in the *New Yorker*, "people in Miami say, 'Codina made Jeb a rich man.'"[24] When Jeb Bush won the governorship in 1998, Codina paid him a bonus of $630,000.[25]

Codina has continued to support the Bush family—a fund-raiser at his house for George W. Bush as he geared up for the 2004 campaign netted $2 million—and he has served on numerous *Fortune*-level boards, including Winn-Dixie, BellSouth Corp, American Airlines, Florida Power and Light, and, as of 2002, General Motors (#3 on the 2005 *Fortune* list).[26]

Several directors are Spanish Americans from New Mexico. These include Katherine Ortega, whose paternal grandparents settled in New Mexico in the late 1880s. Her father owned a café, then a furniture business. Because he was a lifelong Republican, Ortega likes to say she was "born a Republican."[27] After graduating from Eastern New Mexico State University in 1957 with a degree in business, she started an accounting firm with her sister, which the family turned into the Otero Savings and Loan Association in 1974.

Ortega moved to California in the late 1960s, working first as a tax supervisor for the accounting firm of Peat, Marwick, Mitchell & Company and then as a vice president for Pan American Bank, where her bilingualism was valuable in working with the local Latino community. In 1975, she gained visibility as the first woman president of a California bank, the Latino-owned Santa Ana State Bank. Four years later, she returned to New Mexico as a consultant to her family's saving and loan association, and in 1982, Reagan named her to his Advisory Committee on Small and Minority Business Ownership.[28] From 1983 to 1989, she served in the Reagan administration in the largely ceremonial position of treasurer of the United States. That office gave her the public stature to give one of the keynote speeches at the 1984 Republican presidential convention. In 1989, she left her government position and marketed herself as a corporate director who could provide both Hispanic and female perspectives. By 1995, she sat on no fewer than six boards: Diamond Shamrock, ITT Raynier, Kroger Company, Long Island Lighting, Paul Revere Insurance Group, and Ralston Purina (by 2005, she was only on one *Fortune* 500 board: Kroger).

There are some rags-to-riches stories among the Latino directors. Most of them concern Mexican Americans. Edward Zapanta, for example, was told by his high school counselor that he should become a mechanic like his father, but he went on to earn a BA from UCLA and an MD from USC. He founded a medical clinic in a predominantly Mexican American neighborhood near where he grew up, and he has been on the boards of Southern California Edison and the Times Mirror Company. William S. Davila provides another example. Neither he nor his parents graduated from college. Davila started as a stock boy at Von's Markets in 1948 and ended up CEO of the company in 1987 at the age of fifty-six. He retired from the position in 1992 but continued to serve as a director at various companies. As of 2004, he sat on the boards of three *Fortune* 500 companies (Home Depot, Hormel Foods, and Pacific Gas and Electric); as of 2005, he was only on the board of Home Depot.

Luís Nogales provides another example of a Mexican American rags-to-riches story. Nogales was born in 1943 in the central valley of California where his parents were farm workers, albeit farm workers who bought books on literature and history, in both English and Spanish, and "traveled with their own small library."[29] Nogales attended San Diego State University on a scholarship and graduated from Stanford Law School in 1969. After working for three years as Stanford's liaison to Mexican American students, he went to Washington, D.C., as a White House fellow and then became assistant to the secretary of the interior. He returned to the West Coast in 1973 to work for Golden West Broadcasting, owner of the California Angels baseball team, as well as radio and television stations. In 1983, he became executive vice president and in 1985 president of United Press International (UPI). When UPI was sold in 1986, he went to work in Spanish-language television for Univision. After negotiating the sale of Univision to Hallmark in 1988, he formed his own investment and consulting company, Nogales Partners. As of 2005, he was on the boards of two *Fortune* 500 companies: KB Home, Inc., and Edison International.

But not all of the Mexican Americans in the sample started at the bottom. Shortly after his graduation from Notre Dame in 1947, Ignacio E. Lozano Jr. became the assistant publisher of *La Opinión*, the highly successful newspaper his father founded in 1926. Now retired, he has served as a director of Bank of America, Walt Disney Company, Pacific Mutual Life, and Pacific Enterprises. His son, José, became the publisher of the paper, and his daughter, Monica, became first the managing editor of the paper (in 1987) and then the president and chief operating officer. In late 2003, the Los Angeles-based *La Opinión* merged with the New York-based *El Diario/La Prensa*, bringing the country's two largest Spanish-language newspapers under one umbrella company called ImpreMedia. At the time of the merger, José became vice chairman and executive vice president of ImpreMedia, and Monica became senior vice president. At that time, she also became the publisher and CEO of *La Opinión*. She has served on the boards of Disney, First Interstate Bank of California, Fannie Mae, and Tenet Healthcare.

Similarly, Enrique Hernández Jr. and Roland Hernández are Mexican Americans who had the advantage of being raised in a well-to-do family. Enrique Hernández Sr., a former police officer, created Inter-Con Security Systems, a company with offices in twenty-five countries that employs more than twenty-five thousand workers. As of 2005, Enrique Jr., a graduate of Harvard, sat on the boards of four *Fortune* 500 companies: McDonald's, Nordstrom, Tribune Company (of Chicago), and Wells Fargo. Roland, also a Harvard alumnus, was a director at Wal-Mart and MGM Mirage in 2004.

LATINO CEOS AND THE CORPORATE PIPELINE

As of July 2005, there have been six Latino CEOs of *Fortune* 500 companies, all of them men.[30] The first, Roberto Goizueta, the Cuban-born immigrant who served as president and CEO of Coca-Cola from 1981 to 1997, we have already discussed earlier in this chapter. Carlos Gutierrez, also born in Cuba to a wealthy family, became CEO of Kellogg Corporation in April 1999. As we will see later in this chapter, early in 2005, Gutierrez left his position at

Kellogg to become the secretary of commerce after George W. Bush was re-elected in 2004.[31]

Two of the Latino CEOs are from South American countries. Claudio Osorio, CEO of CHS Electronics, was born in Venezuela, where he studied law and business. Alain Belda, the son of a Spanish Republican father who fled Spain in the late 1930s and a Portuguese mother, has been the CEO of Alcoa since 2001, when he succeeded Paul O'Neill (who left to become George W. Bush's secretary of the treasury). Belda was born in French Morocco but moved to Brazil when he was three. The family then moved to Canada when he was thirteen and back to Brazil when he was seventeen (he is a Brazilian citizen).[32]

Two are Mexican Americans, and both seem to have authentic rags-to-riches stories. Carlos Cantu, the CEO of Servicemaster from 1993 until he retired in 1999, is the son of Mexican immigrants. He worked his way through Texas A&M, in part as a custodian (in 1999 he gave a million dollars to his alma mater for a study of the root causes of Hispanic high-school dropouts). Some considered Solomon Trujillo, who became the CEO of U.S. West in 1998, to be the most powerful Hispanic in America after the company merged with Qwest, but by February 2000, after citing "differences with the new owners," he announced that he was leaving the company. In June 2005, Trujillo became the CEO of Telstra, the dominant telecommunications provider in Australia. Trujillo is the son of a railway laborer (he earned both an undergraduate and business degree from the University of Wyoming).[33]

If we expand our list of Latino CEOs to include those who have been CEOs of companies that ranked between #501 and #1000 on the annual *Fortune* list, we add another six men. In 1991, Richard Carrion became the CEO of Popular, Inc., the holding company for Puerto Rico's largest bank chain, Banco Popular. Carrion is from one of the richest families in Puerto Rico (both his father and his grandfather served as presidents of the same bank). Benjamin Montoya, a Mexican American from Indio, California, who attended the Naval Academy and served in the navy for thirty-one years, rising to the rank of admiral, upon leaving the military became CEO of the Public Service Company of New Mexico in 1993 and served in that capacity until 2000. During his military career, he earned bachelor's degrees from the Naval Academy and Rensselaer Polytechnic Institute, a master's degree from Georgia Tech, and a law degree from Georgetown. Walter Kissling, CEO of H. B Fuller from 1994 to 1998, grew up in Costa Rica, the son of German immigrants. Although he "attended" a class at the Harvard Business School at one point and spoke four languages, he did not have a college degree (he died in 2002). J. Philip Samper, whose father was Colombian and whose mother was Anglo and who grew up in Salt Lake City, became the CEO of Cray Research in

1995. He is a graduate of the University of California, Berkeley, and of MIT. Tony White, whose mother was from a wealthy Cuban family and whose father was from a working-class family in western North Carolina, has been the CEO of a company now called Applera (it was formerly called Perkin-Elmer) since 1995. Hector Ortino, who became CEO of Ferro in 1999, is from Venezuela.[34]

These twelve CEOs reflect some of the patterns seen in previous chapters. Like the African American CEOs, all are men. They are mostly well educated, though only two went to elite schools in the United States (Goizueta to Yale and Samper to Berkeley and MIT). The most noteworthy pattern that emerges with this group is their international makeup and the extent to which these international men of business grew up in economically and socially privileged circumstances in Venezuela, Brazil, Puerto Rico, and, of course, Cuba. Because of their worldly backgrounds and their fluency in languages other than English, they seem to be ideal corporate leaders in the current global economy. Consider, for example, these comments from Alain Belda, Alcoa's CEO: "Our board today is 50% American-born and 50% foreign-born. Our top management is 40% foreign-born and over 50% international, if we consider Americans that have lived long periods abroad. We have shared business systems and a common infrastructure applied across a globally connected workforce."[35]

A few, especially the Mexican Americans, grew up poor, but most, especially the Cubans, are from wealthy families (though the Cubans, of course, left after the revolution and often, though not always, left with very little money).[36]

Below the CEO level, the numbers of Latino executives remains small. Recent studies by the Hispanic Association on Corporate Responsibility (HACR), a coalition of eleven Hispanic community-based organizations, show that "the pipeline is thin." As the CEO of HACR put it in describing the findings of a study of *Fortune* 1000–level companies in 2003, "We also see the pipeline as a concern. If the pipeline extends beyond the CEO ranks to the ranks of Executive Officers — the future growth remains constrained knowing that only 1 percent of total Executive Officers are Hispanic." A year later, the organization found that Hispanics held only 1.8 percent of the board seats of *Fortune* 1000 companies and constituted "an even smaller percentage of executive officers (1.1 percent)."[37]

To develop a more general and long-term picture of Latino involvement in the corporate community, we drew on the Distinctive Hispanic Names technique developed by sociologist Abraham Lavender.[38] We used fifteen distinctive Hispanic names to estimate the number of Latinos listed in *Standard & Poor's Register of Executives and Directors*, the most comprehensive and readily accessible list of top managers and directors at more than fifty thousand public companies. We first determined that these fifteen names (Alvarez, Díaz, Fernández, Flores, García, González, Hernández, López, Martínez, Pérez, Ramírez, Rivera, Rodríguez, Sánchez, and Torres) accounted for 23 percent of the names appearing on lists of corporate directors and executives in *Hispanic Business* for 1993, 1994, and 1995, which gave us a factor of 4.35 (4.35 × 23 percent equals 100 percent) for estimating the total number of Latinos listed in *Poor's* at the midpoint in each decade since the 1960s.

According to this analysis, the total number of Latinos listed in *Poor's* rose from 78 in 1965, to 131 in 1975, to 235 in 1985, to 374 in 1995, and to 726 in 2004. Although these raw estimates provide a generally accurate picture of the rising rate of Hispanic participation in the business community from 1965 to 2004, one that indicates that there are almost ten times as many Latinos in *Poor's* as there were forty years ago, they in fact slightly underestimate the overall increase in the rate of participation because there were approximately 4,800 fewer names in *Poor's* in 2004 (70,823) than there were in 1965 (75,639). This notable increase reflects not only that there has been greater Latino involvement in non-Hispanic companies but that there are more Latino-owned businesses. Still, our estimates indicate that Latinos represented only 1.2 percent of executives and directors at publicly owned companies large enough to be listed in *Poor's* in 2004.

It is clear that Latinos have come a long way in forty years: some are in the corporate elite, and the number is increasing; some are or have been CEOs of non-Hispanic *Fortune*-level companies; and there are more and more Hispanics moving through the pipeline. Given the many Hispanics in America, though, a percentage of the population that is increasing substantially, they remain very much underrepresented in the higher levels of the corporate world.

Skin Color among Hispanics

Taking our cue from the findings on skin color and income presented earlier in this chapter, we examined the skin color of 188 magazine-quality photographs of people who were selected as "top influentials" by *Hispanic Business* for 1993 and 1994. First, we wanted to see whether those identified as influential Hispanics in general were light skinned, and second, we wanted to see whether those who were *Fortune*-level directors were even lighter skinned than the other "influentials." We used the same nine color cards and the same two raters that we used to assess the photographs of African Americans in chapter 4.[39]

We used the average score based on the two raters' responses to each photograph. As was true for the African American sample, the two had a high level of agreement (89 percent of their ratings were within one point of one another on the nine-point color scale). As expected, the influentials as a group were light skinned. The overall mean score was 3.5 (on a 10-point scale), and less than 5 percent had ratings higher than 5; in contrast, the overall mean score for the African Americans rated in chapter 4 was 5.9. In order to compare the scores of these Hispanic influentials with a group of whites, the photographs that accompanied the biographical sketches of those on the 1994 and 1995 *Forbes* "400 Richest Americans" lists were rated. Not every sketch included a photograph, and we omitted the one African American on the list for whom there was a photograph (Oprah Winfrey), but we were still left with 170 photographs to rate (96 in 1994, and 74 in 1995). The range of scores was from 1 to 6, and the mean score was 2.9. Thus, the skin-color ratings of Hispanic influentials were much closer to those of non-Hispanic rich whites than to those of prominent African Americans.

We also looked to see whether there were differences based on gender and whether those Hispanic influentials who sat on *Fortune*-level boards were rated as lighter skinned than the other influentials. Both variables were significant: the Latinas were rated as lighter (with a mean score of 2.82) than the Latinos (3.58), and the nine men and three women who sat on *Fortune*-level boards were rated as lighter (2.92) than the other Hispanic influentials (3.42).[40]

We were struck not only by the light skin color of the Hispanic corporate directors but by how overwhelmingly "Anglo" they appeared. We were sure we would have a hard time identifying some of them as Hispanics if we did not have other clues, like Hispanic-sounding names or inclusion of their photos in a magazine called *Hispanic Business*. In order to test this more systematically, we constructed a booklet with twenty-eight photographs of CEOs, chairpersons, or directors of large corporations, all of which we cut out of issues of *Fortune*, *Ebony*, or *Hispanic Business*. We collected seventeen photos of white men and women, three of black men, three of black women, three of Hispanic men, and two of Hispanic women. One of the Latinos was Cuban, and the other two were Mexican American; both Latinas were from New Mexico. We showed these to ten current or recent students at Guilford College in Greensboro, North Carolina, and asked them to tell us which of the twenty-eight people were white, which were black, and which were Hispanic. As expected, the accuracy rate was quite high for whites (87 percent); the relatively few errors were made because some students thought certain of the darker-skinned men or women were Hispanic. The accuracy rate was also quite high for black men (90 percent) and fairly high for black women (60 percent); the blacks who were misidentified were thought to be Hispanic, especially one of the three black women. In sharp contrast, and confirming our own less systematic observations, the accuracy rate for identifying Hispanics was only 40 percent for the men and 30 percent for the women; in every case but one, when errors were made, the Hispanics were thought to be white. (In the one exception, a Hispanic male was perceived by one of the raters as black.) We replicated this little study on the campus of the University of California, Santa Cruz (UCSC), and found that the students were a bit more accurate in identifying Hispanics but still thought they were white about half the time.[41]

LATINOS IN THE CABINET

It was not until 1988 that there was a Hispanic member of the cabinet, and he was an unexpected and unlikely one at that. On the eve of the Republican convention that year, as his eight years as president were about to end, Ronald Reagan's sudden announcement of Lauro Cavazos, a Democrat and college president, as the new secretary of education may have seemed a bit unusual to the casual eye. But his friend George Bush, who was then vice president, was struggling in his campaign for president at the time, especially in Texas. Because the Democratic nominee for vice president, Lloyd Bentson, was a popular senator from Texas, the Republicans feared that Bush would lose the state and its many electoral votes. Since Bush had already proclaimed that he would become "the education president" and that he would appoint a Latino to his cabinet, Reagan decided to help matters along with a person who just happened to be a registered Democrat from Texas. In the words of Alicia Sandoval, a spokeswoman for the National Education Association, the appointment of Cavazos was "just a ploy to help get Bush elected and carry Texas . . . a classic case of tokenism."[42] Bush did carry Texas on his way to victory, and he reappointed Cavazos, who served until December of 1990, when he was forced to resign because Bush's advisers considered him ineffectual.[43]

Cavazos grew up on an eight-hundred-thousand-acre ranch, where his father worked for forty-three years as a foreman in the cattle division. He was educated in a one-room schoolhouse for the children of the ranch's Mexican laborers until, when he was eight years old, his father persuaded reluctant officials in a nearby town to let his children attend what had been up to that time an all-Anglo school. After graduating from high school in 1945, Cavazos served for a year in the army, then began what was to become a lengthy and conventional climb through the ranks of academe. First, he received a BA and an MA in zoology from Texas Technological College (now Texas Tech University) and a PhD from Iowa State. After teaching at the Medical College of Virginia for ten years, he left to become professor and chairman of the anatomy department at the Tufts University School of Medicine. He rose through the administrative ranks over the next sixteen years, becoming the dean in 1975. He left in 1980 to return to Texas Tech as president, the position he held when Ronald Reagan came calling.

Not content with one Latino cabinet member, Bush appointed Republican congressman Manuel Lujan of New Mexico as his secretary of the interior. Born in 1928, Lujan first won election in 1968. He is another example of a conservative Spanish American from New Mexico. In spite of twenty years as a member of the House Committee on Interior and Insular Affairs, where he usually sided with developers in their battles with environmentalists, Lujan showed little understanding of any important land, water, or environmental issues when he assumed his cabinet post. *Time* declared that his record was "dismal" and that he was "clueless on environmental issues and often embarrassed himself making policy statements on matters of which he was ignorant." The conservative British magazine the *Economist* said he had a "blank interior." An article in the *Audubon* spoke of his "incompetence," and the *New Republic* called him "the dregs of the Bush cabinet."[44]

Lujan was raised near Santa Fe in privileged circumstances. His father ran a successful insurance agency and served three terms as mayor of Santa Fe, although he did fail in his bids for Congress and the governorship. Lujan joined his father's business in 1948 after graduating from the College of Santa Fe and worked there for twenty years, eventually moving the business to Albuquerque. He won a seat in Congress in the 1968 elections by making an ethnic appeal to the traditionally Democratic Mexican American voters in his district. By 1995, he was a *Fortune* 1000 director for the Public Service Company of New Mexico, a gas and electric utility.[45]

In January 1993, two Latino men, Henry Cisneros and Federico Peña, became members of Bill Clinton's cabinet. There are some striking similarities between the two. Both were born in Texas in the spring of 1947 into stable middle-class families (Cisneros's father was a civilian administrator for the army, and Peña's father was a broker for a cotton manufacturer). Both attended Catholic schools, received BAs from universities in Texas, went on to earn postgraduate degrees (a doctorate for Cisneros, a law degree for Peña), became the first Latino mayors of the cities in which they lived in the early 1980s (Cisneros of San Antonio in 1981, Peña of Denver in 1983), were reelected throughout the 1980s, and, by the early 1990s, were partners in private investment companies (Cisneros in Asset Management, Peña in Investment Advisors, Inc.). By spring 1995, both were out of the investment business and were being investigated by the Justice Department, Cisneros for allegations that he misled federal investigators during his prenomination interviews about payments he made to a former mistress and Peña in connection with a contract awarded in 1993 to an investment firm he had just left.[46]

In 1996, Janet Reno appointed an independent counsel to look into the accusations against Cisneros. After the election, he resigned from the cabinet and became president of Univision, the largest Spanish television broadcaster in the United States. Although he initially faced eighteen felony counts for having lied to the FBI about the payments he made to his former mistress, in September 1999 the case was settled when he pleaded guilty to one misdemeanor count of lying to the FBI about the payments; he was fined $10,000 (Clinton pardoned him as he was leaving office). In August 2000, he left Univision to run a newly formed housing company, American-City Vista, that would build affordable housing in downtown urban areas.[47] He is one of the directors included on the *Hispanic Business* "Boardroom Elite" list: in 2005, he sat on the board of Countrywide Financial (#150 on the 2005 *Fortune*-500 list), one of the largest mortgage lenders in the United States.

Peña continued as secretary of transportation throughout Clinton's first term and became the secretary of energy at the beginning of Clinton's second term. He resigned from that position after eighteen months, joining Vestar Capital Partners, a New York– and Denver-based investment firm. He became a managing director with Vestar in 2000 and, as of June 2005, was still working with them. He, too, is among the "Boardroom Elite"; as of June 2005, he was on the board of Principal Financial Group (#253 on the *Fortune* list in 2005).

In 1998, after Peña resigned as secretary of energy, Clinton replaced him with another Mexican American. William Blaine Richardson, known as Bill, was quite an atypical Mexican American. Richardson's father, an Anglo, was a well-to-do banker, and his mother was a Mexican citizen. Richardson, born in Pasadena, California, grew up in Mexico City, where his father was an executive for Citibank, the only foreign-based bank in the city at the time. He went to Middlesex, an exclusive New England prep school, then to Tufts for a BA in 1970 and an MA in international relations in 1971. After graduation, he spent three years in the State Department as a liaison with Congress, followed by three more years as a staff member for the Senate Foreign Relations Committee. Obviously looking for a place to settle where he could win a seat in Congress, Richardson moved to Santa Fe in 1979 to become executive director of the Democratic State Committee. In 1980, despite charges that he was a classic carpetbagger, he almost unseated the Republican incumbent, Manuel Lujan, outspending the affluent Lujan by more than $200,000. In 1982, he won a seat in a newly created district, carefully crafted by his Democratic friends in Congress to give him a strong Latino base, and in 1985, he was elected to a term as chair of the Congressional Hispanic Caucus. In 1997, Clinton appointed Richardson chief delegate to the United Nations, replacing Madeleine Albright. In 2002, Richardson became governor of New Mexico, winning by the largest margin of any candidate for that office since 1964. Many thought John Kerry would choose him as his vice presidential running mate in 2004.[48]

As of July 2005, George W. Bush had appointed three Latinos to his cabinets: Melquiades ("Mel") Martinez as secretary of housing and urban development, Carlos M. Gutierrez as secretary of commerce, and Alberto Gonzales as attorney general. Martinez, who was born in Cuba a few years before the revolution, is described on the HUD website as "a leader in implementing President Bush's faith-based initiatives." In December 2003, at the urging of White House strategists, Martinez resigned from his cabinet position so that he could run for the open Senate seat in Florida (created when Bob Graham sought the Democratic nomination). Martinez ran a senatorial campaign that was so negative about his Republican primary challenger that Jeb Bush asked him to take one of his television ads off the air, and the *St. Petersburg Times* rescinded its previous endorsement, accusing him of "hateful and dishonest attacks."[49] Still, he won the primary and then won a close race against Betty Castor, the Democratic nominee.

Shortly after the 2004 election, when Bush's secretary of commerce, Donald Evans, announced his resignation, the president named Carlos M. Gutierrez, one of the Latino CEOs discussed earlier in this chapter, as his replacement. As we have noted, Gutierrez was from a wealthy family in Cuba: his father was an exporter of pineapples, and his family was part of what he refers to as "Cuba's high society." When Bush named him, he had been president and CEO at Kellogg since 1999.[50] Ileana Ros-Lehtinen, a Republican member of Congress from Florida, was quick to claim that Gutierrez's appointment "says a great deal about the president's commitment to the Hispanic community and to the Cuban exile community in particular."[51]

Bush's third Latino cabinet appointment, Alberto Gonzales as attorney general (to replace John Ashcroft), was his most controversial. Gonzales is a genuine rags-to-riches story. The son of a migrant worker, he received his undergraduate degree from Rice and a law degree from Harvard. He became a partner at what the *New York Times* calls "one of the premier law firms in Texas" before he became general counsel to Bush when he was governor of Texas, and he was counsel to him when he became president in 2001. The controversy that surrounded his nomination was based especially on some of the legal advice he provided the president about the treatment of prisoners and about torture: in one memo, he advised the president that the Geneva Conventions did not apply to Al Qaeda or Taliban soldiers in Afghanistan or to the prisoners at Guantanamo; along the same lines, he solicited and participated in the preparation of another memo that redefined torture in such a narrow way that it only included physical abuse that produced the kind of pain that accompanies "serious physical injury, such as organ failure" or death. Despite editorial opposition, the Senate confirmed Gonzales.[52]

Thus, there have been eight Latinos in cabinets, three Democrats (Cisneros, Peña, and Richardson) and five Republicans (Cavazos, Lujan, Martinez, Gutierrez, and Gonzales).

LATINOS IN THE MILITARY ELITE

There have been few Latinos of general officer rank in the armed forces of the United States. Of the 1,067 people who held that rank in 1985, only two were Latinos (one in the navy, the other in the air force). Over the next decade, the number of Latinos with general officer rank increased steadily, but only to ten; the corresponding percentage increase was from 0.2 percent to 1.1 percent. None of the Latino general officers during that decade was a marine, and none of the ten in 1995 was a woman. (From 1986 through 1988, there was one Latina in the air force with general officer rank.) By September 2004, the number of Hispanics with general officer rank had increased to 15, which represented 1.7 percent of the 898 men and women at that level in the military hierarchy.[53]

In the spring of 2004, it appeared that Lt. Gen. Ricardo S. Sanchez, a three-star general and the commander of 160,000 American and allied troops in Iraq, would be promoted to four-star rank and thus become the army's highest ranking Hispanic officer. Sanchez rose from the bottom. He grew up in Rio Grande City, a southern Texas town a few miles from the Mexican border. His father, a welder, had abandoned the family when he was in elementary school, and his mother worked in a hospital to support Sanchez and his four siblings. To augment his mother's salary and the family's welfare payments, young Ricardo worked various odd jobs. The first in his family to graduate from high school, he won an ROTC scholarship to Texas A&I, and upon graduation, he joined the army. Over the years, he rose steadily through the ranks, though not without difficulty, for there was still, especially in his early years, "a lot of racial stuff within the ranks." His promotion, however, was derailed when the Abu Ghraib prison scandal broke. Sanchez had issued an order in November 2003 that officially gave tactical control over the prison to the 205th Military Intelligence Brigade (an order criticized by Maj. Gen. Antonio M. Taguba, who wrote a devastating report on the conditions at the prison); he had also authorized the presence of attack dogs during interrogation sessions. On May 25, 2004, it was announced that he was being replaced as U.S. commander, and he handed over command in early July. Two subsequent reports on the prison scandal, one by three army generals and the other by an independent panel headed by former secretary of defense James Schlesinger, were highly critical of Sanchez. Although he was cleared of wrongdoing in an army inspector general's report that came out in April 2005, it appeared that his promotion to four-star general had been permanently derailed.[54]

In late June 2005, however, the *New York Times* reported that Donald Rumsfeld, confident (as always) that the military had put the Abu Ghraib prison scandal behind it, was considering nominating Sanchez for a promotion to four-star. This appealed to many in the military because Sanchez, it was assumed, would serve as a valuable role model for potential Mexican American recruits. The army was having great difficulty persuading young people to enlist, and the percentage of Hispanic Americans among new recruits had increased over the previous decade from about 8 percent to about 13 percent. Many, including some in the military and some Republicans, were against such a promotion. The *New York Times* editorialized against promoting Sanchez: "He set aside American notions of decency and the Geneva Conventions, authorizing harsh interrogations—including forcing prisoners into painful positions for long periods, isolating them, depriving them of sleep and using guard dogs to, as he put it, 'exploit Arab fears.'"[55]

An examination of the next few levels of the officer ranks for the same years (1985 to 1995) suggests that Latino generals and admirals will remain rare. The percentage of Latinos at those levels increased from a meager 1.6 percent to only 2.5 percent. Because there are high attrition rates for all ethnic groups between colonel and general, there is very little chance of a substantial increase in Latinos at the elite level of the military in the near future.

As we did with African Americans in chapter 4, we considered the longer-term prospects for an increasing Latino presence in the top levels of the military by looking at the makeup of current classes at the three major service academies. At West Point, approximately 6.4 percent of the members of the entering class of 2008 were Hispanic; at the Naval Academy, approximately 9 percent of the members of the entering class of 2007 were Hispanic; and at the Air Force Academy, 6.3 percent of the entering classes of 2005 to 2009 were Hispanic.[56] Although the number of Hispanics in the military has increased dramatically in recent years, this increase has not been matched by corresponding increases in their enrollment at the three major service academies.

LATINOS IN CONGRESS AND ON THE SUPREME COURT

Due to a concentrated population base in the state of New Mexico and in some congressional districts, Latinos have gradually developed a small amount of political representation in Congress. The story could begin with those few who were elected from the territories of Florida and New Mexico in the nineteenth century or with those elected to the House from Louisiana or New Mexico after 1912, but we will restrict ourselves to the four senators elected since 1935 and the twenty-two members of the House first elected after 1960.

The Senate

Until the 2004 elections, there had been two Latino senators, Dennis Chávez and Joseph Montoya, both Democrats from New Mexico whose families had lived in the area for several generations. Chávez, first appointed to the Senate in 1935, was born in 1888 on a family-owned ranch in New Mexico that traced back to a land grant from the king of Spain in 1769. Still, his parents were poor; he was one of eight children, and he was forced to drop out of school in the eighth grade to go to work. He drove a grocery wagon and then was hired to work in the Albuquerque Engineering Department. In the 1916 election, he worked as a Spanish interpreter for Democratic senator A. A. Jones. When Jones won the election, he took Chávez to Washington, D.C., where he became a Senate clerk. He studied law at Georgetown University (which required that he pass a special examination because he held no high school diploma) and received his LLB in 1920.

Chávez then returned to Albuquerque, set up a law practice, and was elected to the New Mexico House of Representatives and then the U.S. House of Representatives as a Democrat. In 1934, he ran for the U.S. Senate and lost a bitterly contested election to Bronson F. Cutting. While he was in the process of challenging the election, Cutting was killed in a plane crash, and Chávez was appointed to replace him. He went on to win a special election and was reelected to serve four more terms in the Senate. Although he had been ill with cancer for more than a year, he ran again for the Senate in 1962, was reelected, returned to the hospital the day after the election, and died a few weeks later.[57]

Montoya's parents were descended from Spanish immigrants who settled in New Mexico in the eighteenth century. His father was a sheriff. Montoya won election to the Senate in 1964. Like Chávez, he studied law at Georgetown Law School. While still a student there, he was elected to the New Mexico House of Representatives on the Democratic ticket. He moved from the state house to the state senate, became lieutenant governor, and, in 1957, was elected to the U.S. House of Representatives. After serving four terms in the House, he was elected to the Senate in 1964. Montoya was defeated in 1976 after a series of newspaper articles detailed alleged improprieties involving a shopping center he owned in Santa Fe, claiming that he had received "special treatment" from the IRS, whose budget was reviewed by a committee he headed. In addition, Montoya's name was one of those mentioned when South Korean businessman Tongsun Park was accused of attempting to buy influence in the United States by making contributions to the election campaigns of politicians. When Montoya died in 1978, he was "said to be a millionaire," according to the *New York Times*.[58]

There were no Hispanics in the Senate from Montoya's death until 2004, when two Hispanic men were elected. One, Mel Martinez, we have already mentioned: after being appointed George W. Bush's secretary of housing and urban development, he left that position to run for the Senate in Florida, where he won a close race against the Democratic nominee, Betty Castor, a politically moderate former state education commissioner. The other was Ken Salazar, a Democratic lawyer from a ranching family that has been in the Southwest for four centuries—thus, like Joseph Montoya, he is of Spanish heritage—who beat Republican beer executive (and heir) Peter Coors to become Colorado's first Hispanic senator.

The House

Since 1960, thirty-seven Latinos have been elected to the House, thirty-two as Democrats and five as Republicans. In 1985, there were eleven Hispanics in the House; the number increased to seventeen in 1995, and to twenty-three in 2005 (thus, the percentage of Hispanics has risen from 2.5 to 5.3).[59] Typically, the Democrats have been Mexican Americans from Texas or California and Puerto Ricans from New York, although a Mexican American from Arizona was elected to the House in 1990 and a Puerto Rican from Illinois was elected in 1992. Until 1996, none of the Mexican Americans had been from a well-to-do background. The five Latino Republicans have tended to come from solidly middle-class or higher backgrounds. As we have indicated, Manuel Lujan who served as Reagan's secretary of the interior, was a member of Congress before he served in the cabinet; his father ran an insurance agency and served three terms as mayor of Santa Fe. Three of the other four have been Cuban Americans, an unsurprising finding given the prominence of Cuban Americans in the corporate elite.

There are some exceptions to these generalizations, but they turn out to be very atypical. Robert Menéndez, elected in 1992 as the first Hispanic American from New Jersey to serve in the House, is an unusual Cuban American Democrat. But Menéndez was born in New York City in 1954, before Castro came to power, and he did not have to leave his parents' native land under pressure. He grew up in New Jersey (his father was a carpenter, his mother a seamstress) and was elected to the school board in Union City in 1974 while he was working on his BA at St. Peter's College. After receiving his law degree from Rutgers in 1976, he became mayor of Union City in 1986 and a member of the state legislature in 1987, moving from the assembly to the senate in 1991. He is married to a non-Hispanic white, the former Jane Jacobsen. About 22 percent of the voters in his district are Latinos.[60] And, as we have noted above, former congressman Bill Richardson, the son of a Citibank executive and a graduate of an elite prep school, is even more atypical.

The second Republican Hispanic elected to the House since 1960, Ileana Ros-Lehtinen, a Cuban American from Miami who had served in the state legislature since 1982, was seated in 1989 just as Lujan was leaving to become secretary of the interior. A 1975 graduate of Florida International University, she owned a private school in Miami. She was joined on the Republican side of the aisle in 1992 by a second Cuban American from southern Florida, Lincoln Díaz-Balart. Díaz-Balart's father, Rafael, was considered one of the founding fathers of Florida's anti-Castro, pro-embargo Republicans. His animus was personal as well as political. His sister, Mirta, was married to Fidel Castro and bore Castro's first son, Fidelito. Thus, Lincoln Díaz-Balart is Fidel's nephew and Fidelito's first cousin.[61]

Lujan, Ros-Lehtinen, and Díaz-Balart are prototypical Republicans, but another Republican Hispanic, Henry Bonilla of Texas, most decidedly is not. His victory over an incumbent Latino Democrat, however, was an unlikely one based on very unusual circumstances. Born in 1954 in San Antonio into a low-income Mexican American family, Bonilla graduated from the University of Texas in 1976, started as a radio announcer in Austin, and worked his way up in the television industry, including jobs in New York and Philadelphia, before returning to San Antonio in 1986 as an executive producer of the news and later a public relations officer for a network affiliate. His wife, Deborah Knapp, a non-Hispanic white, was well known as the station's nightly newscaster.

Bonilla jumped into the 1992 election as a rare Mexican American Republican because the four-term Democratic incumbent, Mexican American Alberto Bustamante, had been caught in a House banking scandal. He also was exposed for building a $600,000 home just outside his district in a wealthy neighborhood, and he was convicted of taking $340,000 in bribes. Under these circumstances, Bonilla attracted the votes of angry Mexican American Democrats (who overwhelmingly supported the Clinton-Gore ticket), even though he was an extremely conservative candidate. Sensing Bustamante's vulnerability, leading Republicans from around the country came to the area to boost Bonilla's candidacy.[62]

The three Mexican Americans first elected to Congress in 1996 follow the patterns described so far in some ways, but they are distinctive in others. Like most Mexican Americans, all three were elected as Democrats. Silvestre Reyes started as a farm worker as a youngster but was regional chief of the Border Patrol in El Paso when he retired to run for office. He won his spurs with Mexican Americans and Anglos alike in 1993 when he stationed his staff one hundred yards apart, twenty-four hours a day, along the border to halt illegal immigration.

The second Mexican American elected in 1996, Ruben Hinojosa, is also a Democrat, but he came from more fortunate economic circumstances than any of the Mexican Americans previously elected to Congress. Hinojosa's family had owned and operated a successful family meatpacking company, H & H Meats of Mercedes, Texas. In the mid-1990s, with Hinojosa as its president, it was the thirty-ninth-largest Hispanic business, with $52 million in sales and 320 employees. Hinojosa was the first Hispanic business leader of major stature to be elected to Congress.

The third Mexican American elected in 1996 was Laura Sánchez, who, like Reyes, was the child of immigrant parents (she was one of seven children). But Sánchez had married Stephen Brixey III, a bond salesman, earned an MBA, and become a Republican. In 1996, she switched her registration to Democratic, dropped her Anglo married name, and defeated an extreme right-wing incumbent in the Republican stronghold of Orange County, California, with the help of donations from women's groups, environmentalists, and gays and lesbians, all of whom found her opponent, "B-1 Bob" Dornan, to be one of their worst enemies in Congress. Sánchez got into some trouble with her Democratic colleagues during the 2000 Gore campaign when she scheduled a Democratic fund-raiser at the Playboy mansion in southern California. After considerable bad press, the event was cancelled.[63]

In 2002, Linda Sánchez, Laura Sánchez's younger sister, a lifelong Democrat, who did her undergraduate work at the University of California, Berkeley, and who has a law degree from UCLA, was elected to the House from a nearby district, making them the first sister team in the history of the House of Representatives. Unlike her middle-of-the-road, Republican-turned-Democrat sister, Linda is an authentic liberal who has been a union lawyer and handled civil rights cases.

In that same 2002 election, the arrival of a liberal Democratic Sánchez sister was matched by the arrival of a conservative Republican Díaz-Balart brother. Mario Díaz-Balart, the younger brother of Lincoln Díaz-Balart, having served in both the Florida House and Senate, was elected to a newly created seat in Florida. Mario, one of the few members of the House without a college degree (he attended the University of South Florida, but did not graduate) is, like his older brother, a Cuban American Republican and (as noted above) Fidel Castro's nephew.

Laura Sánchez and Mario Díaz-Balart are but two of ten Hispanics elected to the House since the 1996 elections. Díaz-Balart is the only Republican, though one of the Democrats, Henry Cuellar, who won a seat in Texas in 2004, endorsed Bush in 2000 and served in the administration of Bush's Republican successor as governor. After Cuellar almost defeated GOP incumbent Henry Bonilla in 2002, the Republicans redrew the district lines to protect Bonilla from a rematch. Cuellar then barely defeated the Democratic incumbent, Ciro Rodriguez, in the primary (Cuellar won by fifty-eight votes) and went on to win the November election.

The Supreme Court

As of July 2005, there had been no Latino members of the Supreme Court. Among the many concerns raised about Alberto Gonzales's nomination to be attorney general was that George W. Bush had him in mind for a Supreme Court nomination. Ironically, although moderates and liberals opposed Gonzales's appointment as attorney general, when Sandra Day O'Connor announced her resignation and many people mentioned Gonzales's name as a possible replacement for her on the Supreme Court, it was the conservatives who reacted negatively, saying he was not conservative enough.

CONCLUSION

Hispanic Americans are part of the corporate community and will continue to be included, especially those with light skin, high-status social backgrounds in their ancestral countries, or both. Such people are racially and culturally similar to the Europeans who came directly to the United States. However, due to their origins in several different Latin American countries, they add an international flavor to the American power elite in an age of increasing corporate globalization. In the case of Cuban Americans, they build on a strong immigrant business community in southern Florida that will continue to generate a disproportionate number of new members in the corporate elite. This point is underscored by the fact that only eleven of the seventy-five wealthiest Latinos for 1995 sat on a *Fortune* 1000 board, so there is a large pool of likely directors ready to be tapped.

The acceptance of light-skinned Hispanic Americans into American society in general and the corporate elite in particular can be seen most clearly in the marriage partners of the three women corporate directors we have highlighted in this chapter. Vilma Martínez married Stuart Singer, a fellow lawyer, in 1968. Patricia Díaz married Michael Dennis, also a lawyer, also in 1968, and she goes by the surname of Díaz Dennis. Katherine Ortega also married a lawyer, Lloyd Derrickson, in 1989.

The military has not been as important an avenue of upward mobility for Latinos and Latinas as it has for African Americans, but it has not been notable for discrimination against Latinos in the past either. As for participation in the political arena, our conclusions are more tentative because there are too few cabinet appointees and elected officials to study. As with the other groups, though, appointed officials tend to come from higher socioeconomic backgrounds and to be present in both Republican and Democratic administrations. Elected officials, on the other hand, with the important exception of Cuban Americans, tend to come from the middle and lower levels of the society and to be Democrats. It is likely that Mexican Americans from the labor movement will play an increasing role in the Democratic Party, forcing the Republicans to redouble their efforts to recruit well-to-do Hispanics of all ethnic backgrounds to maintain their claims to diversity and inclusiveness.

NOTES

1. *Statistical Abstract of the United States* (Washington, D.C.: U.S. Government Printing Office, 1985), 86; see, also, www.census.gov/prod/www/abs/statab1951-1994.htm.

2. Pauline Jelinek, "Hispanics One-seventh of U.S. Population," *Greensboro News & Record*, June 9, 2005, A1. As we noted in the first chapter, when he died, Goizueta was eulogized as representing the American dream, with little or no attention paid to his privileged background in Cuba before the revolution. See Richard Zweigenhaft, "Making Rags out of Riches: Horatio Alger and the Tycoon's Obituary," *Extra!* January–February 2004, 27–28.

3. Janet Morey and Wendy Dunn, *Famous Mexican Americans* (New York: Dutton, 1989), 65–67.

4. Morey and Dunn, *Famous Mexican Americans*, 70.

5. James A. Gross, *Broken Promise: The Subversion of U.S. Labor Relations Policy, 1947–1994* (Philadelphia: Temple University Press, 1995), 250–63.

6. "Emerging Wealth: The Hispanic Business Rich List," *Hispanic Business* (March 1996): 18. We recognize, of course, that Puerto Ricans are U.S. citizens and, thus, those who settle in the United States cannot technically be termed immigrants, but we adopt that term in order to avoid the repeated syntactical gymnastics that would otherwise be necessary. See, also, Roberto R. Ramirez and Patricia de la Cruz, "The Hispanic Population in the United States: March 2002," *Current Population Reports*, issued June 2003, U.S. Census Bureau.

7. Rodolfo de la Garza, Louis De Sipio, F. Chris Garcia, John Garcia, and Angelo Falcon, *Latino Voices: Mexican, Puerto Rican, and Cuban Perspectives on American Politics* (Boulder, CO: Westview, 1992), 13–14. See, also, Suzanne Oboler, *Ethnic Labels, Latino Lives* (Minneapolis: University of Minnesota Press, 1995).

8. See www.ncccusa.org/news/050330yearbook.html.

9. Carlos H. Arce, Edward Murguia, and W. Parker Frisbie, "Phenotype and Life Chances among Chicanos," *Hispanic Journal of Behavioral Sciences* 9, no. 1 (1987): 19–32; E. A. Telles and Edward Murguia, "Phenotypic Discrimination and Income Differences among Mexican Americans," *Social Science Quarterly* 71 (1990): 682–96; Aida Hurtado, "Does Similarity Breed Respect? Interviewer Evaluations of Mexican-Descent Respondents in a Bilingual Survey," *Public Opinion Quarterly* 58 (1994): 77–95.

10. For excellent accounts of the association of color and racial exclusion in Latin America, see Laura A. Lewis, "Spanish Ideology and the Practice of Inequality in the New World," in *Racism and Anti-Racism in World Perspective*, ed. Benjamin Bowser, 46–66 (Thousand Oaks, CA: Sage, 1995); Vânia Penha-Lopes, "What Next? On Race and Assimilation in the United States and Brazil," *Journal of Black Studies* 26, no. 6 (1996): 809–26.

11. Telles and Murguia, "Phenotypic Discrimination and Income Differences."

12. Sonya Tafoya, "Shades of Belonging," Pew Hispanic Center, Washington, D.C., December 2004.

13. As Mike Caplinger, research supervisor for *Hispanic Business* magazine, explained to us in an e-mail on August 31, 2004, they "narrowed down the listing from *Fortune* 1000 companies to *Fortune* 500 companies in an effort to further focus on the 'elite' Hispanics at the very top of the game."

14. Juan Solana, J. Tabin Cosio, Michael Caplinger, and Cynthia Marquez, "The Honored Few," *Hispanic Business*, January–February 2004, 48; "Ready for Progress," *Hispanic Business*, January–February 2005, 44–48. The *Hispanic Business* estimate of 1.6 percent is similar to that based on the data that we received from the Investor Responsibility Research Center, which found that 154, or 1.1 percent, of the seats on the S&P 1500 were held by Hispanics in 2004.

In a study of the directors of twenty-seven of the top hundred companies on the 2004 *Fortune* list, the Hispanic Association on Corporate Responsibility (HACR) found that 3.85 percent of the total available seats were held by Hispanics, compared to 1.97 percent of the total available seats on the top thousand companies. As is the case with African Americans, the larger companies are more likely to include members of previously excluded groups than the smaller companies. None of the 27 companies had a Hispanic woman as one of its ten highest-paid executives, and most did not have a Hispanic woman as one of its top hundred executives. Alfonso E. Martinez, "HACR Corporate Index 2004," *HACR* (online), at www.hacr.org/mediacenter/pubID.86/pub_detail.asp.

15. Reply to letter to the editor, *Hispanic Business*, April 1995, 8.

16. Personal communication from director of community affairs, Sears, July 29, 1996. Despite this, in 1998, *Hispanic Business* included Martinez on its list of five Latinos who were CEOs of *Fortune* 1000 companies. See Maria Zate, "The Big Jump," *Hispanic Business*, January–February 1998, 32. Similarly, *Hispanic Business* included David Fuente, the CEO of Office Depot, as one of the five Latino CEOs in 1998, but the Office Depot public relations officer informed us that Fuente was born and raised in Chicago and is a Sephardic Jew. In all likelihood, his ancestors were ex-

pelled from Spain or Portugal in the fifteenth century, which stretches the meaning of "Hispanic" beyond the usual boundaries. Although *Hispanic Business* continues to include him on its "boardroom elite" list, he is listed as Caucasian, but not Hispanic, on the IRRC's S&P 1500 list.

17. "Who's News," *Wall Street Journal,* June 8, 1995.

18. The IRRC data for the directors who sit on the boards of the S&P 1500 yield comparable results. Hispanic men hold 83 percent of the 154 seats held by Hispanics, but, on average, Hispanic women directors sit on 2.0 seats, and Hispanic men sit on 1.4.

19. Jane Mayer, "Sweet Life: First Family of Sugar Is Tough on Workers, Generous to Politicians," *Wall Street Journal,* July 29, 1991.

20. Phyllis Berman, "The Set-Aside Charade," *Forbes,* March 13, 1995, 78–80, 82, 86; Phyllis Berman, "The Fanjuls of Palm Beach," *Forbes,* May 14, 1990, 56–57, 60, 64, 68–69; Eric Alan Barton, "From Bitter to Sweet: Forget the Awful Past, Say Alfonso and Pepe Fanjul, Florida's Sugar Barons," *Miami New Times* (online), August 26, 2004, at www.miaminewtimes.com/issues/2004-08-26/feature.html.

21. Leslie Wayne, "Foreign G.O.P. Donor Raised Dole Funds," *New York Times,* October 21, 1996; Barton, "From Bitter to Sweet"; Timothy L. O'Brien, "The Castro Collection," *New York Times,* November 21, 2004, section 3, 1; Alexei Barrionuevo and Elizabeth Becker, "Mighty Lobby Is Losing Some Luster," *New York Times,* June 2, 2005, C1, C4.

22. J. P. Faber, "Chairman of the Board: Armando Codina," *South Florida CEO,* January 2004, 44–51.

23. Faber, "Chairman of the Board," 44–51.

24. William Finnegan, "Castro's Shadow," *New Yorker,* October 14, 2002, 101ff.

25. David Pedreira, "Strait-out Country; Bush Pals Vie for Charters," *Tampa Tribune,* March 28, 1999, 1.

26. Dusko Doder, "Our Tropical Terrorist Tourist Trap; As Fidel and His Critics Creak toward Irrelevance, the Push for Normalized U.S.-Cuban Relations Grows Stronger," *The American Prospect,* October 7, 2002, 26.

27. Susan Rasky, "A 'Born' Republican: Katherine Davalos Ortega," *New York Times,* August 21, 1984.

28. Morey and Dunn, *Famous Mexican Americans,* 100–101.

29. Morey and Dunn, *Famous Mexican Americans,* 76.

30. We are not including David Fuente or Arthur Martinez. See n. 16 above.

31. Elizabeth Llorente, "The Breakfast Champ," *Hispanic Magazine* (online), January–February 2004, at www.hispaniconline.com/magazine/2004/jan_feb/CoverStory. See Carlos M. Gutierrez, "The Boss: My Many Citizenship Quests," *New York Times,* August 22, 2001, C6.

32. Shailaja Neelakantan, "Picking His Targets," *Forbes* (online), August 11, 1997, at www.forbes.com/forbes/1997/0811/6003122a.html. In April 2000, CHS filed for bankruptcy. See Simon Robinson, "CHS Files for Bankruptcy Protection," *Hoovers* (online), April 5, 2000, at www.vnunet.com/crn/news/2006410/chs-files-bankruptcy-protection. Phyllis Berman, "The Cosmopolitan Touch," *Forbes* (online), June 21, 2004, at www.forbes.com/business/global/2004/0621/024.html.

33. Wayne Arnold, "Ex-Chief of US West to Lead Australian Telephone Giant," *New York Times*, June 10, 2005, C4; "Hispanics at the Top," *Hispanic Magazine* (online), September 1999, at www.hispanicmagazine.com/1999/sep/CoverStory. Henry Cisneros also called Trujillo "the most important Hispanic in corporate America today." See "U.S. West Elects New Chairman," *New York Times*, May 12, 1999, C8. According to *Hispanic Business*, Robert D. Glynn Jr., CEO at PG&E from 1997 until the end of 2004, is Hispanic. Glynn was born in Orange, New Jersey, and received a BA from Manhattan College and an MA from Long Island University. Although he was listed as one of five Hispanic CEOs of *Fortune*-level companies by *Hispanic Business* magazine in 1998 and included in a September 1999 cover story in *Hispanic Magazine* titled "Hispanics at the Top," we were unable to find any evidence of his Hispanic background. His biographical sketch on the PG&E website makes no mention of either Hispanic background or Hispanic affiliations, and the public relations people at PG&E did not respond to our queries. He is included in the IRRC's list of S&P 1500 directors as Caucasian.

34. "Hispanics at the Top"; www.incae.ac.cr/EN/40anios/walter_kissling_gam.shtml; Andrew Pollack, "The Genome Is Mapped. Now He Wants Profit," *New York Times*, February 24, 2002, section 3, 1.

35. Tonya Vinas, "Three Quick Questions with Alcoa CEO Alain Belda: Prepare for a Hard Landing," *IndustryWeek* (online), May 1, 2005, at www.industryweek.com/ReadArticle.aspx?ArticleID=10180.

36. Gutierrez's family, for example, was able to leave Cuba with more than the clothes on their back. According to Llorente in "The Breakfast Champ," "While many Cubans speak of coming to the United States with little more than pocket change and the clothes on their back, Pedro and Olga Gutierrez and their two sons were able to leave with $2,000 and 22 suitcases in 1960."

37. See the annual reports of the Hispanic Association on Corporate Responsibility, 2003 and 2004.

38. Abraham D. Lavender, "The Distinctive Hispanic Names (DHN) Technique: A Method for Selecting a Sample or Estimating Population Size," *Names* 40, no. 1 (1992): 1–16.

39. The use of color cards to assess skin color is described in Selena Bond and Thomas F. Cash, "Black Beauty: Skin Color and Body Images among African-American College Women," *Journal of Applied Social Psychology* 22, no. 11 (1992): 874–88.

40. These differences were statistically significant. When we ran a regression analysis in which skin color was the dependent variable and both gender and presence or absence on *Fortune* boards were predictive variables, the resulting F was 9.83 ($p < 0.0001$). As was the case with African Americans, sex was a stronger predictor (beta $= 0.29, p < 0.0001$) than presence on *Fortune* boards (beta $= 0.11, p < 0.12$).

41. The accuracy scores of the UCSC students were quite similar to those of the Guilford College students for whites (89 and 90 percent, respectively), black men (97 and 90 percent), and black women (54 and 60 percent). The UCSC students were more accurate than the Guilford College students in identifying both Hispanic men (57 and 40 percent) and Hispanic women (40 and 30 percent). Unable to contain our

curiosity, we showed the photographs to six Latino students at UCSC. They were somewhat less accurate than the other UCSC students in identifying the Hispanic men (44 percent) but more accurate in identifying the Hispanic women (67 percent). Their combined accuracy rate for the Hispanics was 53 percent, virtually the same as that of the non-Hispanic UCSC students.

When a Latino reader in Texas chastised *Hispanic Business* in November 1996 because the 1995 and 1996 stories on the top influentials, top executives, and multimillionaires "failed to include a single dark face," the magazine replied that each of the three lists contained Hispanics with "African ancestry" and claimed that "basing your conclusions on visual evidence alone makes for a faulty argument." But as the reader was saying, and as our evidence shows, there are few "dark faces" at the top, whatever their ancestry. See Gustavo E. Gonzales, "Are Black Hispanics Being Ignored?" *Hispanic Business,* November 1996, 6.

42. "Lauro F. Cavazos, Jr.," *Current Biography* (1989): 97.

43. Maureen Dowd, "Cavazos Quits as Education Chief amid Pressure from White House," *New York Times,* September 13, 1990.

44. Ted Gup, "The Stealth Secretary," *Time,* May 25, 1992, 57; "The Blank Interior of Manuel Lujan," *Economist,* September 22, 1990, 34; "Talk of the Trail," *Audubon,* July 1989, 20; Bruce Reed, "Half Watt: The Dregs of the Bush Cabinet," *New Republic,* October 16, 1989, 20.

45. "Manuel Lujan," *Current Biography* (1989): 354–58.

46. "Henry G. Cisneros," *Current Biography* (1987): 87–96; "Federico F. Peña," *Current Biography* (1993): 460–64.

47. David Johnston, "Concluding That Cisneros Lied, Reno Urges a Special Prosecutor," *New York Times,* March 15, 1995; Steven A. Holmes, "Housing Secretary Resigns, Citing Financial Pressures," *New York Times,* November 22, 1996; Mireya Navarro, "Cisneros Leaving Univision to Run Housing Company," *New York Times,* August 8, 2000, C8.

48. See "Bill Richardson," *Current Biography* (1996): 37–40; James Brooke, "Traveling Troubleshooter Is Ready to Settle Down at the U.N.," *New York Times,* December 14, 1996; Rick Lyman, "An Activist Leader at Home and Nationally," *New York Times,* July 20, 2004, A14.

49. Abby Goodnough, "Ex-Cabinet Member Struggles in Florida Senate Primary," *New York Times,* August 31, 2004, A10.

50. See Gutierrez, "The Boss," C6.

51. Richard W. Stevenson, "Bush Nominates Kellogg Executive for Commerce Secretary," *New York Times,* November 30, 2004, A15. Ros-Lehtinen was less accurate when, in a typical effort to create an Horatio Alger story where there was none, she added, "We're ecstatic because he's a symbol of the Cuban success stories, coming here without a penny to his name and rising up the corporate ladder to become a CEO of a major company." The article notes that the family was allowed to leave Cuba with $8,000 and thirty-one bags of clothing.

52. David Johnston and Richard W. Stevenson, "Riding an Ideological Divide: Alberto R. Gonzales," *New York Times,* November 11, 2004, A28; "The Wrong Attorney General," *New York Times,* January 26, 2005, A20; Mark Danner, "Torture and

Gonzales: An Exchange," *New York Review of Books*, February 10, 2005, 44–46; Jonathan Schell, "What Is Wrong with Torture," *The Nation*, February 7, 2005, 8; David Cole, "Gonzales: Wrong Choice," *The Nation*, December 6, 2004, 5–6.

53. See "Distribution of Active Duty Forces by Service, Rank, Sex and Race, 09/30/04," Department of Defense, DMDC-3035EO (see, also, ch. 3, n. 76).

54. John F. Burns, "In the General's Black Hawk, Flying over a Divided Iraq," *New York Times*, January 11, 2004, A1, A4; "The Abu Ghraib Spin," *New York Times*, May 12, 2004, A22; Seymour M. Hersh, "Chain of Command," *The New Yorker*, May 17, 2004, 37–43; Eric Schmitt and Thom Shanker, "Pentagon Is Replacing Sanchez As the U.S. Commander in Iraq," *New York Times*, May 25, 2004, A1, A11; John F. Burns, "The General Departs, with a Scandal to Ponder," *New York Times*, July 22, 2004, A10; Douglas Jehl and Eric Schmitt, "Army's Report Faults General in Prison Abuse," *New York Times*, August 27, 2004, A1, A10; Josh White, "Top Army Officers Are Cleared in Abuse Cases," *Washington Post*, April 23, 2005, A1.

55. Eric Schmitt and Thom Shanker, "Posts Considered for Commanders after Abuse Case," *New York Times*, June 20, 2005, A1, A9; "Abu Ghraib, Rewarded," *New York Times*, June 22, 2005, A26. A study by the Pew Hispanic Center indicates that while about 10 percent of all enlisted personnel are Latinos, close to 18 percent find themselves on the front lines. See www.pewhispanic.org. Another study, based on the frequency of Hispanic surnames among the casualties, estimates that, as of late 2003, 20 percent of the casualties were Latinos. See Carol Amoruso, "The Military: What's in It for Latinos/as?" *IMDiversity.com*, at www.imdiversity.com/villages/hispanic/careers_workplace_employment/amoruso_latino_military.asp.

56. The figures for the Naval Academy and West Point are taken from their websites; the figures for the Air Force Academy were provided by the school's public affairs office. For some slightly older data on graduation rates, see "Hispanic-American Graduates of the Military Academies, 1966–1989," in *Hispanics in America's Defense* (Washington, D.C.: Department of Defense, U.S. Government Printing Office, 1990), 181.

57. "Dennis Chávez," *Current Biography* (1946): 109–12; "Senator Chávez, 74, Is Dead in Capital," *New York Times,* November 11, 1962.

58. "Joseph M. Montoya Is Dead at 62; Was Senator in Watergate Inquiry," *New York Times,* June 6, 1978.

59. *Congressional Quarterly*, January 31, 2005, 243.

60. In December 2005, Jon Corzine, who gave up his Senate seat to run for governor of New Jersey, appointed Menendez to replace him in the Senate. Menendez thus became the third Latino senator currently serving, along with Mel Martinez (R-FL) and Ken Salazar (D-CO). David W. Chen, "New Jersey's Newest Governor Basks, but only Briefly," *New York Times*, December 10, 2005, A14.

61. Roberto Lovato, "Rocking the Cuban Vote," *The Nation*, November 1, 2004, 24.

62. *Congressional Quarterly,* January 16, 1993, 136.

63. Lizette Alvarez, "Freshman Democrat Is Dogged by Relentless Foe," *New York Times*, October 5, 1997; Leslie Wayne, "The Democrats: The Money; Hefners' Record of Donations Reflects Their Liberal Ideology," *New York Times*, August 14, 2000, A16.

Chapter Six

Asian Americans in the Power Elite

If told that Shirley Young was a graduate of Wellesley College who became a vice president of General Motors in 1988 and has served on the boards of BankAmerica, Bell Atlantic/Verizon, and the Promus Companies, most of us would likely see her as an example of the kind of success story that belongs in our earlier chapter on women. We would think similarly of Seattle resident Phyllis Campbell, the president and CEO of the U.S. Bank of Washington in Seattle from 1993 to 2001 and now president and CEO of the Seattle Foundation; she also has been a director of Safeco and Puget Sound Energy. In fact, although both women might have been included in our chapter 3 on women in the power elite, both are also Asian Americans.

Shirley Young was born in Shanghai in 1935, the daughter of a career diplomat in Chiang Kai-shek's Nationalist Chinese government who was killed by the Japanese in 1942. Arriving in the United States after the war, Young earned a BA in economics from Wellesley in 1955 and became one of the first members of the Wellesley corporate network as a market researcher, first with the Alfred Politz Research Organization, then with Hudson Paper Corporation, and then in 1959 with Grey Advertising, where she helped such companies as Proctor and Gamble, General Foods, and General Motors "understand how consumers go from thinking about a product to actually buying it."[1] In 1988, she left Grey to become a vice president at General Motors, where she worked until 1995. She was lauded in a headline in the *Wall Street Journal* for acting as a bridge to her native country after helping General Motors to "clinch a deal in China."[2] She is now president of Shirley Young Associates, a business advisory company that assists corporations interested in the China market.

Phyllis Campbell, born Phyllis Takisaki in Spokane, Washington, in 1951, is a third-generation Japanese American whose grandfather lost his grocery store when he and his family were taken to a detention camp during World War II. The oldest of five children, she worked for her father after school in his small dry-cleaning business, where she developed a strong interest in accounting and finance. Her mother was a medical technologist. Campbell received her BA and MA, both in business administration, from Washington State University and an MBA from the University of Washington's Executive MBA Program.[3]

As members of underrepresented groups, Shirley Young and Phyllis Campbell are not typical of most women in the power elite. Except for gender, however, they are typical of many Chinese Americans and Japanese Americans who have made it big in the United States. Although some Chinese immigrants before 1965 came from low-income backgrounds, the great majority of the Chinese Americans at the top levels of the U.S. economy are from well-to-do or at least well-educated families in China, Taiwan, or Hong Kong. William Mow, for example, founder of Bugle Boy Industries in 1977, is the son of the man who was chief of Chiang Kai-shek's United Nations military committee when the Communists took over. Mow grew up in Great Neck, New York, studied engineering at Rensselaer Polytechnic Institute, and earned a PhD in that field from Purdue.

By this point in the book, it will come as no surprise to learn that successful Chinese Americans (like other successful businessmen and women) often downplay the advantages they had on the way to the top in America. For example, the late Chang-Lin Tien, who served as chancellor of the University of California and director of Wells Fargo Bank, emphasized that he arrived in the United States at the age of twenty-one as a penniless immigrant, unable to speak English. True, but he also was born into a wealthy banking family in Wanchu, and his wife's father was a high-ranking officer in Chiang's army.[4]

As the very different social backgrounds of highly successful Chinese Americans like Shirley Young and Japanese Americans like Phyllis Takisaki Campbell suggest, the label "Asian American" is no more useful than "Hispanic" or "Latino." The immigrant groups from a wide range of Asian countries included under that label do not share a common language, national heritage, or immigration pattern. Although they have formed some pan-Asian organizations to resist discrimination and ensure a fair share of social services at the local level, they often remain wary of one another because of historic enmities between their native countries.[5]

In this chapter, we concentrate on the immigrant groups that come from China, Japan, and Korea because we could not find more than a few members of other Asian American immigrant groups in top positions. Their populations are too small, too recently arrived, or too low on the income ladder to have had much national-level impact yet. The few exceptions usually come from the higher social levels in their native countries. We also make note of the increasing presence of Asian Indians in the corporate world (and, since the November 2004 election, in the U.S. House of Representatives).

In spite of the many differences among the various Asian American immigrant groups, four generalizations hold at least for the groups on which we shall concentrate. First, they are very highly educated, either in their countries of origin, in the case of immigrants since 1965, or else in the United States.[6] Second, a fact not fully appreciated by those who have sought to understand the acceptance of Asian Americans by white Americans, 63 percent of Asian Americans identify themselves as Christians according to a telephone survey of 113,000 people across the country. Thus, the seeming cultural "gap" between Euro Americans and immigrants from Asian countries does not exist when it comes to this most intimate and important of all culture issues, which provides a collective way to deal with anxiety-arousing transitions (birth, arrival to adulthood, marriage, and death). Christianity is strongest among Korean Americans, whose families in Korea began to adopt the religion at the turn of the twentieth century as a reaction to pressures from China and Japan. Christian churches founded by Korean Americans are also attended by Japanese Americans and Chinese Americans. Exact figures on the religious identification of Japanese Americans and Chinese Americans are not readily available, but it is known that only 4.1 percent of Asian Americans identify themselves as Buddhists.[7]

Third, many Asian Americans have ended up as "middlemen" in the United States in more ways than one, owing partly to their educational backgrounds and partly to their concentration in small businesses. Asian Americans in California, for example, say that in both large corporations and government agencies, they often end up as middle managers, taking orders from white bosses and giving orders — and termination notices — to Hispanic and African American workers; some of them cynically call themselves a "racial bourgeoisie."[8] But Asian Americans also often end up as middlemen in a second and more traditional sense, as small-business owners providing services and retailing in or near ghettoes and barrios, marketing the products of big corporations in areas where companies like Safeway, Sears, and Revco do not wish or dare to tread. This role has been especially common among Korean Americans in major cities like New York and Los Angeles in the past few decades, and this has led to some highly visible confrontations with African Americans and Mexican Americans.[9]

Fourth, there is evidence that most Asian Americans face difficulties in advancing to the highest levels of large organizations. They are stereotyped as lacking in interpersonal and leadership skills and in their written or spoken English. Thus, despite high levels of educational attainment and considerable evidence of their general acceptance by white Americans, it is likely to be very difficult for very many of them to reach the highest levels of the power structure.[10]

ASIAN AMERICANS IN THE CORPORATE ELITE

We have drawn on three sources of information about Asian Americans on corporate boards. For the 1990s (and for the first edition of this book), we drew on two lists, one from Directorship that included Asian Directors of *Fortune* 1000 publicly held companies and the other compiled by the management consultant William Marumoto of Washington, D.C., whose company specialized in executive recruitment and selection. These two lists combined to yield fifty-seven names. In order to update and expand our look at Asian directors for this newer edition, we have drawn primarily on data for 2004 provided to us by the IRRC, which included the names of seventy-nine Asian men and seventeen women who held directorships at S&P 1500 companies. These 96 men and women held 127 board seats at S&P 1500 companies, but since there were 13,820 seats on these companies, this represents less than 1 percent of the total. Eleven of the names appeared on both our earlier and more current lists. In order to be as current as possible, we will look especially at the names of the ninety-six men and women on the 2004 list, though at times we will include information on Asian American directors who were on the two previous lists but not on the more current list.[11]

Fifteen of the ninety-six men and women on our 2004 list were of Indian background. Of the remaining eighty-one men and women on our working list, 54 percent were Chinese Americans, 25 percent were Japanese Americans, and 9 percent were Korean Americans; the remaining 12 percent were distributed among men and women born in Singapore, the Philippines, and Vietnam.

Chinese Americans

The Chinese Americans directors on the list were typically born in either China or Taiwan, though some of the youngest on the list were born in the states. Three have become CEOs of *Fortune* 1000 companies. The first, Andrea Jung, who became CEO of Avon in 1999, we have already mentioned in the chapter on women. Jung was born in Toronto, and her family moved to Wellesley, Massachusetts, when she was ten. Her father was an architect, and her mother was a chemical engineer. After graduating from Princeton with a degree in English literature, she went into retail marketing, first at Bloomingdale's, then at I. Magnin's, and then at Neiman Marcus. She began to work for Avon in 1993 and moved quickly upwards through the corporate ranks of that company. Jung is married to Michael Gould, chief executive of the Bloomingdale's unit of Federated Department Stores. She sits on the board of General Electric (#5 on the *Fortune* 2005 list).[12]

Another Chinese American CEO of a *Fortune*-level company is Jerry Yang, who was born Jerry Chih-y Yan Yang in Taiwan in 1968. His mother, Lily, taught English and drama at the university level. His father, who had come to Taiwan from China, died when he was two, and eight years later Lily, her father, Jerry, and his younger brother came to the states to live in San Jose, California. Yang learned the language quickly, and by the time he was a senior at Piedmont Hills High School, he was the student body president and class valedictorian and played on the tennis team. After completing his undergraduate work at Stanford and a master's degree, he was on his way to a PhD in electrical engineering. He never completed the degree, however, because what started out as a hobby that he was working on in a campus trailer turned out to be the start of Yahoo!, the search engine website that was incorporated in 1995 and already ranked #502 on the 2005 *Fortune* list. Yang appears on the 2005 annual *Forbes* list of the four hundred richest Americans, ranked #97, with an estimated worth of $2.2 billion (by comparison, Oprah Winfrey was ranked #215, with an estimated worth of $1.3 billion). In addition to his seat on the Yahoo! board, Yang is on the Cisco Systems board (#91 in 2005).

The third CEO of a *Fortune* 1000 company who is of Chinese descent is Allen Y. Chao. In 1968, Chao's parents sent him from Taiwan to the United States to study pharmacy sciences so that he could then return and run the family pharmaceutical business, but things did not work out that way. After he received a PhD in 1973 from Purdue, he was employed as a researcher for G. D. Searle & Company, and then borrowed $4 million from family and friends to start his own company manufacturing generic drugs. He called it Watson Pharmaceuticals. (Chen's mother's maiden name was Hwa; thus, the company derives from "Hwa's son.") After a series of purchases and mergers, the company ranked #878 on the *Fortune* 2005 list, with market capitalization of over $3 billion.[13]

Andrea Jung, Jerry Yang, and Allen Chao are atypical in that they have reached the very apex of wealth and power in America, but they are similar to most of the Chinese American directors on our list who, like them, grew up in families that were well-educated and economically privileged. Some have worked at, are working at, or are the beneficiaries of companies started by their parents or grandparents. They are, as UCLA sociologists Min Zhou and Rebecca Kim explain, the children and grandchildren of the approximately thirty thousand Chinese who were admitted to the United States during and after "the Chinese civil war . . . many of whom were members of the Chinese elite, including top military officers, government officials, diplomats, capitalists, large business owners, and other members of the Chinese upper class." These "transnational capitalists," Zhou and Kim note, "stand at the forefront of the global economy, serving as the 'gateway to the Pacific Rim' on the US shore and, by the same token, the gateway to the US on the other side of the Pacific."[14]

For example, Leslie Tang Schilling, who sits on the board of Golden West Financial Corporation, is the granddaughter of Ping Yuan Tang, an MIT graduate (class of 1923) who returned to Shanghai and built up a textile, cement, and flour conglomerate. When the Chinese revolution came, he left Shanghai for Hong Kong, where he started the South Sea Textile Manufacturing Company. His son, Jack C. Tang, also graduated from MIT (in 1959) and became chairman of South Sea Textile in Hong Kong when his father died. Leslie was born in New York, but her family moved back to Hong Kong before she was one year old. She went to high school there and then came to the United States, where she received a BA from the University of California, Berkeley, and later earned an MA in international management.[15]

Marjorie Yang, the chairman and CEO of Esquel, a shirt manufacturer that produces sixty million shirts a year, was born in Hong Kong, the daughter of a prominent textile manufacturer. Like Leslie Tang Schilling's father and grandfather, as well as a number of the Asian American directors on the IRRC list, she attended MIT, and then she earned an MBA from Harvard. She worked for First Boston Corporation (now Crédit Suisse First Boston) before returning to Hong Kong to help her father set up Esquel Group. In 2004, she also sat on the board of Gillette (#215 in 2005).

And, to give just one more example, there is John S. Chen, born in Hong Kong to a family successful enough to send him to the United States to attend an elite boarding school (Mount Hermon in Northfield, Massachusetts), after which he received his BA from Brown University and an MS from the California Institute of Technology. Chen is now the CEO and president of Sybase, Inc., one of the largest global, independent software companies, and he is on the board of Disney (#54 in 2005).

However, not all of the Chinese American corporate directors are from privileged backgrounds. Sue Ling Gin, who is on the board of Exelon (#145 in 2005) and has been on the boards of Commonwealth Edison, a public utility in Chicago, and the Michigan National Corporation, a banking company, started working in her family's small restaurant outside Chicago at the age of ten and took on major responsibilities as a teenager after her father died. She also worked in a sewing factory and a Laundromat to help make ends meet. She went to DePaul University in the fall of 1959 but dropped out to work at a variety of jobs before opening her own real estate firm. She hired an all-female staff—not, she explained to one interviewer, out of feminist principles, but "because women would work for lower wages."[16] She made her first million speculating in run-down Chicago real estate and acquired two restaurants. In 1983, she started Flying Fare Foods to provide food services for airlines flying in and out of Chicago's Midway Airport. In 1984, at age forty-three, she married for the first time. Her husband, William McGowan, thirteen years older than she, was born into a working-class Irish American family, but by then he was CEO of MCI.

Some of those considered Chinese Americans live or grew up in Hawaii. A number of those on our list serve on the boards of relatively small companies like Hawaiian Electric Industries, Bancorp of Hawaii, and First Hawaii Bank. Connie Lau, for example, is the president and CEO of Hawaii's third largest bank, American Savings Bank, and sits on two mid-level S&P companies, Alexander & Baldwin and Hawaiian Electric Industries. Lau, the daughter of a real estate broker, attended Punahou, an elite prep school in Honolulu, on whose board she now sits and where she met her husband. She received a bachelor's from Yale, a law degree from the University of California, and a business degree from Stanford.[17]

There have been a few other prominent Chinese Americans worthy of mention. Of the fifty-seven people on the list we drew on for the first edition of this book, five people (almost 10 percent) were directors at Wang Laboratories, founded in 1951 by Chinese American immigrant An Wang, who died in 1990 at the age of seventy. Wang was a 1947 PhD in applied physics from Harvard whose invention of magnetic core memory was the basis for major advances in the computer industry. Wang's innovative work helped make him one of the five richest people in the United States in the early 1980s, but his company failed to follow the market's turn to smaller personal computers and had to be transformed into a software and services provider in 1993 to escape bankruptcy. In 1999, the company was sold to a Dutch firm, Getronics, for about $2 billion, leaving the Wang heirs with money to invest in new ventures.[18]

Pei-yuan Chia, who appeared on our earlier lists and is also on our current list of 2004 directors, is the former vice chairman of Citibank. He was the highest-ranking Asian American executive and corporate director at a world-class U.S. corporation until his unexpected retirement in 1996 at age fifty-six. He continued to serve on various corporate boards, including Baxter, Singapore Airlines, and the American International Group (#9 on the 2005 list). He also was a prototypical Chinese American member of the power elite. Born in Hong Kong in 1939, he grew up in a banking family. After receiving his BA from a university in Taiwan in 1961, he came to the United States in 1962 and earned an MBA from the Wharton School of Business at the University of Pennsylvania in 1965. He became a U.S. citizen in 1970, and from 1965 to 1973, he was a products group manager for General Foods. In 1973, he moved to Citibank, where he worked in consumer banking, which was then secondary to corporate accounts. He caught the tidal wave of growth in credit cards and helped Citibank develop consumer banks for upscale customers in three dozen countries, making large profits in the process. In 1992, he was elevated to the six-person management group that runs Citibank, and in 1994, he became one of four vice chairmen.[19]

A handful of Asians have appeared on the annual *Forbes* lists of richest Americans. As we have already noted, Jerry Yang is on the 2005 list. In 1995, the richest Asian American was developer Ronnie Chan, forty-five years old at the time, a naturalized U.S. citizen with an MBA from USC. Chan was a director on a number of corporate boards, including Enron, but after the Enron scandals, he, like some other Enron board members, became pariahs and lost their seats on some of these boards. Still, he continues to be a very rich man as he and his family are the majority owners of the Hong Kong–based Hang Long Development Corporation, a company that he inherited from his father.[20]

Charles B. Wang of New York (no relation to An Wang) also appeared on the 1995 list. Wang, estimated by *Forbes* to be worth $410 million in 1995, was born in 1944 in Shanghai, where his father was a supreme court justice, and he came to New York at the age of eight. After graduating from Queens College in 1967 with a degree in mathematics, he worked for Columbia University's Riverside Research Institute and for Standard Data Corporation. In 1977, he founded Computer Associates International, which develops software for businesses and is today a *Fortune* 1000 company (#520 in 2005). In 2000, Wang was at the very top of *Forbes'* annual list based on executive pay—he pulled in a cool $650 million that year, all but $1 million of which was allegedly based on the "performance" of the company's stock (from 1996 to 2000, he was also paid almost $30 million in salary and bonus grants, in addition to the money he received based on stock performance). But Computer Associates was found to have used very dubious accounting practices, Wang was fired, and in 2004, the company announced that it would restate its revenue for 2000 and 2001, lowering it by $2.2 billion.[21]

The 2005 *Forbes* list includes three other Asians of Chinese background, Patrick Soon-Shiong, Min Kao, and Victor Fong. Soon-Shiong's parents left China during World War II for South Africa, where Patrick was born. He went to college and medical school there, becoming one of the first nonwhite surgical residents at Johannesburg's General Hospital. By 1983, he had joined the faculty of the medical school at UCLA, and by 1991, he had left UCLA to start a firm specializing in diabetes research. A decade later, he was the chief executive and largest shareholder of two companies, American Bioscience and American Pharmaceutical Partners; in 2004, he was ranked #234 on the Forbes list with an estimated worth of $1.2 billion. Min Kao, a native of Taiwan, earned his BA at the National Taiwan University and then came to the United States to study electrical engineering at the University of Tennessee. While earning his MS and PhD at Tennessee, he did research for NASA and the U.S. Army. Kao led the team that developed the first global positioning system receiver certified by the Federal Aviation Administration for use in planes. The profits from the company he cofounded, Garmin, helped put him on the 2005 *Forbes* list (#327, estimated worth, $950 million). Victor Fong, also on that *Forbes* list (#340, estimated worth at $900 million), heads a Hong Kong distribution company, Li & Fung, founded by the family patriarch Fung Pak-liu in 1906.[22]

Japanese Americans

One-fourth of those on our list are Japanese Americans, only one of whom, Phyllis Campbell, mentioned at the beginning of this chapter, is female. For the most part, the experiences of the Japanese American directors have been dramatically different from those of the Chinese American corporate directors.

When Robert Nakasone was appointed president and CEO of Toys R Us (#192 in 2005) in February 1998, he became the highest-ranking Japanese American corporate executive. His tenure in that position, however, did not last for long—the company, struggling when he was hired, continued to struggle, and he resigned in August 1999, replaced by the man he had succeeded, who had stayed on the board and with whom Nakasone allegedly had considerable conflict. Nakasone grew up in the San Fernando Valley in California, and his mother was among the 120,000 Americans of Japanese ancestry who spent time in internment camps during World War II. He obtained a BA from Claremont College in 1969 and an MBA from the University of Chicago in 1971, then worked for Jewel Foods before joining Toys R Us in 1986.

In 2004, another Japanese American, Wayne Inouye, became the CEO of a *Fortune*-level corporation. Both of Inouye's parents were sent to an internment camp during World War II. After the war, they bought a farm in Yuba City, California, about an hour north of Sacramento. As he recalls, "Farming was a tough life. We'd have money one year and be flat broke the next." Inouye differs from the other Japanese Americans on our list and, indeed, from almost every person on the list of Asian directors in that he does not have a college degree. He started at Berkeley but dropped out after two years to join a blues band. After the band broke up, he worked at various music stores and bought and sold vintage guitars out of his car.

He turned out to be a very persuasive salesman (he managed to sell guitars to Joni Mitchell, various members of the Grateful Dead, and Carl Wilson of the Beach Boys). As he got older, he found more secure jobs, one of which was at Best Buy, where he built a reputation as a number cruncher. In March 2001, he became CEO of eMachines, a company that was in deep trouble, and managed to turn things around. When Gateway (#495 in 2005), also in deep trouble, bought eMachines in 2004, Inouye became the CEO of the newly merged company.

In an interview in 2004, Inouye, a third-generation American, revealed both the advantages of being a transnational capitalist working in Japan and the misconceptions that have been part of his cross-cultural endeavors. When asked if he felt "any affinity toward the Japanese market," he replied, "I do, and they seem to feel a greater affinity toward me than I do them. It's crazy, it's nuts. I really get the sense that they're trying to help me because I look like them: the press, the dealers, everybody. The first thing they tell me is, 'You speak perfect English.' Well, it's because I don't speak any Japanese."[23]

Robert S. Hamada, a third-generation Japanese American, has followed an academic pathway to the corporate elite. He was born in San Francisco in 1937, but when he was a youngster, his family was sent to an internment camp in Colorado. When the war ended and the family was released, his parents did not want to return to California. Instead, they moved to New York, and Robert and his younger brother were raised in New Rochelle (his father was an accountant and his mother a bookkeeper). Robert went to Yale, then to MIT for an MS in business and a PhD in finance. He has been a professor in the business school at the University of Chicago since 1966, where he has done research and taught about corporate finance (one of his students was Robert Nakasone, the former CEO of Toys R Us). An award-winning teacher, he has also held a number of administrative positions at the business school (he was the dean from 1993 until 2001), and he has served on the boards of many corporations, including TIAA-CREF (#81 in 2005) and Northern Trust (#587 in 2005).[24]

Another Japanese American director on our 2004 list is Eric Shinseki, a retired four-star general who is the highest-ranking Asian American in military history. Shinseki grew up in Hawaii, and attended public schools (unlike those Hawaiians on our list who attended the elite Punahou school). His father managed a Ford dealership, and his mother was a beautician. An excellent student, a fine athlete, and a student leader at Kauai High School, he won an appointment to the U.S. Military Academy at West Point and later earned a master's in English literature from Duke University. We will say more about his remarkable career in the military, which included differing publicly with Donald Rumsfeld and Paul Wolfowitz about the number of troops that would be required to stabilize Iraq, later in this chapter. For now it is noteworthy that, having retired from the military, in what C. Wright Mills would see as a typical move from the military elite to the corporate elite, he sits on the board of Honeywell (#75 in 2005), a major defense contractor.[25]

Although we found relatively few multimillionaires on the list of Japanese American directors, Tomio Moriguchi, the chairman of Uwajimaya, the Northwest's largest Asian grocery company, is the third generation to be involved in what has become a multi-million-dollar family business. Moriguchi's grandfather owned a local import-export business in Seattle. His mother, born in Seattle in 1907, was sent back to Japan at the age of five in order to receive a traditional Japanese education. She returned to live in Seattle when she was in her twenties and married; she and her husband (who had been in the grocery business in Japan) began a business in 1928 in which they sold Asian goods off the back of a truck to Japanese laborers in Tacoma, Washington. They were sent to an internment camp in northern California during World War II, and, after the war, they relocated to Seattle, where they opened a grocery store, Uwajimaya. The store, a family business, did well.

Tomio Moriguchi, one of the sons, was an engineer at Boeing when his father died. He quit at Boeing and joined the family business, and under his leadership as CEO (his brother is president and chief operating officer), the company continued to expand. In 2000, already the region's largest Asian grocery company, with stores in Seattle and Bellevue in Washington and in Beaverton, Oregon, the company opened a new store in Seattle, twice as big as its former Seattle store. By 2001, the company's sales had increased to $75 million, and by 2002, to $88 million.[26]

As we have indicated, there are at least four Chinese Americans on the 2004 *Forbes* list of the four hundred richest Americans (Jerry Yang, Patrick Soon-Shiong, Min Kao, and Victor Fong). There are no Japanese Americans on that list, but there was one on the 1995 list when we did the research for the earlier edition of this book, Katsumasa "Roy" Sakioka, a farmer and developer with a net worth estimated at $350 million. Sakioka, who kept out of the limelight and did not sit on any major boards, was born in a farm village in Japan in 1899 and came to the United States at the age of eighteen. He had been a tenant farmer for more than two decades when he was interned during World War II, but, after the war, he and his children were able to buy farmland in Orange County, California, in anticipation of urban growth spilling over from Los Angeles. When Sakioka died in late 1995, his businesses were taken over by his surviving family of five children and seventeen grandchildren. Except for the founder's death, the only mention of any Sakioka in the *Los Angeles Times* since 1980 concerned a violation of state labor laws in 1983 by Sakioka Farms for asking migrant farm workers to use short-handled hoes to weed crops, putting its workers at risk for painful back injuries.[27]

One of the most prominent Japanese Americans of great wealth in the post–World War II era, George Aritani, who is now in his late eighties, would have inherited the thriving import-export business that his father founded in 1936, but he had to start all over again, albeit with cash in hand, because the business was sold when the family was put into an internment camp. Fortunately for Aritani, his parents had sent him to college in Japan in the 1930s, so after the war he was able to use his contacts there and his knowledge of Japanese business to create the Mikasa Corporation, which specialized in importing Japanese china. In 1995, when Aritani was still a director, the company had sales of $331 million and eighteen hundred employees, but in 1985 he had been bought out by his predominantly European American executives for $32 million, so there is no family presence in the company. Aritani also founded Kenwood, a leading electronics company. Over the years, Aritani and his wife have made major contributions to the UCLA Asian American Studies Center, including an endowed chair whose specialty is the Japanese American internment, redress, and community.[28]

We could name a few other multimillionaires in the Japanese American community, especially in Los Angeles and Seattle, but they are neither as numerous nor as visible as their Chinese American counterparts, and they rarely serve on major corporate boards.

When we compare the careers of Chinese American and Japanese American directors, we see that they tend to follow different pathways to the top. The Chinese Americans are more likely to be investors or founders of their own companies who are later invited to serve on the boards of other companies. The Japanese Americans are more likely to have climbed the corporate ladder in established companies or to come from legal or academic backgrounds.

Korean Americans and Filipino Americans

There are five Korean Americans on our list, four men and one woman, none of whom is on a board of the largest companies on the S&P list (the top five hundred); all are on what are called "mid-cap" or "small-cap" boards.

The best-known Korean American, Wendy Lee Gramm, is not on our list, but she has been a corporate director of major companies (and will, no doubt, be again). Gramm is an economist who is married to the ultraconservative former Republican senator from Texas, Phil Gramm. Born in Hawaii in 1945, she comes by her Republican and conservative leanings naturally. Her father was a vice president of a sugar company, her mother a librarian. She received her BA from Wellesley in 1966 and her PhD from Northwestern in 1971. She met and married Gramm in the 1970s, when they both taught economics at Texas

A&M. George H. W. Bush appointed her in 1988 to the Commodity Futures Trading Commission. When she left the commission in 1993, she joined the board of Enron, where she served on the Audit and Compliance Committee, helped approve financial statements, and acted as the liaison to the company's corrupt auditors, Arthur Andersen. When Enron collapsed, destroying the pension funds and jobs of tens of thousands of employees, she became chairman of regulatory studies for the Mercatus Center, a conservative think tank affiliated with George Mason University in Virginia. Ironically, she is heavily involved in the debate over proper "corporate governance."

Perhaps the most intriguing of the Korean directors is Masayoshi Son, for his story reveals the difficulties Korean Americans have faced as a result of powerful discrimination from the Japanese. Son is a second-generation Korean, but he was born in 1957 in Japan, where he encountered the harsh treatment Koreans typically received in Japan; for example, his family had been forced to adopt a Japanese name (Yasumoto) in order to become Japanese citizens. Then, as a *Washington Post* profile put it, "Son moved to the United States at age 16, fleeing to San Francisco to live with family friends and escape the racism directed against Koreans in Japan."[29] In California, Son began using his Korean name, finished high school, and then graduated from Berkeley in 1980. Hooked on computers, he accumulated more than a million dollars by inventing an electronic multilingual pocket translator and selling it to Sharp Corporation and by importing arcade games from Japan and installing them around the Berkeley campus. He then returned to Japan to start his own business, Softbank, a software distributor that has been successful enough to make Son one of Japan's wealthiest businessmen. By the late 1980s, he was still not a Japanese citizen, but he had his Japanese fiancée change her name to Son, married her and then legally assumed her last name, all so that he could become a Japanese citizen without having to adopt a Japanese surname as is typically required of Koreans who become Japanese citizens.

There is one Korean-born Asian on the current *Forbes* list of the richest Americans, James J. Kim. Born in 1936, Kim came to the United States to study economics at the Wharton School of Business at the University of Pennsylvania. He taught at Villanova for six years before he founded Amkor, a manufacturer of microchips for companies like Motorola and Toshiba. Amkor went public in 1998 and is currently a $1.64 billion company with more than twenty thousand employees. Kim also applied his entrepreneurial skills to Electron Boutiques, a video games company with more than eight hundred stores.

Two Filipino Americans appear on the list, both women. One of them, Marissa Peterson, made it without the advantages of an economically privileged background. She won a scholarship to come to the United States to attend the Kettering Institute, formerly called General Motors Institute, from which she earned a BA before going on to earn an MBA from Harvard. (Kettering is the same school that African American CEO Stanley O'Neal attended, and he, too, went on to earn an MBA from Harvard.) She worked for GM, then became a management consultant at Booz, Allen, and, in 1988, she became a senior executive at Sun Microsystems (she retired in June 2005).

Asian Indians

As we have indicated, another group of directors appears on the 2004 list of directors, some of whom are Indian Americans, some of whom are Indians, and (even more so than for those we have discussed so far in this chapter) it is often difficult to tell what their citizenship is. We include mention of them here, for they do in fact add to the diversity in the American corporate elite, but they are clearly a subgroup that is separate from the other Asians considered in this chapter. Indians were not included in the two lists we drew on for the first edition of this book; nor do various studies of Asian Pacific Americans include Indians—for example, the Committee of 100's Asian Pacific American (APA) Corporate Board Report Card. We think it is important, however, to acknowledge that Asian Indians are rising through the corporate ranks.

Most of the Asian Indian men and women on the list were born in India to educated and well-off families, did their undergraduate work in India, and then came to the United States to earn master's and in some cases doctoral degrees. They then worked for multinational corporations, often in the United States, but sometimes elsewhere, and some have risen to positions that are at, or near, the tops of major companies. Many have lived much of their adult lives in America. For example, Ramani Ayer, who received a BA from the Indian Institute of Technology in Bombay and then earned an MS and PhD from Drexel University, has been the CEO of the Hartford Financial Services Group since 1997 (#88 on the *Fortune* 2005 list). Rakesh Gangwell, who also received his BA from the Indian Institute of Technology before earning an MBA from the Wharton School, became the CEO of USAirways (#295 in 2005) in 1998 (he left USAirways in 2001). Rajiv Gupta, whose BA is also from the Indian Institute of Technology and who has an MS from Cornell and an MBA from Drexel, became CEO of Rohm and Haas (#287 in 2005) in 1999.

All but one of the Asian Indians on our list are men, but the one woman, Indra Nooyi, generated more publicity than any of the men by pointed remarks she made at a graduation ceremony in 2005. Born in Madras, Nooyi spent her first twenty-three years in India. She received a BA from Madras Christian College and then an MBA from the India Institute of Management in Calcutta before she came to the United States to study at the Yale School of Management. As a Brahmin from a traditional family, she was surprised that her parents allowed her to study in the United States. As she says, "It was unheard of for a good, conservative, south Indian Brahmin girl to do this. It would make her an absolutely unmarriageable commodity." After she received her master's degree from Yale, she worked for Boston Consulting Group, then Motorola, and then, beginning in 1994, PepsiCo, where she rose through the ranks to become president and chief financial officer. She was ranked #4 on *Fortune* magazine's 2005 "50 Most Powerful Women in Business" list, and many assumed she would emerge as another of the handful of women who head *Fortune* 500 companies (PepsiCo was #61 in 2005).

She still might, but she may have hurt her chances by the candid remarks she made as commencement speaker at the May 2005 Columbia University Business School graduation. She compared the various continents to the fingers on a hand, noting that each was different, but all had to work together. After comparing Africa to the little finger ("when our little finger hurts, it affects the whole hand"), Asia to the thumb ("strong, powerful"), Europe to the index finger ("the pointer finger . . . pointed the way for Western civilization"), and South America to the ring finger ("symbolizes love and commitment"), she turned to North America, "the long, middle finger." She made a few positive comments about the strength and importance of the middle finger but then stressed that "the middle finger can convey a negative message and get us in trouble. You know what I'm talking about." "Unfortunately," she went on to say, "I think this is how the rest of the world looks at the U.S. right now. Not as part of the hand—giving strength and purpose to the rest of the fingers—but instead, scratching our nose and sending a far different signal." After giving some specific examples of culturally insensitive behavior on the part of American business executives while visiting other countries, she said to the graduates, "It pains me greatly that this view of America persists. Although I'm a daughter of India, I'm an American businesswoman. My family and I are citizens of this great country." She then encouraged the MBA graduates to be aware of the global effects of their actions when they became business leaders.

Firestorm city. The graduates and their families did not like the analogy, they did not like being told that Americans are perceived negatively, and they lit up the phone lines to Columbia University and PepsiCo. The blogosphere was hopping. The reaction was not unlike the furor that ensued when one of the members of the Dixie Chicks criticized George W. Bush and his decision to go to war in Iraq (though the furor was not orchestrated by Clear Channel Communications, a huge and conservative media conglomerate, as was the case with the protests against the Dixie Chicks). Over the next few days, Nooyi issued a clarification, and when that did not appease her critics, she offered her "sincere apologies." It is not clear if this will impede her rise through the corporate ranks at Pepsi, but it is unlikely to help.[30]

The Corporate Pipeline

There is little systematic information available on Asian American executives below the top echelon of the corporate community. At a very general level, however, it is likely that Asian Americans are underrepresented in management positions, even though they have excellent educational backgrounds and are well represented in the professional ranks of corporations. This has even been the case in Silicon Valley, where one study revealed that only 22 percent of the Asian American professionals became officers and managers, as compared to 35 percent of the white professionals.[31]

To explore possible increases in Asian American representation in higher management, we studied distinctive Chinese, Japanese, and Korean names listed in *Poor's* for 1965, 1975, 1985, 1995, and 2004, paralleling our use of distinctive Jewish and Hispanic names in earlier chapters (we did not include distinctive Asian Indian names for this study). In the case of Chinese Americans, we used the names Wang, Wong, Woo, and Wu, which account for 13 percent of the 2,801 Chinese American entries from China, Taiwan, and Hong Kong in *Who's Who Among Asian Americans*, giving us a multiplier of 7.7 to obtain estimates of the total number of Chinese Americans in *Poor's* for those years.[32] For Japanese Americans, we used any name beginning with seven distinctive prefixes: Haya, Kawa, Koba, Miya, Naka, Taku, and Yama. These names account for 17 percent of the 882 Japanese Americans in *Who's Who Among Asian Americans*, giving us a multiplier of 5.9. Finally, we sampled Korean Americans with the distinctive surname Kim, which accounts for fully 25 percent of all Koreans and Korean Americans at all levels of the social ladder.[33]

Table 6.1 presents our estimated total number of Chinese Americans, Japanese Americans, and Korean Americans in *Poor's* for 1965, 1975, 1985, 1995, and 2004. To provide a further comparison, we include our earlier estimates for Hispanic Americans for the same years. As we noted in the previous chapter, some of the raw figures underestimate the rise in the rate of participation because of fluctuations in the number of names in *Poor's* over time. We therefore include for the first three groups in the table a percentage in-

Table 6.1.   Estimated Number of Asian Americans and Hispanics in Higher Management, 1965–2004

Group	1965	1975	1985	1995	2004	2004N/1965N
Hispanics	78	131	235	374	726	9.9
Japanese Americans	24	65	88	112	177	7.9
Chinese Americans	15	69	92	177	346	24.6
Korean Americans	0	0	20	20	68	
Estimated Poor's Total	75,639	73,649	76,449	68,423	70,823	

crease from 1965 to 2004, adjusted for the decline in total entries. Because there were no Kims in *Poor's* until 1985, no such adjustment was possible for Korean Americans.

As might be expected on the basis of group size, there were more than twice as many Hispanic Americans in *Poor's* than the largest Asian American group, Chinese Americans (726 as opposed to 346). But the Chinese American group grew the most, by a factor of 24.6 (Hispanics increased by a factor of 9.9 and Japanese Americans by a factor of 7.9). Still, taken together, the three Asian American groups collectively account for less than 1 percent of the total number of executives, officers, and directors listed in *Poor's* in 2004. There seem to be no more Asians in the pipeline than there are current directors of S&P 1500 companies.

The positions held by those Asian Americans listed in *Poor's* below the level of director, president, or CEO were primarily confined to finance, accounting, and research. They tended to be in financial or technical firms, especially electronics. This finding is consistent with the fact that 20 to 40 percent of the engineers and technical staff in some major companies in the electronics industry are Asian American.[34]

Our findings on Asian directors and those in the pipeline allow us to draw a few conclusions. First, given the relatively small numbers of Asian Americans who have been in the United States long enough to arrive at the top, as well as the negative stereotypes they face, their record of corporate involvement is impressive. As we noted at the outset of the chapter, subtle forms of discrimination have kept all but a few Asian immigrants from making it to the very top. But a considerable number, particularly those who entered American society at its middle or higher levels thanks to wealth or educational credentials or who have acquired a good education since coming to the United States, have done well.

Some have worked their way up through the ranks. Still other directors come from foundations, law firms, and academic institutions, common routes to the top for directors of all social backgrounds. But the most frequent pathway for Asians to take to become directors of *Fortune*-level companies is that of the immigrant entrepreneur, that is, to have started their own businesses or to have worked in businesses started by their parents or grandparents.

There are scores of immigrant entrepreneurs in the computer and electronic industries. At one point, it was estimated that three hundred of the nine hundred high-technology firms in Santa Clara County, California, or Silicon Valley, were headed by Asian American immigrants. As we have indicated, many emigrated with a strong educational background, acquired further education in the United States, and then worked for established firms before venturing out on their own.[35]

THE POLITICAL ELITE

Patsy Takemoto Mink, named assistant secretary of state for ocean and international, environmental, and scientific affairs by Jimmy Carter in 1977, was the first Asian American whose executive-branch appointment required Senate confirmation. Mink was born in 1927 into modest circumstances in Hawaii, where her father was a civil engineer. After graduating from high school as class valedictorian, she earned a bachelor's at the University of Hawaii and a law degree at the University of Chicago, where she met and married John Mink, a graduate student of Eastern European extraction studying geophysics. In spite of her excellent educational credentials, she had difficulty obtaining a legal position in either Chicago or Honolulu, so she finally started her own practice in Honolulu.

Mink was elected president of the Young Democrats in Honolulu in 1954. In 1957, she was elected to the state legislature, where she sponsored a law mandating equal pay for equal work. In 1965, she became the first woman from a minority background to be elected to Congress. After serving six terms in the House, she failed in a bid for the Senate and, at that point, received her State Department appointment. Mink left the State Department in 1978 to serve three consecutive terms as the national president of Americans for Democratic Action. In 1983, she was elected to the Honolulu City Council, and in 1990, she returned to the House of Representatives, where she served until 2002 (when she died of pneumonia in late September 2002, she was heavily favored to win reelection).[36]

It was not until 2000, however, that there was an Asian American in a presidential cabinet. In the final months of his second term, President Clinton nominated Norman Y. Mineta, a Japanese American, to be secretary of commerce. After the Supreme Court finally settled the 2000 election, George W. Bush named Mineta to be secretary of transportation. In addition, as we noted in the chapter on women, Bush named Elaine Chao to be his secretary of labor.

Mineta, born in 1932, was ten years old when he and his family were taken from their home in California to an internment camp in Wyoming. After graduating from Berkeley, he joined the army, where he served as an intelligence officer in Korea and Japan. He returned home to San Jose, California, where he worked in his father's insurance agency until he became active in politics, rising from city council, to mayor, to the U.S. Congress, in which he served from 1976 to 1995. While in the House, he helped to pass legislation that granted $20,000 to every Japanese American who had been interned during World War II. He resigned from the Congress in 1995 with a year to go in his term to become a senior vice president at Lockheed Martin (a decision that made many of his Democratic colleagues and constituents unhappy, especially when a Republican was chosen in a special election as his replacement). After five years in the corporate world, he joined Clinton's cabinet in 2000.[37]

As we explain in chapter 3, Elaine Chao, a Chinese American, was born in Taiwan and came to the United States when she was eight. Hers is a classic Chinese American success story: her parents were well-educated and well-connected, and after leaving China and then Hong Kong, her hard-working father came to the United States and built a thriving international shipping and trading business. Chao received a BA from Mt. Holyoke and an MBA from Harvard. She became an investment banker with Citicorp from 1979 to 1983 and then spent 1983 and 1984 in Washington, D.C., as a White House Fellow during Reagan's first term. She then took a job as a vice president for syndications at the Bank of America and, while working for the bank in California, became more involved in Republican politics, chairing a national committee of Asian Americans for George H. W. Bush and Dan Quayle in 1988. This earned her appointments as deputy administrator of the Maritime Administration and later as deputy secretary of the Department of Transportation before she became the director of the Peace Corps, a position she held for less than a year, and then, from 1992 to 1996, the president of the United Way of America (and a director at Dole Foods). In 1993, she married Kentucky senator Mitch McConnell, a conservative Republican who is best known for his opposition to campaign finance reform. Prior to her appointment to the cabinet, she had become an expert on philanthropy at the Heritage Foundation, a right-wing think tank.[38]

ASIAN AMERICANS IN THE MILITARY ELITE

In spite of the aspersions cast upon their patriotism and their bitter internment experience, Japanese Americans volunteered for service in World War II and fought courageously throughout Europe. Two future Democratic senators from Hawaii, Daniel Inouye and Spark Matsunaga, both decorated for bravery on the field of battle, used veterans organizations in Hawaii as their political base in winning election. Japanese Americans also served in important roles as intelligence officers and interrogators of prisoners in the war with Japan. Nonetheless, the military has never been an avenue of mobility for Japanese Americans, and none had reached the highest levels of the military elite until Eric K. Shinseki became army chief of staff (and, thus, a member of the Joint Chiefs of Staff).

Shinseki, as we noted earlier in this chapter, grew up in Hawaii and then attended the U.S. Military Academy. During his thirty-eight-year career in the army, he won two Purple Hearts for life-threatening injuries in Vietnam, commanded NATO soldiers in Germany and in Bosnia-Herzegovina, and, as chief of staff, spent four years on the Joint Chiefs of Staff.

Shinseki's years on the Joint Chiefs of Staff were marked by disagreements with the civilian leadership in the Pentagon, especially George W. Bush's secretary of defense, Donald Rumsfeld. Because Shinseki had already challenged Rumsfeld on earlier decisions (for example, he continued to speak out for the Crusader artillery system even after Rumsfeld canceled it), Rumsfeld was particularly annoyed when Shinseki and other military men publicly differed with his confident assertion that the United States needed no additional troops to stabilize Iraq after the initial invasion. In fact, Shinseki drew rebukes from Rumsfeld and other administration officials when he told a congressional committee that the United States would need as many as two hundred thousand troops as a peacekeeping force in Iraq. In a speech that Shinseki gave at his retirement ceremony in June 2003, he did not mention Rumsfeld by name (he did not have to) as he warned against arrogance: "You can certainly command without that sense of commitment, but you cannot lead without it. Without leadership, command is a hollow experience, a vacuum often filled with mistrust and arrogance."[39]

Shinseki is now retired, as are six other Asians who had achieved general officer rank.[40] As of September 2004, there were six generals of Asian background in active service, five in the army and one in the air force (there have been no admirals). Among them were two Filipino immigrants.

Edward Soriano was the first Filipino general in the U.S. Army. Soriano was born in a province about one hundred miles north of Manila. When he was seven, his father, who was in the Filipino military, was captured by Communist troops invading Guam (this was during the Korean War). Soriano's mother took Edward and his sister back to the Philippines. When his father was released three years later, the family moved to Salinas, California. Soriano graduated from Salinas High School and from San Jose State, then joined the army. During his army career, Soriano has commanded units in North Carolina, Washington, Georgia, New York, Texas, Korea, and Germany. Along the way, he earned a master's degree in public administration from the University of Missouri.

The other Filipino general is Antonio Taguba. Taguba was born in Manila, and his family moved to Hawaii when he was ten. After graduating from Leilehua High School and from Idaho State University, he, too, joined the army and, like Soriano, followed in the footsteps of his father, Tomas, a career military man (Tomas was captured and tortured by the Japanese when they invaded the Philippines in 1941). Taguba rose through the ranks, accumulating three master's degrees as he did so, emerging as an acting director of the army staff during the Iraq war. He was appointed to inquire into the activities of the police brigade at the Abu Ghraib prison. The report that he issued chronicled a long list of "sadistic, blatant and wanton criminal abuses," including "egregious acts and abuses of international law." Seymour Hersh, in a *New Yorker* article, referred to Taguba's report as "devastating" and praised Taguba for "fearlessly" taking issue with orders that were given at the prison by various people in charge, including three-star general Ricardo Sanchez. A retired army major general interviewed by Hersh explained that Taguba's report flew in the face of pressures from the Pentagon: "He's not regarded as a hero in some circles of the Pentagon. He's the guy who blew the whistle, and the Army will pay the price for his integrity. The leadership does not like to have people make bad news in public."[41]

This handful of Asian American generals, however, represents a very small percentage of the total number of those with general officer rank in the United States military (less than 1 percent). There has been an increase in the number of Asians at the three service academies: 4 percent of the entering class of 2007 at the Naval Academy, 7.4 percent of the entering class of 2008 at West Point, and 6 percent of the entering classes of 2005 through 2009 at the Air Force Academy were of Asian background.[42] Despite the reputation of the armed forces as the most diversified institution in America and the recent increase in the number of students at the three service academies, there is little evidence that the military represents a likely route to the power elite for Asian Americans. As one writer put it, "Asian Pacific Americans are at the bottom of the totem pole in the military ranks."[43]

ASIAN AMERICANS IN CONGRESS

Five Asian Americans have been elected to the Senate, four from Hawaii and one from California. Ten have been elected to the House, four from Hawaii, five from California, and one from Oregon. Three of the four House members from Hawaii went on to be senators, so the total number of Asian Americans elected to Congress is twelve.

Asian American elected officials tend to be from more modest social and educational backgrounds than Asian American members of the corporate world or appointed government officials. Although the first Asian American elected to the U.S. Senate, Hiram Fong of Hawaii, a Chinese American, became a millionaire, his father had been an indentured servant on a sugar plantation and his mother a maid. Fong (who changed his name early in his adult life from Yau Leong to Hiram) earned a BA at the University of Hawaii in 1930 and an LLB at Harvard Law School in 1935, then returned to Hawaii to begin his political career. He won his first political race in 1938 for a seat in the Territorial House of Representatives. By 1959, when Hawaii entered the Union as the fiftieth state and Fong won one of the two Senate seats, he had amassed a fortune.[44] Daniel Inouye, a Japanese American born in Honolulu in 1924, served in the House for four years and, in 1963, became the first Asian American Democrat elected to the Senate. His father was a file clerk. Following his service in World War II, where he lost his arm in the fighting in Italy, Inouye earned a bachelor's from the University of Hawaii and a law degree from George Washington University, then entered the political arena, where he has been ever since.

Spark Matsunaga, from a poor immigrant Japanese family, worked many different jobs as a teenager, then graduated from the University of Hawaii in 1941 and served in World War II. After the war, he used the GI Bill to earn a law degree at Harvard and returned to Hawaii to serve as a Honolulu prosecutor and involve himself in Democratic Party politics. He won a seat in the House in 1962 and defeated Hiram Fong in 1976 to join Inouye in the Senate. When Matsunaga died in 1990, Daniel Akaka, of Hawaiian and Chinese heritage, won his seat. Akaka, whose father had a third-grade education and worked in a machine shop, went to the University of Hawaii on the GI Bill, earning his BA in education, and worked as a teacher, principal, and program specialist for the state's Department of Education before winning a seat in the House in 1976 with 80 percent of the vote. He became the first native Hawaiian in Congress (native Hawaiians, who constitute 20 percent of the population, are defined as those with indigenous ancestors who lived in the islands before the U.S. Marines toppled the monarchy in 1893).[45]

The fifth Asian American senator, and the only one from a mainland state, would have to be classified as atypical whatever his social or ethnic background, and he was not born in the United States. S. I. Hayakawa, a one-term Republican senator from California from 1975 to 1981, was born in 1906 in Canada, where his well-to-do Japanese parents had an import-export business. Hayakawa completed his BA and MA in Canada, then came to the United States to earn a PhD in English and American literature at the University of Wisconsin in 1953. He somehow developed a fascination with pseudoscientific claims about "general semantics," and in 1949, he wrote a best-selling popular book, *Language in Thought and Action.* Hayakawa taught at San Francisco State University starting in 1955 and became a vice president there in 1968. His confrontational stance toward antiwar and civil rights protesters made him a conservative celebrity. His theatrics led to his elevation to the presidency of the campus. He switched his registration from Democratic to Republican and won his Senate seat in 1974, receiving little support from Japanese American voters. He was an abysmal failure as a legislator, falling asleep at inopportune moments, making inappropriate remarks, and generally ignoring the details of his position. Voters rejected him for a Democrat in 1980, despite the general Republican sweep that year.

Although generalizations are premature at this point, it is noteworthy that the only Chinese American senator, Hiram Fong, was a well-to-do, conservative Republican, whereas the senator of mixed heritage, Daniel Akaka, and the two Japanese American senators from Hawaii were moderate-to-liberal Democrats. Hayakawa blurs the picture somewhat because he became a Republican in the 1970s, but he was also a Japanese Canadian with a very atypical personality and career.

Ten Asian Americans and two Asian Indians (one in the 1950s and one more recently) have been elected to the House. In addition to Inouye, Matsunaga, and Akaka, each of whom became a senator after serving in the House, seven other Asian Americans have served there: Patsy Mink (1966–1977 and 1991–2002), Norman Mineta (1976–1995), Robert Matsui (1978–2005), Jay Kim (1993–1998), David Wu (1999–present), Michael Honda (2000–present), and Doris Matsui, the widow of Robert Matsui (2005–present). Nine of the ten have been Democrats; four have been from Hawaii, five from California, and one from Oregon; and seven have been Japanese Americans (Inouye, Matsunaga, Mink, Akaka, Mineta, and both Matsuis). All seven of the Japanese Americans either came from low-income circumstances or had parents who did.

The Republican, Jay Kim, who founded his own engineering firm in Southern California, is of Korean ancestry. After being convicted of what prosecutors called the largest case of campaign violations in U.S. history, Kim became the first member of Congress to wear a court-ordered electronic monitoring bracelet on the House floor.[46]

David Wu, elected to the House from Oregon, is the first Chinese American to serve in the House. Born in Taiwan in 1955, he spent his first six years separated from his father, a scientist who had emigrated to the United States (his mother was also a scientist). He and his mother were only able to join his father in New York after immigration laws were changed in the early 1960s during John F. Kennedy's presidency. After a few years in New York, the family moved to Westminster, California. Wu was the valedictorian of a class of seven hundred students at Westminster High School and then graduated from Stanford in 1977. He started medical school at Harvard but changed his mind and went to Yale for a law degree (he told one interviewer, "When I was being sworn into Congress, it was the proudest moment of my life. But I recall thinking, 'Do my parents still wish I had finished medical school?'").

Despite his accomplishments and his status, Wu, like other Asian Americans, encounters stereotypes, often in unexpected places. In May 2001, more than two years after he became a member of the House, Wu tried to enter the

Energy Department, where he was scheduled to give a speech in celebration of Asian Pacific American Heritage Month. The guards refused to let him in the building, asking him and his aide, who was also an Asian American, if they were Americans. The guards refused to accept his congressional identification. After about fifteen minutes, Wu and his aide persuaded them to get a supervisor, things were worked out, and Wu was able to give his speech.[47]

As we mentioned earlier in the chapter, an Asian Indian was elected to the House in 2004. A Republican from Louisiana, Bobby Jindal, the son of immigrant parents from India, became the second Asian Indian elected to the House (the other, Dalip Singh Saund, born in India in 1899, served as a Democrat from California from 1957 to 1962). Jindal was born in Baton Rouge. As a small child, he informed his parents that he was going to be called "Bobby" rather than his given name, Piyush. In his teens, he converted to Catholicism. He graduated from Brown in 1991 and won a Rhodes Scholarship, receiving a master's from Oxford in 1994. He worked as a management consultant at McKinsey & Company for a year and a half and then was asked by the Republican Louisiana governor to run the state's Department of Health and Hospitals. At twenty-seven, he became the president of the state university system, and at twenty-nine he moved to Washington, D.C., when George W. Bush appointed him assistant secretary for the Department of Health and Human Services. Three years later, he ran for governor of Louisiana but lost a close race; the religious Right endorsed him, but most people of color voted against him because of his conservative views (almost one-third of the voters in Louisiana are African Americans). A year later, however, he ran for, and was elected to, the House. As one commentator put it, a Jindal win in Louisiana "may mean not that race no longer matters in Louisiana, but simply that . . . Asian-Americans now fall on the white side of the racial divide."[48]

CONCLUSION

The patterns among the subgroups encompassed by the term *Asian American* show cleavages similar to those found among Latinos. The wealthier and better-educated immigrants, in this case Chinese Americans, tend to be the corporate directors and appointees in Republican administrations. Immigrants coming to the United States from less privileged socioeconomic backgrounds, in this case Japanese Americans, are more likely to be elected officials. Japanese Americans, with their history of communal sharing to establish small farms and small businesses and with their common experience of arbitrary incarceration during World War II, are defenders of civil liberties who tend to be Democrats.

From the point of view of the power elite, successful Asian Americans have three main functions. First, they serve as "middlemen" in corporate management and in selling corporate products in low-income communities through small retail businesses. Second, they are "ambassadors" for their corporations to Asian countries and to Asian American consumers in the United States. Like some of the Latinos discussed in chapter 5, they add a further international dimension to the power elite. Third, they provide much-needed scientific and technical expertise in corporations, research institutes, engineering schools, and science departments.

We predict that Chinese Americans will become increasingly important members of the power elite. Not only are they growing in numbers, but they often arrive with strong educational credentials, considerable wealth, and conservative outlooks. They also have the ability to obtain loans from Chinese financiers in Hong Kong, Taiwan, and Singapore.[49] Japanese Americans, on the other hand, are likely to stay about where they are now as fourth- and even fifth-generation Americans. The Japanese American community is not being infused with large numbers of new immigrants. Nor does it have strong ties to banks or corporations in Japan that might be a source of loans. Although Japanese Americans have been very successful, especially in obtaining excellent educational credentials, few have amassed large amounts of capital, so they are likely to turn to the professions even more in the future. They are also outmarrying at a very high rate, as we document in chapter 8, and they have a very low birthrate.[50]

Whatever the future may bring, the economic and political achievements of Chinese and Japanese Americans are such that old-line members of the power elite can claim that their circles are now diversified in terms of Asian Americans as well as women, African Americans, and Hispanic Americans.

But does the acceptance of diversity in the power elite extend to differences in sexual orientation on the part of either men or women?

NOTES

1. Jim Henry, "Shirley Young," *Notable Asian Americans* (New York: Gale Research, 1995), 437–38.

2. Gabriella Stern, "GM Executive's Ties to Native Country Help Auto Maker Clinch Deal in China," *Wall Street Journal,* November 2, 1995.

3. Nancy Moore, "Phyllis Jean Takisaki Campbell," *Notable Asian Americans,* 24. For a detailed study of the Japanese American experience that demonstrates just how typical Campbell's childhood was, see Edna Bonacich and John Modell, *The Economic Basis of Ethnic Solidarity: Small Business in the Japanese American Community* (Berkeley: University of California Press, 1980).

4. Chang-Lin Tien, "A View from Berkeley," *New York Times,* Education Life section, March 31, 1996, 30.

5. For an excellent account of efforts to create pan-Asian institutions, see Yen Le Espiritu, *Asian American Panethnicity* (Philadelphia: Temple University Press, 1992). Espiritu begins her account by noting that she is "a Vietnamese American who is married to a Filipino American" (xi).

6. This is true for Asian Americans in general. In "The Committee of 100's Asian Pacific American (APA) Corporate Report Card," updated in April 2004, at www.committee100.org, the authors note that 47 percent of APAs have college degrees compared to 27 percent for all American adults. See, also, Deborah Woo, "The Glass Ceiling and Asian Americans," Glass Ceiling Commission, U.S. Department of Labor, Washington, D.C., 1994.

7. Barry A. Kosmin and Seymour P. Lachman, *One Nation under God: Religion in Contemporary Society* (New York: Harmony, 1993), 148. The overall figure is inflated somewhat by the fact that virtually all Filipino Americans are Christians, but it is the low figure for Buddhism that makes our general point. Most Asian Americans do not maintain a religious tradition that conflicts with the overwhelming predominance of Christianity in the United States. In the United States, 86 percent of all people are Christian, 2 percent are Jewish, 8 percent are secular, 2 percent "decline to state," and 1.5 percent are "other."

8. Benjamin Pimentel, "Asian Americans' Awkward Status," *San Francisco Chronicle,* August 22, 1995.

9. See, for example, Ivan Light and Edna Bonacich, *Immigrant Entrepreneurs: Koreans in Los Angeles, 1965–1982* (Berkeley: University of California Press, 1988).

10. For comprehensive reviews and analyses of the evidence concerning discrimination against Asian Americans in corporate, government, and academic settings, see Woo, "Glass Ceiling and Asian Americans," and Bill Ong Hing and Ronald Lee, eds., *Reframing the Immigration Debate: A Public Policy Report* (Los Angeles: LEAP Asian Pacific American Public Policy Institute and UCLA Asian American Studies Center, 1996). For an earlier summary of the situation facing Asian Americans and other minorities in the corporate world, as well as essays by minority executives on their experience, see Donna Thompson and Nancy DiTomaso, eds., *Ensuring Minority Success in Corporate Management* (New York: Plenum, 1988).

11. As with Latinos, we are aware that there are some people not on our list who should be, and, perhaps, there are some on our list who are not Asian Americans. Our three sources all used slightly different methods to identify these men and women as Asians, but for each of those we include, we have found supporting evidence for the fact that they are, indeed, Asian Americans. Moreover, the percentages estimated on the various lists correspond with other estimates in which we have confidence. For example, the estimate of 1 percent that derives from the 128 seats held by Asians on the IRRC S&P 1500 list of 13,820 directors is exactly the same as the estimate made by the Committee of 100 in their Corporate Report Card for 2004 for Asians on *Fortune* 500 boards. See "The Committee of 100's Asian Pacific American (APA) Corporate Report Card," at www.committee100.org. Similarly, in a study of *Fortune* 100 directors in 2004 by the Alliance for Board Diversity (an alliance consisting of three

organizations, Catalyst, the Executive Leadership Council, and the Hispanic Association of Corporate Responsibility), the researchers found that 12 of the 1,195 seats, or 1.00 percent, were held by Asian Americans (alternatively, 11 of the 995 people, or 1.1 percent, were Asian Americans). See "Women and Minorities on Fortune 100 Boards," May 17, 2005, Executive Leadership Council, at http://216.15.177.66/ABDRelease.html.

12. "Andrea Jung," *Current Biography* (2000): 333–35; Dana Canedy, "Opportunity Re-Knocks at Avon," *New York Times*, November 5, 1999, C1 and C18.

13. Damon Darlin, "Still Running Scared (Watson Pharmaceuticals Inc.)," *Forbes*, September 26, 1994, 127ff.

14. Min Zhou and Rebecca Y. Kim, "Formation, Consolidation and Diversification of the Ethnic Elite: The Case of the Chinese Immigrant Community in the United States," *Journal of International Migration and Integration* 2, no. 2 (Spring 2001): 242.

15. In 1993, the Tang family gave $4.7 million to MIT. See Carla Lane, "Tang Family Gives $4.7M to MIT," *MIT Tech Talk* 37, no. 20 (January 27, 1993).

16. Leslie Wayne, "Together Apart," *New York Times Magazine,* March 27, 1988, 38.

17. Kelli Abe Trifonovitch, "The American President: Hawaii's Third Largest Bank Has a New Leader: Local Girl Connie Lau," *HawaiiBusiness*, February 2002, cover story.

18. Barb Cole-Gomolski, "Dutch Firm Buys Wang in IT Services Deal; Merged Entity Has Big Europe Presence," *Computerworld*, May 10, 1999, 29.

19. Michael Quint, "Moving Up at Citicorp," *New York Times,* January 19, 1992; "Chia, Citicorp's Head of Consumer Banking, Made a Vice Chairman," *Wall Street Journal,* January 20, 1994.

20. "Board Members Become Pariahs," *Business Week*, April 29, 2002, 14.

21. Maya Roney, "The Best Bosses for the Buck: It Paid to Cheat," *Forbes* (online), May 9, 2005, at www.forbes.com/free_forbes/2005/0509/138.html. See, also, Alex Berenson, "A Patriarch's Shadow at Troubled Software Maker," *New York Times*, April 23, 2004, C1.

22. Arik Hesseldahl, "Pinpoint Production," *Electronics Supply & Manufacturing* (online), December 1, 2004, at www.my-esm.com/printableArticle.jhtml?articleID=54201264.

23. Terril Yue Jones, "Gateway Puts Focus on Its Core PC Business," *Detroit News* (online), September 14, 2004, at www.detnews.com/2004/technology/0409/08/technology-263325.htm. See, also, Arlene Weintraub, "Powering Up at eMachines: How Did Wayne Inouye Turn a Reviled, Money-Losing PC Maker into a Winner?" *Business Week* (online), *Businessweek.com*, at www.businessweek.com/magazine/content/03_46/b3858106_mz063.htm.

24. This information comes from Barnaby J. Feder, "Chicago Names Professor as Business School Dean," *New York Times*, March 30, 1993, D4, and from Robert S. Hamada, interviewed by telephone by Richard Zweigenhaft, August 9, 2005.

25. Richard Halloran, *My Name is...Shinseki and I am a Soldier* (Honolulu, HI: Hawaii Army Museum Society, 2004), 9, and Gregg K. Kakesako, "Army Museum Honors Shinseki," *Honolulu Star-Bulletin* (online), March 28, 2004, *Starbulletin.com*, at http://starbulletin.com/2005/01/13/news/story2.html. See C. Wright Mills, *The Power Elite* (Oxford University Press, 1956), 215. The *New York Times* points out that

Shinseki is part of a particularly large current wave of ex-generals joining corporate boards as the Department of Defense and the Department of Homeland Security have billions of contracts to dole out. See Leslie Wayne, "An Office and a Gentleman," *New York Times*, June 19, 2005, section 3, 1, 11. As we note in ch. 4, in their extensive research on blacks in the military, Charles C. Moskos and John Sibley Butler found in *All That We Can Be: Black Leadership and Racial Integration the Army Way* (New York: Basic, 1996) that retired black generals were not asked onto boards as frequently as retired white generals (50). Shinseki's presence on the Honeywell board may reflect yet another example of the gap between blacks and the other groups we are studying.

26. Florangela Davila, "Uwajimaya Celebrates Its 'Dream' Store," *Seattle Union Record* (online), November 30, 2000, at www.unionrecord.com/biz/display.php? ID=422; Carol Tice, "Cash Registers Ring at Uwajimaya's New Grocery Store," *Puget Sound Business Journal* (online), June 14, 2002, at www.bizjournals.com/ seattle/stories/2002/06/17/focus4.html; Alex Fryer, "The Guiding Force at Landmark Store," *Seattle Times*, July 27, 2002, A1.

27. Bill Billiter, "Workers on Farm in Orange County Issued Illegal Hoes," *Los Angeles Times,* April 9, 1983; J. R. Moehringer, "Katsumasa Sakioka: Made Fortune in O.C. Real Estate," *Los Angeles Times,* November 1, 1995.

28. Damon Darlin, "Accessorizing the Dinner Table," *Forbes,* December 19, 1994, 288–90. See, also, Naomi Hirahara, *An American Son: The Story of George Aritani: Founder of Mikasa and Kenwood* (Los Angeles, CA: Japanese American National Museum, 2001).

29. Sandra Sugawara, "Masayoshi Son," *Washington Post*, May 9, 1999, H1.

30. "Indra Nooyi's Graduation Remarks," *Business Week* (online), May 20, 2005, at www.businessweek.com/bwdaily/dnflash/may2005/nf20050520_9852.htm. Joe Kovacs, "Pepsi President Likens U.S. to Middle Finger: Food Giant Now Doing Damage Control," *WorldNetDaily.com*, May 20, 2005, at www.worldnetdaily.com/ news/article.asp?ARTICLE_ID=44356.

31. Edward Jang-Woo Park, "Asians Matter: Asian American Entrepreneurs in the Silicon Valley High Technology Industry," in Hing and Lee, *Reframing the Immigration Debate,* 166–67. See Woo, "Glass Ceiling and Asian Americans," for further details. For a quantitative study using logit regression analysis to show that Asian American scientists and engineers are less likely than their white counterparts to be advanced to management positions, see Joyce Tang, "Glass Ceiling in Science and Engineering," *Journal of·Socio-Economics* 26, no. 4 (1997): 383–406. Tang's work shows that being native born or, in the case of immigrants, being a longtime resident of the United States does not improve one's odds of moving into a management role.

32. See ch. 5, "Latino CEOs and the Corporate Pipeline," for details on the generation and use of this multiplier.

33. Eui-Hang Shin and Eui-Young Yu, "Use of Surnames in Ethnic Research: The Case of Kims in the Korean-American Population," *Demography* 21, no. 3 (1984): 347–59.

34. Melanie Erasmus, "Immigrant Entrepreneurs in the High-Tech Industry," in Hing and Lee, *Reframing the Immigration Debate*, 180.

35. Park, "Asians Matter," 165–67.

36. Samuel R. Cacas, "Patsy Takemoto Mink," *Notable Asian Americans*, 261–62.

37. Marc Lacey, "First Asian-American Picked for Cabinet," *New York Times*, June 30, 2000, A15.

38. Christopher Marquis, "A Washington Veteran for Labor; a Tested Negotiator for Trade," *New York Times*, January 12, 2001; "Elaine L. Chao," *Current Biography* (2001): 84–86.

39. Thom Shanker, "Retiring Army Chief of Staff Warns against Arrogance," *New York Times*, June 12, 2003, A22.

40. The six retired generals are Lt. Gen. Allen K. Ono, Maj. Gen. William S. C. Chen, Maj. Gen. John L. Fugh, Maj. Gen. Theodore S. Kanamine, Brig. Gen. Paul Y. Chinen, and Brig. Gen. Frederick G. Wong. See Bert Eljera, "Army Appoints Its Second Fil-Am General," *Asian Week News* (online), August 1–7, 1997, at www.asianweek.com/080197/news.html. Both Gen. William Chen and Maj. Gen. John Fugh came from high-ranking families in China and acquired advanced degrees in engineering, law, or medicine. Fugh, for example, was judge advocate general of the army before he retired in 1993 to join a corporate law firm in Washington, D.C.

41. Seymour M. Hersh, "Chain of Command: How the Department of Defense Mishandled the Disaster at Abu Ghraib," *The New Yorker*, May 17, 2004, 37, 42, 43.

42. The data for the Naval Academy and West Point are drawn from their websites; the data for the Air Force Academy were provided by the school's public affairs office.

43. Eljera, "Army Appoints Its Second Fil-Am General."

44. "Hiram L. Fong, 97, Senator from Hawaii in 60's and 70's," *New York Times*, August 19, 2004, C13.

45. Lawrence Downes, "In Hawaii, a Chance to Heal, Long Delayed," *New York Times*, July 12, 2005, A22.

46. Lizette Alvarez, "Lawmaker Votes in Congress after Conviction for a Crime," *New York Times*, March 11, 1998, 12; Frances X. Clines, "Confined by Ankle Bracelet, in a Tight Race for Congress," *New York Times*, April 8, 1998.

47. Sam Chu Lin, "Congressman Warns against Stereotypes," *AsianWeek.com*, April 1, 1999; "The Freshman: David Wu," *A Magazine*, August 2, 1999; Al Kamen, "DOE Trips on Security Blanket," *Washington Post*, May 25, 2001, A37.

48. Adam Cohen, "A New Kind of Minority Is Challenging Louisiana's Racial Conventions," *New York Times*, September 12, 2003, A10.

49. Park, "Asians Matter," 167.

50. Norimitsu Onishi, "Japanese in America Looking beyond Past to Shape Future," *New York Times*, December 25, 1995.

Chapter Seven

Gay Men and Lesbians in the Power Elite

On Monday, January 24, 2005, Margaret Spellings, a longtime political adviser to George W. Bush, joined his cabinet as secretary of education. The next day she sent a chilling letter to the president of the Public Broadcasting System (PBS), warning him, "You can be assured that in the future the department will be more clear as to its expectations for any future programming that it funds."

And what led to this letter? She was outraged by an episode of "Postcards from Buster," an animated cartoon about a bunny who travels the United States with a digital camera and reports back on what he discovers about people of different regions of the country, different backgrounds, and different religions. In the offending episode, Buster traveled to Vermont where he learned about how to make maple sugar, and, along the way, encountered two lesbian couples. "Many parents," explained Spellings in the letter, "would not want their young children exposed to the lifestyles portrayed in the episode."[1]

George W. Bush won the election in 2004 in no small part because of the large turnout of conservative Christians, many of whom were motivated to go to the polls to support the constitutional amendment that Bush advocated, which would assure that marriages could only take place between a man and a woman. Bush's victory and Spellings' threat to PBS were thus signs of the times in that they revealed the widespread antagonism toward the very real gains gay men and lesbians have made in recent decades. In fact, another sign of the times was that in the same election that brought Bush back to the White House and Margaret Spellings to his cabinet, Lupe Valdez, a Democrat and a lesbian, was elected sheriff of Dallas County in Texas.[2]

It is apparent that doors have opened for gays and lesbians since Mills wrote *The Power Elite*, but fears and prejudices remain. Presumably, there have always been homosexuals in the power elite, but there is no way to know how many or who they were. The best research on this topic indicates that the prevalence of homosexuality is less than 5 percent of the population, although the estimates vary based on whether one is assessing behavior, desire, or identity.[3] What we do know is that, over the past few decades, many gays and lesbians have chosen to be public about their sexual orientation, and this openness and the accompanying political activism have contributed to changes in the lives of institutions as well as individuals. There are now openly gay men and women in almost all walks of life in America, but are there openly gay men and women in the power elite or Congress?

For the most part, the answer is no, but this depends on what one means by "open." People tend to assume that homosexuals are either "in the closet" or "out" (and thus "open"), but, in reality, there are many shades in between. One study of hundreds of gay men and women in the corporate world found that most of those who remained closeted had revealed their sexual orientation to some of their coworkers. Many told the researchers that although they were out at work, they still did not want their real names published.[4] So, there are gay men and women in the corporate world who are open about their homosexuality to certain colleagues, or even to most of their colleagues, but this information is not public in the sense that it is accessible to researchers trying to understand the extent to which the power elite has diversified.

Although the existence of a well-to-do and highly educated community of gay doctors, lawyers, entertainers, and business executives makes it possible in theory to determine who is and who is not gay in the power elite, our interest was not to "find" those who are homosexual but to explore whether or not people who happen to be homosexual and who have made it into the power elite are willing to be public about their homosexuality. So, by "openly homosexual," we really mean "publicly homosexual." And, of course, we were interested in determining the extent to which continuing prejudices and barriers prevent gay men and lesbians from rising to the top.

GAY MEN AND LESBIANS IN THE CORPORATE ELITE

There can be no doubt that the experiences of gay men or lesbians working for *Fortune* 500 companies these days are likely to be different from those of their counterparts in the 1950s. The larger culture has undergone dramatic changes in attitudes about sexuality in general, and so have many corporations.[5] Support groups for gay and lesbian employees have formed in many corporations, and according to the 2004 annual "State of the Workplace" report compiled by the Human Rights Campaign, fifty-one of the *Fortune* 500 companies included sexual orientation in their written antidiscrimination policies.[6]

More significantly (and not unrelated to the growing influence of gay employees' organizations), many companies have extended health benefits to the live-in partners of homosexual employees, a development that for many was unthinkable in the late 1980s.[7] Annette Friskopp and Sharon Silverstein conducted interviews between 1990 and 1994 for their study of gay and lesbian graduates of the Harvard Business School. They found that none of those interviewed in 1990 even mentioned the lack of domestic-partner benefits. When asked, they said that they did not think it was likely that such benefits would be provided in very many companies in the foreseeable future. But many of those interviewed in 1993 and 1994 raised this as an issue, and they were well aware that the number of companies providing such benefits had increased.[8] By 1995, not only had various West Coast companies already known for progressive corporate policies—Lotus, Apple Computer, and Levi Strauss, for example—added domestic-partner benefits, but even the Walt Disney Company, known throughout the years for its conservatism, had done so.[9] By the end of 2004, 216 of the *Fortune* 500 (43 percent) offered domestic-partner benefits for same-sex mates (a tenfold increase since 1995).[10]

In spite of these changes, considerable evidence demonstrates that gay men and lesbians continue to encounter prejudice and discrimination in the corporate world. Moreover, there is reason to believe that the higher one moves in the executive ranks, the less likely it is for homosexuality to be acceptable.

Two studies are especially relevant to our focus on gays in the corporate elite. The first, by James Woods, grew out of a doctoral dissertation for the Annenberg School of Communications at the University of Pennsylvania. In 1990, Woods traveled around the country interviewing seventy gay men who worked as professionals, many (but not all) in law firms and corporations. (His was a snowball sample, in which an initial group of friends and contacts put him in touch with others.) Woods concluded, "They learn to control and monitor outward appearances, to distort them when necessary. They learn to dodge. For many the result is a calculating, deliberate way of approaching social encounters. One can say . . . that they *manage* their sexual identities at work."[11]

Woods identified three groups of gay men in the corporate world, each employing a different coping strategy. The first group, which he called "counterfeiters," fabricate heterosexual identities, at times even marrying to mask their homosexuality. The second group, called "integrators," are known to be gay. And the third group, which he considered the largest and called "avoiders," do not lie or fabricate false identities; nor are they open about their sexual orientation. Instead, they remain somewhat aloof and hope the issue will not come up. In Woods' view, conditions had improved even since his own one-year stint in the corporate world (where he was a counterfeiter, and miserable) in 1985, before he enrolled in graduate school. Still, at the time that Woods wrote a book based on his dissertation, relatively few companies had made major changes. He expressed the hope that "because heterosexism is expensive for both employers and employees, market forces may ultimately achieve what appeals to fairness and civil rights will not."[12]

The second valuable study of particular interest to us is Friskopp and Silverstein's research on the experiences of gay and lesbian graduates of the Harvard Business School. These two graduates of the business school (where they were members of the Gay and Lesbian Student Association) mailed a survey to more than one hundred people who were on the mailing list of the Harvard Gay and Lesbian Alumni Association; sixty-seven were returned. They also interviewed more than one hundred people, including some who had indicated on their returned surveys that they were willing to be interviewed. The authors spoke with gay and lesbian professionals from every graduating class since the late 1960s and with "a number" (they do not say how many) from the 1940s, 1950s, and early 1960s. All had gone to Harvard, and most had worked in the corporate world.[13]

Of their many findings and suggestions for homosexual employees and employers, most relevant for our purposes is their conclusion that "discrimination in the form of a hostile atmosphere, corporate cowardice, and unequal benefits is rampant." As a result, they wrote, "the fear of the lavender ceiling looms large for many," especially at "conservative" *Fortune* 500 companies.[14] Citing the fear of discrimination as one reason gay and lesbian employees remain closeted, Friskopp and Silverstein wrote, "Those employed by America's most prominent conservative companies almost universally believed they would be discriminated against in some fashion if they were completely open about their gay identity in their current work environment. These professionals include those working for *Fortune* 500 manufacturers (both industrial and consumer products companies) and in construction, energy, real estate, transportation, investment banks, and utilities. To a lesser degree this fear is shared by those employed by large banks, insurance companies, pension funds, and major consulting firms."[15]

Woods' study, Friskopp and Silverstein's study, and other, smaller-scale studies indicate that the higher one rises in the corporate hierarchy, the more being open about one's homosexuality serves as an impediment to one's career. As Marny Hall concluded in her study of lesbians in the corporate world, "They could advance to a certain level but not beyond because they could not project the necessary corporate image."[16]

When we looked for openly homosexual men or women who hold senior executive positions on *Fortune*-level boards, we found only Allan Gilmour, and his story is elucidating. Gilmour decided to reveal his homosexuality in an interview in *The Advocate*, a magazine that addresses issues of relevance to the gay and lesbian communities, in December 1996, two years after he had retired from the Ford Motor Company, having worked there for thirty-five years. He had served as chief financial officer and as vice chairman of the board, and on two occasions, he was considered for, but not chosen as, CEO. The son of a Vermont cattle dealer, a graduate of both Harvard and the University of Michigan, and a lifelong conservative Republican, when he came out publicly, he was still on the boards of Prudential Insurance, Dow Chemical, Detroit Edison, U.S. West, and Whirlpool.

Gilmour made clear that he chose to wait until he was no longer working at Ford to reveal his homosexuality. In fact, he noted, he did not even take phone calls at work from his thirty-four-year-old partner until a few months before he retired. As Gilmour put it, "I perceived the risk of coming out in the business world as fairly substantial."[17]

It was, of course, of interest to many people that Gilmour chose to go public and not insignificant that he waited until he retired to do so. So, too, was it noteworthy that none of the chairmen of the boards on which Gilmour sat asked him to leave those boards. He contacted each one after the story broke, and, he said, "I was told uniformly that it makes no difference." He spent the next few years actively involved in fund-raising for gay and lesbian causes, including overseeing an investment fund that supported gay and lesbian groups.

Then, in June 2002, after Ford had lost $5.5 billion the previous year, and with increasing concerns on Wall Street about the company, including its empty product pipeline and demoralized employees, Bill Ford, forty-five years old, who had become CEO the previous October, rehired Gilmour, at the time sixty-seven, to serve once again as chief financial officer to try to help turn the company around. As one Ford executive put it, "Gilmour's return is like Yoda coming back to Earth."

When Gilmour was rehired, Ford's stock shot up, and, according to *Newsweek*, "previously bearish Wall Street analysts issued buy recommendations." Gilmour acknowledged that "this is much less controversial now" but that we as a society "have some good distance to go." In his view, things had improved for gays and lesbians in corporate America, but not enough and not in all segments: "It depends on the company and the nature of the industry. The newer companies and industries pay much less attention to these issues." He worked for two more years and then retired again in 2004.[18]

It is possible that Gilmour will serve as an important role model for younger gay men and lesbians in the corporate world (though, as he noted, "I'm not running for poster boy or poster codger"). But the corporate floodgates have not exactly opened since Gilmour's 1996 interview. Although we assume there are other senior executives at *Fortune*-level companies, including CEOs, who are homosexual, none has followed Gilmour's lead and come out. As we noted at the outset of this chapter, for many, homosexuality is a religious and political issue, and these potential customers and voters see acceptance of homosexuality as an important enough issue on which to boycott products or vote against certain politicians. Our best guess is that a few gay men and lesbians will move up the ranks at some companies, and a few may even become openly gay CEOs, but only in companies marketing certain kinds of products and with younger clienteles.

More likely, gay men and lesbians who are already out will start businesses that are so successful that they become *Fortune*-level companies or are bought out by *Fortune*-level companies. These entrepreneurial innovators may emerge as rich and influential people, and some will be asked onto corporate boards as outside directors.

One such person is the media executive David Geffen. Geffen grew up in a three-bedroom apartment in a Jewish-Italian section of Brooklyn. His mother, Batyam, ran a brassiere and corset shop (and called her son "King David"). "She made the money," Geffen recalls, while his father "read a lot. He wasn't successful or ambitious. He spoke lots of languages. There were times that kids said to me, 'What does your father do?' and I had to make something up because I actually didn't know what he did."[19]

After an undistinguished record in high school, Geffen enrolled at the University of Texas but dropped out after one semester. He headed out to California, where his older brother lived, and held a number of jobs before landing a lowly but coveted position in the mailroom of the William Morris talent agency. He told his employer that he was a graduate of UCLA, then intercepted the expected reply from UCLA denying this claim, steamed open the envelope, and replaced it with a bogus letter that he had prepared on UCLA stationery, stating that he had graduated.[20]

Desperately wanting to be an agent, he followed the astute advice of a more experienced William Morris agent, who told him that, rather than trying to persuade established stars to work with a mailroom boy in his early twenties, he should seek to represent some of the undiscovered musical talent of his own generation.

He became the agent for Laura Nyro, a singer and songwriter who wrote a series of hits for herself and various other artists. When her publishing company, half-owned by Geffen, was sold to CBS in 1969, he received $2 million in CBS stock at the age of twenty-five. Within a year, he had started his own record company, Asylum, which put out records by Joni Mitchell, Jackson Browne, Linda Ronstadt, and the Eagles, among others. Five years later, he sold the company to Warner Communications for $7 million.

In 1980, he started Geffen Records. With a stable that included Don Henley, Guns N' Roses, Rickie Lee Jones, and Aerosmith, this venture, too, was extremely successful, and Geffen branched out to invest in theater (including *Cats* and *Little Shop of Horrors*) and films (including *Beetlejuice* and *Lost in America*). In 1990, Geffen concluded that the time had come to join the massive move toward conglomeration, and he sold the company, the last of the major independent labels. Rather than accepting various lucrative cash offers, he decided on MCA's offer of $550 million worth of stock, foreseeing that MCA would itself be sold in the near future. When the Japanese company Matsushita bought MCA, Geffen, as MCA's largest shareholder, received a check for an estimated $670 million.[21] A 1990 article in *Forbes* described him and his wealth in the following way: "This 47-year-old chap given to blue jeans, T shirts and a fashionable, day-old stubble, will be worth nearly $900 million. David Geffen is well on his way to achieving his well-known ambition of becoming Hollywood's first billionaire. And he's a bachelor to boot."[22]

He was indeed a bachelor, but not an eligible one in the conventional sense. Geffen had not yet gone public about his homosexuality, but over the next few years, he became increasingly involved in fund-raising for the battle against AIDS, and he told a reporter for *Vanity Fair* that he was bisexual. Then, both frightened and energized by the venomous language at the 1992 Republican National Convention, especially a speech in which Patrick Buchanan claimed that there was "a religious war going on in this country for the soul of America," Geffen became involved in Clinton's presidential campaign. Even before the Republican convention ended, he had called Clinton's campaign director, Mickey Kantor, an old friend from Kantor's days as a Los Angeles lawyer. Geffen became a major contributor and fund-raiser.[23]

In late November 1992, just a few weeks after Clinton's election, in a speech to six thousand people at Commitment to Life VI, a benefit for AIDS Project Los Angeles, Geffen went public about being gay. "As a gay man," he told the crowd, "I have come a long way to be here tonight."[24] This declaration generated considerable publicity. *The Advocate* named Geffen "Man of the Year." Friskopp and Silverstein write that many of the Harvard Business School graduates they interviewed cited Geffen as a public role model "for his business success and his candor about being gay."[25]

In chapter 2, we noted that, several decades ago, Laurence Tisch advised young Jewish men interested in business careers to avoid the large "Gentile" companies because they would only get "bogged down." Better, said Tisch, to work for Jews or to be successful enough to buy your own company so that you can call the shots. Similarly, Geffen might advise young homosexual men and women interested in business careers to be selective about whom they decide to work for. A week after the AIDS fund-raiser, when asked whether being gay had influenced his decision to pursue a career in show business rather than another business, Geffen acknowledged that it had been a key consideration: "When I realized as a teenager that it was possible that I might be gay—I wasn't sure until my twenties—I thought, *What kind of career can I have where being gay won't make a difference?* I thought about it a lot, and I decided that the entertainment business was a profession in which being gay was not going to be unusual or stand in my way."[26]

If the richest man in Hollywood is publicly gay, then it sends a message to those who run the many companies that do business with him. But, the entertainment business is only one segment of the corporate world, and given its reputation for liberal politics and lifestyles, the public presence of one homosexual executive, even an extremely wealthy one, does not exactly indicate that the mostly conservative corporate elite is ready to accept openness about homosexuality. Still, given the real changes that have taken place at the lower tier of corporate management and the increasing tendency for younger gay men and lesbians in the corporate world to be open about their sexual orientation, it is likely a few will rise above the lavender ceiling in certain companies in certain industries.

We think that those gay men and lesbians who start at large corporations and do manage to rise through the ranks are likely to go off on their own at some point to begin companies or to work in more comfortable environments. Consider, for example, Kathy Levinson, a 1977 graduate of Stanford, an economics major and the university's only three-sport varsity athlete (field hockey, basketball, and tennis). Levinson held various senior executive positions with Charles A. Schwab & Company, helping that company to become one of the first major corporations to offer domestic-partner health-insurance coverage. After thirteen years with Schwab, she left in 1996 to work for E*TRADE Group, where she was president and chief operating officer from 1999 to 2000. She made enough money to give Stanford $1 million in 1998, and she has been named one of the most influential businesswomen in the San Francisco Bay Area. Now retired from corporate life, she is politically active in the Bay Area and involved in community service (among other activities, she and her partner are involved in creating a new Jewish spiritual community in Palo Alto). She sits on various corporate boards, although none made the 2004 S&P 1500 list.

Similarly, David Bohnett, a self-described electronics geek from the suburbs of Chicago, worked for Arthur Andersen after he graduated with a bachelor's degree in business administration from USC and an MBA from the University of Michigan. Of being a gay man at Arthur Andersen, he said, "It wasn't going to be easy. I would have had to push down who I was, and that didn't seem right to me." So, he left the corporate world, worked for a while for a software company, and then, using his life savings and $386,000 in life insurance money he had inherited when his partner died of AIDS, he created Beverly Hills Internet, the first ever World Wide Web video camera (it overlooked Hollywood and Vine). The idea caught on, the company expanded, the name was changed to GeoCities, and within four years, the first-quarter revenues were almost $8 million. In 1999, GeoCities merged with Yahoo! ("Right company, right culture, right price, right time," said Bohnett). Bohnett's profit from the deal: $350 million.[27]

Bohnett now manages an investment firm called Baroda Ventures. He also started the David Bohnett Foundation, which has an endowment of about $28 million and earmarks money for various forms of social activism. In 1999, Bohnett was asked onto the board of a *Fortune* 500 company, NCR Corporation (#337 in 2005), and he also has been on the boards of Netzero, Inc., Stamps.com in Santa Monica, and several privately held Internet ventures.

It is our guess that the pathways followed by Geffen, Levinson, and Bohnett will appeal more to the next generation of gay men and lesbians than the more confining pathway traveled by Allan Gilmour. Gilmour, now in his seventies, was willing to put up with the segmentation of his work and private lives. As Bohnett's comments about working for Arthur Andersen suggest ("I would have had to push down who I was, and that didn't seem right to me"), younger gay men and women may not be willing to do so. Perhaps they will either find niche settings in the corporate world that accept them (presumably, this was the case for Kathy Levinson at E*TRADE), or they will go out on their own.

GAY MEN AND LESBIANS IN THE POLITICAL ELITE

Contrary to the images of gays and lesbians as outrageous drag queens and butches on the one hand and as left-wing political activists on the other, the great majority of gays and lesbians tend to be straight-looking, mainstream Democrats and Republicans. Like everyone else, gays and lesbians mostly reflect and express their social and educational backgrounds, as well as their occupational training and experience. Since homosexuality occurs randomly in all human groups, gays and lesbians can be from high social levels as well as lower ones. Thus, a wealthy ultraconservative like Phyllis Schlafly can have a gay son; an army brat like Newt Gingrich can have a lesbian half-sister; a psychoanalyst like Charles Socarides, who claimed that he could "cure" one-third of the homosexuals he treated, could have a gay son, Richard, who served in the Clinton administration as the White House liaison to the Labor Department; and Vice President Dick Cheney can have an openly lesbian daughter.[28]

In fact, many prominent gays and lesbians are from comfortable socioeconomic backgrounds, have had excellent educations, and have experienced considerable success in the professions, academia, and business.

There are gay Democratic clubs and gay Republican clubs across the country, but only the Republicans are organized by a national centralized office. The umbrella group is called the Log Cabin Republicans—the name refers to Abraham Lincoln, who is alleged to have grown up in a log cabin and who supported individual rights (but whose father actually was a skilled carpenter and farmer who owned two farms of six hundred acres each and several town lots, as well as horses and livestock).[29] Membership skyrocketed after Buchanan's speech at the 1992 convention, when many formerly closeted gay Republicans decided they had to become more involved in order to combat the antigay views of the religious Right. The president of the Texas Log Cabin Republicans at the time, Paul von Wupperfeld, the son of a Goldwater Republican certain that it would be "unnatural" for him to vote Democrat, claimed that the state organization's membership had more than tripled in the twelve months ending in December 1992, an increase that he attributed in no small part to the Republican convention.[30] That year, the Log Cabin Republicans decided they could not endorse the Bush-Quayle ticket.[31] Twelve years later, in 2004, it was, as Yogi Berra might have put it, déjà vu all over again when, after George W. Bush supported a constitutional amendment banning same-sex marriage, the board of the Log Cabin Republicans voted overwhelmingly against endorsing the Bush-Cheney ticket. According to the group's political director, Bush's endorsement of the marriage amendment had led to the group's doubling in size.[32]

Some Republicans are gay, and so, too, are some staff members who work in the offices of elected Republican officials. This can create anguish for those closeted staffers of particularly homophobic congressmen. Some find themselves preparing antigay briefings for their bosses during the day and returning to their gay partners at night. As one explained, "How would you like to turn on your television and see your boss, or your boss's cohorts, telling you what a horrible person you are every other day? Happens to me all the time." Still, most say nothing, and most remain closeted, for to do otherwise would be to risk their own jobs or the jobs of their partners. Furthermore, they do not want to hurt what they see as the more important cause: conservatism. As one openly gay Washington, D.C., consultant, who worked to gain the support of gay voters for George W. Bush, put it, "They believe in the cause, the president, and the ideals of the Republican party," and to come out might mean they would no longer be seen as "part of the team" or, worse, would be "labeled a liberal."[33]

Some true believers in the conservative movement who are gay not only stay in the closet but use homophobic issues to further the right-wing cause.

The first famous right-wing gay man who was well-known for his support of gay-baiting was Roy Cohn, assistant to Senator Joseph McCarthy (McCarthy made a reputation for himself by pursuing "Communists" and "queers" in the State Department). Terry Dolan, born in 1950, was another right-wing, closeted-gay homophobe. He formed the National Conservative Political Action Committee (NCPAC) during the Reagan years. NCPAC was hostile to all things liberal, and its shrill fund-raising letters railed against feminists and "gay activists" ("Our nation's moral fiber is being weakened by the growing homosexual movement," read one). Dolan, like Cohn, died of AIDs; unlike Cohn, who refused to acknowledge that he had AIDS, Dolan endorsed gay rights before he died in 1986.[34]

But the gay conservative ideologue of greatest use to the current right wing has been political consultant Arthur Finkelstein. Finkelstein previously guarded his private life with care, but, apparently, the attractions of marriage were too great for him once the possibility existed, thanks to the efforts of liberal gays: despite the horrors that the thought of gay marriage creates for most of his conservative clients and for conservative voters, he married his same-sex partner of forty years in Massachusetts in April 2005, which, of course, generated considerable (risky) publicity. Before his marriage, Finkelstein had been a major political strategist for over twenty-five years for a range of conservatives and conservative causes, including former North Carolina senator Jesse Helms (whose use of homophobia outdid that of all other Republicans in the 1990s). He also worked with a group called "Stop Her Now," devoted to preventing the 2006 reelection of Hillary Clinton. Now, he describes himself as a pro-choice, pro-gay-marriage libertarian.

So, just as diehard liberals at times endorse politicians with whom they differ on specific issues because they agree with the overall liberal position, so, too, do diehard conservatives who are gay allow their belief in the overall conservative ideology to trump the more specific issues related to sexual orientation, even though such a stance seems to go against their self-image and their self-interest. As Martin Duberman, a historian who has written extensively about gay issues, explains, being a gay Republican is no longer the contradiction that he and others used to assume it was: "A number of gay people approve of the administration because they are militaristic, they are jingoistic, and they may have grown up in fundamentalist families."[35]

Nonetheless, most gay men and lesbians vote Democratic, and they, too, like the Log Cabin Republicans, have organized politically. In 1977, the Municipal Elections Committee of Los Angeles was formed. Its bland generic name disguised the fact that it was a gay and lesbian political-action committee, the first in the country, and made it easier for politicians to accept money from the group without having to acknowledge support from homosexuals.

The adviser to this early gay Political Action Committee was David Mixner, a very different political consultant from Arthur Finkelstein. Fifteen years later, Mixner emerged as Bill Clinton's liaison to gays and lesbians during the 1992 campaign.[36]

Mixner was born in 1946 in southern New Jersey (three days after Bill Clinton was born in Arkansas). His father managed the workers on an absentee-owner farm. After graduating from the local public high school in 1964, Mixner attended three different colleges before finally dropping out of Arizona State to work in Eugene McCarthy's 1968 presidential campaign. He became a key McCarthy organizer, was thrown through a window by police at the 1968 Democratic National Convention in Chicago, and became one of the four organizers of the Vietnam moratorium in October 1969.

Later that year, at a reunion of those who had worked on McCarthy's presidential campaign, Mixner met Bill Clinton. Clinton had not worked on the campaign but came to the reunion on Martha's Vineyard with a friend who had. The two twenty-five-year-olds, one a Yale Law School student, the other a college-dropout political activist, hit it off, and because both had political aspirations, they kept in touch over the years as their respective political careers unfolded. In October 1991, Mixner arranged a meeting in Los Angeles between Clinton, by then governor of Arkansas, and a small group of wealthy southern Californians known as Access Now for Gay and Lesbian Equality. The group was impressed by Clinton, in part because he agreed to their demands, including an end to the ban on homosexuals in the military.

Mixner was able to rally considerable support from the homosexual community for Clinton. Patrick Buchanan's speech at the Republican convention made this task much easier. As Mixner said to one interviewer, "Support crystallized overnight with Pat Buchanan's speech. It created a voting bloc and tripled the money."[37] According to Mixner, gays and lesbians contributed $3 million of the $25 million Clinton raised.[38]

In spite of the money Mixner raised and assurances by Clinton of access to decision makers with regard to gay and lesbian issues, Mixner and other homosexual activists were frozen out and treated badly by most members of Clinton's inner circle, a sordid story that Mixner tells in his book, *Stranger among Friends*. Clinton's youthful and arrogant aides, Rahm Emanuel and George Stephanopoulos, both from white ethnic groups that had been discriminated against in the past, were the worst offenders. In May 1996, when Clinton said he would support a Republican bill denying recognition of same-sex marriages, Mixner called the decision "nauseating and appalling" and an "act of political cowardice."[39]

Although Mixner's public criticisms of Clinton led Rahm Emanuel, at one point, to declare Mixner "persona non grata," by 2002, when Emanuel was running for congress in a Chicago district with a large gay population, the two had nicer things to say about one another. Emanuel claimed his conflict with Mixner was a learning experience and that he hoped to bring people together "for the good of the country." Mixner responded, "Rahm and I will never be friends, but he's running a great campaign, doing all the right things working with and for the gay community."[40]

Mixner, like Geffen, has rallied homosexual support for various Democratic politicians, just as the Log Cabin Republicans have raised money and gotten out the more conservative gay vote. But no openly gay men or women have been appointed to presidential cabinets or been elected to the Senate. Nine gay men have served in the House of Representatives, three Democrats and six Republicans, although each was elected before his homosexuality was publicly revealed. And since 1998, there has been a liberal Democratic woman in the House who won her seat running as a lesbian feminist.

Before the press began reporting in the 1970s on the sexual escapades of politicians, straight and gay, there was little or no information on the sexual orientation of members of Congress. Between 1978 and 1983, however, four men in the House, two Democrats and two (very conservative) Republicans, were revealed to be gay after soliciting sex in public places or having sex with teenage boys. It was not until the spring of 1987 that the House had its first openly gay member, Barney Frank, a liberal Democrat from Boston who had been in Congress since 1980. Given the nature of his district and the climate of the times, with tensions over AIDs and gay rights at the forefront, it apparently seemed to Frank to be the right, and safe, thing to do. As *Newsweek* explained, "the voters shrugged and returned him to Congress by a landslide majority."[41]

In 1980, as part of the Reagan landslide victory, twenty-nine-year-old closeted gay Steve Gunderson, a Republican who had previously served in the Wisconsin state legislature, was elected to the U.S. House of Representatives. His homosexuality was, as the *New York Times* put it, "quietly known in his Wisconsin district and in Washington for years," but it was neither a public nor a political issue in six reelection campaigns, until the spring of 1994. In March of that year, Gunderson gave a speech to the Human Rights Campaign Fund, a gay political group in Baltimore, Maryland, in which he mentioned that his partner of eleven years was in the audience. At that point, the House had its second openly gay member.

That same month, Gunderson spoke on the House floor against a Republican-sponsored amendment to deny funds to schools "encouraging or supporting" homosexuality. When he sat down, a fellow Republican, Robert Dornan of California, leveled a highly personal attack on Gunderson, an attack that added to the fervor with which gays and lesbians across the country supported the Republican-turned-Democrat Laura Sanchez in her successful challenge of Dornan in 1996. "He has a revolving door on his closet," Dornan said. "He's in, he's out, he's in, he's out, he's in. I guess you're out because you went up and spoke to a huge homosexual dinner, Mr. Gunderson."

Though Dornan later withdrew his remarks from the official record, he refused to apologize. Nor was he able to withdraw comments he made later that day to a reporter: "We have a representative on our side who is a homo. I have just had it with him saying he takes second place to no one in this House upholding Christian principles."[42] In spite of hostility from the right wing of his own party, Gunderson won the 1994 election, but he chose not to run for reelection in 1996.[43]

Just as Gunderson was finishing out his term, it became known in August 1996 that another Republican was gay, but this time the information was not entirely voluntary. After voting to deny federal recognition to same-sex marriages, Jim Kolbe, a six-term representative from Arizona, was electronically "outed" by gay activists who distributed the information in e-mail messages. As a result of this campaign, Kolbe publicly acknowledged his sexual orientation. A gay activist described as an architect of the outing campaign happily noted that after Kolbe's announcement, there were as many openly gay Republicans, two, as openly gay Democrats in Congress: "I think it's a terrific development that we now have an equal number of openly gay G.O.P. members of Congress."[44] (The other gay Democrat besides Barney Frank was Gary Studds, also from Massachusetts, who was censured by the House in 1983 for having had sex with a seventeen-year-old male congressional page a decade earlier. He was subsequently reelected six times before retiring in 1996).

Outing also brought two more gay Republicans into the public arena. In the spring of 2003, a Florida weekly magazine revealed that Mark Foley, a fifth-term Republican congressman who was considering a run for the Senate, had a long-time same-sex companion and had been seen regularly at gay bars in Washington, D.C., and Fort Lauderdale. Foley's record on gay issues was mixed: in 1996, he had voted in favor of the antigay Defense of Marriage Act, but since that time, his voting record on gay rights had been liberal. The journalist who outed him wrote that since he was running for the Senate, "I felt that telling the truth about Foley presented a good test for the Republican Party: is it really—with its Christian Right/Rick Santorum wing—as inclusive as it claims to be?"[45] Foley's response to the article—"I'm not going to be dragged into the gutter by rumormongers"—did not, however, endear him to those in the gay community (denying the allegation was one thing, although he did not actually deny it; comparing homosexuality to the gutter was another). A few months later, Foley dropped out of the race for the Senate (he continues to serve in the House).

In the fall of 2004, a blogger revealed that Ed Schrock, a married, two-term, Republican congressman from Virginia who was running for reelection, had placed a voice mail ad for gay sex (he had it on tape: "Nothing real heavy, but just a fun time"). Schrock had supported the Bush administration's attempt to ban gay marriage, and he had criticized the military's "don't ask, don't tell" policy as too pro-gay. In defending himself from those who criticized him for outing Schrock, the blogger put it bluntly: "Why should my community protect him? He's the enemy." Schrock declined all comment for eleven days and then dropped out of the race.[46]

In 1996, the same year that Kolbe was outed and Gunderson and Studds retired, two openly gay Democratic candidates won their primaries. Rick Zbur then lost the general election by ten points to the Republican candidate in California, and Paul Barby lost by thirty points to the Republican opponent in Oklahoma. In 1998, there were four more homosexual candidates, all Democrats and all lesbians: Margarethe Cammermeyer, a retired career military woman, ran in a district north of Seattle; Christine Kehoe, a San Diego city councilwoman (and childhood television star), ran for a seat in southern California; Susan Tracy, a former state legislator, ran for an open seat in Massachusetts; and Tammy Baldwin, a state representative in Wisconsin ran in a district that included the liberal city of Madison, home of the University of Wisconsin. Only Baldwin won, but that represented a genuine breakthrough: she was the first lesbian elected to Congress and the first openly gay politician to win election as a nonincumbent (that is, all the others were outed or came out after having been elected). She was reelected in 2000, 2002, and 2004 (winning 63 percent of the vote in 2004).[47]

Baldwin's parents divorced shortly after her birth in 1962, and she and her mother moved in with her maternal grandparents (both grandparents worked at the University of Wisconsin, her grandfather as the chair of the biochemistry department and her grandmother as a costume designer for the theater department). When she was nine, her mother married again, this time to an African American. Baldwin graduated first in her class at Madison West High School and then went to Smith, where she completed a double major in political science and math. She returned to Wisconsin, and just two years later, she was elected to the first of four terms on the Dane County Board of Supervisors. During her first two terms, she also completed a law degree at the University of Wisconsin. In 1993, she won election to the Wisconsin state legislature, thus becoming the first openly gay member of that body.[48]

Therefore, with Baldwin joining Barney Frank and Jim Kolbe in the House, there are three openly homosexual members of Congress. When we completed work on the first edition of this book, there were four (as noted, two of those four, Gunderson and Studds, retired in 1996). There are no openly gay men or women in the Senate. Given the absence of openly gay men and women in the Senate and their minimal presence in the House, it is not surprising that no openly gay men or women have been appointed to presidential cabinets.

Back in 1992, however, whether as a political payback for the support he received from gay voters or out of a genuine commitment to diversity in his administration, or both, Clinton appointed an openly gay man and an openly gay woman to positions senior enough to require confirmation by the Senate. Both were confirmed, making them the highest-ranking openly gay people to serve in the executive branch. Roberta Achtenberg, a former law professor at the New College of California School of Law and a member of the San Francisco Board of Supervisors, became an assistant secretary at HUD. She was confirmed by the Senate in a 58–31 vote, although Jesse Helms called her a "militantly activist lesbian" who "tried to bully the Boy Scouts of America" into permitting homosexual Scout leaders.[49] After less than two years, when she and others became disillusioned by Clinton's policies toward gay men and lesbians, she quit the job and returned to California to run for mayor of San Francisco. She lost that race (to Willie Brown) and then became a senior vice president for public policy at the San Francisco Chamber of Commerce. Although David Mixner and Dennis Bailey portray her in heroic terms in the chapter they devote to her in their book *Brave Journeys: Profiles in Gay and Lesbian Courage*, many Bay Area housing and tenant activists have been disappointed by Achtenberg's active support for programs that benefit local developers and real estate owners more than they help low-income people.[50]

The other openly gay Clinton nominee who needed the Senate's approval, Bruce Lehman, also a lawyer, became assistant commerce secretary and commissioner of patents and trademarks. Lehman, who had worked in Washington, D.C., as a congressional aide and as a copyright lawyer and lobbyist for a major law firm, had many friends on Capitol Hill, including Republicans. His confirmation hearings produced none of the conservative wrath that marked those held for Achtenberg's appointment. Lehman noted that a conservative paper in Washington had tried to stir up some outrage from conservative Republicans, but "the problem is, they all know me, and they kind of like me, and they didn't want to make a martyr of me."[51]

It may be that Bruce Lehman received kinder treatment from the Senate than did Roberta Achtenberg simply because she was, in fact, further to the left politically than he was. But, we are also reminded that when homosexuals are considered for positions in or near the power elite, gender is also part of the equation. As both a homosexual and a woman, Achtenberg had two barriers to surmount. As we point out in chapter 3, the more characteristics that differentiate a woman from the dominant, WASP, male majority in the power elite, the more difficult it is for her to gain acceptance. This phenomenon becomes more apparent the closer one gets to the power elite. At a level requiring Senate confirmation, an openly gay woman may pose a greater threat than an openly gay man.[52]

Antagonism toward homosexuality persists, especially from the religious Right, even though exit polls have indicated that about one-third of the voters who identify themselves as gay, lesbian, or bisexual vote for Republicans.[53] As Kathleen Jamieson points out, it has become the pattern that powerful women are accused of being closet lesbians. In her efforts to unseat Barbara Mikulski, the incumbent Democratic senator from Maryland, in 1986, the conservative Republican syndicated columnist Linda Chavez, another Spanish American from New Mexico, married to a Jew, who abhors affirmative action but uses her maiden name to further her own political career, claimed that Mikulski was "a San Francisco-style Democrat," that she was "antimale," and that she should "come out of the closet."[54] In a radio interview, House Majority Leader Richard Armey referred to Barney Frank as "Barney Fag," then gave a lukewarm apology, saying that he had mispronounced Frank's last name.[55] Rather than face the outspoken opposition of Jesse Helms, the Clinton White House backed away from naming James Hormel, an openly gay San Francisco businessman who had contributed heavily to Clinton's election, as ambassador to Fiji.[56] In 2003, Rick Santorum, a Republican senator from Pennsylvania, questioning a Supreme Court decision that challenged a Texas law banning sodomy, complained, "If the Supreme Court says that you have the right to consensual sex within your home, then you have the right to bigamy, you have the right to incest, you have the right to adultery. You have the right to anything."[57] Although the Log Cabin Republicans called on Santorum to "take back his divisive and alarming comments," he did not.

For politicians on the Right, given the continuing hostility toward homosexuals and homosexuality among many of their constituents, even deciding whether to accept campaign contributions can be problematic. This was demonstrated quite clearly in late 1995, when Robert Dole's presidential campaign at first accepted a $1,000 campaign contribution from the Log Cabin Republicans, then months later returned it on the grounds that the group's agenda was "in opposition to Senator Dole's on the issues."[58] Republican congressman Gunderson, who had previously stepped down as chief deputy whip because of the intolerance exhibited by Republicans at the 1992 convention, wrote a pained letter to Dole, noting that he had first heard about this at a dinner party; as he put it, "I assumed my friends had mistaken yours for the campaigns of other, decidedly bigoted candidates. I was embarrassed to learn I was wrong."[59]

It is not only the Right that finds homosexuality a volatile issue. In 1993, the national board of the highly respected Japanese American Citizens League voted to make the league the first civil rights organization to endorse same-sex marriage. The following year, one of the chapters came to the national convention with a proposal to retract this support. There was extensive and heated debate on the issue. Among those who spoke passionately against the resolution (and thus to continue to endorse same-sex marriage) was Norman Mineta, then a congressman (and later to serve in Clinton's and George W. Bush's cabinets). Mineta told the gathered delegates,

> There are those who have argued that gay rights are not Japanese American issues. I cannot think of any more dangerous precedent for the organization to take than a position on an issue of principle that is based on how it will directly affect those of Japanese ancestry. When we fought for redress, we won. We could not have won that battle if we had stood alone. If organizations had taken the position that redress was a Japanese American issue and had nothing to do with African Americans, Hispanic Americans, Jewish Americans, or with gay and lesbian Americans . . . they joined with us because they understood and believed in our argument that a threat to anybody's civil rights is a threat to the civil rights of all Americans. And they acted.

When the votes were counted (while, as one account put it, "JACLers held their breath"), thirty voted for the resolution, but fifty voted against it (eleven abstained). A major split within the organization ensued. Disaffected members elected a new president and several new directors. There was a wholesale firing of national staff members, who were blamed for the resolution even though delegates from Hawaii had introduced it. Membership dropped by 11 percent in the next year, and the organization's attorney resigned because the endorsement conflicted with his Christian beliefs. But the Japanese American Citizens League survived, reaffirmed its support for gay marriage as a matter of fundamental principle in 1998, and continues to stand up for civil rights for all Americans on many difficult issues. In 2005, it had 112 chapters and over 24,000 members in 23 states, with headquarters in San Francisco and an office in Washington, D.C.[60]

GAY MEN AND LESBIANS IN THE MILITARY

Almost immediately after he entered office, Bill Clinton blundered into a firestorm over gays in the military. After initially taking a clear and principled stand, he crumbled in the face of opposition led by a traditional southern Democrat, Senator Sam Nunn of Georgia. Nunn, then chairman of the Senate Armed Forces Committee, had a lot of support, including the Joint Chiefs of

Staff, various congressmen, and the entire religious Right. Colin Powell was also against allowing openly homosexual men and women in the military, although he later tried to sugarcoat his vigorous opposition by telling Henry Louis Gates Jr., "I never presented the case in terms of there being something wrong, morally or any other way, with gays. I just couldn't figure out a way to handle the privacy aspect." (As journalist Clarence Page points out, Powell's argument that gays in the military would threaten "discipline, good order, and morale" was the very same language that Gen. Dwight Eisenhower had used in the 1940s to justify maintaining racial segregation in the army.[61]) Others in the military were much more blunt, and crude, about their opposition to homosexuals in the military: Adm. Thomas Moore, former chairman of the Joint Chiefs of Staff, once referred to homosexuality as "a filthy, disease-ridden practice."[62]

The result was Clinton's endorsement of an ambiguous policy generally referred to as "don't ask, don't tell" that went into effect in November 1993 whereby gay men and lesbians could be in the military as long as they did not acknowledge their sexual orientation. It did not take long for many to conclude that things had gotten worse, not better, for gay men and lesbians in the military. In Mixner's view, by mid-1995, "It was clear to everyone, except perhaps the President and his staff, that the 'Don't Ask, Don't Tell' policy was a disaster." As he went on to note, the number of dismissals of homosexuals from the military had not, as intended, decreased but instead had increased.[63]

The pattern of increased dismissals continued until 2001. Whereas 617 service members had been dismissed for being homosexual in 1994, by 2001, that number had more than doubled to 1,273. Then, clearly because the country was at war, first in Afghanistan and then in Iraq, and because meeting goals for new recruits had become more and more difficult, the numbers declined, first to 902 in 2002, then to 787 in 2003, and to 653 in 2004 (the same decline in discharges for gays and lesbians occurred in World War II and during every war since then). Despite this decline based on military needs, a government study revealed that more than three hundred foreign-language specialists considered critical in the war on terrorism had been dismissed since 1993 because of their sexual orientation, including fifty-four who spoke Arabic; another four hundred or so with critical skills, such as specialists in code breaking and air traffic controllers, were also dismissed.[64]

By late 2003, on the tenth anniversary of the policy, nearly ten thousand service members had been dismissed. The Servicemembers Legal Defense Network, a group that has monitored the policy since its inception, held a news conference at which three retired military officers, two generals and one admiral, criticized the policy as ineffective and demeaning and disclosed that they had been forced to hide their sexual orientation from family and friends.[65] And by 2005, critics of the policy had gained new allies, including conservatives, in part because of the cost of recruiting replacements (according to the Government Accountability Office, it cost nearly $100 million to replace those dismissed between 1993 and 2003, and this did not count the costs of investigating them, providing counseling for them, or handling legal challenges).[66] Others, like Wayne Gilchrest, a conservative Republican member of the House from Maryland, said that he had changed his views on the policy out of respect for gay marines with whom he had served in Vietnam and for his brother, who is gay.[67]

Even though Clinton later came to regret the policy—in 1999, while still in office, he acknowledged that the implementation of the policy was "out of whack," and in 2000, after the election, he simply referred to it as that "dumb ass policy"—it is still in effect, and even though a number of legal efforts are underway to change the policy, the Bush White House and, especially, Donald Rumsfeld, Bush's secretary of defense, have made it clear that they have no interest in revisiting the policy. By way of contrast, after a European court ruled in 1999 that it was a violation of human rights laws to ban gays from the military, Britain lifted its ban. By early 2005, the Royal Navy was actively recruiting gay men and lesbians.[68]

Needless to say, no openly homosexual men or women have risen very far in the military hierarchy, and, certainly, none have made it into the military elite.

CONCLUSION

Gay rights activism, like the women's movement of the late 1960s, was emboldened by the civil rights and antiwar movements, and, in fact, some gay and lesbian leaders, in addition to Mixner, were part of those other movements to begin with. As the movements of the 1960s took on various forms, they affected one another and, to varying degrees, contributed to cracking the monolithic nature of the power elite.

The problem facing openly gay men and women as they move closer to the power elite, while unique in some ways, is, at a deeper level, similar to the problems facing others who were previously excluded. They, too, will have to find ways to enter the comfort zone of the upper- and upper-middle-class, Ivy League–educated, white, heterosexual males at the center of the power elite. They will have to do so by asserting as many similarities as possible and by managing differences that might rekindle discomfort. Most of all, they must behave in traditionally masculine or feminine ways. Woods makes this point about identity management when he asserts that while many in the corporate world "don't care if someone's gay or not," that they do care "how effeminate you are."[69] It is likely that a similar problem faces lesbians in making sure they do not appear too "masculine." But, as we concluded in chapter 3, this is a key issue for heterosexual women as well.

Our assumption is that there are, and have always been, homosexuals in the power elite, but to stay there, they have had to "manage" their image by remaining closeted. Whether openly gay men and women will be allowed into the power elite in the coming decades remains to be seen.

NOTES

1. Ben Fuller, "Education Secretary Condemns Public Show with Gay Characters," Associated Press, January 25, 2005, at www.AP.org; Frank Rich, "The Year of Living Indecently," *New York Times*, February 6, 2005, section 2, 7.

2. Ralph Blumenthal, "An Improbable Victor Becomes a Texas Sheriff," *New York Times*, November 10, 2004, A13.

3. See Edward O. Laumann, John H. Gagnon, Robert T. Michael, and Stuart Michaels, *The Social Organization of Sexuality: Sexual Practices in the United States* (Chicago: University of Chicago Press, 1994), 292–97. See, also, Stuart Michaels, "The Prevalence of Homosexuality in the United States," in *Textbook of Homosexuality and Mental Health*, ed. Robert P. Cabaj and Terry S. Stein, 43–63 (Washington, DC: American Psychiatric Press, 1996). For more recent data based on 12,571 in-person interviews with men and women fifteen to forty-four years of age, see "Sexual Behavior and Selected Health Measures: Men and Women 15-44 Years of Age, United States, 2002," National Center for Health Statistics, at www.cdc.gov/nchs/products/pubs/ad/361-370/ad362.htm.

4. Annette Friskopp and Sharon Silverstein, *Straight Jobs, Gay Lives: Gay and Lesbian Professionals, the Harvard Business School, and the American Workplace* (New York: Scribners, 1995), 21, 24.

5. See, for example, John D'Emilio and Estelle B. Freedman, *Intimate Matters: A History of Sexuality in America* (New York: Harper and Row, 1988); Bruce Bawer, *A Place at the Table* (New York: Poseidon, 1993), 52–54; M. V. Lee Badgett, *Money, Myths and Change: The Economic Lives of Lesbians and Gay Men* (Chicago: University of Chicago Press, 2001); John Simons, "Gay Marriage: Corporate America Blazed the Trail," *Fortune*, June 14, 2004, 42–43; Nicole C. Raeburn, *Changing Corporate America From the Inside: Lesbian and Gay Workplace Rights* (Minneapolis, MN: University of Minnesota Press, 2005).

6. Daryl Herrschaft, *The State of the Workplace for Lesbian, Gay, Bisexual and Transgender Americans: 2004* (Washington, D.C.: Human Rights Campaign Foundation, 2005), 30–31; Andres R. Martinez, "Gay Workers Finding Workplace Friendlier," *Greensboro News & Record*, June 9, 2005, B8.

7. Late in 1991, Lotus became the first publicly held major corporation to extend benefits to domestic partners of gay and lesbian employees. In February 1992, Levi

Strauss became the second. Over the next few years, other companies also extended such benefits. James D. Woods, *The Corporate Closet: The Professional Lives of Gay Men in America* (New York: Free Press, 1993), 236–37. When IBM announced in October 1996 that it would extend benefits to the partners of gay and lesbian employees in its 110,000-person domestic workforce, it became the largest employer to extend health-care coverage to same-sex couples. See David Dunlap, "Gay Partners of I.B.M. Workers to Get Benefits," *New York Times,* September 20, 1996.

8. Friskopp and Silverstein, *Straight Jobs, Gay Lives,* 71.

9. Thomas A. Stewart, "Gay in Corporate America," *Fortune,* December 16, 1991, 42–56, 50; Woods, *Corporate Closet,* 236–37; Mireya A. Navarro, "Disney's Health Policy for Gay Employees Angers Religious Right in Florida," *New York Times,* November 29, 1995.

10. Herrschaft, *The State of the Workplace,* 15.

11. Woods, *Corporate Closet,* 28.

12. Woods, *Corporate Closet,* 241.

13. Friskopp and Silverstein, *Straight Jobs, Gay Lives,* 18–23.

14. Friskopp and Silverstein, *Straight Jobs, Gay Lives,* 110–11.

15. Friskopp and Silverstein, *Straight Jobs, Gay Lives,* 157. In a study of 284 respondents to a survey in *Out/Look* magazine, economist Lee Badgett found that "those whose employer has a sexual orientation nondiscrimination policy are much more likely to disclose their sexual orientation." See Badgett, *Money, Myths and Change,* 67.

16. Marny Hall, "Private Experiences in the Public Domain: Lesbians in Organizations," in *The Sexuality of Organization,* ed. Jeff Hearn, Deborah L. Sheppard, Peta Tancred-Sheriff, and Gibson Burrell, 125–38 (Newbury Park, CA: Sage, 1989), 134.

17. Steve Friess, "Executive Decision," *The Advocate,* April 29, 1997, 24–26, 31 (quotations appear on p. 26 and p. 25, respectively).

18. Danny Hakim, "Ford Is Said to Reappoint Ex-Executive," *New York Times,* May 18, 2002, B3; Danny Hakim, "Executive Leaves Retirement to Help Ford," *New York Times,* May 21, 2002, C10; Alex Taylor III, "Ford Finds Everyone Old Is New Again," *Fortune,* June 10, 2002, 40; "The Last Prejudice: Ex-Vice Chairman of Ford Comes Out," *Newsweek,* June 3, 2002, 8.

19. Bernard Weinraub, "David Geffen: Still Hungry," *New York Times Magazine,* May 2, 1993, 28–31, 38–43, 68, 78 (quotation appears on p. 43).

20. Lisa Gubernick and Peter Newcomb, "The Richest Man in Hollywood," *Forbes,* December 24, 1990, 94–98; Weinraub, "David Geffen," 68.

21. Geraldine Fabrikant, "The Record Man with Flawless Timing," *New York Times,* December 9, 1990.

22. Gubernick and Newcomb, "Richest Man in Hollywood," 94.

23. Weinraub, "David Geffen," 40. The Buchanan quotation appears in David Mixner, *Stranger among Friends* (New York: Bantam, 1996), 249.

24. Brendan Lemon, "Man of the Year: David Geffen," *The Advocate,* December 29, 1992, 35.

25. Friskopp and Silverstein, *Straight Jobs, Gay Lives,* 196.

26. Lemon, "Man of the Year," 38.

27. Michael Kearns, "Out on the Web," *LAWeekly.com*, November 26–December 2, 1999, at www.laweekly.com/ink/00/01/cyber-kearns.php.

28. Laura Blumenfeld, "Schlafly's Son Out of the Closet," *Washington Post*, September 19, 1992; "Gingrich's Half-Sister Now Gay Activist," *Greensboro News and Record*, March 6, 1995; David W. Dunlap, "An Analyst, a Father, Battles Homosexuality," *New York Times*, December 24, 1995; David Kirkpatrick, "Cheney Daughter's Political Role Disappoints Some Gay Activists," *New York Times*, August 30, 2004.

29. The log cabin myth is to presidents what the Horatio Alger myth is to captains of industry. See Edward Pessen, *The Log Cabin Myth: The Social Backgrounds of the Presidents* (New Haven, CT: Yale University Press, 1984), 25.

30. As has been the case with other gay Republicans, Von Wupperfeld has encountered antagonism from liberals in the gay community. Francis X. Clines, "For Gay G.O.P. Members, a 2d Closet," *New York Times*, September 4, 1992.

31. Kathy Sawyer, "Dole Campaign Returns Gays' Donation," *Washington Post*, August 27, 1995.

32. David Kirkpatrick, "Gay Activists in the G.O.P. Withhold Endorsement," *New York Times*, September 8, 2004, A20. According to this article, as a result of Bush's support for the marriage amendment, membership doubled from six thousand to twelve thousand.

33. Tim Bergling, "Closeted in the Capital: They're Powerful, Republican, and Gay," *The Advocate*, May 11, 2004, 45.

34. Frank Rich, "Just How Gay Is the Right?" *New York Times*, May 15, 2005, section 4, 14; Sarah Wildman, "A Roy Cohn for our Time?" *The Advocate*, May 24, 2005, 32.

35. Patrick D. Healy, "Gay Republicans Soldier On, One Skirmish at a Time," *New York Times*, April 17, 2005, Week in Review section, 3.

36. The information in this and the next two paragraphs is drawn from Daniel Golden's profile of Mixner, "Mixner's Moment," *Boston Globe* (online), June 6, 1993, magazine section, 14, and from Mixner, *Stranger among Friends*.

37. Bawer, *A Place at the Table*, 52.

38. Golden, "Mixner's Moment," 4; Mixner, *Stranger among Friends*, 250.

39. Golden, "Mixner's Moment"; Mixner, *Stranger among Friends*, chs. 16–18. Todd Purdom, "Clinton Would Sign Bill Barring Recognition to Gay Marriages," *New York Times*, May 23, 1996.

40. Chris Bull, "Baby Bills: A Crop of Candidates from the Clinton Administration Could Add New Life to Gay Political Causes," *The Advocate*, October 29, 2002, 22.

41. This quotation and the material in the previous two paragraphs are drawn from "Barney Frank's Story," *Newsweek*, September 25, 1989, 14–18; Jonathan Alter, "Gays in Washington: Voters Aren't as Alarmed as Politicians Think," *Newsweek*, September 25, 1989, 19.

42. Chandler Burr, "Congressman (R), Wisconsin. Fiscal Conservative. Social Moderate. Gay." *New York Times Magazine*, October 16, 1994, 43–45; John McCormick, "'Poster Boy,'" *Newsweek*, July 11, 1994, 19.

43. Frank Rich, "On the Bright Side," *New York Times*, November 10, 1994.

44. See David W. Dunlap, "A Republican Congressman Discloses He Is a Homosexual," *New York Times*, August 3, 1996.

45. Bob Norman, "Out with the Truth, the Epilogue," *New Times Broward–Palm Beach*, June 6, 2003.

46. Charles Kaiser, "When Outing Works," *The Advocate*, October 12, 2004, 112.

47. Erika Niedowski, "Four Walk Out of the Closet and toward the House," *CQ Weekly*, April 25, 1998, 1051–52; Timothy Egan, "Uphill Race Despite Lesbian's Past Success," *New York Times*, July 22, 1998, A1, A12; Adele Stan, "Baldwin's New Battle," *The Advocate*, June 8, 2004, 26–29.

48. Linda Rapp, "Tammy Baldwin," *glbtq.com*, February 16, 2005, at www.glbtq.com/social-sciences/baldwin_t.html; see Tammy Baldwin's government website at http://tammybaldwin.house.gov; the information about Baldwin's grandfather was provided by Baldwin's press secretary.

49. "Lesbian Confirmed in Housing Position with Votes to Spare," *New York Times,* May 25, 1993.

50. David Mixner and Dennis Bailey, *Brave Journeys: Profiles in Gay and Lesbian Courage* (New York: Bantam Books, 2000), 169–219; Rachel Brahinsky, "The Great Housing Hoax: How a Group of Developers, Hiding behind Worker-Friendly Rhetoric, Is Poised to Usher in the Next Wave of San Francisco Gentrification," *San Francisco Bay Guardian* (online), February 11, 2004, at www.sfprogressives.com/mt/archives/000049.html. In that article, Brahinsky says of Achtenberg that she "once was a relatively progressive city supervisor and a senior housing official in the Clinton administration."

51. Teresa Riordan, "Even in a 'Big Tent,' Little Insults, Little Compromises," *New York Times,* May 29, 1994.

52. Badgett's research suggests that gay men and lesbians have differing labor-market experiences. Using data from surveys conducted by the National Opinion Research Center at the University of Chicago, she found that, in terms of labor-market experiences, for lesbians, the fact that they were women was more important than the fact that they were lesbians. For gay men, sexual orientation had a much more powerful labor-market disadvantage than it did for lesbians. See Badgett, *Money, Myths and Change*, 49–50, tables 2 and 3.

53. David W. Dunlap, "For Gay Republicans, the Ideological Sniping Comes from Both Camps," *New York Times,* October 4, 1995.

54. Kathleen Hall Jamieson, *Beyond the Double Bind: Women and Leadership* (New York: Oxford University Press, 1995), 72

55. "The Republican Week That Was," *New York Times,* January 29, 1995.

56. David W. Dunlap, "Nomination of Gay Man Is Dropped," *New York Times,* January 1, 1995. Helms's opposition was not the only problem. Fiji has harsh laws against homosexuality that might have complicated Hormel's ambassadorship.

57. Sheryl Gay Stolberg, "Persistent Conflict for Gays and G.O.P.," *New York Times*, April 23, 2003, A20.

58. Sawyer, "Dole Campaign Returns Gays' Donation." Dole later said that an aide had made this decision, but that he did not want to object publicly because he did not want to embarrass the aide. See "Dole Changes His Tune on Donation," *Greensboro News and Record,* October 18, 1995.

59. Richard L. Berke, "Gay Congressman of His Own Party Brings Fire on Dole," *New York Times,* September 7, 1995.

60. Dennis Akizuki, "Turning Point for Asian Civil Rights Group," *San Jose Mercury News,* August 6, 1996; Dennis Akizuki, "Japanese Group Heals Internal Divisions," *San Jose Mercury News,* August 11, 1996; Chizu Iiyama, "Nikkei Heritage," *National Japanese American Historical Society* 14, no. 3 (summer 2002); see, also, www.gapsn.org/project2/discussion/jacl.asp. The quoted paragraph is from Iiyama.

61. Henry Louis Gates Jr., "Powell and the Black Elite," *New Yorker,* September 25, 1995, 63–80 (quotation appears on p. 74). Clarence Page, "Don't Ask, Don't Tell, Don't Leave," *Greensboro News & Record,* April 29, 2004, A11.

62. Quoted in Bawer, *A Place at the Table,* 149.

63. Mixner, *Stranger among Friends,* 350. See, also, Philip Shenon, "New Study Faults Pentagon's Gay Policy," *New York Times,* February 26, 1997.

64. Page, "Don't Ask, Don't Tell, Don't Leave," A11; John Files, "Number of Gays Discharged from Services Drops Again," *New York Times,* February 11, 2005, A21; Bryan Bender, "'Don't Ask' Policy Leaves Gap in Military," *Greensboro News & Record,* February 25, 2005, A1; Gary L. Lehring, *Officially Gay: The Political Construction of Sexuality by the U.S. Military* (Philadelphia: Temple University Press, 2003), 3.

65. John Files, "Gay Ex-Officers Say 'Don't Ask' Doesn't Work," *New York Times,* December 10, 2003, A14.

66. John Files, "Rules on Gays Exact a Cost in Recruiting, A Study Finds," *New York Times,* February 24, 2005, A16.

67. Associated Press, "Push On to Let Openly Gay Soldiers Serve," *Greensboro News & Record,* June 15, 2005, A3.

68. Lehring, *Officially Gay,* 117; John Kifner, "Clinton Said He Felt Pushed into Gay Policy," *New York Times,* December 7, 2000, A22; Sarah Lyall, "New Course by Royal Navy: a Campaign to Recruit Gays," *New York Times,* February 22, 2005, A1.

69. Woods, *Corporate Closet,* 14.

Chapter Eight

The Ironies of Diversity

As the preceding chapters have shown in detail, the power elite and Congress are more diverse than they were before the civil rights movement and the social movements that followed in its train brought pressure to bear on corporations, politicians, and government. Although the power elite is still composed primarily of Christian, white men, there are now Jews, women, blacks, Latinos, and Asian Americans on the boards of the country's largest corporations; presidential cabinets are far more diverse than was the case fifty years ago; and the highest ranks of the military are no longer filled solely by white men. In the case of elected officials in Congress, the trend toward diversity is even greater for women and the other previously excluded groups that we have studied. At the same time, we have shown that the incorporation of members of the different groups has been uneven.

In this final chapter, we look at the patterns that emerge from our specific findings to see if they help explain the gradual inclusion of some groups and the continuing exclusion of others. We also discuss the impact of diversity on the power elite and the rest of American society. We argue that most of the effects were unexpected and are ironic. The most important of these ironies relates to the ongoing tension between the American dream of individual advancement and fulfillment ("liberal individualism") and the class structure: we conclude that the racial, ethnic, and gender diversity celebrated by the power elite and the media actually reinforces the unchanging nature of the class structure and increases the tendency to ignore class inequalities.

229

WHY ARE SOME INCLUDED?

The social movements and pressures for greater openness at the higher levels of American society have led to some representation for all previously excluded groups, but some have been more successful than others. Four main factors explain why some people come to be included: higher class origins, elite educations, a lighter skin color, and the ability to make oneself acceptable to established members of the power elite, which we call "identity management."

The Importance of Class

Those who have brought diversity to the power elite have tended to come from business and professional backgrounds, like the white, Christian males C. Wright Mills studied more than fifty years ago. Fully one-third of the women who have become corporate directors are from the upper class, and many others are from the middle and upper-middle classes. Most of the Cuban Americans and Chinese Americans who have risen to the top have come from displaced ruling classes, a far cry from the conventional image of immigrants who start with nothing. The Jews and Japanese Americans in high positions have mostly been the products of two- and three-generational climbs up the social ladder. The first African American members of the corporate elite and the cabinet tended to come from the small black middle class that predated the civil rights movement. Although there is no systematic information on the social backgrounds of gay and lesbian leaders, who are treated in most studies as if they have no class origins, our anecdotal information suggests that many visible activists and professionals come from business and professional families as well.

A high-level social background, of course, makes it easier to acquire the values, attitudes, and styles that are necessary to hire, fire, and manage the work lives of employees with blue, white, and pink collars. This point can be extended to include even those from more modest circumstances, like Lauro Cavazos, whose father was a ranch foreman, or Katherine Ortega, Sue Ling Gin, and David Geffen, whose families owned small businesses, or David Mixner, whose father was in charge of minority farmhands on a farm he did not own. Most of those we studied, in other words, learned firsthand that a few people boss the majority or have independent professions based on academic credentials and that they were expected to be part of this managerial and professional stratum.

When we compare the newly arrived members of the power elite with their counterparts in Congress, however, two further generalizations emerge. First, members of the power elite tend to come from more privileged social backgrounds than elected officials. Second, the elected officials are more likely to be Democrats than Republicans. These two findings suggest that there are class and political dimensions to our findings on the differences between the power elite and Congress that cut across gender and ethnic lines. Now that the power elite is housed almost exclusively in the Republican Party and the liberal-labor coalition has become more important within the Democratic Party, the country's traditional regional, racial, and ethnic politics is being replaced by a more clear-cut class-and-race politics, with both the Republicans and Democrats now able to say that they are diverse in terms of leaders and candidates from all previously excluded groups. (Even the Republican Party can claim gay and lesbian members thanks to the Log Cabin Republicans, although many conservative Republicans would prefer not to.) And as everyone knows, the number of African Americans who are Republicans is very small, but they are important to the success of the party with centrist white voters because they "prove" that the party is trying to be inclusive of everyone.[1]

The Importance of Education

Class by no means explains all of our findings, however. Education also matters a great deal. The members of underrepresented groups who make it to the power elite are typically better educated than the white males who are already a part of it. This was seen with the European American women and African Americans on corporate boards and in presidential cabinets, as well as the successful Asian American immigrants. Education seems to have given them the edge needed to make their way into the power elite. In the case of many of the African Americans, new educational programs in elite private high schools, created in response to the disruptions of the 1960s, were more than an edge. They were essential. In effect, these scholarship programs in part compensated for the wealth they did not have.[2]

Moreover, it is not merely having academic degrees that matters but also where those degrees are from. Again and again, we saw that a significant number were from the same few schools that educate Christian, white, male leaders, such as Harvard, Yale, Princeton, and MIT on the East Coast, the University of Chicago in the Midwest, and Stanford on the West Coast. Whether it is Bill Clinton or George W. Bush in the White House, Hillary Clinton in the Senate from New York or Joseph Lieberman in the Senate from Connecticut, or Clarence Thomas on the Supreme Court, they all went to Yale in the 1960s.

These elite schools not only confer status on their graduates but also provide contacts with white male elites that are renewed throughout life at alumni gatherings and on other special occasions. School connections, in turn, lead to invitations to attend exclusive social events and join expensive social clubs, which extend the newcomers' social networks even further. With success in business or a profession comes invitations to serve on boards of trustees of elite foundations and universities, and the circle is completed.

In short, they have acquired the full complement of what is now called "social capital," the network of friends and contacts that provides access to jobs, financial capital, and marriage partners of high social standing. The newcomers thereby become part of the ongoing institutional framework that defines and shapes the power elite in the United States, even though only a few of them are likely to reach the very top. The individuals in the power elite may come and go, and they may diversify in gender, race, ethnicity, and sexual orientation, but there is stability and continuity in terms of the types of people who are fed into the set of institutions that define the power elite and dominate the American social structure.

As was true of social class origins, there is a difference in educational attainment between those in the power elite and those in Congress: the men and women elected to Congress are not as likely as those in the power elite to have attended elite colleges and universities or to have earned postgraduate degrees.

The Importance of Color

Just as class alone cannot explain all of our findings, neither can the combination of class and education: color also matters. African Americans and darker-skinned Latinos find it more difficult than others to use their educational credentials and social capital as passports to occupational success. This can be seen poignantly in our skin-color comparisons of successful blacks and Latinos. Even among those who had achieved some level of prominence (measured by inclusion in *Ebony*'s fiftieth anniversary issue or the *Hispanic Business* listing of "Hispanic influentials"), those who had made it into the power elite were lighter skinned than those who had not. On this score, our data simply reinforce earlier work by others. As the Glass Ceiling Commission reported, "Our society has developed an extremely sophisticated, and often denied, acceptability index based on gradations in skin color."[3]

Julia Alvarez, a writer whose novels have captured the difficulties of leaving one's Latin American home and coming, with far fewer material resources, to the United States to start anew, understands well the importance of one's class background in the old country and of light skin in the new country. In an essay about leaving the Dominican Republic and coming to the United States as a young girl, Alvarez acknowledges the advantages her family had over other immigrant families because they were well educated, had access to money, and (as she says, "most especially") were light skinned: "My family had not been among the waves of economic immigrants that left their island in the seventies, a generally darker-skinned, working-class group, who might have been the maids or workers in my mother's family house. We had come in 1960, political refugees, with no money but with "prospects": Papi had a friend who was a doctor at the Waldorf Astoria and who helped him get a job; Mami's family had money in the Chase Manhattan Bank they could lend us. We had changed class in America—from Mami's elite family to middle-class spics—but our background and education and most especially our pale skin had made mobility easier for us here."[4]

Alvarez's perceptive and honest assessment of the advantages she had (so different from the public relations stories put out by many corporate chieftains), coupled with the findings we have described on color discrimination, may help to explain why so few people of color have made it into the power elite. The failure of American society to accept darker-skinned citizens, especially African Americans, is the most difficult issue that needs to be understood by social scientists. We return to this issue in the next section, "Why Are Some Still Excluded?"

Identity Management

Finally, we have seen that the newcomers who join the power elite have found ways to demonstrate their loyalty to those who dominate American institutions—straight, white, Christian males. They know how to act and interact using the manners, style, and conversational repertoire of the already established elite, and they can hold their own in discussing the fine points of literature and the arts; that is, they have the "cultural capital" that comes from high-class origins or an elite education. When William T. Coleman recited great poetry with his fellow law clerk, Boston Brahmin Elliot Richardson, he was not only sharing a mutual love of poetry with a colleague and friend, he was demonstrating his elite educational background. Reading between the lines of traditional stereotypes, we can imagine Jewish and black executives being properly reserved, Asian American executives acting properly assertive, gay executives behaving in traditionally masculine ways, and lesbian executives acting in traditionally feminine ways. Within this context of identity management, we also can see why Cecily Cannan Selby decided to reduce tension at a dinner meeting with the previously all-male Avon Products board by lighting up a cigar and why Hazel O'Leary decided she had to learn to play golf if she wanted to advance in her corporate career. In all these ways, the newcomers are able to meet the challenge of moving into a "comfort zone" with those who decide who is and who is not acceptable for inclusion.

At the same time, in chapter 3 we drew on research on the sociology of organizations to stress that the demand for demonstrations of outward conformity by established leaders is not primarily a matter of personal prejudice or cultural heritage. It is, instead, the need for trust and smooth working relationships within complex organizations that leads to the marked preference for women and people of color who think and act like the straight, Christian males running those organizations. Such demonstrations may be especially important when there are suspicions that the newcomers might have lingering loyalties to those they have left behind. The social movements that arose in the 1960s were able to rock the boat enough to open up some space for nontraditional leaders, but not enough to change the way in which work is structured and institutions are managed. Unless, and until, changes are made in work structure and institutional cultures, underrepresented groups will be at a disadvantage in climbing the managerial hierarchy, even though they are now able to enter the competition.

In summary, class origins, an excellent education, and the proper appearance, especially in terms of lighter skin tone, are the building blocks for entry into the power elite, but identity management is the final step, the icing on the cake.

WHY ARE SOME STILL EXCLUDED?

How is the continuing exclusion of African Americans and Latinos who are darker skinned to be explained? From the power-structure perspective that we favor, the answer is to be found in the economic and political domination of darker-skinned people that began when European settlers took North and South America from the Native Americans and imported an estimated ten to twelve million slaves from Africa in order to make the southern United States, the West Indies, and parts of Latin America even more profitable to them. This economically driven subjugation, which unfolded in brutal fashion shortly after 1492 in ways that are all too familiar, created the "racial hierarchy" that persists to this day based on a jumble of prejudices, cultural stereotypes, strategies of exclusion, and feelings of superiority on the part of those who are white.

The fact that both indigenous Indians and African slaves were conquered and subjugated in the United States is less visible today because there are so few Native Americans left. They are now often regarded positively as brave and heroic warriors, but until fairly recently, they were treated as less than human due to the first (and most successful, along with that in Australia) large-scale ethnic cleansing by a modern democracy. Their numbers dropped from an estimated 4 to 9 million in the pre-Columbian era in what is now the United States to 237,000 in 1900, when they were no longer a threat to the land hunger of the white settlers. Today, most of the approximately 1.5 million self-identified Native Americans not living on reservations are of mixed white and Indian heritage, and 59 percent of those who are married are married to whites.[5]

In the United States, then, and unlike many Latin American countries, where both Indians and former African slaves mostly occupy the bottom rungs of society or are complete outcasts, the brunt of the persistent sense of group superiority on the part of Euro Americans is on the significant percentage of the population — 12 percent, as we noted earlier — who are descendants of slaves (and slave masters in some cases). In this country, being "black" means being stigmatized because the dishonored status of being a slave became identified with the racial features of "blackness."[6] In particular, skin color became the major means by which enslaved and conquered groups could be identified and stigmatized for purposes of keeping them subordinated. Hair texture and facial features were also part of the subordinating racial stereotyping, but "color" came to stand for the ensemble of identifying markers. (By contrast, the Slavic peoples enslaved by the Greeks and Romans, from whose language the word "slave" is derived, were able to blend in when their masters released them from bondage.)

In addition to carrying the legacy of slavery, which stripped people of any group or personal identity, rendered them subject to constant surveillance and violence, and regularly broke up roughly one-third of all nuclear families as a way to destroy feelings of kinship, African Americans also continued to endure subordination to white Americans in the postslavery era. In the South, that subordination began with the exploitative system called "tenant farming," which left African Americans with little more than their freedom, a mule, and a few farm implements.[7] In the North, African Americans were kept out of the best-paying construction jobs, often with the use of violence by white workers, despite their having the necessary skills. They also encountered cross burnings, race riots, and racial covenants in deeds of trust when they tried to live in white neighborhoods, which meant they were excluded from predominantly white public schools and forced to pay higher prices for housing that depreciated in value because whites would not live nearby.[8]

Under these circumstances, and until the 1960s, it was rare that any but a small number of African Americans could accumulate any wealth at all. Although the civil rights movement brought formal equality and voting power to African Americans, which in turn led to improved treatment in many social spheres and better jobs, especially with the government, the fact remains that it has been impossible for African Americans to close the socioeconomic gap with whites. According to detailed work on wealth accumulation by sociologist Thomas Shapiro, based on his own interviews in several cities, along with national surveys and government statistics, the typical African American family has only one-tenth the wealth of the average white family (a net worth of $8,000 versus $81,000 for whites). This is because whites were able gradually to accumulate wealth throughout the twentieth century with the help of government-backed mortgages, large tax deductions on home mortgages, the GI Bill, and other programs that were available to very few, if any, African Americans at the time. Moreover, whites were able to pass down this wealth to their children through inheritance, not only at the time of death, but also in the form of what Shapiro calls "transformative assets," which include help with college tuition, down payments on new homes (which then appreciate in value), and gifts or loans to survive unexpected crises that cause a temporary drop in income.[9]

On the other hand, the historic legacy of income and wealth discrimination means that African Americans lack similar transformative assets. In addition, more black wealth goes to helping relatives and friends in need and to taking care of aging parents, so the little wealth African Americans do accumulate is less likely to be given to young adult children as transformative assets or eventually inherited by them. Even when blacks and whites are at the same level in terms of earnings, they are at different starting points in terms of wealth, making it impossible to close the gap through earnings. Both black and white families increased their financial wealth between 1988 and 1999, but there was nonetheless a $20,000 increase in the asset gap. Racial inequality is growing worse, not better, because of both the initial advantages enjoyed by whites and their greater capacity to pass on these advantages as transformative assets. As Shapiro concludes, "it is virtually impossible for people of color to earn their way to wealth through wages."[10]

This huge wealth differential is further compounded by continuing discrimination and exclusion on the part of whites, especially in the area of employment, where many whites wrongly think there is now color-blind fairness.[11] Although the official racist ideology of the past is now gone, or at least not verbalized in public, there is strong evidence that more covert forms of racism still persist that make many blacks feel uncomfortable or unwanted in white settings. In covert racism, which also has been called free-market and color-blind racism, traditional American values, especially those concerning the fairness of markets, including labor markets, are blended with antiblack attitudes in a way that allows whites to express antagonism toward blacks' demands ("Blacks are getting too demanding in their push for civil rights") or resentment over alleged special favors for blacks ("The government should not help blacks and other racial minorities—they should help themselves") without thinking of themselves as racists. White Americans say they simply want everyone to be treated the same, even though most of them know that African Americans are not treated equally.[12]

Then, too, more subtle forms of racial discrimination are uncovered in various kinds of social psychology experiments that have revealed "aversive racism," in which whites express egalitarian beliefs but also hold unacknowledged negative feelings about blacks. The resulting ambivalence means that they avoid blacks, especially when the norms are conflicting or ambiguous. The evidence for aversive and other subtle forms of racism is important because it reveals the persistence of cultural stereotypes about blacks and demonstrates that these stereotypes affect behavior, often at an unconscious level. These stereotypes, in turn, convey to African Americans that they continue to be seen as "different." They come to feel they are not respected, which naturally breeds resentment and hostility, which is then sensed by whites and said to be groundless in this day and age.[13]

This cycle of discrimination, exclusion, resentment, and mutual recrimination is very different from what happens to most of the groups who come to the United States as immigrants from Europe, Asia, or Latin America. They arrive with a sense of hope, often as families or in extended kin networks, and with an intact culture; these combine to enable them to endure the discrimination and exclusion they often face at the outset. As they persist in their efforts, the dominant majority grudgingly accepts some of them. The difference can be seen in the two most revealing indicators of acceptance by the dominant group, residential patterns and rates of intermarriage.

The most comprehensive study on residential patterns demonstrates that African Americans continue to live in predominantly black neighborhoods, but this is not the case for Latinos or Asian Americans. In *American Apartheid: Segregation and the Making of the Underclass,* sociologists Douglas Massey and Nancy Denton reveal just how persistent residential segregation has been in the United States. Using computerized data from the U.S. Censuses of 1970 and 1980, they looked at the thirty metropolitan areas with the largest black populations. Based on two different measures ("black-white segregation" and "spatial isolation"), they conclude that the 1970s showed virtually no increase in integration, "despite what whites said on opinion polls and despite the provisions of the Fair Housing Act."[14] Moreover, they did not find that degree of segregation for Hispanics and Asian Americans. "In fact," Massey and Denton conclude, "within most metropolitan areas, Hispanics and Asians are more likely to share a neighborhood with whites than with another member of their own group." In the final chapter of their book, Massey and Denton update their work to include 1990 Census data. They conclude that "there is little in recent data to suggest that processes of racial segregation have moderated much since

1980. . . . Racial segregation still constitutes a fundamental cleavage in American society."[15] This conclusion still holds based on data from the 2000 Census, which shows only a slight decline in residential segregation for African Americans, along with increasing segregation for everyone along class lines.[16]

There have been dozens of studies focusing on the recent marriage patterns of underrepresented groups. All of them point to increasing intermarriage occurring between the large white population and each previously excluded group except African Americans. The exact percentage of "outmarriage" varies with a number of factors, including country of birth, years of residency in the United States, region of residence, educational level, and income. For our emphasis on intermarriage as a sensitive indicator of integration and acceptance, research by sociologists Jerry Jacobs and Teresa Labov, using a 1 percent sample from the 1990 Census (539,279 marriages), provides an ideal test case. Table 8.1 summarizes the findings of their analysis of marriages to non-Hispanic white partners by American-born minorities under the age of forty.[17]

There are many dramatic findings in this table, including the very high percentage of native-born Asian Americans marrying non-Hispanic whites, but none is more germane to our point than the continuing low levels of intermarriage by African Americans to non-Hispanic whites. In a sample that focuses only on married couples, thereby excluding any distortion by the high percentage of unmarried males and females in the African American community, only 5 percent of married African American males and 2 percent of married African American females under age forty were married to non-Hispanic whites. This is less than one-sixth the percentage for the next-lowest group, Mexican Americans, and far below the 44 to 66 percent figures for various

Table 8.1.   Intermarriage by U.S.-Born Members of Ethnic and Racial Minorities

	Percentage Married to Non-Hispanic Whites	
Group	Male (N)	Female (N)
Filipino Americans	61 (106)	66 (103)
Native Americans	57 (1,212)	58 (1,234)
Cuban Americans	61 (92)	47 (137)
Chinese Americans	47 (140)	52 (152)
Japanese Americans	44 (216)	54 (266)
Puerto Rican Americans	42 (528)	35 (602)
Mexican Americans	31 (4,793)	28 (5,261)
African Americans	5 (9,804)	2 (9,581)

Source: Adapted from Jacobs and Labov, "Asian Brides, Anglo Grooms," 23, table 4.
Note: The table includes only individuals under age forty and excludes war brides and grooms.

groups of Asian Americans. Even among African American college graduates, only 11 percent of the males and 3 percent of the females had married whites, whereas the percentages for all married Asian American college graduates as a group were 51 percent for males and 59 percent for females.[18]

As might be deduced from the higher percentage of Asian American college graduates marrying whites, there is a strong tendency for affluent immigrant minorities to marry affluent whites and for less affluent groups, like Mexican Americans and Puerto Ricans, to marry less affluent whites. The same pattern holds for marriages between African Americans and whites: the partners usually have similar education and occupation levels.[19]

To make matters more complex, most recent immigrant groups bring similar negative attitudes toward African Americans from their home countries, as in the case of nonblack Latinos, or soon adopt them once they are in the United States, as seen in the case of some Asian American groups. They often claim that African Americans do not see the "opportunities" that lie before them and do not work hard. Thus, most immigrants come to share the stereotypes and prejudices of the dominant white majority.

This point is demonstrated for Mexican Americans in an analysis of information in the 1990 Latino Political Survey, where 60 percent of all Mexican Americans felt "warmly" toward whites on a "feeling thermometer scale," compared to only 36 percent who felt that way toward African Americans; those with lighter skin or born outside the United States expressed even less warmth toward African Americans.[20] Similar findings are reported in a study of attitudes toward African Americans on the part of both Latinos and Asian Americans in Los Angeles.[21] This distancing from African Americans is also seen in a study that asked Latinos and Asian Americans to construct their "ideal" neighborhood, which included no African Americans for 33 percent of Latinos and 40 percent of Asian Americans.[22]

The power of this comparison between African Americans and immigrant groups is demonstrated in studies of the different course of events for most dark-skinned immigrants of African heritage, as studied most carefully in the case of West Indians. Based on their experience of their home countries, where there are few blacks at the top and few whites at the bottom, they expect to encounter obstacles in occupational advancement due to what is called "structural racism" by sociologist Mary Waters,[23] who conducted revealing interviews with West Indians, African Americans, and their white supervisors at a food service company in New York. Despite their expectations about structural racism, however, West Indian immigrants arrive hopeful and with positive attitudes towards whites as individuals, leading to pleasant interactions with most of the whites they encounter. But their initial hopeful attitudes are gradually shaken by the unexpected "interpersonal racism" they encounter in some of their interactions with whites. They are also made wary by the degree to which everything is "racialized" in the United States. Although most of them still retain a hopeful stance, they develop greater sympathy for what they see as the more defensive stance towards whites taken by African Americans.

As black immigrants come to realize the depth of the problem they face, they strive to preserve their accents and try to retain their "foreign" identities in an attempt to avoid the stigmatization applied to African Americans. They also attempt to socialize their children so that white Americans do not see them as African Americans. Earlier generations of West Indian immigrants, for example, sent their children back to the Caribbean to be educated. More recently, West Indians in New York who arrive from middle-class backgrounds have founded private schools that are based on the educational system "back home" in the islands. These schools often emphasize that their teachers have been trained in the West Indies, the curricula are rigorous, the students wear British-style school uniforms, and there is strict discipline.[24]

But these strategies are not always successful. Although some children of middle-class West Indians are able to resist racialization and end up among the blacks of African descent at the most selective universities in the United States (where as many as 25 percent of the black students have at least one parent who is foreign born), many others, as well as the children of other black immigrants, begin to view American society the same way working-class African Americans do because they face the same situation: high rates of unemployment, lack of good jobs, and not-so-subtle racism.[25] Treated like African Americans, many black West Indians, black Puerto Ricans, black Dominicans, and black Cubans come to see themselves subjectively as African Americans. As Waters concludes, "It is in the second generation that this process of rapid cultural change is most evident. The children of these immigrants do grow up exhibiting the racialism their parents are concerned with preventing. Indeed, the rapidity of the change in attitudes about race between parents and children is quite dramatic."[26]

Those white Americans who say that racism is a thing of the past and blame African Americans for creating problems for themselves by dwelling on it often point to their good interpersonal relations with immigrant groups, including West Indians, as evidence for their claim. However, as Waters demonstrates, the persisting racial discrimination practiced (and denied) by whites is in fact the root of the problem, generating the tensions that whites attribute to African Americans:

> It is the continuing discrimination and prejudice of whites, and ongoing structural and interpersonal racism, that create an inability among American, and ultimately West Indian, blacks to ever forget about race. The behavior and beliefs about race among whites, and the culture of racist behaviors among whites, cre-

ate the very expectations of discomfort that whites complain about in their dealing with their black neighbors, coworkers, and friends. That expectation is not some inexplicable holdover from the long-ago days of slavery, but rather a constantly re-created expectation of trouble, nourished by every taxi that does not stop and every casual or calculated white use of the word "nigger."[27]

Based on the findings on how differently black and nonblack immigrants are treated, it seems likely to us that, over time, the overwhelming majority of the children and grandchildren of nonblack immigrants to the United States will blend together with non-Hispanic whites into a common cultural pool and then sort themselves out along class and educational lines, using ethnic and racial identities for mostly symbolic and strategic purposes. On the other hand, Americans of African descent, whether African Americans or immigrants, will find themselves struggling to hold on to whatever class standing they are able attain. Race, as well as class, will continue to determine their life chances.[28] We therefore agree with those who argue that people of African descent have been treated very differently from all other previously excluded groups. In making this point, we are fully aware that other groups have suffered many forms of discrimination and exclusion, and we do not want to diminish the depth of personal anguish that such mistreatment has caused, but the fact remains that people of African heritage are the only ones to experience the combined effects of race, slavery, and segregation.[29] This confluence is unique because the "dishonored" or "stigmatized" status attached to slavery everywhere it has been practiced cannot easily be overcome or forgotten when there is the constant reminder of skin color.

Based on this analysis, we can see why the gains made by African Americans since the civil rights movement are in constant peril in a context where they have not been able to accumulate sufficient wealth to help their children or provide support in times of crisis. Given the ongoing discrimination and accumulated disadvantages, it may be that even the current rate of entry into the power elite will be difficult to maintain. Upwardly mobile black Americans could continue to be the exception rather than the rule without the strong support of affirmative action laws and programs at the federal level.[30] But such laws and programs have been trimmed back since the new conservative era began in the 1980s, making further progress problematic.

However, in a clear demonstration of the concerns members of the power elite have on this score, a small part of the decline in government support for equal opportunity has been offset by a set of corporate-sponsored programs for identifying and educating academically talented African American youngsters who can be groomed for elite universities and possible incorporation into the power elite. These programs begin in elementary school in some areas of the country, then carry through to private high schools, Ivy League universities, and corporate internships. They are financed by donations from the large charitable foundations that the corporate rich in turn influence through financial donations and directorship positions. Since we have written about these programs elsewhere, with a special emphasis on the first and largest of them, A Better Chance, founded in the early 1960s by a handful of New England boarding school headmasters with help from the Rockefeller Foundation, we will provide only three examples here.[31]

The Black Student Fund in Washington, D.C., places students in 42 private schools in Maryland, Virginia, and the District of Columbia with the help of foundation grants and personal gifts. Since its founding in 1964, it has served over two thousand students, 84 percent of whom have earned at least a BA. The Steppingstone Foundation in Boston and Philadelphia has a program for children in the fourth and fifth grades, who are prepared through two six-week summer sessions, Saturday classes, and after-school classes once a week for acceptance into both private and elite public schools that will see them through their high school years with the help of scholarship support. Between 1997 and 2005, 125 graduates of the Steppingstone program had enrolled in college. About one-third had attended prestigious schools (five went to Columbia or Barnard, four to Yale and Penn, three to Tufts, two to Harvard, Wellesley, Bowdoin, Bates, Georgetown and Williams, and one to Brown, Dartmouth, Duke, Hamilton, Johns Hopkins, Mt. Holyoke, and Wesleyan), and about 10 percent had attended traditionally black colleges and universities (including four who went to Spelman, three to Hampton, and two to Morehouse). The others had attended a wide range of public and private institutions (five went to the University of Massachusetts, three to George Washington, and two to Temple, Boston College, Boston University, Fordham, and Pine Manor).

Prep for Prep in New York City may currently be the largest and most comprehensive of these programs. Created in 1978 as a pilot project under the auspices of Columbia University's Teachers College just as the full-scale attack on affirmative action was beginning, it takes in about 150 fifth graders and 60 seventh graders in New York City each year for a fourteen-month program to prepare them for placement in 36 private day schools and 10 boarding schools. Like the Steppingstone program, it includes two intensive, seven-week, summer programs, as well as after-school classes one day a week and Saturday classes during the school year. It sponsors a leadership institute and offers counseling services. Its program of summer job placements is meant to introduce students to the business and professional worlds. Alumni participate in a summer advisory program to help create what is called the "Prep Community," a support group and sense of group identification, and 75 percent of the children complete the program and go to college.

As of 2003, Prep for Prep had worked with more than 2,500 students, and 951 had graduated from college. Fully 84 percent of those college graduates had attended schools characterized as "most selective" on the annual list published by *U.S. News & World Report*, and 40 percent had attended Ivy League schools. Among the schools with the most Prep for Prep alumni (as of 2005) are Wesleyan (58), the University of Pennsylvania (36), Harvard (32), Columbia (30), Brown (27), Princeton (22), and Dartmouth (18).

Wall Street lawyers and financiers direct the program. For example, its chairman, John L. Vogelstein, is the vice chair of the board of directors of the investment bank E. M. Warburg, Pincus, & Company and sits on the board of directors of three other corporations. The program received $2.8 million from 29 foundations in 2002–2003, starting with $1.5 million from the Goldman Sachs Foundation.

Once African American students are in college, there are programs that encourage any interest they may have in going to law school or business school. A joint program between major corporations and the Harvard Business School is one good example of how African Americans are recruited for the business community. For almost twenty years, the Harvard Business School has sponsored the Summer Venture in Management Program, a weeklong program designed to expose talented minority students to management in the business world. The participants are "underrepresented minority U.S. citizens" who have completed their junior year of college, been hired as interns during the summer by sponsoring companies (generally *Fortune*-level companies), and been nominated by those companies to spend a week at the Harvard Business School learning what a high-powered business school is like. Participation in the program does not guarantee subsequent acceptance into the Harvard Business School, but it does allow the school to identify and encourage applications from highly qualified individuals.

Taken as a whole, this elementary to graduate school pipeline may produce several thousand potential members of the corporate community each year, if successful graduates of public high schools who receive business and law degrees are added to the prep school graduates. However, these programs are not large enough to provide opportunities for more than a tiny fraction of all African Americans without much more help from the government at the national, state, and local levels. They are primarily a way to provide a few highly educated Americans of African descent with the educational credentials to rise in the corporate community. For example, despite all these programs, the percentage of master's degrees awarded to blacks has been flat at about 6.5 percent since 1977, which demonstrates a significant underrepresentation. A shorter time series available from the government for master's degrees in business reveals a slight but steady increase between the

1994–1995 and 1999–2000 school years. During these six years, the percentages of black students receiving business degrees rose from 5.2 to 7.1 percent. We therefore believe that the potential pool of African Americans who can make their way into the power elite is growing at a much slower rate than for the other previously underrepresented groups.

THE MANY IRONIC IMPACTS OF DIVERSITY

The impetus for greater diversity, as we have stressed, did not come from within the power elite but was the result of external pressures brought to bear by the civil rights movement. The fact that the American power elite was in competition with the Soviet Union for access and influence in previously colonized Third World countries also played a role, but that factor can easily be exaggerated in historical hindsight. Faced with the possibility of continuing massive disruption and rioting in the inner cities of major urban areas, most members of the power elite reluctantly accepted integration, and later diversity, as a goal only because they had little choice.

This point is best demonstrated in the case of the affirmative action programs originally designed to create more job opportunities for African Americans. Despite hesitations about breaking the taboo on quotas and preferences, affirmative action policies were adopted by political and business elites very hurriedly in the face of the estimated 329 major disturbances in 257 cities between 1964 and 1968, which resulted in 220 deaths, 8,371 injuries, and 52,629 arrests.[32] At the urging of first President Kennedy and then President Johnson at off-the-record meetings with the Business Council, at the time the most central organization in the power elite, corporate CEOs took the lead in calling on all businesses to provide more jobs for African Americans as quickly as possible. They thereby helped legitimize what they knew was preferential hiring because job programs were seen not only as the fastest and surest way to restore domestic tranquility but also as a means of avoiding larger government programs and expanded welfare benefits as well. Moreover, it was the corporate-backed Nixon administration in 1969 that created the stringent guidelines for hiring by government contractors (under the guise of "good faith" efforts at meeting numerical "targets"), which were soon attacked as a "quota" system.[33]

Once the concern with urban unrest subsided, however, the elite origins of the plan were soon ignored. It was at this point, too, that Nixon abandoned his guidelines, and ultraconservative Republicans began to attack affirmative action as unfair to whites and unconstitutional, a mere experiment by liberals and professors. The fear of disruption was gone, so now the rewriting of history could begin, along with attempts to capitalize on the increasing backlash among white workers. In the first of the many ironies arising from the saga of diversity, African Americans and white liberals, who had been very hesitant about preferential hiring in the beginning, ended up defending a program created and endorsed by white male elites in a time of crisis.[34] In a related irony, the successful Republican campaign to place the "blame" for the affirmative action program on African Americans and white liberals helped to dislodge angry whites from the Democratic Party.

Although it was African Americans and their white allies who created the disruption and pressures that led to government programs, including affirmative action, other previously excluded groups soon became eligible for consideration and benefited greatly, perhaps even more so than African Americans in terms of higher-level jobs.[35] This change, which was gracefully accepted by most African American leaders and even seen by some of them as a way to expand their coalition, not only ended up marginalizing African Americans within the programs they created, but it added to the opposition by middle-American white males, who deeply resented the increased competition they had to face for good blue-collar and government jobs.

In response to this growing resentment, defenders of the program in and around the corporate world began to talk about the need for "diversity" in management circles and to emphasize its importance for business reasons rather than social-justice goals. At this point, the focus shifted to such business advantages as having managers who could interact with an increasingly heterogeneous set of lower-level wage earners. Proponents of diversity also emphasized that a "multicultural" management team would be essential for competing in the many non-European countries that were part of the rapidly expanding global economy. But for all the changes in rationale and the emphasis on bottom-line business objectives, the actual practices of the corporations (and universities and large nonprofit organizations) remained about the same, based on the procedures and programs initially established by social movements and government laws.[36]

Although African American management consultants were part of this effort to redefine the affirmative action programs as diversity programs and thereby fend off the right wing of the Republican Party, a further irony developed: diversity no longer needed to include African Americans. The new goal was to have a high percentage of nonwhites and women. And it was not long before foreign-born executives and professionals, even those who came to the United States as young educated adults from foreign universities, were included in the statistics, driving the numbers even higher.[37]

In what may be the greatest and most important irony of them all, the diversity forced upon the power elite may have helped to strengthen it. Diversity has given the power elite buffers, ambassadors, tokens, and legitimacy. This is an unintended consequence that few insurgents or social scientists foresaw. As recent social psychology experiments show and experience confirms, it often takes only a small number of upwardly mobile members of previously excluded groups, perhaps as few as 2 percent, to undermine an excluded group's definition of who is "us" and who is "them," which contributes to a decline in collective protest and disruption and increases striving for individual mobility. That is, those who make it are not only "role models" for individuals, but they are safety valves against collective action by aggrieved groups.[38]

Tokens at the top create ambiguity and internal doubt for members of the subordinated group. Maybe "the system" is not as unfair to their group as they thought it was. Maybe there is something about them personally that keeps them from advancing. Once people begin to ponder such possibilities, the likelihood of any sustained group action declines greatly. Because a few people have made it, the general human tendency to think of the world as just and fair reasserts itself: since the world is fair, and some members of my group are advancing, then it may be my fault that I have been left behind. As liberal and left-wing activists have long known, it is hard to sustain a social movement in the face of "reforms," which has led to long-standing debates about how activists should proceed.[39]

DO MEMBERS OF PREVIOUSLY EXCLUDED GROUPS ACT DIFFERENTLY?

Perhaps it is not surprising that when we look at the business practices of the members of previously excluded groups who have risen to the top of the corporate world, we find that their perspectives and values do not differ markedly from those of their white male counterparts. When Linda Wachner, one of the first women to become CEO of a *Fortune*-level company, the Warnaco Group, concluded that one of Warnaco's many holdings, the Hathaway Shirt Company, was unprofitable, she decided to stop making Hathaway shirts and to sell or close down the factory. It did not matter to Wachner that Hathaway, which started making shirts in 1837, was one of the oldest companies in Maine, that almost all of the five hundred employees at the factory were working-class women, or even that the workers had given up a pay raise to hire consultants to teach them to work more effectively and, as a result, had doubled their productivity. The bottom-line issue was that the company was considered unprofitable, and the average wage of the Hathaway workers, $7.50 an hour, was thought to be too high. (In 1995, Wachner was paid $10 million in salary and stock, and Warnaco had a net income of $46.5 million.) "We did need to do the right thing for the company and the stockholders," explained Wachner.[40]

Nor did ethnic background matter to Thomas Fuentes, a senior vice president at a consulting firm in Orange County, California, a director of Fleetwood Enterprises, and chairman of the Orange County Republican Party. Fuentes targeted fellow Latinos who happened to be Democrats when he sent uniformed security guards to twenty polling places in 1988 "carrying signs in Spanish and English warning people not to vote if they were not U.S. citizens." The security firm ended up paying $60,000 in damages when it lost a lawsuit stemming from this intimidation.[41] We also can recall that the Fanjuls, the Cuban American sugar barons, have no problem ignoring labor laws in dealing with their migrant labor force, and that Sue Ling Gin, one of the Asian Americans on our list of corporate directors, explained to an interviewer that, at one point in her career, she had hired an all-female staff, not out of feminist principles but "because women would work for lower wages." Linda Wachner, Thomas Fuentes, the Fanjuls, and Sue Ling Gin acted as employers, not as members of disadvantaged groups. That is, members of the power elite of both genders and of all ethnicities practice class politics.

CONCLUSION

The black and white liberals and progressives who challenged Christian, white, male homogeneity in the power structure starting in the 1950s and 1960s sought to do more than create civil rights and new job opportunities for men and women who had previously been mistreated and excluded, important though these goals were. They also hoped that new perspectives in the boardrooms and the halls of government would spread greater openness throughout the society. The idea was both to diversify the power elite and to shift some of its power to underrepresented groups and social classes. The social movements of the 1960s were strikingly successful in increasing the individual rights and freedoms available to all Americans, especially African Americans. As we have shown, they also created pressures that led to openings at the top for individuals from groups that had previously been ignored.

But as some individuals made it, and as the concerns of social movements, political leaders, and the courts gradually came to focus more and more on individual rights and individual advancement, the focus on "distributive justice," general racial exclusion, and social class was lost. The age-old American commitment to individualism, reinforced by tokenism and reassurances from members of the power elite, won out over the commitment to greater equality of income and wealth that had been one strand of New Deal liberalism and a major emphasis of left-wing activism in the 1960s.

We therefore conclude that the increased diversity in the power elite has not generated any changes in an underlying class system in which the top 1 percent of households (the upper class) own 33.4 percent of all marketable wealth, and the next 19 percent (the managerial, professional, and small business stratum) have 51 percent, which means that just 20 percent of the people own a remarkable 84 percent of the privately owned wealth in the United States, leaving a mere 16 percent of the wealth for the bottom 80 percent (wage and salary workers).[42] In fact, the wealth and income distributions became even more skewed starting in the 1970s as the majority of whites, especially in the South and Great Plains, switched their allegiance to the Republican Party and thereby paved the way for a conservative resurgence that is as antiunion, antitax, and antigovernment as it is determined to impose ultraconservative social values on all Americans.

The values of liberal individualism embedded in the Declaration of Independence, the Bill of Rights, and American civic culture were renewed by vigorous and courageous activists in the years between 1955 and 1975, but the class structure remains a major obstacle to individual fulfillment for the overwhelming majority of Americans. The conservative backlash that claims to speak for individual rights has strengthened this class structure, one that thwarts advancement for most individuals from families in the bottom 80 percent of the wealth distribution. This solidification of class divisions in the name of individualism is more than an irony. It is a dilemma.

Furthermore, this dilemma combines with the dilemma of race to obscure further the impact of class and to limit individual mobility, simply because the majority of middle-American whites cannot bring themselves to make common cause with African Americans in the name of greater individual opportunity and economic equality through a progressive income tax and the kind of government programs that lifted past generations out of poverty. These intertwined dilemmas of class and race lead to a nation that celebrates individualism, equal opportunity, and diversity but is, in reality, a bastion of class privilege, African American exclusion, and conservatism.

NOTES

1. On the continuing importance of class voting in the United States, contrary to recent claims based on weak methods, see Jeff Manza and Clem Brooks, *Social Cleavages and Political Change: Voter Alignments and U.S. Party Coalitions* (New York: Oxford University Press, 1999). On class voting by Latinos, see Barry Kosmin and Ariela Keysar, "Party Political Preferences of U.S. Hispanics: The Varying Impact of Religion, Social Class and Demographic Factors," *Ethnic and Racial Studies* 18, no. 2 (1995): 336–47. In surveys of the CEOs of the largest Hispanic-owned

businesses in 1989 and 1996, *Hispanic Business* found that 78 percent of them voted Republican in 1988 and that 67 percent said they were Republicans in 1996. See "CEOs and the Entrepreneurial 80s," *Hispanic Business,* April 1989, 30; "HB 500 CEOs Opt for Dole," *Hispanic Business,* June 1996, 34. On class voting by Chinese Americans, see Wendy Tam, "Asians—a Monolithic Voting Bloc?" *Political Behavior* 17, no. 2 (1995): 223–49.

2. Richard L. Zweigenhaft and G. William Domhoff, *Blacks in the White Elite* (Lanham, MD: Rowman & Littlefield, 2003), 158–60.

3. Glass Ceiling Commission, *Good for Business: Making Full Use of the Nation's Human Capital, a Fact-Finding Report of the Federal Glass Ceiling Commission* (Washington, D.C.: U.S. Government Printing Office, 1995), 95.

4. Julia Alvarez, "A White Woman of Color," in *Half and Half: Writers on Growing Up Biracial and Bicultural,* ed. Claudine Chiawei O'Hearn, 139–49 (New York: Pantheon, 1998). Alvarez's novels include *How the Garcia Girls Lost Their Accents* (New York: Plume, 1992) and *In the Time of the Butterflies* (New York: Plume, 1994).

5. Michael Mann, *The Dark Side of Democracy: Explaining Ethnic Cleansing* (New York: Cambridge University Press, 2005); Karl Eschbach, "The Enduring and Vanishing American Indian: American Indian Population Growth and Intermarriage in 1990," *Ethnic and Racial Studies,* 18, no. 1 (1995): 89–108.

6. Glenn Loury, *The Anatomy of Racial Inequality* (Cambridge: Harvard University Press, 2002), 69.

7. Michael Schwartz, *Radical Protest and Social Structure: The Southern Farmers' Alliance and Cotton Tenancy, 1880–1890* (New York: Academic Press, 1976).

8. Kevin Fox Gotham, *Race, Real Estate, and Uneven Development* (Albany: State University of New York Press, 2002); Michael K. Brown, Martin Carnoy, Elliott Currie, Troy Duster, David B. Oppenheimer, Marjorie M. Shultz, and David Wellman, *Whitewashing Race: The Myth of a Color-Blind Society* (Berkeley: University of California Press, 2003).

9. Thomas M. Shapiro, *The Hidden Cost of Being African American: How Wealth Perpetuates Inequality* (New York: Oxford University Press, 2004).

10. Shapiro, *Hidden Cost,* 2.

11. Devah Pager and Bruce Western, "Discrimination in Low-Wage Labor Markets: Results from an Experimental Audit Study in New York City" (paper presented at the annual meeting of the American Sociological Association, Philadelphia, Pennsylvania, 2005); Deirdre A. Royster, *Race and the Invisible Hand: How White Networks Exclude Black Men from Blue-collar Jobs* (Berkeley: University of California Press, 2003).

12. Lawrence Bobo and Ryan Smith, "From Jim Crow to Laissez-faire Racism: The Transformation of Racial Attitudes," in *Beyond Pluralism: The Conception of Groups and Group Identities in America,* ed. Wendy Katkin, Ned Landsman, and Andrea Tyree, 182–220 (Urbana: University of Illinois Press, 1998); Eduardo Bonilla-Silva, *Racism without Racists: Color-Blind Racism and the Persistence of Racial Inequality in the United States* (Lanham, MD: Rowman & Littlefield, 2003).

13. James M. Jones, *Prejudice and Racism*, 2nd ed. (New York: McGraw-Hill, 1997); John F. Dovidio, "On the Nature of Contemporary Prejudice: The Third Wave," *Journal of Social Issues* 57, no. 4 (2001): 829–49.

14. Douglas S. Massey and Nancy A. Denton, *American Apartheid: Segregation and the Making of the Underclass* (Cambridge: Harvard University Press, 1993), 61.

15. Massey and Denton, *American Apartheid*, 67, 223.

16. William Clark and Sarah Blue, "Race, Class, and Segregation Patterns in U.S. Immigrant Gateway Cities," *Urban Affairs Review* 39 (2004): 667–88; John Iceland, Cicely Sharpe, and Erika Steinmetz, "Class Differences in African American Residential Patterns in US Metropolitan Areas: 1990–2000," *Social Science Research* 34 (2005): 252–66.

17. Jerry A. Jacobs and Teresa Labov, "Asian Brides, Anglo Grooms: Asian Exceptionalism in Intermarriage," Department of Sociology, University of Pennsylvania, October 1995; Jerry A. Jacobs and Teresa Labov, "Sex Differences in Intermarriage: Exchange Theory Reconsidered," Department of Sociology, University of Pennsylvania, September 1995. For similar findings, based on 1990 survey data with native-born Latinos, that are slightly lower due to a wider age range, see Rodolfo de la Garza, Louis DeSipio, F. Chris Garcia, John Garcia, and Angelo Falcon, *Latino Voices: Mexican, Puerto Rican, and Cuban Perspectives on American Politics* (Boulder, CO: Westview, 1992), 25, table 2.6. Jacobs and Labov find low rates of intermarriage among subgroups of Latinos, and de la Garza and colleagues report similarly low rates among Latino groups in the table cited. There is, however, evidence for a growing number of intermarriages among Asian Americans in California, with the rate being higher than intermarriage with whites when the size of the population is taken into account. See Larry Hajima Shinagawa and Gin Yong Pang, "Intraethnic, Interethnic, and Interracial Marriages among Asian Americans in California, 1980," *Berkeley Journal of Sociology* 13 (1988): 95–114. Inter-Asian marriages are also high in Hawaii; see Morrison G. Wong, "A Look at Intermarriage among the Chinese in the U.S. in 1980," *Sociological Perspectives* 32, no. 1 (1989): 87–107.

18. Jacobs and Labov, "Sex Differences in Intermarriage," 11.

19. Jerry A. Jacobs and Teresa Labov, "Gender Differentials in Intermarriage among Sixteen Race and Ethnic Groups," *Sociological Forum* 17 (2002): 621–46. On black-white marriages and socioeconomic similarities, see also James H. Gadberry and Richard A. Dodder, "Educational Homogamy in Interracial Marriages: An Update," *Journal of Social Behavior and Personality* 8, no. 6 (1993): 155–63; Matthijs Kalmijn, "Trends in Black/White Intermarriage," *Social Forces* 72, no. 1 (1993): 119–46; Kristyan M. Kouri and Marcia Lasswell, "Black-White Marriages: Social Change and Intergenerational Mobility," *Marriage and Family Review* 19, no. 3–4 (1993): 241–55.

20. Edward Murguia and Tyrone Foreman, "Shades of Whiteness: The Mexican-American Experience in Relation to Anglos and Blacks," in *White Out: The Continuing Significance of Race*, ed. Ashley Doane and Eduardo Bonilla-Silva, 63–79 (New York: Routledge, 2003).

21. Lawrence Bobo and Devon Johnson, "Racial Attitudes in a Prismatic Metropolis: Mapping Identity, Stereotypes, Competition, and Views on Affirmative Action,"

in *Prismatic Metropolis*, ed. Lawrence Bobo, Melvin L. Oliver, James H. Johnson, Jr., and Abel Valenzuela, 81–166 (New York: Russell Sage Foundation, 2000).

22. Camille Zubrinsky Charles, "Neighborhood Racial-Composition Preferences: Evidence from a Multiethnic Metropolis," *Social Problems* 47 (2000): 379–407.

23. Mary C. Waters, "Explaining the Comfort Factor: West Indian Immigrants Confront American Race Relations," in *The Cultural Territories of Race: Black and White Boundaries*, ed. Michelle Lamont, 63–96 (Chicago: University of Chicago Press, 1999); Mary C. Waters, *Black Identities: West Indian Immigrant Dreams and American Realities* (Cambridge: Harvard University Press, 1999).

24. Philip Kasinitz, *Caribbean New York: Black Immigrants and the Politics of Race* (Ithaca, NY: Cornell University Press, 1992), 76, 220–21.

25. For information on the children of foreign-born blacks at twenty-eight highly selective colleges and universities, see Douglas S. Massey, Camille Z. Charles, Garvey F. Lundy, and Mary J. Fischer, *The Source of the River: The Social Origins of Freshmen at America's Selective Colleges and Universities* (Princeton, NJ: Princeton University Press, 2003), 40. At a forum during a 2004 reunion of black Harvard alumni, law professor Lani Guinier and Henry Louis Gates Jr., the chairman of the African and African American Studies Department, reported that at least a majority, and perhaps as many as two-thirds, of the then current undergraduates at Harvard were either West Indian and African immigrants, their children, or the children of biracial couples. See Sara Rimer and Karen W. Arenson, "Top Colleges Take More Blacks, but Which Ones?" *New York Times*, June 24, 2004, A1.

26. Waters, "Explaining the Comfort Factor."

27. Waters, "Explaining the Comfort Factor," 82.

28. Eduardo Bonilla-Silva, "'New Racism,' Color-blind Racism, and the Future of Whiteness in America," in Doane and Bonilla-Silva, *White Out*, 271–84; Herbert Gans, "The Possibility of a New Racial Hierarchy in the Twenty-First Century United States," in Lamont, *The Cultural Territories of Race*.

29. Thomas F. Pettigrew, "Integration and Pluralism," in *Modern Racism: Profiles in Controversy*, ed. Phyllis A. Katz and Dalmas A. Taylor, 19–30 (New York: Plenum, 1988), 24–26. For detailed evidence on the difficulties black Americans, including members of the middle class, still face, see Lois Benjamin, *The Black Elite* (Chicago: Nelson Hall, 1991), and Joe R. Feagin and Melvin P. Sikes, *Living with Racism* (Boston: Beacon, 1994).

30. See Sharon Collins, *Black Corporate Executives: The Making and Breaking of a Black Middle Class* (Philadelphia: Temple University Press, 1997). For a systematic empirical demonstration of the importance of such government policies using time series data, see Martin Carnoy, *Faded Dreams: The Politics and Economics of Race in America* (New York: Cambridge University Press, 1994).

31. Zweigenhaft and Domhoff, *Blacks in the White Elite*, 2003.

32. Brian T. Downes, "A Critical Re-examination of the Social and Political Characteristics of Riot Cities," *Social Science Quarterly* 51 (1970): 349–60.

33. John D. Skrentny, *The Ironies of Affirmative Action: Politics, Culture, and Justice in America* (Chicago: University of Chicago Press, 1996), ch. 4 and 7.

34. Skrentny, *The Ironies of Affirmative Action*, 78–91.

35. John D. Skrentny, *The Minority Rights Revolution* (Cambridge: Harvard University Press, 2002).

36. Erin Kelly and Frank Dobbin, "How Affirmative Action Became Diversity Management: Employer Responses to Antidiscrimination Law, 1961–1996," in *Color Lines: Affirmative Action, Immigration, and Civil Rights Options for America*, ed. John D. Skrentny, 87–117 (Chicago: University of Chicago Press, 2001).

37. Skrentny, *The Minority Rights Revolution*, ch. 10.

38. Stephen C. Wright, "Restricted Intergroup Boundaries: Tokenism, Ambiguity, and the Tolerance of Injustice," in *The Psychology of Legitimacy: Emerging Perspectives on Ideology, Justice, and Intergroup Relations*, ed. John Jost and Brenda Major, 223–54 (New York: Cambridge University Press, 2001); Stephen C. Wright, "Strategic Collective Action: Social Psychology and Social Change," in *Blackwell Handbook of Social Psychology: Intergroup Processes*, ed. Rupert Brown and Samuel Gaertner, vol. 4, 409–30 (Malden, MA: Blackwell, 2001).

39. Jost and Major, *The Psychology of Legitimacy*.

40. Sara Rimer, "Fall of a Shirtmaking Legend Shakes Its Maine Hometown," *New York Times,* May 15, 1996. See, also, Floyd Norris, "Market Place," *New York Times,* June 7, 1996; Stephanie Strom, "Double Trouble at Linda Wachner's Twin Companies," *New York Times,* August 4, 1996. Strom's article reveals that Hathaway Shirts "got a reprieve" when an investor group stepped in to save it.

41. Claudia Luther and Steven Churm, "GOP Official Says He OK'd Observers at Polls," *Los Angeles Times,* November 12, 1988; Jeffrey Perlman, "Firm Will Pay $60,000 in Suit over Guards at Polls," *Los Angeles Times,* May 31, 1989.

42. Edward N. Wolff, "Changes in Household Wealth in the 1980s and 1990s in the U.S." (working paper 407, Levy Economics Institute, Bard College, 2004), at www.levy.org.

Index

About the Authors

Richard L. Zweigenhaft is the Charles A. Dana Professor of Psychology at Guilford College in Greensboro, North Carolina, where he also serves as the Director of the Social Science Division and of the Communications Concentration. He received his BA at Wesleyan University, his MA at Columbia University, and his PhD at the University of California, Santa Cruz. He is the coauthor of *Jews in the Protestant Establishment* (1982), *Blacks in the White Establishment?: A Study of Race and Class in America* (1991), *Diversity in the Power Elite: Have Women and Minorities Reached the Top?* (1998) and *Blacks in the White Elite: Will the Progress Continue?* (2003).

G. William Domhoff is a research professor at the University of California, Santa Cruz. He received his BA at Duke University, his MA at Kent State University, and his PhD at the University of Miami. He is the author of numerous books on power in the United States, including *Who Rules America? Power, Politics, and Social Change* (fifth edition, 2006).